Demography

Techniques & Analysis

Demography

Techniques & Analysis

Asis Kumar Chattopadhyay, M.Sc., Ph.D.
Professor, Department of Statistics
Calcutta University

Anuj Kumar Saha, M.Sc., M.P.S., Ph.D.
Formerly Associate Scientist-B
Population Studies Unit
Indian Statistical Institute, Kolkata

Viva Books

New Delhi | Mumbai | Chennai | Kolkata | Bengaluru | Hyderabad | Kochi | Guwahati

Publisher's note

First Published 2012
Reprinted 2015, 2016, 2017, 2019, 2021, 2023, 2024

Viva Books Private Limited

- 4737/23, Ansari Road, Daryaganj, New Delhi 110 002
  Tel. 42242200, 23258325, 23283121, Email: vivadelhi@vivagroupindia.net
- 76, Service Industries, Shirvane, Sector 1, Nerul, Navi Mumbai 400 706
  Tel. 27721273, 27721274, Email: vivamumbai@vivagroupindia.net
- Megh Towers, Old No. 307, New No. 165, Poonamallee High Road, Maduravoyal
  Chennai - 600 095 E-mail: vivachennai@vivagroupindia.net, Tel. 23780991, 23780992
- B-103, Jindal Towers, 21/1A/3 Darga Road, Kolkata 700 017
  Tel. 22816713, Email: vivakolkata@vivagroupindia.net
- 7, GF, Sovereign Park Aptts., 56-58, K. R. Road, Basavanagudi, Bengaluru 560 004
  Tel. 26607409, Email: vivabangalore@vivagroupindia.net
- 101-102, Moghal Marc Apartments, 3-4-637 to 641, Narayanguda, Hyderabad 500 029
  Tel. 27564481, Email: vivahyderabad@vivagroupindia.net
- First Floor, Beevi Towers, SRM Road, Kaloor, Kochi 682 018
  Tel. 0484-2403055, 2403056, Email: vivakochi@vivagroupindia.net
- 232, GNB Road, Beside UCO Bank, Silpukhuri, Guwahati 781 003
  Tel. 0361-2666386, Email: vivaguwahati@vivagroupindia.net

www.vivagroupindia.com

ISBN: 978-81-309-2118-1

Published by Vinod Vasishtha for Viva Books Private Limited, 4737/23 Ansari Road, Daryaganj, New Delhi 110 002.

Printed and bound by Replika Press Pvt. Ltd.

S0000/S1020/S1000

in the sacred memory of my parents
"late Narendranath and Protima"

Asis Kumar Chattopadhyay

in memory of my beloved parents
"late Amalangshu and Mihirkana"

Anuj Kumar Saha

Contents

Preface

We, the authors, have sincerely and carefully tried to write this book on technical and analytical demography for the readers. Our principal aim of this book is to serve the readers better than any other book available so far in the market because we know; no single book has ever tried to cover most of the aspects of technical demography in a book at a time. So we value the book honestly. This book has tried to employ almost all the basic as well as advanced techniques for the estimation of demographic parameters along with their applications and illustrations as well as with some important notes given, wherever possible, which are not only useful but also helpful for the readers of demography as well, in a single book. We know, the subject of Demography is regarded as one of the important disciplines in the academic arena that deals with the scientific study of human population. Hence, government and non-government organizations as well as colleges and universities over the world, have understood its importance. That is why, most of the colleges and the universities in the world have introduced this subject at the undergraduate and graduate level. That apart many national and international organizations have been actively involved in demographic analysis.

Overall, this book clearly outlines the methods used to study population structure and change by presenting the major descriptive and analytical models developed by demographers to investigate the interrelationships between fertility, age-structure, mortality, nuptiality, migration, socio-economic mobility and projection. With illustrations, tables, figures and data drawn from a few constituent states of India and a neighbouring country, namely, Bangladesh, "**Demography: Techniques and Analysis**" explicates the potential uses and limitations of the current models for population analysis, estimation, and forecasting.

We have divided the whole book into nine chapters. The Chapter One has dealt with the 'Introduction to demography', which covers broadly the definition and scope, historical background of the subject, data sources, some basic concepts and their measurements, age-sex composition, sex-ratio, proportion, life expectancy at birth, defining migration, population growth and decline, along with various measures, concept of stable population, models, demographic transition and the need for indirect techniques as well. The Chapter Two has employed 'Age Distribution' which initiates with introduction, age structure of the population, analysis of the age structure, dependency ratio, sex composition, evaluation and adjustment of age data by various indices with illustration, smoothing and adjustment of age distribution along with various polynomials and curve fitting, estimation of base population by age and sex by Newton's Halving method and, Dual Record System based on Sample Registration areas and surveys (Chandra Sekar and Deming Method). The Chapter Three has dealt with 'Mortality: Basic Measures and Indirect Estimation'. This chapter initiates with introduction, mortality and life tables, need for mortality analysis, sources of death statistics and its quality with reference to developing countries, measurement of mortality, concepts and various measures of mortality, standardization techniques, construction of life tables, use of various mortality models, limitations of data and their adjustments, childhood mortality estimation by various methods and models with illustrations, estimation of reference time periods for child mortality estimates, use of logit smoothing technique and its application; adult mortality estimation by various methods, reference time period to which the mortality estimates refer, application of logit smoothing technique and construction of smoothed abridged life tables by sex generated by Brass Two Parameter Logit Life Tables System. The Chapter Four, which, has dealt with 'Reproductivity'. Measures of reproduction, GRR, NRR; and Timing of Fertility, Bongaarts Proximate Determinants of Fertility, estimation of the indices along with remarks. Chapter Five has dealt with 'Fertility'.

Introduction, sources of fertility data, basic measures, period and cohort fertility, sex-age adjusted birth rate, Coale's indices of fertility, birth order and parity, and parity progression ratios have been discussed. It has dealt with the indirect estimation of fertility (Brass Method), smoothing of fertility estimates generated by Gompertz relational fertility model, use of Gompertz relational fertility model to estimate Total Fertility Rate, Parity Ratio methods of fertility, methods of checking accuracy of fertility estimates, fertility estimation by reverse survival method, Rele's procedure of fertility estimation and Coale's model of marital fertility. Next one is the Chapter Six, which covers the description and analysis of nuptiality. This chapter covers the need for the study of nuptiality, data sources and its uses. It has discussed and defined its definition, estimation of nuptiality probabilities, construction of nuptiality tables, age patterns of marriage, derivation of a cohort schedule and its analysis, analysis of marriage pattern by means of a model nuptiality schedule, estimation of nuptiality parameters, estimation of proportion evermarried, age structure of the first marriage frequencies and the risk of first marriage etc. Chapter Seven has dealt with 'Migration': causes of migration, estimation and evaluation of net migration, differential migration, migration rates, concept of mobility, terms related to migration, measurement of internal migration, effectiveness of migration, indirect methods, data sources and data analysis. Next, Chapter Eight has dealt with 'Population Projection'. It discusses population growth, female population projection by age, discrete analysis, growth of female population, length of female generations and population estimation by various methods. At the end, Chapter Nine deals with 'Social and Occupational Mobility'. It has dealt with social processes, mobility and man power planning, mobility models and measures, some perfect situations, measures of career pattern based on entropy, model based job market situation, measure of occupational mobility, modelling survey data and computation of various measures etc.

In writing this book, the authors have consulted many national and international journals, text books, research papers, country monographs and unpublished Ph.D. dissertations, mimeographed papers and various notes available from different scholars and teachers of various universities and institutes as well. The authors are indebted to those whose continuous support has come in great use for writing this book. (1) Professor A.K. Chattopadhyay is grateful to his teacher Professor S.P. Mukherjee and co-worker Dr. Shahjahan Khan whose contributions helped a lot in writing this book. Professor Chattopadhyay also expresses his gratitude to Dr. Arindam Gupta, Assistant Professor, Department of Statistics, Burdwan University and Mr. Saptarshi Mandal, Research Scholar, Department of Statistics, Calcutta University for helping him in the preparation of the typescript and (2) Dr. Anuj Kumar Saha, former Associate Scientist–B, Indian Statistical Institute, Kolkata expresses his gratitude to his teachers, namely, Prof. K. Srinivasan, Late Prof. K.B. Pathak, Prof. S. Lahiri, Guide of his Doctoral Dissertation, Prof. T.K. Roy, Prof. Arvind Pandey, Prof. F. Ram, Mr. K.B. Gotpagar and others in International Institute for Population Sciences, Mumbai, and his senior colleagues of his unit, ISI, namely, Prof. S. Guha Roy, Co-guide of his Doctoral Dissertation and Prof. C.R. Malakar for their valuable advice as and when needed during his stay in the institutes. Dr. Saha wishes to express his special gratitude to his wife, Sova and his son, Shounok for their active involvement in typing the manuscript and inspiration in writing this book. At the end, both the authors would like to express their endless regards and gratitude to the publisher, Viva Books Private Limited, 4737/23 Ansari Road, Daryaganj, New Delhi 110002 for their special care of undertaking this publication.

Asis Kumar Chattopadhyay
Professor, Department of Statistics,
Calcutta University
e-mail: akcstat@caluniv.ac.in

Anuj Kumar Saha
Former Associate Scientist–B
Indian Statistical Institute, Kolkata
e-mail: sahaanui@hotmail.com

1
Introduction to Demography

1.1 DEFINITION AND SCOPE OF DEMOGRAPHY

The term 'DEMOGRAPHY' has been extracted from the Greek word 'demos'. The word 'demos' means 'a human being' and 'description of the people'. A Belgian Statistician 'ACHILLE GUILLARD' was the first man in 1855 to pronounce and designate the term 'Demography' in the article entitled ***'Eléments de statistique humaine, ou démographique comparée'*** (Elements of human statistics or comparative demography – Shryock and Siegel, 1971) which, anyone of nominal stature, would not be able to explain the meaning of physics or chemistry. We have profound sense of knowledge about the subject matter with which physical sciences deal. Demography, however, has, thus, spanned over several areas of multiple academic disciplines that have interlinkages with it. Therefore, it should necessarily clarify its subjects of study in detail. Duncan and Hauser (1972, p. 2) write:

'Demography is the study of the size, territorial distribution, and composition of population, changes therein, and the components of such changes, which may be identified as natality, mortality, territorial movement (migration), and social mobility (change of status). Three features of this definition merit brief explanation. First, the omission of reference to population "quality" is deliberate, to avoid bringing normative considerations into play. "Population composition" encompasses consideration of variation in the characteristics of a population, including not only age, sex, marital status, and the like, but also such "qualities" such as health, mental capacity, and attained skills or qualifications. Second, interest in "social mobility" is made explicit because population composition changes through movements by individuals from one status to another, e.g., from "single" to "married," as well as through natality, mortality, and migration. Third, the term "territorial movement" is preferred to "migration" because the latter ordinarily applies to movements from or to arbitrarily defined areal units rather than to the totality of movements.'

Over the past years, the empirical documents for demographic studies were censuses and vital registration only. As the World War II is over, sample surveys have started increasing the substantial progress of providing the data for demographic studies and researches. Since then, the surveys have started providing demographic data sufficiently with useful and insight information.

Demography, as a subject agrees, in principle, that it has two definitions: such as, a narrow and a broader definition like all other disciplines. In narrow terms 'demography' is defined as the scientific study of human populations, primarily with respect to their size, their structure and their development' (Van de Walle, 1982). Thus, it is a scientific study of human populations in their aggregate with regard to their size, composition or structure, spatial distributions and developments or changes in these over time. In its broader definition, when it is also called 'POPULATION STUDIES', it does not only deal with the levels and changes in the size, composition and distribution of the population but also does deal with the causes and consequences of the levels and changes. In it's broader view, demography overlaps with a number of other disciplines such as Economics, Sociology, Social Psychology, Statistics, Mathematics, Geography, Medicine, Political Science, Law, Anthropology, and Reproductive Physiology (Bogue, 1969; UN 1958) etc. Thus, demography, in its broader definition, known as 'Population Studies', is multidisciplinary in nature, and of late, as well as, from the recent past; it has attracted researchers from different disciplines such as Economics and Sociology who have made valuable contributions to its development. These researchers, though, are primarily associated with their main disciplines but find interest in population phenomena.

The practical central focus of demography known, as 'FORMAL DEMOGRAPHY'— a set of techniques, by which, data collected in censuses, surveys and vital registration systems are described, summarized and manipulated. The ***Multilingual Demographic Dictionary*** of the IUSSP defines formal demography as 'the treatment of quantitative relations among demographic phenomena in abstraction from their association with other phenomena' (Van de Walle, 1982). It assumes as a toolbox, containing the tools generally employed by demographers and others, in their 'scientific study of human populations'. Thus, the main features of formal demography are that it is basically descriptive or analytic rather than explanatory in nature and, thus it is concerned with demographic phenomena in isolation, not with their interaction with economic, social and other phenomena. It answers questions of 'what' instead of 'how' regarding the population phenomena. Hence, we focus our interest in this formal demography in describing and illustrating some of the basic demographic techniques and their utility in the planning and management of public health and population programme.

In demography, by the terminology 'Demographic Process' we mean the phenomena of fertility or births, mortality or deaths and migration or movement of people from one place to another that contributes to changes in the size and structure of a population. The variables of age, sex (gender) and marital status are thought to be the three basic demographic variables. Usually most of the methods of formal demography are restricted to an idea of the interrelationships between demographic process and size; growth and the age-sex marital structure of a population. Thus, by an analysis of a population in demography, we mean the analysis of its size, growth, spatial distribution, age-sex marital structure of the population and changes in these over time.

1.2 HISTORICAL BACKGROUND OF FORMAL DEMOGRAPHY

The development of Formal Demography that had started just before the late nineteenth century is now essentially known as the story of the evolution of the life table as a means of analyzing and presenting mortality data. Largely because of the commercial interests of the actuarial profession drove this process. Prior to 1900 the topics of fertility, nuptiality, migration and age-structure were rarely studied with any degree of mathematical sophistication, though one famous exception is Leonard Euler's (a Swiss Mathematician) invention in 1760 of the concept of Stable Population. Euler's remarkable achievement occurred some 150 years before Lotka, who, is generally regarded as the Father of Stable Population Theory, published his first paper. Smith and Keyfitz (1977) reproduced the original paper in their invaluable collection of, and commentary on, dozens of important historical papers tracing the development of Mathematical Demography.

The tables at the very earliest, which can be said to bear any resemblance to modern life tables dated back to Roman Times, but the first real demographic work was that of JOHN GRAUNT – the father of demography, whose analysis, in 1662, of London's 'Bills of Mortality' included the production of a life table of sorts, though the rather obscure method of calculation, discussed at length by Glass (1950), is very different, to say the least. Another important development in the late seventeenth century includes that of Edmund Halley (1693)—an Astronomer, and Royal of comet fame. He calculated, for the city of Breslau (now Wroclaw in Polish Silesia), the first life table was based on the actual numbers of deaths by age.

If Graunt, thought to be the father of demography, the Reverend Thomas Malthus (1766–1834) is generally thought to be the father of substantive demography, and is certainly better known. He achieved this position not because of what he said was all new, not because of what he said was all true, but because he initiated tremendous controversy and debate over the relationship between **food and population** – debate which was continued from his lifetime to the present day and is as relevant today as it was when first proposed. As a matter of fact, Malthus's essay **on the Principle of Population** was that human populations tended to increase at a more rapid rate than the food supply needed to sustain them. To balance these two, checks would be imposed on population growth and these were all resolvable into vice and misery and moral restraint. The only moral restraint recognized by Malthus was the postponement of marriage with no extramarital sex during the postponed period. Moral restraint was to be the saviour of mankind. The checks on population growth noted by Malthus were described as 'preventive' and 'positive' checks or, as they are now called, factors affecting fertility and mortality respectively. Positive checks were identified as causes that shorten human life, e.g., diseases, epidemics, famine, plague, etc. (all forms of misery) and wars excesses of all kinds, etc.(forms of misery brought about by vice). Preventive checks were the kind, which reduced fertility and – apart from moral restraint – included promiscuity, homosexuality, adultery, abortion and birth control (all vices). Malthus recognized that preventive and positive checks varied inversely, i.e. fertility and mortality must be either both high or both low. Finally, it should be noted that Malthus' great hope, 'moral restraint' or delayed marriage, did not encompass abstinence or any birth control after marriage, partly because of their immorality and partly because of their tendency to remove a necessary stimulus to industry. The fear of having a large number of children causes man to work much harder than he would if the family size could be knowingly controlled. From the technical methods of John Graunt and the substantive arguments of Malthus the subject of demography has developed to a major field of study in the social sciences.

There were few important developments in the eighteenth century, but in the early nineteenth century, Milne (1815) is generally credited with formalizing the conventional calculation and presentation of the life table, as we know it today. Thus, by 1841, when William Farr, the famous Victorian Registrar General of England, started producing the decennial series of English life tables, which continue to the present, the life table was recognizably similar to its present form. By 1900 the distinctive notation used for life tables today had come established.

After 1900 the major developments in formal demography are first attributable to Alfred Lotka, who in three papers totaling just thirteen pages (Lotka, 1907; Lotka, 1922; Sharpe and Lotka, 1911) developed the mathematics of a Stable Population, showing how does a closed population tend, if the schedules of age-specific mortality and fertility remain constant, to develop along a predictable path to a final, fixed age-structure. Later, in 1925, Lotka with Louis Dublin (Dublin and Lotka, 1925) incorporated the concepts of 'intrinsic' (or 'true') rates into theory.

In the field of fertility analysis, The Total Fertility and Net Reproduction Rates, which had been developed by German demographers in the late nineteenth century, were widely used largely through the work of Kuczynski (1935). Cohort analysis of fertility data only really was widely used after the Second World War, especially in American Fertility Surveys, the classic first application there being by Whelpton (1954). Another post-war development is that of Hajnal's Singulate Mean Age at Marriage (Hajnal 1953). This is noteworthy as first of many demographic 'Indirect' techniques whereby information on one topic (here proportions single by age) is used to estimate another (here mean age at first marriage).

The first widely used demographic models (if Lotka's stable population is excluded) were the model life tables published by United Nations (1955, 1956). These were followed by the Princeton Regional Model Life Tables' (Coal and Demeny, 1966), whose continued importance and usefulness is attested by the publication of a second, extended edition in 1983. The mortality models were followed, also from Coale and his Princeton Colleagues, by somewhat similar models of Nuptiality and Marital Fertility (Coale, 1971; Coale and McNeil, 1972; Coale and Trussell, 1974). Along parallel but quite different lines, Brass and his colleagues in London were developing their 'Relational' models of mortality (Brass, 1971) and fertility (Brass, 1981), whereby age-patterns of fertility or mortality are related, via mathematical transformations, to a standard pattern.

By the 1980s the main areas of advance in formal demography are in the areas of model building, much of it made possible by the ever-increasing power and sophistication of computing and related statistical and database tools. An excellent example of this is multi-regional demographic modeling of Rogers (1975) and others, which uses accounting techniques within a framework of matrix algebra.

1.3 SOME BASIC MEASURES

Nearly all-demographic data take the form of frequencies of either qualitative or discrete (i.e. counted) quantitative variables used. The statistics used to manipulate such data are rates, ratios and proportions. They, thus, constitute the most basic tools of formal demography. Essentially, they enable comparison by eliminating differences due to population size. The basic measures have also been discussed in the relevant chapters later. Here only a snapshot of some basic measures has been given below.

1.3.1 Ratio

A ratio is simply any number divided by any other number. An example is the sex ratio – the number of males per 100 females.

$$\text{Sex Ratio} = \frac{\text{Males}}{\text{Females}} \times 100$$

The overall Sex Ratio is simply the ratio of males to females in the population. The overall sex ratio is entirely determined by

1. Sex ratio at birth.
2. Sex differences in mortality.
3. Differential migration.

Each will be discussed in turn.

1.3.2 The Sex Ratio at Birth

It is just the number of male births per 100 female births. It is normally around 105, that is, 105 boys are born for every 100 girls, but it does vary somewhat between populations and sub-groups. For example, in England and Wales in 1985 there were 336,835 male and 319,582 female births, so the Sex Ratio at Birth was

$$\text{Sex Ratio at Birth} = \frac{336{,}835}{319{,}582} \times 100 = 105.4$$

1.3.3 Proportion

A proportion is a special type of ratio in which the numerator is included in the denominator. That is, it has the form:

$$\text{Proportion} = \frac{X}{(X+Y)} \quad \text{where, X = Males and Y = Females}$$

$$\text{Proportion} = \frac{336{,}835}{(336{,}835 + 319{,}582)}$$

where, $X = 336{,}835$ and $Y = 319{,}582$

$$= 0.513$$

Note that the proportion can only range from 0.0 to 1.0. It is, though, very common to express proportions as percentages simply by multiplying by 100, in which case the range of possible values is from 0 per cent to 100 per cent.

The term *rate* is used very loosely in demography (as elsewhere) and this can cause confusion. Strictly, the numerator of a *rate* is a number of events, such as births or deaths, occurring during a period of time. The denominator is the number of 'persons-years of exposure to risk' experienced by the population during the period under consideration. The crucial point is that some time, period has to be specified.

In demography, rates are most frequently calculated for periods of one year. This means that the total number of person-years of exposure to risk can usually be approximated by the population at mid-year. To understand this, consider the calculation of an annual death rate. Each person surviving for the whole year will contribute one year to the total number of years of exposure to risk, while those dying during the year will contribute only a fraction of a year. This fraction will be, on average, half a year if people die evenly throughout the year. The total number of years of exposure to risk arrived at by adding these fractions to the total contributed by those who survived is the same as taking the average population total during the year and letting each person in that average contribute a whole year of exposure. And, since the average population can normally be approximated closely by the population total at mid-year, the mid-year population can, under most circumstances, be used for calculating annual rates. This is why Government Statistical Services produce annual population estimates relating to the middle of each year, rather than the beginning or the end.

It should be reiterated that many measures, which are commonly called 'rates' in demography, are strictly ratios, proportions or more complex indices. For example, the 'Literacy Rate' is just the proportion of the population that is literate.

1.3.4 Life Expectancy at Birth

Life expectancy at birth (e_0^0) measures the average number of years that a newborn baby can expect to live. We can think of cohort life expectancy at birth, which would be the average age at death of a cohort of individuals (equal to the total number of person-years lived by the cohort divided by the size of the initial cohort).

More common is a period measure of life expectancy at birth. Like the period TFR, this is a synthetic measure, showing the hypothetical experience of a cohort passing through life subject to the relevant age-specific rates from a given period. Hence, if life expectancy at birth for 1996 were, say, 75 years, this would mean that a cohort of individuals experiencing the age-specific death rates that prevailed in 1996 would live for an average of 75 years.

A more general aspect of life expectancy is the notion of **remaining life expectancy** as of age x (e^0_x). This simply shows the average number of years of life remaining for individuals who reach age x and then experience a given set of age-specific death rates.

1.3.5 Migration

The definition of the word can be 'the movement of people from one place to another'.

There are two main types of migration: first, internal migration, i.e. migration within one country, and secondly international migration, which means the movement from one country to another.

A good example of internal migration is the movement from East Germany to West Germany, which causes big problems for East Germany.

A good example of international migration is the movement from third-world countries to Europe or America.

The next question is: What makes people migrate from one place to another?

The reasons for migration can be divided into two main aspects, the so-called 'push' and 'pull' factors.

Push factors are those in their old place, which force people to move. For example, there may be civil wars or wars in general in the country, but political or religious oppression, climate changes, lack of jobs or simply poverty are all important push factors.

Pull factors are factors in the target country, which encourage people to move; these include peace and safety, a chance of a better job, better education, social security, a better standard of living in general as well as political and religious freedom.

Migrants are people who change their place of residence. In-migrants (I) move into a place, while out-migrants (O) leave that place. Gross migration flows measure movement in both directions, while net migration reflects the difference between two opposing gross migration flows. Thus, for example, if during a particular period 300,000 people moved from New York to California and 100,000 moved from California to New York, we would characterize the situation as one with a net migration of 200,000 from New York to California.

When migration entails crossing an international border, we speak of immigration or emigration, depending on whether the place we are focused on is the one migrant are moving into or out of, respectively.

1.3.6 Age and Sex Composition

Age and Duration. An individual's **age** at any given time is the time elapsed since this individual's birth. **Age in completed years** (or 'at last birthday') refers to the greatest integer less than an individual's age. Age may be referred to as **exact age** to emphasize the distinction between age and age in completed years. 'Age' in demography is often used to mean either exact age or age in completed years, the appropriate interpretation being given by context. The same terminology applies to any time unit, so that we may refer, for example, to 'exact age in months' or 'age in completed weeks.'

An age pyramid reflects the age and sex composition of a population. These diagrams are drawn with age (ascending) on a central vertical axis, horizontal bars showing the number or proportion of males on the left, and bars showing the number or proportion of females on the right. They are an extremely useful means of depicting the age and sex composition of a population, and typically will provide a good deal of information about the past history of fertility and perhaps also mortality and migration in a population.

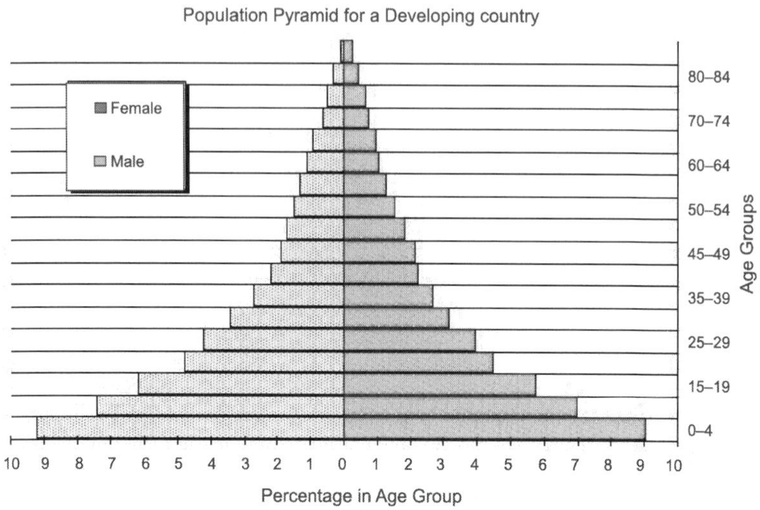

Fig.1.1 Population Structure – Developing Countries

This population pyramid (Figure 1.1) is wide at the base, which means there are a large proportion of young people in the country. It tapers very quickly as you go up into the older age groups, and is narrow at the top. This shows that a very small proportion of people are elderly.

This shape of pyramid is typical of a developing country, such as Kenya or Vietnam.

1.3.7 Concept of a Stable Population

Lotka defines a stable population as a particular case of a broader category of populations, called ***Malthusian populations***. A Malthusian population is a population where the survivorship curve and the age structure are invariable. There are an infinite number of such populations, which can be classified, initially, in two ways: (1) Given a survivorship function, there corresponds a sub-set (H) of all the Malthusian populations based upon that survivorship function. By varying the survivorship function, an infinite number of sub-sets (H) embracing all Malthusian populations will then be obtained; (2) Given an age structure, there corresponds a subset (F) of all the Malthusian populations based upon that age structure. By varying the age structure an infinite number of sub-sets (F) covering all Malthusian populations will then be obtained. In a given sub-set (Ho) or (Fo) an additional condition is needed in order to determine a particular population.

The stable population of a sub-set (Ho) is a particular population for which the fertility function is known. It can be demonstrated that for any given fertility function there exists one, and only one, stable population. By varying the fertility function, on the other hand, all the populations of the sub-set (H) can be obtained. Thus, any Malthusian population can be considered a stable population, and indeed there are an infinite number of ways of doing this. That is why the two concepts are often confused, and such confusion has, in fact, become traditional. In this introduction, following the tradition, we have made references to a stable population, whereas in some cases the expression 'Malthusian population' would have been more accurate. For the same reason, the expression 'stable population' here is not entirely in keeping with the contents.

Therefore, a population is called **stable** when both its growth rate and its relative age distribution do not change over time. Hence the size of a stable population grows or diminishes at a constant rate, but each age group has a constant **share**. The **size** of each age group grows or diminishes with the same (constant) rate as the size of the whole population.

Property 1: The number of births and the number of deaths in a stable population change with the same rate. The rate is constant and it equals the growth rate of the population. Thus the Crude Birth Rate (CBR) is also constant, and so is the Crude Death Rate (CDR) – although the CBR and the CDR are usually not equal to each other.
In other words
growth rate (= natural growth rate) = CBR – CDR = constant

Property 2: Any two-sets of time-constant age-specific birth rates and age-specific death rates, when applied to a population with a certain initial age distribution, will in the long run result in a stable population, of which the growth rate and the age distribution only depend on the birth rates and the death rates. The ultimate (stable) age distribution will have a regular form. This is the case even if the initial age distribution was not stable—for instance was very irregular.

The Use of Stable Population Theory

We usually use stable population theory when we find deficiencies in certain population data (for example, the CBR) and when we know some of other data (for example, the age distribution) with certainty.

Stable age distributions can be applied in the way as follows:

The age distribution of a stable age distribution is usually written as

$$c\,(a)\,da = b \exp(-ra)\, s\,(a)\, da \qquad \text{(A)}$$

where c (a) da is the proportion of the population aged between a and a + da.

$$\text{From (A) it follows that } s\,(a) = \frac{c\,(a)\, e^{ra}}{b} \qquad \text{(B)}$$

Euler has noted that if an age distribution can be available from a census and if the corresponding crude birth rate and rate of population growth are known, the population's survivorship can be inferred. Since then Euler, became an early inventor of indirect estimation. It will be noted that

$$\ln \frac{c\,(a)}{s\,(a)} = \ln b - ra \qquad \text{(C)}$$

the equation (C) given above can be used to estimate the crude birth rate and the rate of population growth from the age-distribution c (a) based on using a standard statistical package, (A) or (B) can be used for simultaneous estimation of survivorship, the crude birth rate and the natural rate of population increase (requires well-behaved data). Stable relationships like (C) have been used for estimation of mortality and fertility in nations with incomplete vital registration (Brass 1975).

1.3.8 Some Related Definitions

Replacement-level fertility: The level of fertility at which a couple has only enough children to replace themselves, or about two children per couple.

Stable population: A population in which the percentage of people at each age and sex category does not change over time.

Stabilized population: Common term for stationary population, in which the birth rate equals the death rate and in addition where net immigration equals net emigration so that the population does not increase or decrease over time. Usually used in the context of stabilizing increasing populations, where the net population growth rate is zero.

Stationary population: A type of stable population in which the birth rate equals the death rate.

1.3.9 Population Growth

1.3.9.1 *History and Evolution*

The increase in general population in the world was negligible until the industrial revolution. From the era of the Roman Empire to the colonization of America, the population of the world grew from about a quarter billion to a half billion persons. By the mid-19th century, however, it had grown to about one billion, and by 1930 it had risen to 2 billion; the United Nations estimates the population of the world will reach 10 billion in 2200. In world terms, the population is growing at about 1.2 per cent annually (compared with 0.1 per cent in ancient times and a rate of 1.75 per cent as recently as the 1990s) in population. Though a 1.2 per cent growth rate may appear small, it annually adds some 77 million persons to the population of the world and all of this growth will be taking place in less developed nations mostly.

During the period of industrial revolution, developments in sanitation, technology, and the means of food distribution that made possible a drop in the death rate significantly between 1650 and 1900, the population of Europe almost quadrupled (from about 100 million to about 400 million) despite considerable emigration. As the population growth rate increased, so did concern that the earth might not be able to sustain future populations. The phenomenal increase in numbers led Thomas Robert Malthus to predict that the population would eventually outstrip the food supply. Karl Marx emphatically rejected this view and argued that the problem was not one of overpopulation but of unequal distribution of goods, a problem that even a declining population would not solve.

1.3.9.2 *Modern Population Growth*

In the late 20th century, difference in a major population arose in the comparative growth rates of the developed (0.6 per cent) and developing (2.1 per cent) nations. Africa's annual growth rate is about 3 per cent, compared to 1.7 per cent for Asia, 0.7 per cent in Latin America, and 0.3 per cent in Europe. If the present rates hold constant, many developing countries will double their populations in 25 years or less, compared to 50 years or more for industrialized nations. As for example, Great Britain has a present doubling rate of 140 years, while Costa Rica has one of 19 years.

Great Britain has accomplished its demographic transition, i.e., it has moved from a situation of high birth rate and high death rate (prior to the industrial revolution), to one of high birth rate and low death rate (during industrialization), and finally it has reached one of low birth rate and low death rate (as a postindustrial society). Most of the Third World countries are in a situation of high birth rate and declining death rate, contributing to the population explosion.

1.3.9.3 *Population Control*

An indication of declining birth rate depends largely on the availability and use of birth control and on high living standards that makes unnecessary the production of additional children to provide necessary and inexpensive labour. Family planning is national policy in many industrial countries, such as Japan and most of Europe. At the end, in most cases the birth rate has declined. Many developing countries have followed the lead of India (which has since 1952 conducted an extensive, but not totally successful, birth control programme) in trying to promote family planning as national policy. The developing countries that had followed India, by name, are China, Kenya, Pakistan, Taiwan, Turkey, Egypt, and Chile respectively.

In the United States, aspects of the population question, such as birth control and abortion, are among the most bitterly debated subjects. The United States has opposed at times the use of foreign aid appropriations for family planning overseas; private groups such as Planned Parenthood mainly run domestic family planning.

A number of nongovernmental organizations concerned with population growth have also appeared. Zero Population Growth, an educational group founded in 1970, aims to stop population growth, first in the United States and then in other countries. On the international level, besides the International Planned Parenthood Federation, the United Nations Economic and Social Council provides birth control aid to underdeveloped nations.

1.3.9.4 *Population Change*

The change in population from one year to the next equals the excess of births over deaths plus the amount of net in-migration:

$$\Delta P = B - D + I - O.$$

The first portion of the right hand side of the equation (B – D) equals the natural increase in the population. Note that the rate of natural increase in the population equals the difference between the crude birth rate and the crude death rate. The overall rate of population growth equals the rate of natural increase plus the rate of net immigration.

Further, note that because of the effects of age composition, it is possible for a population to manifest below-replacement fertility and yet still experience natural increase (in the demographic short and medium run). This has been the case for most of the past two decades and more in the U.S.

1.3.10 Basic Measures of Growth and Decline

1.3.10.1 *Arithmetic Growth*

A population that grows arithmetically will increase by a constant number of people in each period. If a population of 5000 grows by 100 annually, its size over successive years will be: 5100, 5200, 5300, . . . Since the annual increases are the same, these numbers form an arithmetic progression or series; the size of the population in the example is also increasing at a constant *arithmetic rate* of 2 per cent (100/5000 = 0.02 or 2 per cent). Arithmetic growth is analogous to 'simple interest', whereby interest is paid only on the initial sum deposited, the principal, rather than on accumulating savings. Five per cent simple interest on INR100 merely returns a constant INR5 interest every year.

Real examples of arithmetic population growth are uncommon and necessarily limited to settings where administrators have the option of establishing targets to increase or decrease numbers by a constant amount. For instance during a phase of expansion, budgets could support a linear increase in numbers – such as of employees in an organization, enrolments at a college or soldiers in an army. Despite its limitations for describing actual population changes, arithmetic growth is the basis for a widely used measure in demography, namely *average annual increase*. It was also an important concept in Malthus's (1798) population theory.

Thomas Robert Malthus (1766–1834), an English clergyman, and professor of history and political economy, is the best known among the pioneers of demography. His *Essay on the Principle of Population* (1798) is one of the most important and influential books ever written on the subject of human numbers (Grebenik, 1989: 1); it was the first to stimulate interest in the relationship between population and resources (Keyfitz, 1972). Malthus wrote to oppose prevailing ideas about the benefits of population growth. His 'gloomy thesis' was that population growth threatened prosperity because it inevitably outran increases in food supplies. He reasoned that, at best, agricultural production grew arithmetically, by the same amount every 25 years, while population grew geometrically, doubling every 25 years (Malthus, 1798: 16). Thus the implications of his 'principle of population' arose from the differences between arithmetic and geometric growth.

Table 1.1 Basic measures of population growth and decline.

Definitions	Male, West Bengal
P_0 = population at the start, e.g. year zero	P_0 = 23435987 (1st March, Year 1971)
P_n = population at the end, e.g. after n	P_n = 28560907 (1st March, Year 1971 to 1st April, Year 1981)
n = number of intervals (e.g. years) between P_0 and P_n	Years n = 10.08 years (1st March, Year 1981 to 1st April, 1981)
1. Absolute change $P_n - P_0$ 28560907 – 23435987 = 5124920	2. Percentage change $\left(\frac{P_n - P_0}{P_0}\right) \times 100$ (5124920/23435987) × 100 = 21.87%
3. Average annual increase $\left(\frac{P_n - P_0}{n}\right)$ 5124920 /10.08 = 508,425	4. Arithmetic growth rate $\left(\frac{P_n - P_0}{n}\right) \div P_0 \times 100$ 508,425/23435987 × 100 r = 2.1694% for Male, West Bengal

1. Absolute change is simply the difference between the size of the population at the start and end of a period of time. This represents the *net growth* of the population. It is not a measure to be ignored because of its simplicity: sometimes the main implications of population changes arise from the extra numbers to be fed, housed, educated, employed or supported. Table 1.1 presents an example of absolute change in numbers in Male Population, West Bengal.
2. Percentage change (absolute change/initial population × 100) provides a means of comparing developments in different populations or different periods of time by gauging the amount of change relative to initial numbers. Percentage change is always based on numbers at the start of the period. It is a measure frequently used in census atlases and other maps of intercensal population change, because percentages are comparable and intelligible to a wide readership.

3. Average annual increase (or decrease) is based on the concept of arithmetic change. It assumes constant annual gains or losses – ignoring the notion that growth is self-reinforcing. The measure provides a rough-and-ready indication of the numbers being added to a population, but the longer the period of observation, or the greater the amount of change, the more likely the average is misleading. Average annual change is sometimes used to provide a quick estimate or projection of the size of a population in a particular year, but the same caveats apply. Estimates of average annual increase really have claims to accuracy only when the interval is short or where little change has occurred.
4. The arithmetic growth rate included in Table 1.1 is mainly for comparison with other rates: it is seldom used in demographic calculations. The rate compares the annual average increase with the size of the initial population. The result is multiplied by 100, since population growth rates are usually expressed as rates per cent.

In calculating measures of population change there are several potential sources of error arising from the nature of the data. Firstly, boundary changes are common and may call for many adjustments to data for geographical analyses of population change within cities or across regions. For example, incorporation of new territory, such as a neighbouring town, can greatly change the population of a city. The main strategy in such situations is to use constant boundaries, typically the most recent, for establishing the size of the population at the start and at the end of the period.

Secondly, changes in the dates of censuses and population estimates affect the length of the interval, which should be expressed as accurately as possible (Pollard et al. 1990: 21). Thus if the first estimate is for 30th June 2000 and the second for 10th August 2001, the length of the interval (n) is 1 year plus 41 days, or 1.11 years.

Thirdly, definition changes can have dramatic effects that may be difficult to resolve. Statistics on the growth rate of the labour force will vary greatly if the first population includes the unemployed, part-time workers and unpaid workers while the second population includes only people in full-time paid employment.

Similarly, the apparent growth of ethnic minority groups will vary according to whether the source data are based on self-identification, degree of descent, birthplace, language or religion, or a combination of these. Inclusion or exclusion of children of mixed descent can also affect results considerably. Adjustments may be essential to achieve a consistent definition of the population at the start and at the end.

1.3.10.2 *Geometric Growth*

More accurate measures of population growth avoid the limiting assumption of constant annual increments or decrements and facilitate better estimates of intermediate values. Measures of population change based on the geometric growth rate are widely used, as are those based on the exponential growth rate. The former are slightly easier to understand and calculate yet yield similar results where the time interval is short or the rate is within the typical range for national populations (from about 1 to 4 per cent). Also, the collection of official statistics on population size is inevitably periodic – at regular intervals such as census dates – and the intervening pattern of change need not be continuous and cumulative, especially where migration contributes substantially. Measuring growth somewhat crudely, as a geometric process, acknowledges the nature of the source data and the imprecision of estimates between dates.

Rates of change are not the only needed measures from the geometric growth formula. Analyses of population trends often require other information about the past or future size of the population, the time required to reach a given size and the population's doubling time. Table 1.2 therefore presents variations of the geometric growth formula for calculating the initial and end-of-period populations, together with time intervals. As in Table 1.1, definitions are at the top, together with the values employed in the accompanying examples. The footnotes to the table provide brief explanations of the derivation of each formula. Some of the formulas need to be calculated using logarithms; the table shows the logarithmic form of all of the formulas for comparison, as well as for use where a scientific calculator or computer is not available. Results of calculations vary according to the number of decimal places retained in intermediate steps.

1. End of period population: Formula 1 in Table 1.1 has applications in estimating intercensal numbers, or projecting the future population, assuming that the growth rate remains constant. This assumption becomes increasingly untenable as n increases, because growth rates typically vary through time. In the table, example 1 estimates population numbers in 1981 from information on the

initial population in 1971 together with the rate of growth and the time period. The growth rate per cent must be divided by 100. Changing the value of n would permit estimates of the size of the West Bengal male population in other years, such as 1990 (n = 9) and 2009 (n = 19).

2. Initial population: The second formula works backwards in time to calculate what past population numbers would have been if numbers had been growing at a particular rate. The assumption of constant growth rates is too constraining to allow back-projection to proceed very far. Thus, reconstructing the past in this way is best confined to shorter intervals, all the more so in populations where substantial growth derives from migration – the most variable and unpredictable of all components of population change.

Table 1.2 Measures of population change from the geometric growth rate.

Formulas	Examples
Definitions	*Male, West Bengal*
P_0 = population at the start	P_0 = 23435987 (1st March, Year 1971)
P_n = population at the end	P_n = 28560907 (1st March, Year 1971 to 1st April, Year 1981)
n = number of intervals between	n = 10.08 between P_0 and P_n
r = annual growth rate	r = ?
1. End of period population $P_n = P_0 (1 + r)^n$ $= 23435987 \times (1 + r)^{10.08}$	$P_n = 28560907$
2. Initial population $P_0 = \dfrac{P_n}{(1+r)^n}$	$P_0 = \dfrac{28560907}{(1+r)^{10.08}}$
3. Geometric growth rate $\sqrt[n]{\dfrac{P_n}{P_0}} - 1$	$r = \sqrt[10.08]{(28560907/23435987)} - 1$ $= \sqrt[10.08]{1.21867737} - 1$ $= 1.01981338 - 1$ $= 0.0198$
4. Interval between two populations $n = \dfrac{\log\left(\dfrac{P_n}{P_0}\right)}{\log(1+r)}$	n = 0.085888746/0.008515007631 = 10.08 years

5. Doubling time

$$n = \frac{\log 2}{\log(1+r)}$$

$n = 0.301029995/0.008515007631$

$= 35.35$ years

Derivation of formulas:

1. End of period population: 'compound interest' formula.
2. Initial population: divide both sides of formula 1 by $(1 + r)$ n.
3. Geometric growth rate: divide both sides of formula 1 by P_0 and make r the subject.
4. Interval: make *n* the subject of the logarithmic form of formula 3.
5. Doubling time: in formula 4, $(P_n/P_0) = 2$, since the population doubles.

3. Growth rate: The growth rate provides an informative basis for comparisons between countries, since it gives an impression of stage of development in terms of progress through the demographic transition. However, the contribution of migration to national population growth is not known accurately for some countries, and cross-national data on rates of natural increase are sometimes published instead of figures on overall growth rates.
   In contemporary national populations, the highest growth rates occur where the demographic transition is yet to be completed, but more developed countries receiving substantial flows of international migrants, such as the United States and Australia; also have rates higher than other 'post-transition' populations (World Bank, 1994).
   New towns and suburbs have the most spectacular growth rates on account of low initial numbers, but their growth rates typically fall as the population increases. Canberra, the capital of Australia, had an annual growth rate that peaked at 14 per cent during the 1960s, because of substantial government investment in establishing the new city. Subsequently, Canberra's growth rate declined rapidly from this peak, mainly because the larger the population, the greater the increments needed to sustain a particular rate. In the West Bengal example in Table 1.2, the growth rate calculation proceeds either by finding the 10.08^{th} root of P_n/P_0, or by raising P_n/P_0 to the power of 1/10.08 (the reciprocal of the power).
4. Interval between two populations: This denotes the time taken to change from one specified total to another. Thus the example in the table addresses the question of how long it will take a population

to reach a particular size. Applications arise in planning when seeking to anticipate the date that numbers will reach consequential levels. For instance, population size determines the rights of communities to self-government or separate political representation. The passings of size thresholds, such as a million or a billion, are also occasions for reflection and action.

5. Doubling time: After the growth rate, the doubling time is the most widely mentioned measure of national and global population growth, because it is readily comprehended. In 2000, the world population doubling time was 51 years, compared with 49 years in 1999 (Population Reference Bureau 1999: 2; 2000: 2).

Transitional populations in Africa have most of the fastest contemporary doubling times of 20–23 years. Malthus (1798: 16) made effective use of doubling time to convey the implications of population growth.

In the United States of America, where the means of subsistence have been more ample, the manners of the people more pure, and consequently the checks to early marriages fewer, than in any of the modern states of Europe, the population has been found to double itself in twenty-five years.

A well-known shortcut formula for calculating doubling times is to divide 70 by the growth rate per cent. Thus annual growth rates of 2 per cent and 1 per cent give doubling times of 35 years and 70 years respectively. This approximation, which assumes an exponential, rather than geometric, growth rate, is improved slightly by using 69 instead of 70. The approximation is based on the doubling time formula from the exponential growth rate, as discussed below.

1.3.10.3 *Exponential Growth*

Exponential growth refers to the situation where growth compounds continuously – at every instant of time. Accordingly, it is sometimes called 'instantaneous growth' (Krebs, 1978). Geometric growth is a special case of exponential growth (Pressat, 1985: 74), because compounding occurs at intervals much longer than an instant. The shorter the interval over which increments occur, the faster the population increases – just as the balance in a bank account with daily interest grows more quickly than one with yearly interest.

By 2010, exponential growth at an annual rate of 50 per cent results in a total of nearly three quarters of a million, compared with 288325 from geometric growth – compounding annually – and 30000 from arithmetic growth. As in geometric growth, the ratio between adjacent populations is constant: 5000 : 8244, and 8244 : 13591, for example, are equivalent to ratios of 1: 1.649. In other words, numbers increase by about 65 per cent annually. Continuous compounding explains why a 50 per cent annual growth rate actually creates a 65 per cent increase. Exponential growth was prominent in one of the late twentieth century statements of a mathematical principle of population growth, namely the book *The Limits to Growth* (Meadows, et al. 1974, first published 1972) and its sequel *Beyond the Limits* (Meadows, et al. 1992). Whereas Malthus believed that populations tend to grow geometrically, the authors of the *Limits to Growth* argued that the world's population is growing exponentially, and consumption of resources is also increasing exponentially (Meadows, et al. 1974: 25). They went further in saying that the world's population is really increasing 'super-exponentially', by which they meant that far from being constant, growth rates have increased through time such that 'the population curve is rising even faster than it would if growth were strictly exponential' (Meadows et al. 1974: 34). To explain the implications of exponential growth for population numbers the authors quoted the following story (Meadows, et al. 1974: 29; 1992: 18).

There is an old Persian legend about a clever courtier who presented a beautiful chessboard to his king and requested that the king give him in return 1 grain of rice for the first square on the board, 2 grains of rice for the second square, 4 grains for the third, and so forth. The king readily agreed and ordered rice to be brought from his stores. By the fortieth square a million rice grains had to be brought from the storerooms. The king's entire rice supply was exhausted long before he reached the sixty-fourth square. Exponential increase is deceptive because it generates immense numbers very quickly.

This story, however, is misleading when applied to population growth. It implies that numbers tend to keep doubling at short intervals indefinitely. Population growth does not occur in this way, since the rates seldom remain constant for long. Also, national population doublings normally take decades rather than years. The world's population growth rate has never exceeded 2.1 per cent (doubling time 33 years), and the growth rate has been falling since the mid-1960s; in 2001 it was estimated to be 1.3 per cent (Population Reference Bureau 2001b).

Table 1.3 Measures of population change from the exponential growth rate.

Formulas	Examples
Definitions	***Male, West Bengal***
P_0 = population at the start	P_0 = 23435987 (1st March, Year 1971
P_n = population at the end	P_n = 28560907 (1st March, Year 1971 to 1st April, Year 1981)
n = number of intervals between P_0 and P_n	n = 10.08 years
r = annual growth rate	r = ?
ln = natural logarithm	
e is a constant (2.718 28)	
1. End of period population $P_n = P_0 e^{rn}$ or $\ln(P_n/P_0) = r \times 10.08$	or ln (1.21868) = r × 10.08 0.197768305 = r × 10.08 r = 0.197768305/10.08 = 0.01962
2. Initial population $P_0 = \frac{P_n}{e^{rn}}$ $\ln P_0 = \ln P_n - r\,n$ $16.9697833 = 17.16754945 - r\,n$ or $0.197766152 = r\,n$	
3. Exponential growth rate $r = \frac{\ln\left(\frac{P_n}{P_0}\right)}{n}$	r = 0.197766152/10.08 = 0.01961
4. Interval between two populations $n = \frac{\ln\left(\frac{P_n}{P_0}\right)}{r}$	n = 0.197768305/0.01961 = 10.08 years
5. Doubling Time $n = \frac{\ln 2}{r}$	= 0.69314718/0.01961 = 35.36 years

1.3.10.4 *A Paradox of Growth*

A 100 per cent exponential growth rate per annum generally produces more than a 100 per cent increase a year, which is apparently seemed to be a paradox. Because the growth amounts to 100 per cent over a single interval of a year with the exponential growth, as there is an infinite number of intervals over which the growth is compounding. As for example, if a 100 per cent annual increase on an initial population of 100 was split into two intervals of six months, the rate for each interval would be 50 per cent ($r = 0.5$) but based on the geometric growth formula, the population comes to 150 (100×1.5) at mid-year and 225 (100×1.5^2) when the year ends. So likely, on the basis of calculation of the increments quarterly (i.e. 25 per cent growth per quarter) the population in total should stand at 244 (100×1.25^4) when the year ends. Hence, the greater the number of points at which increments are added, the greater the growth. But in case of exponential growth it produces higher outcomes for the same reasons that daily interest payments cause a bank balance to grow faster than monthly or yearly payments (Krebs, 1978).

1.4 DEMOGRAPHIC TRANSITION

The notion of the demographic transition refers to the long-term process of transition from a demographic regime of high birth and death rates to one of low birth and death rates. Every industrialized country has undergone this transition, and developing countries may be seen as being in various stages of the transition. In developed countries this transition began in the eighteenth century and continues today. Less developed countries began the transition later and are still in the midst of earlier stages of the model.

CBR and CDR

The model is based on the change in crude birth rate (CBR) and crude death rate (CDR) over time. Each is expressed per thousand population. Taking the number of births in one year in a country, dividing it by the country's population, and multiplying the number by 1000 determine the CBR. In 1998, the CBR in the United States is 14 per 1000 (14 births per 1000 people) while in Kenya it is 32 per 1000. The crude death rate is similarly determined. The population divides the number of deaths in one year and that figure is multiplied by 1000. This yields a CDR of 9 in the U.S. and 14 in Kenya.

Stage I

Prior to the industrial revolution, countries in Western Europe had a high CBR and CDR. Births were high because more children meant more workers on the farm and with high death rate, families needed more children to ensure survival of the family. Death rates were high due to disease and a lack of hygiene. The high CBR and CDR were somewhat stable and meant slow growth of a population. Occasional epidemics would dramatically increase the CDR for a few years (Represented by the 'waves' in Stage I of the model).

Stage II

In the mid-18th century, the death rate in Western European countries dropped due to improvement in sanitation and medicine. Out of tradition and practice, the birth rate remained high. The dropping death rate but stable birth rate in the beginning of Stage II contributed to skyrocketing population growth rates. Over time, children became an added expense and were less able to contribute to the wealth of a family. For this reason, along with advances in birth control, the CBR was reduced through the 20th century in developed countries. Populations still grew rapidly but this growth began to slow down.

Many less developed countries are currently in Stage II of the model. For example, Kenya's high CBR of 32 per 1000 but low CDR of 14 per 1000 contributes to a high rate of growth (as in mid-Stage II).

Stage III

In the late 20th century, CBR and CDR in developed countries both leveled off at a low rate. In some cases the CBR is slightly higher than the CDR (as in US, 14 versus 9) while in other countries the CBR is less than the CDR (as in Germany, 9 versus 11). Immigration from less developed countries now accounts for much of the population growth in developed countries that are in Stage III of the transition. Countries like China, South Korea, Singapore and Cuba are readily approaching Stage III.

1.5 MODEL

As with all models, the demographic transition model has its problems. The model does not provide 'guidelines' as to how long it takes a country to get from Stage I to Stage III. Western European countries took centuries through some rapidly developing countries like the Economic Tigers are transforming in mere decades. The model also does not predict that all countries will reach Stage III and have low birth and death rates. There are factors such as religion that keep some countries' birth rate from dropping.

Though this version of demographic transition is composed of three stages, you will find similar models in texts as well as ones that include four or even five stages. The shape of the graph is consistent but the divisions in time are the only modification.

An understanding of this model, in any of its forms, will help you to better understand population policies and changes in developed and less developed countries around the world.

1.6 THE BASIC DEMOGRAPHIC EQUATION

This is one of the most fundamental relationships in formal demography. It can be written as:

$$P_{t+1} = P_t + B - D + IN - OUT$$

That is, the population of an area at time t + 1 is just the population at time t plus the number of births between t and t + 1, minus the number of deaths, plus the number of migrants entering the area, minus the number leaving. The difference between the number of births and deaths gives the **'natural increase'**, while the difference between the numbers of migrants **in** and **out** gives the **'net migration'**. Thus the equation can be written as:

Natural Increase = Births – Deaths and,

Population Change = Natural Increase + Net Migration

In some parts of the world, population is dominated by the rate of natural increase, but on the other hand net migration is more important, and in some parts they are of roughly equal importance.

Occasionally the Basic Demographic Equation is called the **'Balancing Equation'**, though it is a characteristic of the equation but it never balances exactly. Taking the population at one census and adding it to the natural increase and net migration that occurs during the inter-censal period will never give exactly the population recorded at the next census. The extent to which the figures differ is known as the **'Error of Closure'**. Its magnitude is a sensitive indicator of the consistency of demographic data and of the quality of data collection. The inconsistencies may be due to differences in definitions of the populations being used, or to errors and omissions. The measurement of births, deaths, migrants and population size is a very imprecise and error-prone process, even in highly developed societies.

The equation can also be expressed in terms of rates, by dividing each element by the mid-year population (***MYP***). Then the rate of population change is just

$$\frac{P_{t+1} - P_t}{MYP} = \frac{B}{MYP} - \frac{D}{MYP} + \frac{IN}{MYP} - \frac{OUT}{MYP}$$

The difference between the **Birth Rate** and **Death Rate** is the rate of natural increase, and the difference between the **IN** and **OUT-Migration Rates** is the **Net-Migration Rate** so the equation can also be written as:

Growth Rate = Rate of Natural Increase + Net Migration Rate.

These are all, in fact, Crude Rates.

1.7 TYPES OF DEMOGRAPHIC DATA

The raw materials of demographic data are collected in censuses, surveys, registration systems and elsewhere. They can be presented in a wide variety of ways, but divide into two fundamentally different forms. First, there are the data collected in population censuses or census-like surveys. A census produces a record of individuals at a particular instant in time. It yields a static, cross-sectional snapshot of the population stock, its size and structure, as it was on census night. Comparisons within or between censuses usually involve either absolute numbers or frequently, the calculation of proportions.

Second, there are the data usually collected by registration systems. The data produced are a record of events during a particular time-interval, usually a year. They are essentially dynamic in nature, because they give information on flows over time. Because the number of births, deaths, moves or whatever, occurring during a period are affected by the numbers 'at risk' of having a birth, dying, moving or whatever, it is common to calculate rates. This enables comparison of levels of mortality, fertility, mobility or whatever, rather than just births, deaths or moves.

1.8 THE DEFINITION OF 'POPULATION'

The term 'population' is used in different senses in demography and in statistics. In demography the term relates to the number of people in a given area, while in statistical usage, particularly when talking about sampling, it means the universe of units under consideration, which may be people, light bulbs, rats or whatever. The demographic usage is thus very similar to normal English usage.

However, the phrase used in the previous paragraph—'number of people in a given area'—is vague in several ways and a definition of 'population' for demographic purposes has to be much more precise. There actually exist numerous ways of population, mainly depending on whether one includes or excludes groups such as visitors, seamen, armed forces, diplomats, institutional populations, those temporarily away or those missed by the census.

Broadly, though, there are just two types of population counts – *de facto* and *de jure.* The former is the population actually present at some moment – the population 'in fact' there i.e. the main advantage of the *de facto* method is that it offers less chance of double counting or omission of persons and the main advantage of *de jure* method is that it gives a picture of the permanent population. The latter is a vaguer term. It means the populations who belong to the area, or have a right to live there through citizenship, legal residence or whatever. In order to try to obtain some comparability between nations, the United Nations recommends that each country should produce, from its census, a population total which excludes foreign military and diplomatic staff currently living in the country, but includes its own armed forces, merchant seamen and diplomats who are currently abroad.

In the United Kingdom several different population definitions are used. In the census it is usual to publish some tables, particularly early results, on the basis of the 'Enumerated Population', while most tabulations are based on the population of 'usual residence' where visitors, students, armed forces, diplomats, travellers, and seamen are included, excluded or moved to their 'usual residence' as asked for a specific, extra question in the census.

Mid-year population estimates for England and Wales used to be made for three different population definitions—'total', 'civilian' and 'home'—but since 1981 only the last is used. The 'home' population includes all those who are usually residents in England and Wales, allocating armed forces to the area in which they are stationed and students to their term-time address. This is the definition to use when calculating vital rates, as it is the population at risk of experiencing the events.

In United States there are also three definitions in use. The 'resident' population is used in census reports, and for the calculation of the vital rates. It comprises the residents of the fifty states and the district of Columbia. It thereby excludes the populations of Puerto Rico, Guam, the

US Virgin Islands and so on, and also American citizens living overseas, both military and civilian. Including all these groups with the resident population produces the 'total population including armed forces overseas'. Excluding US armed forces based in the US from the resident population yields the third definition, the 'civilian population'.

But in India, the decennial series of census covering the whole country has been conducted since 1881 and the latest census was conducted in 2001. Though the census count is a costly affair, involving great administrative efforts with disruption of normal services, it is considered as essential for any modern state interested in the security, welfare and development of its citizens and is also an activity of national pride.

The census refers to the population at a particular point of time. In the Indian Census of 2001, this point of time was the sunrise of 1st March 2001. This is called the census reference date and time. In general, census enumeration can adopt two types of counts. One method is to count the population according to where the persons are staying at the time of census enumeration or the night before, irrespective of their usual place of residence. This count is called the *de facto* method. Another method is to collect information about the people who are the normal residents of a specified area, irrespective of whether they are present at the time of the census enumeration time in that particular household or not. This type is called the *de jure* method. Thus in a *de jure* census, information about all the persons who usually live in a household is collected, whether or not they are present at the time of enumeration. In practice, it is impossible to count the entire population at any instant of time. Usually, it is achieved by starting the enumeration sufficiently early and then adjusting for the deaths, births and movements that occur between enumeration and the census moment through additional inquiries soon after the census moment.

The primary unit of census enumeration is the individual. For the final classification and analysis of census data, information regarding each person is required. For studying the characteristics that are common to the whole household or family, the unit of enumeration could be the household or the family itself. The usual minimum questions asked in the census about each individual are: name, age, sex, relationships to the head of household, marital status, religion, education, employment status, occupation, and migration; and at family level: housing conditions and amenities. In addition to these questions, general questions about the number of children everborn, children surviving out of everborn, and births occurred during last 12 month-period during the census time are also asked to the married women. Questions are also asked on the employment status of the individuals, whether working full-time or part-time, nature of work they are engaged in and whether he or she is seeking work. The questionnaire can be filled in by the enumerator or by the respondent himself, handed-over by the enumerator personally or sent by mail. The quality of the responses seems to be better and the extent of error lower where the questionnaires are kept short, the questions are simple and factual, and trained enumerators administer the questionnaires.

It is important to distinguish the difference between censuses and sample surveys. As mentioned, the census is a complete count of the entire population and does not involve sampling. Censuses relate to a single point of time, not a period, even though the enumeration itself may be spread over days or weeks. In a census, each individual should be enumerated separately. The success of census depends upon the efficiency of its fieldwork. Many countries, including India, have a large census organization as a part of their permanent statistical system. This ensures the supply of trained technical persons, improved documentation and reduced expenditure.

Once the census enumeration has been done, all data collected by the enumerators are carefully checked and edited by supervisors. A post-enumeration check is usually carried out for assessing the coverage errors. The processing of data collected involves entering the data into computers, validation and producing the final tabulations. A detailed tabulation may be prepared well before the enumeration. The final publication of the census will be produced from the tabulation plans initially formulated and funded for, by appropriate analysis of the data collected. Usually, the final publication of the results may take a long time, even many years, but provisional figures are generally published by the census organization as early as possible after the census enumeration. For a country with a large population like India, the census enumeration demands a large number of enumerators (approximately a million was used for the 2001 Census) and to maintain homogeneity in collecting data through them is really a difficult task. Population census in most countries is preceded by an enumeration of the households, a mapping of the villages and the urban blocks and in many situations by a housing census, wherein data on the conditions of the house in terms of number of rooms, construction materials used, etc., are gathered. It has to be recognized that censuses provide the basic data needed on the structure of the population of the country in terms of size, age-sex, marital status distribution in different areas and are essential for the planning of various developmental programme, such as the number of children in school-going ages in an area and the number of those to be brought under schooling, the number of people seeking work, the number of aged persons, etc. The census also provides the population size of different areas which forms the basis of division of political constituencies, the number of political leaders to be elected from different states or provinces to the state and central legislative bodies and is in a way crucial in setting up the power base of the country. Thus, the census is fundamental to the politics and planning for development of any country and the fact that it serves an important function in demography is only supplementary to its other administrative functions.

1.9 VITAL STATISTICS

The flow data on the demographic variables are largely derived from the Vital Registration System existing in most countries. Censuses provide only information about the population at one period of time. The gap between two censuses is very large (10 years) and often policy-makers and planners require detailed information about the population in the intervening years for planning of public health programme, implementing social welfare measures and drawing up schemes for distribution of public facilities. In such situations, the aggregates of vital registration along with the latest population census serve as basic data. Vital registration is a system for the registration of the demographic events occurring in a population—births, deaths and marriages—and is the basic source of information on population dynamics. The registration system of developed nations provides elaborate statistical data on many aspects of social change. In most countries, the registration of births and deaths is compulsory, as their information is also necessary for individuals for a variety of legal purposes. In organizational aspects the vital statistics system is different from the census operation.

Vital statistics is the total process of registering, compiling and reporting of the aggregate of vital events, such as births, deaths, marriages, that occur during a specified duration of time among the members of the population residing in an area. The parents or a relative can report births, and a relative can report deaths. A period of time is allowed to report the event after its occurrence. In case of marriage, divorce, etc., the informant could be the individual himself. A Registrar is the official authorized to register the occurrence of a vital event and to record the required details with respect to the event. The quality of the vital statistics data generally depends upon the educational levels of the Registrar and the informant and the level of enforcement of the law on registration. A standard proforma is used to collect necessary information on a birth, death or marriage. Vital registration is mainly carried out for administrative and legal purposes, and only a few selected questions is asked. The questions on a birth include: the date of the event, date of registration, place of birth, sex of the child, birth order and characteristics of the parents including their name, age, marital status (in some societies), religion and occupation. For a death, the minimal information includes: name of the deceased, age at death, sex, marital status, date and place of death, date of registration, cause of death and characteristics of the parents in the case of the death of a child.

The Registrar transmits the information either in a duplicate form or as a statistical summary to the higher level of administration on a periodic basis. Generally, in India, in the urban areas the municipalities or the corporations are the places for registering the events, while in rural areas, the officials authorized to register the events vary from state to state; from the village's headman, the village panchayat, the Auxiliary Nurse Midwife (ANM) or the health inspector of the public health department. Usually, it is the village headman from the revenue department who has to report births and deaths to the next higher authority, viz., the tehsildar. The Registration of Births and Deaths Act of 1969 gave the Registrar General of India the statutory authority to coordinate civil registration work throughout the country. According to this Act, registration of births and deaths has become compulsory, births to be registered within 14 days and deaths within a week; violators are punishable. Yet, the registration of events is usually far from complete. In India, and many other countries, the vital statistics system forms part of the general administration of statistics collection.

1.10 SAMPLE SURVEY

Third type of data generally used by demographers is the information collected in Sample Surveys. In general, a sample survey involves taking a sample of the population to be enumerated with more trained investigators interviewing them more intensely in a few selected areas. The major advantage of this type of data collection is that it requires less resource of money and manpower than required in censuses and in registration. Data accuracy will also be enhanced since more time can be spent at each household or with the individual, and more skilled persons can hold the interviews in greater detail. However, this type of data involves a sampling error since only a sample is studied, but recent development in sampling theory makes it possible to get estimates of any characteristics in the population, called a Parameter, with a fairly high degree of precision even with relatively small sample sizes. For example, it is possible to get estimates of fertility rates in most of the developing countries within 5 per cent error from a sample survey of 2000 women in reproductive ages. The advantage of the sample survey method is that the sample size needed for the estimation of most demographic parameters does not depend on the size of the population as a whole which estimation is needed. A sample survey with 2000 women in India with a population of over 950 million and from Srilanka with a population of 15 million will have almost the same degree of sampling error. The other advantages of sample surveys are that they can be organized and executed quickly compared to other, and can collect information in much more detail than is possible in a census. The example of large-scale surveys conducted almost simultaneously in many countries of the world on nationally representative samples and providing internationally comparable data are the W.F.S. and DHS's. In India, a similar large-scale sample survey, called the National Family Health Survey (NFHS), was carried out in the most of the larger states and the National Capital Region Territory (NCRT) of Delhi during 1992–93. These surveys are designed not only to provide estimates of various demographic parameters but also with a view to testing a number of research hypotheses. Sample surveys are generally designed with a view to assessing the impact of existing policies, to aid the planning of those yet to be implemented, to influence governmental or other agencies, or for academic purposes. They generally look into the levels and patterns of health, fertility, mortality, contraceptive use and the impact of economic, social, environmental and specific programme-related factors on them. Since the data are generally collected from a sample, in order to produce fairly reliable results, the sample size cannot be too small. In a majority of sample surveys, the unit of observation has been household and interviews within the households have been focused on married women in reproductive ages and their children.

Demographic sample surveys are also diverse in design as well as in their objectives but two main types of surveys are worth mentioning. First, there is a single-round survey, which involves only one interview with the respondents. Such types are generally known as Retrospective Surveys.

This design permits the use of larger samples and is especially suitable in countries where addresses are not well defined or the population is highly mobile. Another type is multi-round survey, which encompasses a great variety of survey designs; surveys, which re-interview the same respondent several times, or surveys that take different samples in each round or a combination of both. Modifications on these are sometimes referred to as Follow-Up or Panel or Prospective surveys. These surveys primarily produce information on trends in the parameters over time.

1.11 INDIRECT ESTIMATION TECHNIQUES AND ITS NECESSITY

Traditionally, demographic estimation is based on the data collected by census and vital registration system. A continuous registration system usually has the task of recording vital events (births, deaths, marriages and divorces etc.,) as they occur. When the system is coupled with periodic counts of the population, the estimation of demographic parameters becomes possible. But unfortunately, however, in many developing countries including India, the performance of data collection systems is so poor that the estimates obtained directly from the data they produce are severely flawed. It was to be expected that the advances in the techniques of estimating demographic measures in non-conventional ways would have an impact on methods of data collection. This was, in fact, the case though the changes were not striking. An important reason was the argument that the primary function of the new indirect methods was to extract information from existing and unpromising material, which is described as 'disaster rescue' by Brass (1996). The recognition that these methods that were relatively easy to apply to produce reasonably good estimates came slowly. However, the momentum continued, and the provision of satisfactory data designed to be analyzed with the new indirect techniques (U.N., 1983) is being increasingly extended. Thus, we have applied indirect techniques, which are necessary to get reasonably good estimates (techniques with their assumption have been discussed in the chapters concerned). The indirect estimates have been smoothed further by applying different suitable techniques and adjustment procedures, which eliminate or minimize the irregularities often present in the preliminary estimates.

2
Age Distribution

2.1 INTRODUCTION

Following the recommendations of the United Nations (1958), we first examine the age structure of the population of a country, state, district or of a local area of interest. Many social scientists have a special interest in the age-structure of a population as the relative numbers considerably affect social relationships within a community at each age. Many types of planning, particularly planning of community institutions and services require data on age composition. Furthermore, it is important to estimate and project some functional age segments of population, such as school age, working-age, voters and elderly. The importance of Census data on age in studying of population growth is even greater when adequate vital statistics from a registration system are not available. As with data on sex, a large part of the usefulness of the age classification lies in its cross-classifications with marital status, labour force, migration etc., and make it possible a much more effective use of census data on these subjects. Age-sex structure is one of the most important characteristics of population composition. Almost all population characteristics vary significantly with age. Age statistics form an important component of population analysis, as most of the analysis is based on age-sex structure of the population. The usefulness of age data is more noticeable when it is cross-classified by variables like marital status, literacy, educational attainment, economic activity that vary with age in different patterns.

Apart from purely demographic concerns, the age-sex data structure is required for age specific analysis of data for planning, scientific, technical and commercial purposes. The dependency ratio, which is the ratio of economically active to economically inactive persons, is dependent on age composition. India has one of the largest proportions of population in the younger age groups in the world. 35.3 per cent of the population of the country have been in the age group 0–14 years and 41 per cent of the population account for less than 18 years of age at the Census 2001. Census 2001 data on marital status of persons show that out of over a billion population of the country, 513 million (49.8 per cent) have reported as 'Never married', mainly due to high proportion of young people. The 'Married' constitutes about 45.6 per cent of the total population.

Although the concept of chronological age is precise and unambiguous, census reports on age are subject to errors arising from a variety of causes; these include deliberate mis-statement, a tendency to ages ending in certain preferred digits and to avoid others, exaggeration of age at older ages, carelessness in reporting, and ignorance of correct age. Therefore, for a worthwhile analysis of age data for a country, state, district or of a local area of interest, we, generally, test their accuracy and apply various smoothing and adjustment techniques in order to eliminate, at least, some of the effects of faulty age reporting.

2.2 AGE STRUCTURE OF POPULATION

As age is very essential variable in demographic analysis it is necessary to distinguish the difference between the age of an individual and, the age structure and distribution of a population. For demographic purposes, age is defined as the number of full years lived by an individual. In other words, it is the 'age at last birth day' that is generally used. So an age given as 30 years means that the person is at present somewhere between 30 and 31 in terms of completed years of life. In developing countries with a high prevalence of illiteracy, age is one of the most difficult personal characteristics to be ascertained by direct inquiries. There are considerable errors that have been observed in the reported ages. In a population, the average of its population distribution by age is called its Man Age. The age of population can increase or decrease with time, unlike that of individual. There seems to be interdependence between the demographic process and age structure of a population. Clearly the age structure of a population at a particular point of time is the result of past demographic process of births and deaths. Also, the age structure of the population at present can affect the future trends of demographic events. The change in the number of births first affects the child age group. After many years this effect can be seen in older age groups as well. In general, a decline in the number of births has the effect of narrowing the size of the child population. If the decline is quite rapid, the effect of age structure will be quite dramatic. Decline in the level of infant deaths, also, produces the same result as caused by increase in the number of births, affecting the first years of life and then filtering towards higher ages. The effect of changes in deaths is generally to produce less variation than births in developed and developing nations. This is because deaths affect most age groups uniformly but births affect only the younger age groups. In developing countries, it is possible that a large number of deaths in a particular year is due to epidemics and natural catastrophes, and these may have a big impact on some ages, which is noticeable in the age structure for many years. Migration can also cause a big distortion in the age structure, as it is normally age selective. Migration is normally concentrated among young adults. Thus the age structure of a population is primarily dependent on births to a great extent, and deaths and migration to a lesser extent. We tend to think of a population growing older when people live longer, but it is when fertility declines, resulting in fewer births, that a population begins to age.

Age structure influences future demographic events as well. For example, a larger proportion of women in the childbearing ages will contribute to an increase in the number of births. High birth rate during one period will produce, a generation later, a comparative larger number of women of childbearing ages and consequently, a comparatively higher number of births could occur even if current birth rates have declined. In a number of developing countries, the birth rates are very high and as a consequence the proportion of young children is high, because of high fertility in the past. Hence, even under rapid declines in fertility in the future, the number of births might keep on increasing because of rise in the number of women in the reproductive age in future. This is simply because there is an increasing number and the proportion of potential parents who will enter the child bearing ages, who are already born and thus the population will continue to grow in size. This aspect is generally known as *Population Momentum*. The population size in these countries will continue to grow rapidly for many years to come, irrespective of future levels and trends in births, deaths and migration. This is very much similar to the distance it takes for a fast speeding vehicle to come to a halt even after breaks are applied. Age distribution of a population determines its momentum of growth.

Age is also a crucial variable in determining the size of the potential school-going children population, manpower population, voting population, women in the child bearing ages, older population requiring pension or other types of old age assistance, etc. Tabulations by age are essential in the computation of basic measures relating to the factors of population change and in the study of economic dependency. Since the study of social and economic characteristics vary much with age and also vary in time and place, populations cannot be meaningfully compared with respect to these characteristics unless age has been controlled. Accordingly, age is considered to be the variable of highest priority in demographic analysis. Tabulations by age are also very useful in the evaluation of the quality of data. Age composition of a population is of particular interest to the planner, as the planning of public institutions and services, is largely dependent on it.

2.3 ANALYSIS OF THE AGE STRUCTURE

Age data are usually available in single years i.e. the number of persons in the population of age 10,11 and 12 etc. For demographic analysis age data are often used in this form. It is customary to classify them in 5-year age groups, such as, 0–4, 5–9, 10–14, 15–19, 20–24 and so on. The age data thus classified in mutually exclusive age groups are used for an analysis of the age structure of a population, and are useful for a wide variety of analytical purposes.

The age structure of a population is most commonly studied with the help of a simple mathematical measure like per cent distribution and equally simple measure like the age pyramid. The other measures used for an analysis of the age structure are the average age (mean, median, mode), and a few other indices based on the distribution of persons in different age groups.

The simplest measure is the percentage distribution of the population based on the absolute numbers in different 5-year age groups, and indicates the number of persons in an age group, if the total number of persons considered is 100. This measure is helpful in forming an idea about the age structure of a population, and is used for describing it. It is also used to compare the age structures of two or more populations at a point of time or to compare the age structure of the same population at different points of time. The age-sex histograms, known as the age-sex pyramids may be used for precisely the same purposes.

Another measure to study the structure of the population is the dependency ratio. This measure indicates the number of dependents per 100 workers, and may be computed on the basis of three broad age groups, i.e., below 15, between 15–59 or 64 and 60 or 65 and above. The population in the age group 15–59 or 64 is considered to be the working population; that below 15 as the young dependents, and that above either 60 or 65 is considered to be old dependents.

2.4 DEPENDENCY RATIO

The dependency ratio, which is useful in economic studies, is defined as the number of persons in a population who are not economically active for every 100 economically active persons in that population. The estimate of the dependency ratio can be calculated from the age distribution of the population. The method of calculating dependency ratio is given below:

$$\text{Child-Dependency Ratio} = \frac{\text{Population aged 0–14}}{\text{Population aged 15–59}} \times 100$$

$$\text{Old Dependency Ratio} = \frac{\text{Population aged 65+}}{\text{Population aged 15–59}}$$

$$\text{Dependency Ratio} = \frac{\text{Population aged 0–14 + population aged 65+}}{\text{Population aged 15–59}}$$

2.5 SEX COMPOSITION

Sex of the individual holds an important place in demography. Data on sex are required for planning purposes, particularly health services. Sex is considered to be a biological characteristic that divides human beings into males and females. Demographic events are generally differentiated by sex. Fertility or the number of children born to a couple is measured in relation to the characteristics of the woman/wife, her age, duration of marriage and spacing between births. There are also substantial differences between the death rates of the sexes, especially at older ages that are considered to be largely due to biological differences. Hence, it is important to consider the effect of variation in the sex composition of populations while comparing their fertility and mortality levels. The common measure, which is used to represent the sex composition of a population, is the sex ratio that is already discussed earlier.

2.6 EVALUATION AND ADJUSTMENT OF AGE DATA

Introduction

A greater part of the distortion results mainly from 'age-misreporting' but irregularities in age distribution may be real and caused by past changes in the levels or patterns of fertility, mortality and migration. Age misreporting can take two basic forms, namely, 'age heaping' and 'age shifting'. With 'age heaping' or digit preference, too many people report ages ending in 'zero (0)' or in 'five (5)' while relatively few give ages ending in one (1), three (3), seven (7), and in nine (9), and, one can also see preference for ages ending in two (2) and in eight (8).

'Age shifting' is a more serious problem than 'age heaping' in various cultures, largely because, it is harder to detect and adjust for. Typically, older people tend to exaggerate their ages particularly where age confers status or prestige, young men understate their ages for getting employment, for children, parents report or understate their ages for admission in schools, and young women understate their ages until they are getting married etc. So, of the plethora of measures, techniques of adjustment and smoothing generally used to get corrected age distribution are as follows: Whipple's Index and Myers' Blended Index along with Age Ratio Score, Sex Ratio Score and U.N. Joint Score.

(A) Whipple's Index

Whipple's Index is a simple measure of preference for ages ending in certain digits such as 'Zero (0)' and 'Five (5)'. Only the ages 23 to 62 are used by comparing the sum of the populations at the ages ending in '0' or '5' employing the assumption of either rectangularity or linearity in a 10-year range separately for '0' and '5'; and in a 5-year range for both '0' and '5'.

The index is as follows:

Whipple's Index (W_0) =

$$\frac{\sum(P_{30}+P_{40}+P_{50}+P_{60})}{1/10\sum(P_{23}+P_{24}+P_{25}+{*}{*}{*}{*}{*}+P_{60}+P_{61}+P_{62})}\times 100 \text{ for '0' and,}$$

Whipple's Index (W_5) =

$$\frac{\sum(P_{25}+P_{35}+P_{45}+P_{55})}{1/10\sum(P_{23}+P_{24}+P_{25}+{*}{*}{*}{*}{*}+P_{60}+P_{61}+P_{62})}\times 100 \text{ for '5'}$$

In the same way, employing the assumptions of rectangularity or linearity in a 5-year range,

Whipple's Index ($W_{0, 5}$) =

$$\frac{\sum (P_{25} + P_{30} + **** + P_{55} + P_{60})}{1/5\sum (P_{23} + P_{24} + P_{25} + ***** + P_{60} + P_{61} + P_{62})} \times 100 \text{ for '0' and '5'}$$

The Index varies between 100, representing no preference for '0' or '5'. According to United Nations' Scale given as follows:

Quality	Whipple's Index
Highly accurate	Under 105
Fairly accurate	105–110
Approximate	110–125
Rough	125–175
Very rough	Over 175

An example of the Whipple's Index for West Bengal, 1991 is given in Table 2.1 below.

Table 2.1 Whipple's Index for heaping on digits '0','5' and both by type of residence and sex in West Bengal, 1991.

Index	Sex	1991		
		Total	Rural	Urban
W_0	Male	243.93	245.95	239.58
	Female	267.80	275.99	248.52
W_5	Male	241.12	246.80	229.40
	Female	268.60	277.96	246.80
$W_{0, 5}$	Male	242.53	246.37	234.49
	Female	268.20	277.03	247.66

Table 2.1 shows that preference on digits ending in '0' or in '5' as well as in (0, 5) combined by male, is less than those of females by types of residence but the responses made by both males and females in West Bengal, 1991, are very much poor compared to United Nations' Scale. So it may be concluded that quality of reporting either in urban or in rural areas is still much beyond the reach of United Nations Scaling of reliability of age data that may cause from lack of education, low education or lack of awareness of the actual meaning of age or ignorance of age and its importance.

(B) Myers' Blended Index

Myers' (1951) has developed a 'blended' index to avoid the bias in the index computed in the way that just described in Whipple's Index which is due to the fact that numbers ending in '0' would normally be larger than the following numbers ending in '1' to '9' because of the effect of mortality. Hence the results from Myers' blended index for West Bengal, 1981 and 1991 by types of residence are shown in Table 2.2 as an example.

Table 2.2 Myers' Blended Index by sex and types of residence for West Bengal in 1981 and 1991.

Myers' blended index				
Census Year	Sex	Total	Rural	Urban
1981	Male	51.66	52.55	51.09
	Female	56.34	59.50	50.41
1991	Male	49.82	50.03	49.31
	Female	56.19	58.71	49.83

The principle employed in the index is to begin the count at each of the 10 digits (from 0 to 9) in turn and then to average the results. The method involves determining the proportion, which the population ending in a given digit is of the total population 10 times, by varying the particular starting age for any suitable 10-year age groups. The first step in calculating the index is to derive a 'blended population'. For this reason, a suitable age range (arbitrary) is selected from 10–59,10–69,10–79 or 10–89. But for this study the age range from 10–59 has been selected and subdivided this age range into two groups as 10–49 and 20–59, which has a 10-year time lag and has ages 20–59 as the overlapping part of the two age ranges.

Taking first, the age range from 10–49, population totals are computed for ages ending with each of the ten digits (0 to 9) and the ten totals corresponding to the digits (0, 1, 2, ..., 9) are multiplied by the ten co-efficients 1, 2, 3, ..., 10 respectively; similarly, the corresponding totals in the age range 20–59 are multiplied by the co-efficients 9, 8, 7, 6, ..., 0 respectively. Then adding together so as to get the 'blended' populations against each digit fuses the two series. Lastly, taking the per cent distribution of the 'blended' population corresponding to each digit, the deviation from 10 per cent is obtained with a view to, if the population numbers decrease linearly with age, the expectation is that in the absence of any digital preference about 10 per cent of the population will have reported in the ages ending with any of the digits 0 to 9. The deviations from the expected 10 per cent for each terminal digit are added (irrespective of sign) to arrive at Myers' Index.

Theoretically Myers' Index can vary from 0, representing no heaping to 90 which, would result, if all ages are reported at a single digit, for example at '0' or '5'. But the values of the index for males and females in West Bengal by types of residence indicate a tendency to concentrate towards the high range because the results in all cases are above 50 in 1981. The results suggest that the concentration at '0' or '5' may be of equal share for both are very close to each other in 1981. A remarkable heaping is exhibited by rural females (59.50), which is much more than that of either rural or urban male. This extent of heaping tending to be high may be the effect of low or no education among rural females in 1981. But in 1991, the index value is around 50 for male which suggests an improvement in age reporting while on the other hand female's index value is around 50 only in urban area but in rural area it follows the same pattern as that of 1981. On the other hand, it is interesting to note that the urban males have heaping slightly more than urban females as indicated by the values of 51.09 for males and 50.41 for females in 1981. The reason for this is probably that being a mere literate does not cause any qualitative change in reporting of age unless a certain threshold of education is attained (S. Guha Roy, 1986). But the reporting of ages indicated by index values for males in 1991 is better than that of females.

The distribution of the blended population for each digit is presented in Table 2.3 and 2.4. Tables show that the digits 0, 5, 2 and 8 account for more than two third of total blended males and females respectively. The greatest preference has always shown for '0', followed by '5', with lesser heaping on ages ending in 2 and 8 by both males and females; greatest avoidance of those ages ending in 9 by males and 1 by females in West Bengal as a whole, as well as in rural and urban areas in 1981 and 1991. In 1991, the digits 0, 5, 8 and 2 account for slightly less than two third of the total blended males and females respectively. Nonetheless the pattern of heaping on digits 0 and 5 is almost the same in 1991 as that in 1981.

Table 2.3 Distribution of Myers' Blended population by terminal digits, sex and types of residence in 1981: West Bengal.

Terminal Digits	Males			Females		
	Blended Population		Order of preference	Blended Population		Order of preference
	Figures (000's)	Per cent		Figures (000's)	Per cent	
West Bengal						
0	34254	21.40	1	33263	23.79	1
1	6596	4.12	9	5191	3.71	10
2	19786	12.37	3	16445	11.76	3
3	8248	5.16	8	6445	4.60	8
4	10830	6.77	6	8989	6.43	6
5	31616	19.76	2	29410	21.03	2
6	14030	8.77	5	11686	8.36	5
7	8718	5.45	7	6881	4.92	7
8	19672	12.30	4	16203	11.59	4
9	6248	3.90	10	5329	3.81	9
All digits	159993	100.00		139842	100.00	
Rural						
0	23313	21.21	1	24745	24.48	1
1	4331	3.94	9	3587	3.55	10
2	13945	12.69	3	12137	12.00	3
3	5504	5,00	8	4507	4.46	8
4	7482	6.81	6	6333	6.26	6
5	21943	19.97	2	21894	21.66	2
6	9921	9.03	5	7846	7.76	5
7	5836	5.31	7	4687	4.64	7
8	13636	12.41	4	11738	11.61	4
9	3992	3.63	10	3623	3.58	9
All digits	109903	100.00		101097	100.00	
Urban						
0	10941	21.41	1	8517	22.39	1
1	2265	4.43	9	1604	4.22	10
2	5841	11.43	4	4308	11.32	4
3	2743	5.37	8	2141	5.63	8
4	3347	6.55	6	2656	6.98	6
5	9673	18,93	2	7516	19.76	2
6	4109	8.04	5	2941	7.73	5
7	2882	5,64	7	2193	5.76	7
8	7035	13.77	3	4465	11.74	3
9	2257	4.42	10	1705	4.48	9
All digits	51093	100.00		38046	100.00	

Table 2.4 Distribution of Myers' Blended population by terminal digits, sex and types of residence in 1991: West Bengal.

Terminal Digits	Males			Females		
	Blended Population		Order of preference	Blended Population		Order of preference
	Figures (000's)	Per cent		Figures (000's)	Per cent	
West Bengal						
0	44348	21.63	1	41409	23.12	1
1	8186	3.99	9	6398	3.57	10
2	25197	12.29	4	21402	11.95	4
3	10108	4.93	8	8494	4.74	8
4	13625	6.65	7	11800	6.59	6
5	38818	18.94	2	37602	21.00	2
6	17461	8.52	5	14880	8.31	5
7	13790	6.73	6	8932	4.99	7
8	25773	12.57	3	21532	12.02	3
9	7690	3.75	10	6620	3.70	9
All digits	204996	100.00		179069	100.00	
Rural						
0	29149	20.73	1	29870	23.61	1
1	5314	3.78	9	4286	3.39	10
2	17644	12.55	4	15353	12.14	3
3	6690	4.76	8	5678	4.49	8
4	9320	6.63	7	8170	6.46	6
5	26906	19.13	2	27304	21.59	2
6	12183	8.63	5	10356	8.19	5
7	10802	7.68	6	5932	4.692	7
8	17731	12.61	3	15203	12.02	4
9	1890	3.48	10	4340	3.43	9
All digits	140629	100.00		126492	100.00	
Urban						
0	13399	21.17	1	11256	21.53	1
1	2872	4.54	8	2104	4.02	10
2	7560	11.95	4	6056	11.58	4
3	3424	5.41	9	2828	5.41	8
4	4305	6.80	6	3620	6.92	6
5	11912	18.82	2	10302	19.70	2
6	5278	8.34	5	4521	8.65	5
7	3692	5.83	7	3000	5.74	7
8	8042	12.71	3	6328	12.10	3
9	2800	4.42	10	2270	4.34	9
All digits	63284	100.00		52285	100.00	

A method of testing the accuracy of population enumerated at ages 0, 1, 2, 3, and 4 is to use an appropriate life-table. Thus, if B_{1991-x} is the number of births x years preceding the 1991 census, then the expected population ($\hat{P}$) aged x–1 to x at the time of census is

$$_1\hat{P}_{x-1} = B_{1991-x}\,(L_{x-1}/l_0)$$

The accuracy of age reporting of children can be tested in this manner, but the lack of complete and accurate birth registration data makes the application of the method complicated.

In many countries, populations are often tabulated in 5, or 10-year age groups simply because of reducing errors in age reporting. The detection of errors in grouped age data is much more difficult than for single year age data. Numerous methods can be employed in the evaluation of data for age groups such as intercensal cohort analysis and comparison with estimates based on birth statistics. These all involve comparison with another set of data.

(C) Sex-Ratio Score

An index developed by United Nations Population Division (1952) for measuring the accuracy for age-distribution grouped in 5-year ages requires only the census data. It uses both sex ratio for each age group and age-ratio for each sex. The index is based on the assumptions that the sex- ratio and the numbers in each age group should change smoothly with increasing age and it attempts to measure the absolute difference which occur from a steady trend. The sex ratio (S.R) for each age group (a, a + 5) is defined as

$$_5(\mathrm{S.R})_a = \frac{_5P^m_a}{_5P^f_a} \times 100, \text{ and}$$

the first absolute differences calculated as

$$_5\Delta_a = {_5(\mathrm{S.R})_{a+5}} - {_5(\mathrm{S.R})_a}$$

give, on averaging, what is called the sex ratio score. This makes no allowance for the fact that the sex ratio is expected to decline by age. But the sex ratios that appeared in Table 2.5 show irregularities and do not decline by age. The sex ratios in West Bengal starting from age group 0–4 to the age group 55–59, besides only minor fluctuations in one age group (50–54) have been consistently increasing with the age increases. This discrepancy in sex ratio might have varied between ages due to differences in mortality among males. But in most parts of the world female mortality is lower than the male mortality at all ages, thus women on average, live longer than men. Thus, sex ratios decline with age. In West Bengal, almost in all ages sex ratio is much higher than that of the U.N. Standard value of 1.05 at birth but it does not only mean that the mortality among females is higher, it might be also due to the smaller in proportion in each age group than those of males. This pattern of sex ratio in urban areas is increasing with age up to 55–59 but fluctuations in rural areas are observed in age groups 20–24, 30–34, 40–44 and 50–54. This may be due to mortality among males or, due to males' out-migration from rural to urban or any other places outside the state. But the sex ratio score of 4.80 for the state as a whole indicates rather poor quality of reporting ages as according to U.N. criterion which states that a score of 1.05 implies a highly accurate system of reporting.

Table 2.5 Age and residence-specific sex ratio scores for West Bengal, 1981.

Age group	West Bengal		Rural		Urban	
(x, x + 5)	Sex ratio	${}_5\Delta^*_x$	Sex ratio	${}_5\Delta^*_x$	Sex ratio	${}_5\Delta^*_x$
0–4	100.90	2.30	100.58	1.34	102.18	5.93
5–9	103.20	2.83	101.92	3.13	108.11	1.15
10–14	106.03	2.35	105.05	2.38	109.26	1.67
15–19	108.38	1.68	107.43	1.27	110.93	9.12
20–24	110.06	3.95	106.16	4.09	120.05	3.48
25–29	114.01	4.20	110.25	2.86	123.65	5.86
30–34	113.81	5.68	107.39	2.11	129.39	15.38
35–39	119.49	1.53	109.50	2.96	144.77	14.88
40–44	121.02	5.10	106.54	8.51	159.65	3.19
45–49	126.12	4.20	115.05	5.22	156.46	1.51
50–54	121.92	6.82	109.83	8.45	157.97	3.19
55–59	128.74	23.67	118.28	19.48	161.16	36.74
60–64	105.07	2.07	98.80	3.04	124.42	18.09
65–69	103.00		101.84		106.33	
Sex Ratio Score		4.80		4.99		9.24

*Absolute differences of sex ratios

(D) Age Ratio Score

The age ratio for age group (a, a + 5) is defined as

$$_5(\text{A.R.S})_a = 100 \times {}_5P_a / [1/3({}_0P_{a-5} + {}_5P_a + {}_5P_{a+5})]$$

A summary measure (S.M) of age ratio scores

$$S.M = \frac{1}{n}\sum\left|\left({}_5(A.R.S)_a - 100\right)\right|$$

Ideally age ratios should be approximately equal to 100 provided the reporting is perfect though, actual variation might be caused by fluctuations in past births, deaths or migration (United Nations, 1952). An overall degree of accuracy of the age reporting can be judged by the United Nations Standard Age Ratio Scores of around 2.4 to 2.6 for a population with almost perfect age reporting.

(E) United Nations Joint Score (U.N.J.S)

United Nations proposed a summary measure, known as age-sex accuracy index or United Nations Joint Score (U.N.J.S) for measuring the accuracy of the age distribution of the reported population in combination with the two scores namely, the age-ratio scores and sex-ratio scores. The U.N. Joint Score is defined as

$$U.N.J.S = T_m + T_f + \frac{3}{n}\sum {}_5\Delta_a,$$

where T_m and T_f are the age ratio scores for males and females respectively and the third component is the three times the sex ratio scores. The census age-sex data were considered by the United Nations as

(a) accurate when U.N.J.S < 20
(b) inaccurate when U.N.J.S will lie between 20–40 and,
(c) highly-inaccurate when U.N.J.S will be > 40

This index is only an approximate indicator of the smoothness of the reported data, affected by digital bias, variations in under-enumeration by age, etc.The results of other scores like Sex Ratio Score, Age Ratio Score and Joint Score for West Bengal, 1961–1991 are presented in Table 2.6 as an example, to view the extent of age reporting errors.

Table 2.6 Sex ratio score, age ratio score and joint score by sex for West Bengal during 1961–1991.

Years	Sex Ratio Score	Age Ratio Score		U.N.
		Males	Females	Joint Score
1991	4.69	6.95	9.47	30.49
1981	4.80	7.26	9.56	31.22
1971	8.67	7.95	10.89	44.85
1961	10.93	9.74	16.78	59.31

2.7 SMOOTHING AND ADJUSTMENT OF AGE DISTRIBUTION

It is not recommended to smooth or adjust the age distributions prior to applying any analytical procedure in the grounds that their results may be distorted by smoothing and adjustment process; an age distribution that is smooth and nearly correct is still useful, particularly as a basis for population projections (United Nations, 1983).

As the age distribution is distorted by the preferential digits, heaping, mis-reporting etc. that is evinced from the result obtained by the use of various indices in the earlier section of this chapter, it is felt necessary to use smoothing and adjustment techniques so that we can get the corrected age distribution of the population of a country, state, district or any area of choice. The techniques of smoothing and adjustment may be applied to age data for male and female as well as age data for total population are as follows:

2.7.1 Fitting of a Third Degree Polynomial to the Cumulated Data for Total Population, Male and Female Populations

2.7.2 A Stable Population Model as Standard is Used for Y-transformation to Compare with the Reported Male and Female Population

2.7.3 Estimation of Base Population by Age and Sex (Newton's Halving Method)

(A) Adjustment for Heaping by Using Third Degree Polynomial

Step 1: Cumulation of population counts: For each sex, the population under each age ending in three (viz. 3, 13, 23, 33, and so on) and in eight (viz. 8, 18, 28, 38 and so on) is needed and by cumulating the numbers in successive single-year ages up to, but not including the upper boundary of the age group. Thus, if N (Y) is the population of age y and N (x–) is the population under age x is

$$N(x-) = \sum_{y=0}^{x-1} N(y),$$

Thus, $N(3-) = N(0) + N(1) + N(2)$, and

$$N(8-) = N(3-) + N(3) + N(4) + N(5) + N(6) + N(7)$$

Step 2: Fitting of polynomials to the cumulated age distributions: Estimates of population under ages 15, 20 and so on, up to age 75 can be obtained from polynomials fitted to the numbers under ages ending in three or eight by using equation.

$$N((a+12)-) = -0.048N(a-) + 0.864N((a+10)-) + 0.216N((a+20)-) - 0.032N((a+30)-) \quad 1(a)$$

and

$$N((a+17)-) = -0.0455N(a-) + 0.3315N((a+10)-) + 0.7735N((a+20)-) - 0.595N((a+30)-) \quad 1(b)$$

and the population under ages 20 and 25 can be estimated from the populations under ages ending in eight by the equations 1(a) and 1(b).

Equations 1(a) and 1(b) are then applied to the populations under ages 10 years older and the process is repeated up to age 75. Estimates of the population under age 15 based on populations under ages ending in eight and of the population under 10 based on populations under ages ending in three are obtained by applying the equation.

$$N((a+7)-) = 0.1495N(a-) + 1.0465N((a+10)-) - 0.2415N((a+20)-) + 0.0455N((a+30)-) \quad 1(c)$$

The estimates of population under age 10 from populations under ages 8, 18, 28 and 38 are obtained by applying the equation,

$$N((a+7)-) = 0.672N(8-) + 0.504N((18-) - 0.224N(28-) + 0.048N(38-) \quad 1(d)$$

Once two estimates are available for each of the population under ages ending in 'zero' or 'five' from 10 to 70, a best estimate at each age is obtained by averaging the two values corresponding to it. Thus for example,

$$N^*(20-) = N_3\ (20-) + N_8\ (20-)/2.0$$

and the population under age 5 is then found by substituting best estimates of the population under ages 10, 20 and 30 into equation

$$N\ (5-) = 0.9375N\ (10-) - 0.3125N\ (20-) + 0.0625N\ (30-) \quad 1(e)$$

The cumulated population estimates can then be successfully subtracted from each other to provide an age distribution in 5 year age groups, the population aged from x to x + 4 being obtained by subtracting N*(x–) from N* ((x + 5)–).

The procedure described above can be applied to single-year age distribution of population by sex only. An example from West Bengal, 1991 Census Single-year Age returns is presented in Table 2.7.

Table 2.7 Adjustment for heaping, of the age distribution of population of West Bengal, 1991.

Age a	Population under age, a	Age b	Adjusted Population under age b based on ages ending in		Average Population under age, b	Population in age group from b to b + 4		Proportion in age group from b to b + 4	
			Three	Eight		Adjusted	Reported	Adjusted	Reported
(1)	(2)	(3)	(4)	(5)	(6)	(7)	(8)	(9)	(10)
–	–	0	–	–	–	8817384	7820034	0.1303	0.1155
3	4287800	5	9206418	8428350	8817384	8180188	9035220	0.1209	0.1335
8	13313424	10	17485072	16510071	16997572	7701130	8070303	0.1138	0.1192
13	22253575	15	25201648	24195756	24698702	6991030	6307343	0.1033	0.0932
18	28603349	20	31952848	31426616	31689732	6515637	6306997	0.0963	0.0932
23	35708913	25	38334512	38076226	38205369	6104345	6140067	0.0902	0.0907
28	41759115	30	44535219	44084208	44309714	5280214	5042762	0.0780	0.0745
33	47898503	35	49822893	49356963	49589928	4251096	4458485	0.0628	0.0659
38	52112587	40	51001366	53680681	53841024	3376989	3323144	0.0499	0.0491
43	56121683	45	57403769	57032257	57218013	2754191	2914603	0.0407	0.0431
48	58719535	50	60165262	59779146	59972204	2267681	2398591	0.0335	0.0354
53	61552172	55	62399235	62080535	62239885	1818173	1745717	0.0269	0.0258
58	63236747	60	64189252	63926864	64058058	1378403	1607993	0.0204	0.0238
63	65047049	65	65519953	65352968	65436461	949001	974148	0.0140	0.0144
68	66008276	70	66431887	66339037	66385462	586407	729723	0/0087	0.0108
73	66817620	75	67015555	66928183	66971869	706970[a]	803709[a]	0.0104	0.0119
78	67154231	–	–	–	–	–	–	–	–
83	67462448	–	–	–	–	–	–	–	–
88	67564470	–	–	–	–	–	–	–	–

[a] Population aged 75 and above excluding age not stated

Table 2.7 shows that proportion of reported population in age group 0–4 is much lower compared to that of the adjusted proportion in the same age group suggesting under-reporting of the child population (0–4) in 1991 which might not be due to decline in fertility or increase in child mortality as West Bengal has been experiencing almost constant proportion of child population since 1981(Saha, 1997). But in case of young children of age groups 5–9, 10–14 and young adult of age group 15–19 and 20–24 some distortions have been observed in enumerated proportion compared to adjusted proportion since 1981(Saha, 1997). It is due to the cause of age shifting either backward or forward and thus, age shifting is very common to two adjacent age groups keeping the middle most age group in common. Distortion in age group from 20–24 to 45–49 is not so well marked in 1991 without one or two irregularities. But the elderly population aged 60 and over has exaggerated their ages as evinced from the enumerated proportion in 1991 and this typical exaggeration in their reporting ages is not anything new to the demographers of the world. Hence, West Bengal is not at all different from this type of faulty reporting of ages.

(B) Comparison with a Standard Age Distribution

In most developing countries the quality of age data is poor, so the ages often seem to be affected by the systematic mis-reporting other than heaping. Therefore, the most drastic form of adjustment for an age distribution is to compare with a suitable stable population as standard, which has been selected from Coale-Demeny Family of Model Life Tables. Here, the west model stable population with a very close growth rate to that of the reported population by sex has been selected assuming that the standard age distribution will reflect the main features of the reported one while at the same time, it is free from the obvious bias.

The comparison of the reported and model distribution is made easier by the use of a transformation that linearizes the relationship between age and the cumulated proportion of the population under each age. Therefore, the transformation suitable for growing population is given by

$$Y(x) = \ln [(1.0 + C(x)/(1.0 - C(x))]\ldots \qquad 1(f)$$

where C (x) represents the proportion of the population under age x. The transformation as defined in equation 1(f) is referred to as Y-transformation.

Note that the Y-transformation of any proportion C (x) assumes values ranging from zero to infinity.

A second-degree polynomial is assumed to represent the relationship between y-transformation of the reported and the standard age distribution. To simplify the fitting, the two-point group means procedure has been employed, the mean of a first group of eight points and the mean of a second group of eight points (for simplicity fifteen points are assumed to be considered including the middle most in common i.e. two groups of eight will suitably be chosen) from a likely parabola are considered. Therefore, the fitted equation has the form,

$$Y(x) = \alpha (Y_s(x))^2 + \beta Y_s(x) \qquad 1(g)$$

where α and β, the two unknown parameters, can be estimated as,

$$\alpha = \left[\frac{1.0}{\bar{y}_{s1} - \bar{y}_{s2}}\right]\left[\frac{\bar{y}_1}{\bar{y}_{s1}} - \frac{\bar{y}_2}{\bar{y}_{s2}}\right] \qquad 1(h)$$

$$\beta = \frac{\bar{y}_2}{\bar{y}_{s2}} - \alpha.\ \bar{y}_{s2} \qquad 1(i)$$

where $(\bar{y}_{s1}, \bar{y}_1)$ and $(\bar{y}_{s2}, \bar{y}_2)$ are the mean points for the first and second groups respectively, where $\mathbf{Y}_s$ denotes the **Y**-transformation of the standard.

As α and β are estimated, the eqn.1 (g) is used to obtain adjusted values of the **Y**-transformation. $\mathbf{Y}^*(x)$ which in turn, can be used to produce estimates of an adjusted age distribution. For the sake of completeness, the equation,

$$Y^*(x) = \alpha(Y_s(x))^2 + \beta.\ Y_s(x)\ldots \qquad 1(j)$$

indicates how the adjusted values of $Y^*(x)$ are obtained and equation which is reversal of the equation 1(f), is of the form

$$C^*(x) = (\exp[Y^*(x)] - 1.0) / (\exp[Y^*(x)] + 1.0)\ldots \qquad 1(k)$$

has been used to obtain the estimated proportions under each age x. Adjusted proportions in each five-year age group can be obtained simply by subtracting the proportion under each age x-5 from the proportion under age x. The results of the reported, smoothed, standard and adjusted proportion under each age have been presented in Table 2.8 for males in 1981 and Table 2.9 for females in 1981 respectively in West Bengal. Furthermore to relate the transformed proportion to that of the standard selected, a parabola of each sex has been fitted and shown in Figures 2.1 and 2.2 respectively. Figures display the plotted points of the transformation, which have no obvious outliers. Therefore, the parabola passing through the origin, the mean of the first eight points $[\bar{y}_{1(x)}, \bar{y}s_{1(x)}]$ and the mean of the second eight points [$\bar{y}_{2(x)}, \bar{y}s_{2(x)}$] show an acceptable fit for each sex. Again Figures 2.3 and 2.4 show the plots of the reported, smoothed, standard and adjusted proportions in five-year age groups. From the above evidences, it is clear that the proportions of both male and female population are changed, suggesting decline in fertility, so, the procedure of adjustment by Y-transformation that is described above can not be expected to work well at younger ages and above age 50 to 55 for females, but for male excepting the younger ages it has good approximation in 1981. The results show close approximation to the proportion in different age groups that are estimated by a variety of techniques. The smoothed age distribution obtained by removing the effects of age heaping (using third degree polynomial) is very close to that of the observed ones, damping only slightly the effects of de-stabilization at younger ages and retaining the troughs between the ages 50 to 55 for females in 1981, though the irregularities in reporting ages have been tried to smooth out.

Table 2.8 Proportions of reported, smoothed[1], standard[2], and adjusted[3] populations in five-year age groups for males in West Bengal, 1981.

Age group (x, x + 5)	Proportions in five-year age groups			
	Reported	Smoothed[1]	Standard[2]	Adjusted[3]
0–4	0.1116	0.1270	0.1415	0.1410
5–9	0.1328	0.1260	0.1235	0.1247
10–14	0.1334	0.1233	0.1104	0.1127
15–19	0.1033	0.1097	0.0987	0.1017
20–24	0.0946	0.0970	0.0875	0.0906
25–29	0.0847	0.0844	0.0774	0.0804
30–34	0.0650	0.0708	0.0683	0.0708
35–39	0.0613	0.0597	0.0598	0.0616
40–44	0.0517	0.0515	0.0522	0.0531
45–49	0.0463	0.0434	0.0449	0.0449
50–54	0.0367	0.0346	0.0379	0.0369
55–59	0.0253	0.0261	0.0313	0.0294
60–64	0.0222	0.0187	0.0247	0.0220
65–69	0.0125	0.0125	0.0183	0.0151
70+	0.0186	0.0152	0.0236	0.0151

Note: 1. Based on the techniques given in A in the Text
2. Coale-Demeny West Model Stable Population, Level 16, r = 0.0200(where r is growth rate).
3. Using Y-transformation given in B in the Text

Fig. 2.1 Plots of the Y-transformation of the proportions under age x in the reported population against the Y-transformation of the equivalent proportions in the standard, Male, West Bengal, 1981.

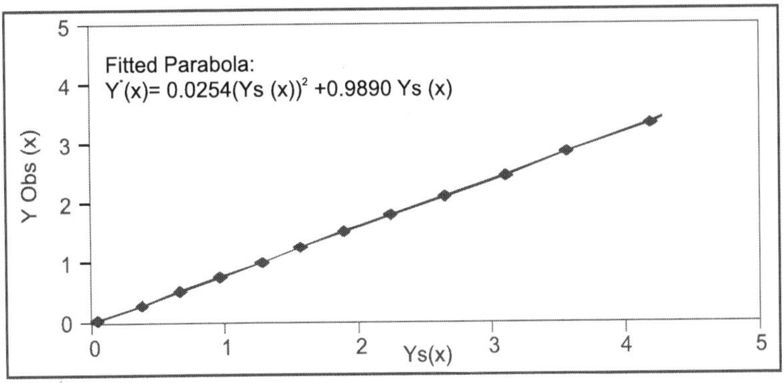

Table 2.9 Proportions of reported, smoothed[1], standard[2], and adjusted[3] population in five-year age groups for females in West Bengal, 1981.

Age group (x, x + 5)	Proportions in five-year age groups			
	Reported	Smoothed[1]	Standard[2]	Adjusted[3]
0–4	0.1214	0.1357	0.1552	0.1531
5–9	0.1412	0.1335	0.1325	0.1322
10–14	0.1380	0.1290	0.1155	0.1164
15–19	0.1046	0.1133	0.1007	0.1023
20–24	0.0944	0.0978	0.0873	0.0892
25–29	0.0816	0.0818	0.0755	0.0775
30–34	0.0627	0.0666	0.0649	0.0666
35–39	0.0563	0.0550	0.0558	0.0572
40–44	0.0469	0.0436	0.0477	0.0487
45–49	0.0403	0.0297	0.0405	0.0410
50–54	0.0330	0.0209	0.0339	0.0338
55–59	0.0216	0.0210	0.0280	0.0274
60–64	0.0232	0.0214	0.0222	0.0211
65–69	0.0133	0.0162	0.0168	0.0153
70+	0.0215	0.0345	0.0235	0.0182

Note: 1. Based on the techniques given in A in the Appendix
2. Coale-Demeny West Model Stable Population, Level 16, r = 0.025(where r is growth rate).
3. Using Y-transformation given in B in the Appendix

In this particular application (Y-Transformation), where the age distribution does not seem poor and where the reported age distribution is not clearly stable, the smoothed age distribution obtained by the technique described for heaping that merely reduces the effects of age-heaping, is probably the best approximation available to the true age distribution. But the actual age distribution of a particular country or its state, is not expected to correspond exactly to the distribution of the stable or quasi-stable population since there may be differences between fertility rates, mortality rates, and growth rates underlying the model and observed rates, as well as errors in the census data that were discussed earlier in this section. The model age distribution is not affected by the errors in age reporting characteristics of census age distributions, but it may be affected by net coverage error if too high or too low a growth rate is employed in deriving or selecting the stable population model.

Fig. 2.2 Plots of the Y-transformation of the proportions under age x in the reported population against the Y-transformation of the equivalent proportions in the standard, Female, West Bengal, 1981.

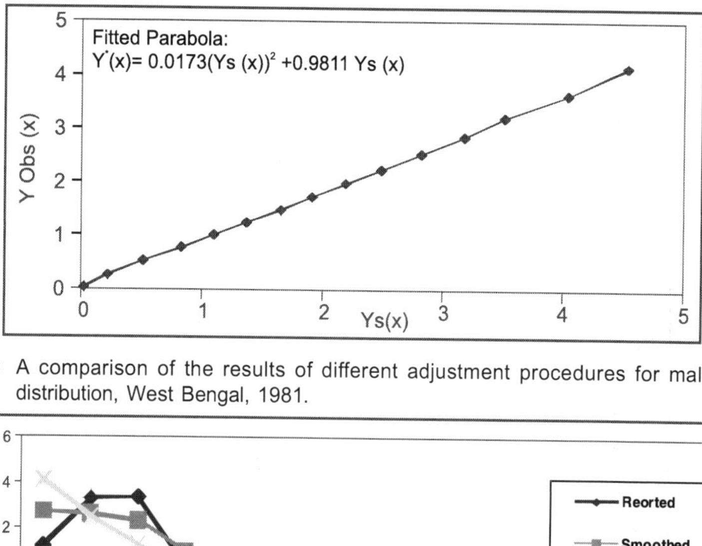

Fig. 2.3 A comparison of the results of different adjustment procedures for male age distribution, West Bengal, 1981.

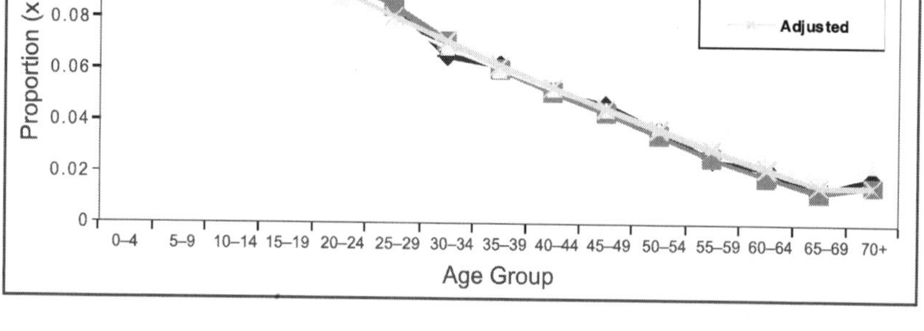

Fig. 2.4 A comparison of the results of different adjustment procedures for female age distribution, West Bengal, 1981.

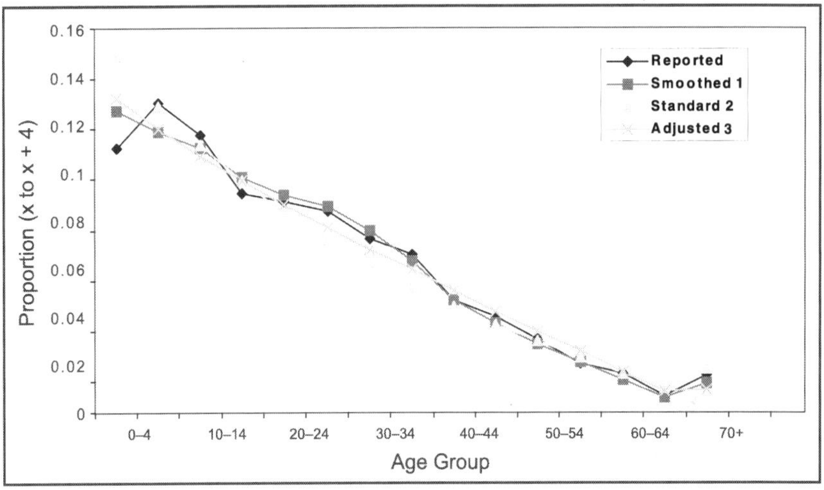

2.8 GENERAL CONFIGURATION OF AGE DISTRIBUTION AND ITS CHANGES (1951–1991)

For the present purpose, the materials indicating the proportions of populations falling into three broad age groups (under 15 years, 15–59 years and, 60 years and above) are important and accordingly the results under sub-total are given in Table 2.10. The decision to employ these three particular categories was influenced by the following considerations: (1) certainly children should be separated from adults, and age 15 is the most practicable point at which to draw the line between the two; (2) in many countries of the developing world the age 59 is rather generally employed as the lower limit of eligibility for social welfare services, such as 'old age assistance' that established for beginning of voluntary or compulsory retirement, and that generally used for statistical purpose to separate 'aged' portion of the population from others; and (3) if these two criteria are employed, the persons in between the stated limits automatically constitute a third category.

On the basis of these criteria, the largest group of nations consists of those in which a high expectation of life is the factor of prime importance in the configuration of the age distribution.

The proportionate age structure of the total population of West Bengal recorded at various dates from 1951 to 1991 is given in Table 2.10. It is being observed that within the span of fifty years between 1951 (the first census after partition in 1947) and1991, the proportionate age structure has changed, but very slowly; about 35 to 43 per cent in the age group under 15 years, around 52 to 60 per cent in the working age group 15–59 years and only around 5 to 6 per cent in the age group 60 and over. The proportion of child population (under 15 years), being the indicator of whether the population is being young or old, has gradually increased up to 1971, that has resulted from the effect of high fertility; and 1971 onwards, it has started declining, which may indicate the decline in fertility and due to out migration of child labour. Mortality might have little impact on this decline. The recorded proportion of child population (35.15) has been observed the lowest for 1951. This proportion, compared to the periods covered by the Table 2.10 is lower by 6, 8, 4 and 2 per cent respectively. The lowest proportion of child population under 15 years in the decade 1941–1951 might have resulted from the loss of infant and child due to deaths caused by the catastrophe of 'Bengal Famine'. The sharp decline in this proportion from 1971 onwards is due to decline in fertility, and out migration of child labour to the industrialized cities outside West Bengal. The proportion under 15 years has declined drastically from 43 per cent in 1971 to 37 per cent in 1991, while the proportion of those aged 15–59 years has dropped to 52 per cent in 1971 from 1951 and, further it has recorded a concurrent increase of 57 per cent (adjusted 58 per cent) in 1991 and those aged 60 years and over, to 6 per cent in 1991 being only little more than 1 per cent higher compared to 1951.

The recorded proportion of working age population (15–59 years) has been the highest in 1951 that has resulted from the influx of refugees from the erstwhile East Pakistan after the partition in 1947. This proportion does not show any consistent decrease or increase during the periods considered for the present study. It has decreased during 1951–1971 and, increased during 1981–1991.

The proportion of aged population (60 years and over), which is also regarded as the indicators of oldness of population, has been increasing very slowly. In the young-old scale the population of West Bengal can be categorized as in the 'intermediate stage (U.N., 1973); this indicates a slight improvement in adult mortality. The proportionate share of this aged 70 years and above in the total old age population has increased since 1951. In West Bengal, the process of aging is slowly underway, while, on the other hand, in the developing countries including Japan (U.N., 1984), this process started before the Second World War.

Table 2.10 Proportionate age structures of unadjusted censuses of 1951*, 1961,1971,1981 and 1991; and adjusted proportionate age structures of 1981 and 1991: West Bengal.

Age group	Unadjusted census proportions					Adjusted proportions	
	1951*	1961	1971	1981	1991	1981	1991
0–4	0.1170	0.1503	0.1459	0.1163	0.1155	0.1310	0.1303
5–9	0.1176	0.1548	0.1527	0.1368	0.1335	0.1295	0.1209
10–14	0.1169	0.1041	0.1310	0.1356	0.1192	0.1262	0.1138
Under 15 years	0.3515	0.4092	0.4296	0.3887	0.3683	0.3867	0.3649
15–19	0.1039	0.0826	0.0925	0.1039	0.0932	0.1114	0.1033
20–24	0.0961	0.0889	0.0765	0.0945	0.0932	0.0974	0.0963
25–29	0.0911	0.0879	0.0759	0.0832	0.0907	0.0832	0.0902
30–34	0.0812	0.0739	0.0670	0.0639	0.0745	0.0688	0.0780
35–39	0.0663	0.0588	0.0591	0.0589	0.0659	0.0575	0.0628
40–44	0.0549	0.0516	0.0503	0.0494	0.0491	0.0477	0.0499
45–49	0.0454	0.0386	0.0403	0.0435	0.0431	0.0369	0.0407
50–54	0.0358	0.0356	0.0335	0.0349	0.0354	0.0281	0.0335
55–59	0.0263	0.0230	0.0222	0.0235	0.0258	0.0237	0.0269
15–59 years	0.6010	0.5407	0.5173	0.5557	0.5709	0.5547	0.5816
60–64	0.0187	0.0226	0.0227	0.0227	0.0238	0.0200	0.0204
65–69	0.0125	0.0109	0.0119	0.0129	0.0144	0.0143	0.0140
70+	0.0163	0.0166	0.0185	0.0200	0.0227	0.0243	0.0191
60 years and over	0.0475	0.0501	0.0531	0.0556	0.0608	0.0586	0.0535

Note: *Age data for 1951 have been converted into conventional 5-year age group by using Newton's Halving Method for the state as a whole to get the data in conformity with other sets of data.

2.9. ADJUSTMENT FOR ERRORS DUE TO INACCURATE AGE REPORTS OR FAULTY ENUMERATION

Procedures for smoothing age distributions affected by errors in age statement, and for correcting the effects of under-enumeration or under-registration in certain age groups are described below, separately with reference to age groups in the range from 10 to74 years, ages 0–4 and 5–9.

(A) Adjustment for Population Aged 0–4 and 5–9

Using the reverse survival ratio techniques, birth rates based on 0–4, 5–9 and 0–9 population may be calculated and the relation given below may adjust the population aged 0–4 and 5–9:

$$P^{A}_{0-4} = P^{E}_{0-4} \times \frac{CBR(0-9)}{CBR(0-4)}$$

Where P^{A}_{0-4}: Adjusted population aged 0–4 and

P^{E}_{0-4}: Enumerated population aged 0–4

Then 5–9 population was adjusted by

$$P^{A}_{5-9} = P^{E}_{5-9} \times \frac{CBR(0-9)}{CBR(5-9)}$$

For the open-ended age groups such as population aged 75 and over, we can adjust the population by using a table for a stationary population (Manual III, Table 7, p.141).

Theoretically, different formulae should be used to smooth data exhibiting different degrees of inaccuracy. The U.N. five-point formula, the three-point formula and the Newton's formula for splitting 10-year of age groups into 5-year of age groups are referred to, off and on in the adjustment of the age-distribution of various countries.

(B) The U.N. Secretariat Recommended Formula

$1/16[-1,4,10,4,-1]$ where $-1/16, 4/16, 10/16, 4/16$ and $-1/16$ are the weights to be applied to the enumerated population in five consecutive five year of age data in order to obtain a smoothed value for the middle five year of age groups. This formula may be used for smoothing data with marked inaccuracies and is derived from a simple parabola. It should be used for smoothing all age groups excepting the first two and the last two. The formula simply says that in order to adjust the figure for one five year age group, data for the two preceding and the two succeeding age groups must be inserted in the formula. This formula is specially designed to deal with errors derived from digital preference. It is based on the assumption that the not gains and losses of alternate quinary age groups are constant, i.e., independent of age (Population Studies XII (3), 1959, pp. 240–285).

The three-point formula developed by Ramachandran (1959) is based on similar premises as the U.N. five point formulas. The formula is obtained by fitting an interated straight line to three points. Like the five point it is based on the assumption that the net gains and losses of alternate quinary age groups are constant, i.e., independent of age. For smoothing the first, middle or last quinary age groups the respective three point formula is as follows:

First group: ¼ [3, 1, 0]

Middle group: ¼ [1, 2, 1]

Last group: ¼ [0, 1, 3]

Where the respective weights as given in the corresponding groups if applied to three consecutive quinary age groups data will produce the required smoothed value.

(C) Ages from 10 to 74 Newton's Halving Formula: For Ten-year Age Groups

Sometimes, particularly in problems of population, where data are classified in ten-year age groups, it is required to find out the number of people in two-five year age groups of a composite ten-year age groups. Newton has developed a single second difference formula for this purpose. The formula requires the number of people in the ten-year age groups preceding and succeeding groups, which has to be broken into two-five year age groups.

The formula may be stated as follows:

$$f_{na} = 1/2\ [f_n + 1/8\ (f_{n-1} - f_{n+1})]$$

where f_{na}: is the number in the first half of the given 10-year age groups to be computed.

f_n: is the given number in the entire 10-year age group.

f_{n-1} and f_{n+1} are full numbers in the preceding and following 10-year age groups.

(D) The Eleven Point Moving Average Methods

This method removes the wide fluctuations and gives a first approximation to the true distribution but contains some systematic biases. This process was not applied to ages above 72, as the census age above this age was considered to be of poor reliability.

Basic Assumptions:

(i) That the total of any 11 consecutive terms represents the true total of the group, i.e., error at the individual ages cancel out within the group,

(ii) The average gives the true population at the mid age.

Assumptions first means that the actual heaping or deficit in the number enumerated at certain age is exactly equal to the next because of deficit and heapings in the numbers counted at the five ages on either side. If the assumptions are correct the 11 term moving average will give the true population at the age. Actually, the assumptions are not strictly true. In fact, the 11-point moving average is very much near the true value, but not exactly equal to it.

(E) Carrier-Farrag Ratio Method

Mathematical graduation of census data can be employed to derive figures for 5-year age groups that are corrected primarily for net reporting error. Carrier-Farrag in 1959 developed a ratio method for adjusting 5-year age data. (Population Studies 12(3): pp. 240–285). The adjustment for 5-year age groups extend only from ages 15–19 to 70–74 or 80–84 because the procedure requires an extra 10-year group at the beginning and end of the age group. The formulas are as follows:

$$v_i'' = v_i \div (1 + k) \quad \text{(i)}$$

$$k = \sqrt[4]{v_{i-1} \div v_{i+1}} \quad \text{(ii)}$$

$$v_i' = v_i - v_i'' \quad \text{(iii)}$$

The meaning of the symbols is made clear from the following description of the steps:

(i) Combine a 5-year census counts in to 10-year census counts = (v_i) beginning with age group 5 to 9 and continuing as far as possible (e.g., (80–84) or 90–94).

(ii) For a given 10-year age groups (v_i), record the ratio (K^4) of the preceding 10-year age group (v_{i+1}).

(iii) Determine the fourth route (k) of the ratios in step (ii).

(iv) Divide the 10-year census count (v_i), by the result in step (iii) increased by (1 + K), age group (v_i''), in the central 10-year group (v_i).

(v) Obtain the estimated figure for the younger 5-year age group (v_i'), by subtracting the estimate for the older group (v_i''), from the 10-year group including it (v_i).

2.10 DUAL RECORD SYSTEM BASED ON SAMPLE REGISTRATION AREAS AND SURVEYS (CHANDRA SEKAR AND DEMING METHOD)

Chandra Sekar and Deming have presented a mathematical theory which, when applied to a comparison (i.e. matching) of individual entries on a register's lists of deaths with individual entries on the lists obtained in a house to house canvass, gives national unbiased estimates of the completeness of registration. The basic procedure is to divide the area covered into subgroups, each of which is highly homogeneous. Within each sub group, the correlation between unregistered and unenumerated events would be very low. The per cent of 'enumerated' deaths, which are registered in each sub group, is assumed to apply to the enumerated deaths, which are registered in the sub group to derive the total number of deaths, which occurred in the sub group. An estimate of the total number of deaths (registered and unregistered) in to the area could then be derived by cumulating the total number of deaths corrected for under registration for subgroups. Relating the figures for registered deaths to this total nationally would then give an unbiased estimate of the completeness of registration. This procedure represents one of the more promising ways of evaluating the reported number of deaths or death rates, or of estimating them, particularly for the statistically underdeveloped areas.

The essential features of this method is summarized as follows:

Suppose that deaths or births are recorded for a given year in a sample registration system and in a corresponding sample survey (conducted at the end of the year) in which a question of deaths or births during twelve months period preceding the survey is asked. Suppose further, the two events of death or birth record are matched event by event and then, from the matching procedure, the following classifications of these events may be obtained:

C: number of events recorded in both registration (R) and survey (S)

N_1: events recorded only by R but not in S,

N_2: events recorded only by S but not in R

X: events missed by both systems of R and S

The classification may be represented in the following schematic table

	In R-System	Not in R-System	Total
In S-Survey	C	N_2	S
Not in S-Survey	N_1	X*	–
Total	R	–	N*

If N represents the total number of events, then Chandra Sekar-Deming (C-D) estimate N may be written as

$$N = C + N_1 + N_2 + \hat{Y}$$

where $\hat{Y}$ represents the number of events missed by both R × S.

i.e. we have $\hat{Y} = \dfrac{N_1 N_2}{C}$ (Assuming independence of the reporting of R and S)

Which may be written as

$$N = \frac{(C+N_1)(C+N_2)}{C} = \frac{RS}{C}$$

assuming the independence of R and S.

The proof is very simple and may be seen as:

Probability of R detecting an event $p_1 = \dfrac{C+N_1}{N}$ and,

Probability of S detecting an event $p_2 = \dfrac{C+N_2}{N}$

∴ The probability of an event being missed by both R × S is given by

$$\left(1-\frac{C+N_1}{N}\right)\left(1-\frac{C+N_2}{N}\right)$$

i.e. $(C + N_1 + N_2 + \hat{Y})\left(1-\dfrac{C+N_1}{N}\right)\left(1-\dfrac{C+N_2}{N}\right)$

i.e. $(C + N_1 + N_2 + \hat{Y})\dfrac{N_1 N_2}{(C+N_1)(C+N_2)} = \hat{Y}$

$$\Rightarrow \hat{Y} = \frac{N_1 N_2}{C}$$

Now, since N = RS/C, rearranging this, it can be seen that the C-D formula estimates the completeness of the coverage of the R-system as the match rate of the S-system, and estimates the completeness of the coverage of the S-system as the match rate of the R-system.

$$R/N = C/S \text{ and } S/N = C/R$$

Validity of the above estimate will depend on the following main conditions:

1. The matching procedure successfully identifies all true matches and conversely, only true matches are identified as matches.
2. All events identified in either of the two systems are true events, i.e., occurred in the population under investigation and in the appropriate time period.
3. The two systems are independent, i.e., the probability of the event being omitted from one system is not related to the chance of the event being omitted from the other system.

The validity of the method mostly depends on the effect of correlation of the events in the list of R and S. It is important to note that this correlation signifies heterogeneity in the population viz the events that fail to be detected by both the agencies do not form a random sample of the events of the whole population. The heterogeneity arises because of the difference in the reporting rates in different segments of the population.

It therefore follows that the correlation can be minimized by dividing the population into homogeneous groups and estimating the total number of events from each group, then by addition of the grand total (for details, see Chandra Sekar and Deming, 1949, JASA).

3
Mortality: Basic Measures and Indirect Estimation

3.1 INTRODUCTION

Mortality as one of the components of population growth has played an important role in determining the growth of a population. The health status of a population has been an obvious bearing on mortality, and hence, on population growth; moreover, its importance as a variable affecting the quality of the population is also recognized. Analyses of the health status of a population have generally been neglected in demographic research, largely because of the poor data and techniques used in measuring health (Linder, 1959). Much more is known about the levels of mortality than about the conditions of health within various countries, because death is a clearly defined event. Hence most of the governments have generally adopted legal provisions for the registration of such events, but still now in many countries such registration is incomplete in practice. Unlike developed countries, registration data available for developing countries such as in India are not reliable.

The concept of social responsibility for health of a population, little dreamed of a century ago, has won gradual acceptance over time, so that nearly everywhere the reduction of disease and lowering of death rates are considered the important tasks of the governments. The continued effort to control diseases and reduce mortality is a universally accepted government policy and because of rapid population growth that presents many serious problems. Apart from the important, and obvious humanitarian consideration, the contribution that better health makes to economic development, for example, through increased labour productivity should not be overlooked (Taylor, 1965; Taylor and Hall, 1967). Several governments policies relevant to health cover a wide variety of matters involving measures, which directly or indirectly promote better health. More than two decades back, in its general conference in Florence, International Union for the Scientific Study of Population (IUSSP, 1985) decided to give mortality studies a prominent position and to review research in the various fields regarding the influence of social and health policies on the levels and patterns of mortality (Vallin and Lopez, 1985a,b). The complicated interplay of various biological, economic, social and cultural factors has an impact on the health of the individuals and hence, on the mortality trends, levels and patterns of the population.

The chapter has been divided into two: (i) Child mortality and, (ii) Adult mortality. Direct estimates of mortality from deficient registration data and census counts often being flawed, indirect methods of estimation based on children everborn (CEB) and children surviving (CS) by age group of mother and marriage duration of mother and, widowhood data by age groups of male/female spouses have been used for the study.

3.2 MORTALITY AND LIFE TABLES

3.3 NEED FOR MORTALITY ANALYSIS

There are three basic components of population change, namely, fertility, mortality and migration that determine the age, sex composition and distribution with respect to various other characteristics of a population. Historical experiences in various countries indicate that the size and growth of a population were largely governed by the change in mortality component than the changes in other two components, viz., fertility and migration. After the industrial revolution in many European countries during the Seventeenth century, the increase in population was mainly due to initiation of decline in mortality. Furthermore, the experiences in the recent past in many developing countries show that the sharp decline in mortality alone rather than any increase in fertility and/or in-migration rates is the most revealing factor responsible for a rapid growth of population. Furthermore, the study of mortality, which deals with the effects of deaths on various aspects of a population, has a key role in analyzing the effects of other two components on the growth of a population.

Study of mortality was the first and foremost subject in demography brought under rigorous analysis and has found commercial applications in the field of insurance. Apart from applications in the field of insurance, many purposes are served by mortality analysis. It is useful in (i) analyzing demographic situation prevailing in a country as well as for assessing the prospects of potential growth and changes in future mortality conditions of the country, (ii) filling the administrative and research needs of public health agencies in connection with the development operations, and evaluation of public health programmes, for death statistics in a population cross-classified by age, sex and causes of death are of great value for the formulation, implementation and evaluation of public health programmes; and (iii) determination of administrative policy and action in connection with the programmes of government agencies other than those concerned with public health. Death statistics are required for forecasting population and other demographic characteristics in future which, are often used in developing plans for housing and educational facilities, managing the social security programmes, producing and providing services and commodities for different sections of a population. Analysis of mortality statistics by cause is essential to control various diseases. Local health authorities make use of mortality statistics reports to assess necessary administrative actions for improving public health in the local area. Finally, mortality analysis has important role in the studies of replacement and population growth and of migration.

3.4 SOME IMPORTANT DEFINITIONS RELATED TO DEATH

Since death is very much related to life, one should know the formal definitions of *life* and *death* even though the meaning of these two terms may appear obvious, at least in a physical sense, to most of persons. However, for ease in analyzing the statistical data on vital events, the United Nations and World Health Organizations have defined the three basic complimentary and mutually exclusive categories of vital event systems, viz., 'live birth', 'death' and 'foetal death' as follows:

Live birth: 'Live birth' is a complete expulsion or extraction from its mother as a product of conception, irrespective of the duration of pregnancy, which after such separation, breathes or show any evidence of life, such as beating of heart, pulsation of umbilical cord, or definite movement of voluntary muscles, whether or not umbilical cord has been cut or the placenta is attached; each product of such a birth is considered 'live birth'.

Death: Death is a permanent disappearance of all evidence of life at any time after birth has taken place (post-natal cessation of vital function without capability of resuscitation).

Foetal death: The definition of a death excludes foetal death, that is, death prior to (live) birth. A foetal death is formally defined as a death (disappearance of life) prior to complete expulsion or extraction from its mother as a product of conception, irrespective of the duration of pregnancy, the death is indicated by the fact that after such separation foetus does not breathe or show any other evidence of life such as beating of the heart, pulsation of the umbilical cord or definite movement of voluntary muscles. These definitions were recommended by WHO Experts' Committee on Health Statistics and adopted by the Third World Health Assembly, Geneva, 08–27 May 1950.

In demographic terminology, the term *foetal death* includes all the events variously called *stillbirths*, *miscarriages*, and *abortions* in popular medical legal usage. According to the United Nations, *stillbirths* refer to foetal deaths of 28 completed weeks of gestation or more, although the term is sometimes used to cover all foetal deaths. The term miscarriage is popularly employed to refer to spontaneous or accidental termination of foetal life occurring in early pregnancy. The term *abortion* is generally used to refer induced early *foetal deaths*, including births, those, which are legal and which are illegal. In medical science an abortion is the foetus prematurely particularly at any time before it is viable or capable of sustaining life. From a technical point of view, abortion and miscarriage could hardly be distinguished. To avoid these ambiguities, the United Nations and The World health Organizations recommended to groups all those events, miscarriages, abortions and still births under the common heading 'foetal deaths' classifying them as early, intermediate and late according to the months of gestation.

3.5 SOURCES OF DEATH STATISTICS AND ITS QUALITY WITH REFERENCE TO DEVELOPING COUNTRIES

For the statistically developed areas, the basic death statistics for mortality analysis are usually obtained through civil registration system of vital events. The analysis of the death statistics collected through civil registration system of vital event requires corresponding appropriate population data from a Census or a Survey, or population estimates for computing rates and ratios of various kind (discussed later on). This dependence on a second data collection system for obtaining requisite population for the purpose of computing various mortality rates and ratios may be avoided provided there exists a scheme that includes other types of events of each individual in addition to vital events only; such a scheme is known as 'Population Register Scheme'.

In developing countries the system of registering vital events are rather poor since many vital events remain unregistered due to poor machinery to collect the requisite data and lack of awareness of the utility of such data among the common persons, a bulk of whom are illiterates. However, in developing countries where death records are poor in quality, mortality conditions are usually measured through some indirect techniques from the age-sex distribution of persons collected in a census or a survey.

3.6 MEASURES OF MORTALITY

There are several measures of mortality based on deaths statistics. They may vary in respect of mortality they describe, their degree of refinement or elaboration, whether they are summary measures or specific measures, and whether they are measures of mortality per se or merely mortality related measures. One can distinguish among the measures of mortality so-called 'observed rates' from so-called 'adjusted rates'. The distinction is only approximate. The observed rates are typically simpler and are computed directly from actual data in a single brief calculation. The adjusted rates are more complicated both with respect to method of calculation and interpretation.

3.7 CONCEPTS AND VARIOUS CONVENTIONAL MEASURES OF MORTALITY

3.7.1 The Crude Death Rate (CDR)

The simplest as well as the most common measure of mortality is the crude death rate (CDR). It is defined as the number of deaths occurring in a locality at Calcutta in a specified year per 1000 of the mid-year population. Hence, Crude Death Rate (CDR) is simply the deaths in a year divided by the total population at mid-year and multiplied by 1,000. That is:

$$\text{CDR} = \frac{\text{Deaths in a year}}{\text{Population at Mid - Year}} \times 1{,}000$$

$$\text{i.e., CDR (X)} = \frac{D^X}{P^X_{\text{Mid-Year}}} \times 1000$$

Where D^X represents the total number of registered deaths among residents in a community during the calendar year x (1st January to 31st December and $P^X_{Mid\text{-}Yr}$. is the total population at the mid-point of the year x (i.e., 1st July). An example, for computing the CDR for a locality at Calcutta in 1979 as shown below:

D^{1979} = Total number of deaths of a locality at Calcutta during the calendar year 1979 (1st January to 31st December) is 61, 931.

$\bar{P}^{1979}$ = Total population of the locality at Calcutta at the middle of the year, i.e., mid-year population (1st July 1979) is 6,551,000.

Therefore, the crude death rate for the locality at Calcutta in 1979 =

$$\frac{61{,}931}{6{,}551{,}000} \times 1000 = 9.50 \text{ (appr.)}$$

The crude death thus expresses the frequency of deaths in an entire population as a single index, which is the most commonly used and widely available index of the level of mortality.

It is, of course, possible to use periods shorter or longer than a year, but then the calculation becomes more complex, involving estimation of years of exposure to the risk of dying.

Although it is easily computed and understood, it is generally a poor measure of mortality, as it does not take age structure into account. In many developing countries it is lower than in highly developed countries just because the former has a much younger age structure. For example, in England and Wales in 1983 the CDR was 11.7, while in Mexico, where mortality is higher, it was just 7.1. The CDR also covers all ages, yet a crucial aspect of mortality is the way it varies by age.

One important use of the CDR is to calculate the Crude Rate of Natural Increase—the difference between the CBR and CDR—a measure of the current rate of population growth if net migration is not substantial.

3.7.2 Infant Mortality Rate (IMR)

Concept and conventional measure of Infant mortality rate (IMR) in Section 3.7.2 and its major subdivision Early-neonatal mortality, Late-neonatal mortality and Post-neonatal mortality in Section 3.7.3.

Infant mortality rate, in the simplest form, is usually expressed as the number of deaths (excluding foetal deaths) during the first one-year of life since birth occurring among residents in a locality during a specified calendar year per 1000 live births during the same calendar year. Symbolically, infant mortality (IMR) is defined by,

$$\text{IMR} = \frac{\text{Deaths under age 1 in year}}{\text{Live births in year}} \times 1{,}000 \qquad \text{(i)}$$

or

$$\text{IMR} = \frac{D_0^X}{B^X} \times 1000$$

Where denotes the number of deaths below one-year of age during the calendar year X; and B^X represents the number of live births during the same calendar year. Because of very high level of mortality in the first few hours, days and weeks of human life and the differences in the causes accounting for infant deaths (i.e., deaths below I year of age) may usually be classified into three groups according to age at death yielding *early neonatal mortality rate occurs under 1 week* (mortality rate per 1000 live births) and *late neonatal mortality rate* (mortality rate between 1–4 weeks) and post neonatal mortality rate (*mortality between 4–52 weeks*). The neonatal mortality has been defined in conventional form in the section 3.7.3. The denominators, of overall infant mortality rate, early neonatal mortality rate, late neonatal mortality rate and post-neonatal mortality rate, are the same number of live births during the calendar year under consideration.

Calculated in this way the IMR is not a proper rate but a ratio, as the denominator is not the population at risk of the events in the numerator: some of the deaths under 1 may be of births which occurred during the previous year, while some of the births which occurred during the year may die in the next year, before their first birth day. Shryock and Siegel (1976: 235) call this the ‘Conventional’ IMR to distinguish it from other measures that more precisely relate the births and deaths. If date of birth is asked on death registration forms rather than just age, then the year of birth of those dying is available, so a ‘true’ IMR—the probability of dying during the first year of life—can be calculated. The extent to which the ‘conventional’ IMR approximates the ‘true’ IMR will depend principally on the magnitude of short-term fluctuations in the number of births over time, but usually they are very similar. In highly developed countries IMRs normally range from about 7 up to 15, while in the poorest countries they vary between perhaps 50 and 200 per 1,000 or even higher. For example, in

Sweden there were, in 1985, 98,463 births and 666 infant deaths. The IMR was thus 6.8. According to UN estimates for the early 1980s in developing countries there are, each year, about 104,000,000 births and 9,500,000 infant deaths. The IMR is thus about 91.

3.7.3 Early Neonatal Mortality Rates, Late Neonatal Mortality Rates, Post-Neonatal Mortality Rates

Deaths occurring during the first year of life tend to be concentrated in the first week or month. Also, during these early weeks the causes of infant deaths tend to be different from those that occur later. Because of this the IMR is often broken down into three parts: the Early, Late, and Post-Neonatal Mortality Rates:

$$\text{Early Neonatal Mortality Rate} = \frac{\text{Deaths under 1 Week}}{\text{Live births}} \times 1{,}000$$

$$\text{Late Neonatal Mortality Rate} = \frac{\text{Deaths within 1–4 Weeks}}{\text{Live births}} \times 1{,}000$$

$$\text{Post-Neonatal Mortality Rate} = \frac{\text{Deaths within 4–52 Weeks}}{\text{Live births}} \times 1{,}000$$

3.7.4 Cause Specific Death Rate

For the control of diseases in any population it is very import to know the cause of death. Thus cause-specific measures of mortality are useful in understanding the relative contributions of different causes to the overall mortality rates in the population and resources to be mobilized for controlling the specific disease. The most commonly used measure is Cause-Specific Death Rate (CSDR) and is defined as

$$\text{CSDR} = \frac{D_c}{P} \times 1000$$

where Dc is the number of deaths in a year due to specific cause 'c' and P is the mid-year population.

CSDR can separately be computed by age and sex. Another measure that expresses the number of deaths due to a specific cause as a proportion of all deaths is defined as the Cause-Specific Death Ratio and is used in the mortality analysis.

3.8 MATERNAL MORTALITY RATIO (MMR)

It is a widely used type of cause-specific mortality rate representing approximately the risk of dying as a result of complications of pregnancy, stillbirth and puerperium. This ratio is generally defined as the number of deaths due to puerperal causes per 100,000 live births.

$$\text{MMR} = \frac{D_P}{B} \times 100{,}000$$

where D_p = deaths due to puerperal causes that occur to mothers within 42 days of delivery associated with pregnancy and child birth during a year.

B = the number of live births in the same year.

3.9 THE LATE FOETAL DEATH RATE

Popularly, and in many parts of the world, this is called the 'Stillbirth Rate'. It is defined as:

$$\text{Late Foetal Death Rate} = \frac{\text{Late foetal deaths}}{\text{Late foetal deaths} + \text{Live births}} \times 1{,}000$$

There are, however, problems with the identification of a late foetal death or stillbirth, a problem compounded by the fact that different countries also often use slightly different definitions. According to the World Health Organization, a late foetal death occurs after twenty-eight week of gestation. Early foetal deaths (popularly known as 'miscarriages') are defined to occur before the twentieth week of gestation, and 'intermediate' foetal deaths between the twentieth and twenty eighth week. Such boundaries are both arbitrary and, in practice, very difficult to determine precisely. Another difficulty is in demarcating the difference between a foetal death and a live birth, which dies very soon after birth.

3.10 THE PERINATAL MORTALITY RATE

This widely used rate avoids the problems of defining a live birth and puts together late foetal and early neonatal deaths because they are thought to be determined by similar causes. It is defined as:

$$\text{Late Foetal Death Rate} = \frac{\text{Stillbirths} + \text{Deaths under 1 week}}{\text{Stillbirths} + \text{Live births}} \times 1{,}000$$

3.11 SPECIFIC DEATH RATES, DIRECT STANDARDIZATION RATE, STANDARDIZED MORTALITY RATIO

As the rates are crude, these rates cover persons of all ages and groups in their denominator. When the rates are specific, these rates refer to a particular group, usually defined at least by age and sex. They may include all causes of death, or just a single one. While these can be very precise, these allow very detailed analyses to be done, to compare, these are also very difficult, simply as these are not single-figure indices. Comparing two columns of Age-Specific Death Rates can become very complex. Hence, these problems can often be overcome by Standardization.

The aim of Standardization is to allow more precise comparison of two or more 'crude' rates by eliminating the effect of, say, the differences in age structure between two or more populations. Usually rates are age-standardized, but many other attributes can also be used.

Standardization is of two kinds, known as 'direct' and 'indirect'. Direct standardization involves taking a standard population and applying to it, the specific rates for the population being to be compared. This produces a number of expected events that can be, compared with the actual number observed in the standard population and the ratio Exp./Obs. Gives, directly, the standardized rate. The ratio of two such standardized rates is a very useful measure. It is known by various names, most commonly the 'Comparative Mortality Ratio' (CMR). Thus:

$$\text{Direct Standardization Rate} = \frac{\text{Expected from index rates}}{\text{Observed in standard population}}$$

With indirect standardization, on the other hand, one takes a set of standard rates and applies these to the populations being compared to produce a number of expected events. The ratio Obs./Exp., then gives, not a standardized rate, but a 'Standardized Mortality Ratio' (SMR). Thus:

$$\text{Standardized Mortality Ratio} = \frac{\text{Observed in index population}}{\text{Expected from standard rates}}$$

Then, to calculate the indirectly standardized rates for the index populations being compared one simply multiplies the crude rate in the standard population by the SMRs. Thus, whereas in direct standardization the standardized rates are found immediately (i.e. 'directly') before the CMR is calculated, in indirect standardization they are only computed after the SMR has been found (i.e. 'indirectly').

The main advantage of indirect over direct standardization is that it is not necessary to know the specific rates in the populations being compared. In general, the two methods of standardization will give similar results as long as the standard chosen is not very strange. The World Health Organization produces standard standards. Note also that if the specific rates being compared vary systematically by age or whatever, then this is important and it should not be hidden by standardizing and reporting only the single standardized rate. Instead, comparisons should be made within each age group.

Standardization has been met earlier elsewhere in the text, most obviously in Coale's Indices, which is just indirect standardization, where the standard is the Hutterite ASFRs. But the TFR is also a standardized rate, as can be seen from the Table given below, where the West Bengal ASFRs from fertility estimates mentioned in chapter 5 are directly standardized on a population with one woman in each age group. Remember that each woman will experience the ASFRs for five years.

Table 3.1 The TFR as a standardized rate, West Bengal: 1991.

Age group	ASFRs	Standard Population* (Sri lanka)	Expected births
15–19	0.0630	79865	5032
20–24	0.1539	63315	9744
25–29	0.1170	51860	6068
30–34	0.0717	44440	3186
35–39	0.0438	38795	1699
40–44	0.0245	32250	790
45–49	0.0115	26720	307
TFR =	2.4270		

*Population of a country is to be likely similar taken as standard.

3.12 THE LIFE TABLES

Perhaps because death is a precise, easily definable event, which occurs just once to each individual, the techniques of analyzing mortality have a longer history and are more developed than those for analyzing fertility. It was early part of the twentieth century that fertility began to be studied to any great extent, but the history of mortality analysis goes back as far as the work of 'John Graunt' in the late seventeenth century, and even to Roman times.

3.13 CONSTRUCTION OF A LIFE TABLE

The life table is a device that describes a cohort's or a population's mortality experience. The life table, sometimes called table of mortality (table de mortalité in French, and similarly labelled in most languages other than English) is one of the oldest and probably the single most valuable tool in demography. It has many applications that range well beyond mortality analysis. The concept of a life table comes from a cohort perspective. If one could follow a birth cohort of 100,000 individuals through time in a closed population (a population without in-and out migration), the number of survivors at various ages would correspond to the 'number left alive at age x,' in the life table l_x column. The difference between survivors at two consecutive ages, x and x + n, would correspond to the number of deaths between x and x + n, in the life table denoted by ${}_nd_x$. The ratio of ${}_nd_x$ to l_x produces another column of the life table, the probability of dying between age x and x + n, denoted by ${}_nq_x$. Thus, data on cohort survival can be readily converted into a life table. The life tables are of two types namely, complete (unabridged i.e., single-year age) and abridged (grouped i.e., 5-year age groups). Traditionally, a life table where n = 1 is called an 'unabridged' or a 'single-year' life table, and the left subscript can be omitted. A common alternative is to use 5-year age groups starting with age 5, and to present information for the age group 0–4 (that is, below exact age 5) in two groups: age 0 (i.e., less than age 1) and ages 1–4. In this case, the life table is called 'abridged'. It formerly was common practice to end a life table with an open-ended age interval starting at age 85. With the large proportions of survivors at age 85 in many low-mortality populations, though, the preferred practice is to present more detailed information above age 85, carrying it up to age 100 and concluding with an open-ended interval above that age (i.e., 85+ or 90+ or 95+ that depends on choice). Because of the distinctive mortality differences between the sexes, life tables are commonly presented separately for males and for females also.

Hence, a life table is simply an elegant and convenient way of analyzing Age-Specific Death Rates (ASDRs), though the technique is now used in many other areas, where it is often called '**Survival Analysis**'. It comprises a set of columns, most of which can be calculated from any of the others. The only raw data involved are the ASDRs.

In its classical form, the life table includes the following columns:

x = exact age

l_x = number still alive at age x

${}_nd_x$ = number dying between ages x and x + n = $l_x - l_x + n$

${}_nq_x$ = probability of dying between ages x and x + n, conditional on survival to age x = l_{x+n}/l_x

${}_np_x$ = probability of surviving from age x to age x + n, conditional on survival to age x = l_{x+n}/l_x

${}_na_x$ = average number of person-years lived in the interval between age x and x + n by those dying in the interval

${}_nL_x$ = number of person-years lived between ages x and x + n = ${}_nl_x + {}_na_x \cdot {}_nd_x$

${}_nm_x$ = death rate between ages x and x + n = ${}_nd_x/L$

T_x = total number of person-years lived above age x (sum of ${}_nL_x$ for ages x and higher)

e^0_x = expectation of life at age x = T_x/l_x

When constructing a life table, the column calculated first is q_x. It gives the probability of dying between exact ages x and x + 1. That is:

$$q_x = \frac{\text{Deaths during year of persons aged x at start of the year}}{\text{Population aged x at start of year}}$$

Note that the denominator is the number alive at the beginning of the year. Thus assume 1,000 persons are born at exactly the same moment. Then there may be say 950 left alive at exact age 30. If ten die before they reach 31, then:

$$q_{30} = \frac{10}{950} = 0.010$$

Now q_xs cannot generally be calculated directly because population estimates normally relate to the middle rather than the start of the year.

Instead, they have to be estimated from simple ASDRs. If ASDRs are called M_x, as is conventional, then:

$$M_x = \frac{\text{Deaths during year of persons aged x}}{\text{Population aged x at mid-year}}$$

The difference between M_x and q_x is simply that with the former the denominator is the population at the middle of the year while with the latter it is the beginning of the year. M_x and q_x will thus generally be very similar to each other with q_x slightly smaller than M_x in growing populations, larger in declining ones. So, to construct the life table we have to adjust the M_xs slightly to produce q_xs. To explain how this is done it is necessary to introduce some notation:

Let D_x be the number of deaths in the year of persons aged x.
Let N_x be the population aged x at the start of the year.
Let P_x be the population aged x at mid-year.
Then:

$$q_x = \frac{D_x}{N_x}$$

and

$$M_x = \frac{D_x}{P_x}$$

Now, N_x is just P_x plus those dying between the start and the middle of the year. For most ages this will be close to $0.5D_x$ since deaths occur roughly evenly throughout the year.

Thus:

$$N_x = P_x + 0.5D_x.$$

Putting D_x over both sides we get:

$$\frac{D_x}{N_x} = \frac{D_x}{P_x + 0.5D_x}$$

$$\Rightarrow \qquad q_x = \frac{D_x}{P_x + 0.5D_x}$$

Dividing top and bottom by P_x gives:

$$q_x = \frac{D_x}{P_x/P_x + 0.5(D_x/P_x)}$$

$$= \frac{M_x}{1 + 0.5M_x}$$

However, if ASDRs (M_xs) are expressed per 1,000 population than per 1, then the equation becomes:

$$q_x = \frac{M_x}{1{,}000 + 0.5M_x}$$

Thus it is possible to estimate q_xs from M_xs using this formula. However, it is only an approximation and its accuracy depends on the extent to which reality differs from the assumption that those who die in the year live on average, half of a year during that year. This will be fairly accurate for all ages except the very young and, to a lesser extent, the very old. The young will, on average, live less than half a year because their deaths will tend to be concentrated in the early part of the year. This fraction of a year lived is usually denoted by a_x. It is therefore possible to generalize the equation to:

$$q_x = \frac{M_x}{1 + (1 - a_x)M_x}$$

The values that a_0, a_1... take, vary from country to country and according to the level of mortality. For developing countries, where mortality is high, values of 0.3 for a_0, 0.4 for a_1 and 0.5 for all the others are normally used. Where mortality is low, 0.1 is a better figure for a_0. In general the values chosen are not critical, except for a_0. Moreover, there is another way to estimate q_0 without using formula above, for it is just the Infant Mortality Rate i.e. it is possible to use:

$$q_0 = \frac{D_0}{\text{Births in year}}$$

As an example, next Table 3.2 shows the top and bottom parts of a life table for California, 1970.

Table 3.2 Life table for California, 1970.

Age interval x to x+1	Mid-year population P_x	Deaths in year D_x	Age-specific death rate M_x	Fraction of last year lived a_x	Probability of dying q_x
0–1	340483	6234	0.018309	0.09	0.018009
1–2	326154	368	0.001128	0.43	0.001227
2–3	313699	269	0.000858	0.45	0.000858
3–4	323441	237	0.000733	0.47	0/000733
4–5	338904	175	0.000516	0.49	0.000516
5–6	362161	179	0.000494	0.50	0.000494
6–7	379642	171	0.000450	0.50	0.000450
...	...	...	...	...	...
...	...	...	...	...	...
83–84	34439	3753	0.108975	0.50	0.103344
84–85	31009	3669	0.118320	0.50	0.111711
85+	142692	22483	0.157564	–	1.000000

Source: Chiang (no date: 76–8)

Thus, for example:

$$q_3 = \frac{0.000733}{1 + (1 - 0.47)\, 0.000733}$$

$$= 0.000733$$

There are several points worth noting in this example. First, M_x and q_x are generally very close to each other, especially in populations with low mortality such as California. However, M_x is always slightly larger in growing populations. Second, the a_xs used here were calculated from California registration data and are specific to California, 1970. They are not generally applicable. Third, the last, open-ended age group, here 85+ have to be treated differently. Because all those alive at the start of the interval will die before its end, simply because it has no end, the last probability, q_x+, will always be 1.00. Fourth, although the general formula has been used here for q_0 the 'conventional' IMR could have been used as an estimate of the true probability. Finally, the life table is extremely useful in that it is for both sexes combined. Almost always the sexes are treated separately because their mortality is different.

There are other methods such as Reed-Merrell method and Greville's method of adjusting M_xs to estimate q_xs. To mention here is that Reed-Merrell method incorporates adjustments for under-reporting at younger ages. The nomenclature of a complete life table and, process of computing complete life table and its relation between columns is provided in the table below.

The process of computation of complete life table and its relations between its columns-Basis 10 and column q_x

x	q_x	l_x	d_x	L_x	T_x	e_x^0
0	q_0	$l_0 = 100000$	$d_0 = l_0.q_0$	$L_0 = l_0 - 0.72d_0$	$T_0 = T_1 + L_0$	$e_0^0 = \frac{T_0}{l_0}$
1	q_1	$l_1 = l_0 - d_0$	$d_1 = l_1.q_1$	$L_1 = l_1 - 0.59d_1$	$T_1 = T_2 + L_1$	$e_1^0 = \frac{T_1}{l_1}$
2	q_2	$l_2 = l_1 - d_1$	$d_2 = l_2.q_2$	$L_2 = l_2 - 0.53d_2$	$T_2 = T_3 + L_2$	$e_2^0 = \frac{T_2}{l_2}$
3	q_3	$l_3 = l_2 - d_2$	$d_3 = l_3.q_3$	$L_3 = l_3 - 0.52d_3$	$T_3 = T_4 + L_3$	$e_3^0 = \frac{T_3}{l_3}$
4	q_4	$l_4 = l_3 - d_3$	$d_4 = l_4.d_4$	$L_4 = l_4 - 0.51d_4$	$T_4 = T_5 + L_4$	$e_4^0 = \frac{T_4}{l_4}$
5	q_5	$l_5 = l_4 - d_4$	$d_5 = l_5.d_5$	$L_5 = l_5 - 0.50d_5$	$T_5 = T_6 + L_5$	$e_5^0 = \frac{T_5}{l_5}$
6	q_6	$l_6 = l_5 - d_5$	$d_6 = l_6.d_6$	$L_6 = l_6 - 0.50d_6$	$T_6 = T_7 + L_6$	$e_6^0 = \frac{T_6}{l_6}$
...	...	...	...	...	...	...
ω-1	$q_{\omega-1}$	$l_{\omega-1} = l_{\omega-2} - d_{\omega-2}$	$d_{\omega-1} = l_{\omega-1}.q_{\omega-1}$	$L_{\omega-1} = l_{\omega-1} - 0.50d_{\omega-1}$	$T_{\omega-1} = T_{\omega-1} + L_{\omega-1}$	$e_{\omega-1}^0 = \frac{T_{\omega-1}}{l_{\omega-1}}$
ω	q_ω	$l_\omega = l_{\omega-1} - d_{\omega-1}$	$d_\omega = l_\omega$	$L_\omega = l_\omega - 0.50d_\omega$	$T_\omega = L_\omega$	$e_\omega^0 = \frac{T_\omega}{l_\omega}$

Note: $l_{\omega-1} = 0$, $d_\omega = 1$, $q_\omega.q_\omega = 1$

3.14 METHOD OF LINKING DEATH RATES WITH MORTALITY RATES

If the census population and the registered death are available by age (not by cohorts), the age-specific death rates (${}^tM_x$) are first computed for males and females separately. Mortality rates are computed as a ratio of deaths by age (${}^{t}D_x$) to the mid-year population by age (${}^{t}\bar{P}_x$). As an age-distribution of deaths, the annual average of a three or five-year period (t – 1, t, t + 1) age distribution of deaths is used, so as to lessen the effects from annual fluctuations of deaths.

As a mid-year age distribution of the population, the census population by age at the census year (t) is used, after a simple estimate either by moving backward to the beginning of the year and then to the end of the year, so as to take a simple average of the two estimates, or by moving the census population directly to the mid-point of the year. i.e.

$$t\bar{P} = \frac{1}{2}({}^{1-1-t}P + {}^{31-12-t}P)$$

Accordingly, death rate age-distribution is

$${}^{t}M_x = \frac{{}^{t}D_x}{t\bar{P}_x}$$

Or, $P_t = P_0 e^{rt}$ where P_t the mid-year population is to be estimated based on the Population-P_0, at initial year, Growth Rate-r, and Time-period from 1 March to 1 July, 1981, t = 0.33 and p_t = Population is to be estimated on 1 July 1981. Therefore,

$$P_t = P_0 e^{rt}$$

(Say, P_0–Total Population of West Bengal in 1981, r = .021 and t = 0.33 years and P_t –the population is to be estimated)

Now taking natural logarithm we get,

$\ln(P_t - P_0) = rt$ Hence, $r = \ln(P_t - P_0)/t$, r = growth rate, t = 0.33 we know

$P_{1\ \text{July, } 1981} = P_{1\ \text{March, } 1981 \times r \times t}$

(Mid-year Population)

If the age interval is greater than one year (n years), the death rate includes the entire interval:

$${}_{n}M_x = \frac{{}_{n}D_x}{{}_{n}\bar{P}_x} \times K$$

The transformation of the age-specific death rates into mortality rates (q_x) should be approximately carried out by means of the commonly used formula:

$$q_x = \frac{2 \times m_x}{2 + m_x}:$$

for age groups

$$_nq_x = \frac{2n \times {}_nm_x}{2 + n.\,{}_nm_x},$$

$$_4q_1 = \frac{2.4 \times {}_4m_1}{2 + {}_4m_1},$$

This link between m_x and q_x is of immense practical value, but it is an approximation not fully satisfactory. An age-specific death rate does not refer to a certain cohort, because registered deaths and the mid-year populations are not exactly matched at that specific age. This approach introduces errors in the values of mortality rates, particularly when they are by single year of age.

Although the life table is in principle a cohort concept, it is not commonly used in this fashion. The reason for this is both practical and substantive. Exhaustive cohort mortality data are rarely available, because that would require systematic death registration for a period spanning 100 years or more. In other words, it would be necessary to wait for a cohort to be extinct or near extinct to be able to construct a full cohort life table and obtain an accurate estimate of its life expectancy at birth. Accuracy would be compromised if the population was not closed–that is, if it were depleted not only by death but also out migration – and if death registration included deaths of immigrants. A further and more substantive drawback of cohort life tables is that they refer to a period stretching over a century, during which mortality conditions are likely to have changed. For descriptive and policy purposes, typically less heterogeneous and more timely information is necessary.

The limitations of cohort life tables have led demographers to design period life tables, based on the concept of 'synthetic' cohorts. A synthetic cohort is a hypothetical cohort of persons subject through their life to the age-specific mortality rates of one specific period. This contrasts with a real cohort where each age-specific rate pertains to a different year. The theoretical construction of synthetic cohorts allows one to construct period life tables and compute life-cycle indexes (such as the life expectancy at birth) on the basis of observations relating to, and hence reflecting the mortality conditions for, a well-defined and relatively short time period. In practice, the period chosen is most often a single calendar year, or a two-year period bracketing a census count, or a quinquennium.

3.15 MORTALITY MODELS

Comparison of life tables in various populations has led demographers to observe regularities of age patterns of mortality. In particular, across populations and time periods, age-specific mortality risks tend to follow a U-shape curve, with higher mortality risks at younger and older ages, with the lowest risks in the neighborhood of age 10. Another observation is that mortality rates are highly intercorrelated within a population. When mortality rates are higher at particular ages, they also tend to be higher at other ages. Although with a given level of mortality–as indexed, for example, by the value of the expectation of life at birth–somewhat different age-specific mortality rates may be associated in different populations, this variability is within relatively narrow bounds.

These observations have led demographers to search for parsimonious representations of mortality patterns, or mortality 'models'. The purpose of mortality models is the representation of complex age/level variations in life table columns with a small number of parameters. Mortality models can permit the estimation of mortality indicators in settings where the data ideally required for life table construction (an accurate census count of the population and accurate death registration for years fairly close to the time of the census, or corresponding statistics derived from an accurate population register) are absent. In such situations it may be still possible to estimate a limited number of population parameters, which, along with a model, can be useful for estimating a full life table.

Mathematical mortality models are the oldest parsimonious representations of mortality patterns. The purpose of such models is to present a functional form relating mortality risks to age, with a small number of parameters adjusting for varying levels and patterns across populations. Mathematical mortality models have not been very successful because the shape of the mortality curve is too complex to be easily summarized in a functional form. An important contribution of mathematical representations of mortality, however, is the Gompertz 'law' of mortality, according to which the logarithm of the death rate is a linear function of age. The Gompertz equation is frequently used to represent or estimate mortality rates at past middle adult ages, although it tends to overestimate mortality rates at older ages.

The most widely used mortality models are model life tables. In their classical form, model life tables are a set of life tables indexed along two dimensions, family and level. A family is a group of model life tables with similar age patterns of mortality, often based on the experience of populations that are geographically close. Within a family, tables are indexed by level, from low to high life expectancy at birth. These model life tables are estimated by grouping high-quality empirical life tables with similar age patterns of mortality, and by observing how age-specific mortality rates typically vary as the over-all mortality level changes. Regression equations are then used to construct model life tables for various families and mortality levels.

The most commonly used sets of model life tables were developed by A.J. Coale and P. Demeny and by the United Nations. Coale and Demeny model life tables are mostly based on the experience of European populations during the first half of the twentieth century, whereas United Nations tables are based on the experience of developing countries during the second half the twentieth century. The model life tables are given as follows:

3.15.1 United Nations Model Life Tables

The first set of model life tables was developed by the Population Division of the United Nations Secretariat during the 1950s: This set, subsequently published in a revised form which is based on a collection of 158 observed life tables for each sex. The model tables were constructed by assuming that the value of each ${}_5q_x$, (the probability of dying between age x and x + 5 in a life table) is a quadratic function of the previous q value, namely, ${}_5q_x$-1 - ~ (except for the first two age groups, ${}_1q_0$ and ${}_4q_1$ all the other groups considered are five years in length). This assumption implies that the knowledge of only one mortality parameter (${}_1q_0$ or an equivalent 'level' that indexes the ${}_1q_0$ values used) would determine a complete life table. The United Nations model life tables are thus a one-parameter system. Since the coefficients of the quadratic equations relating each ${}_5q_x$ value to its predecessor were not known a priori, they had to be estimated on the basis of observed data. Regression was used to estimate these coefficients from the 158 mortality schedules available for each sex. Once they were estimated, calculation of the actual model life tables was straightforward: a convenient value of ${}_1q_0$ would be chosen arbitrarily; it would then be substituted in the equation relating ${}_1q_0$ to ${}_4q_1$ so that a value of ${}_4q_1$ would be obtained which, in turn, would be used to generate a value of $\mathbf{{}_5q_5}$ through the equation relating $\mathbf{{}_5q_5}$ to $\mathbf{{}_4q_1}$, and so on.

There are inherent disadvantages in the 'chaining' technique used in calculating the United Nations model tables, especially when, as in this case, the quadratic equations relating one parameter to the next are not exact. Although the regression method of fitting equations to data does make some allowance for the existence of errors, it assumes that the distribution of these errors is known and that their mean is zero. The presence of systematic errors with non-zero mean (biases) may severely affect the estimates yielded by fitted regression equations, and their adverse effects are very likely to be augmented by the chaining technique described above whereby errors in one estimate would only contribute to accentuated errors in the next.

Furthermore, the 158 tables used as the database from which the regression coefficients of the fitted equations were estimated were not all of the same quality. Because many tables from developing countries were used in the database, mortality data with numerous deficiencies were included; and since large areas of the world did not possess any mortality statistics, life tables for those areas could not be included in the database. Owing to these shortcomings and to the fact that a one-parameter system lacks the flexibility required to approximate adequately the variety of cases encountered in reality, the United Nations life tables were soon superseded by other model sets which, though based on a similar approach, tried to avoid the pitfalls encountered by the creators of the first system. However, the United Nations set established the usefulness of a model life-table system.

3.15.2 Coale and Demeny Regional Model Life Tables

The Coale and Demeny regional model life tables were published in 1966. They were derived from a set of 192 life tables by sex recorded for actual populations. That set included life tables from several time periods (39 of them relate to the period before 1900 and 69 refer to the period after the Second World War) and was heavily weighted towards Western experiences. Europe, Northern America, Australia and New Zealand contributed a total of 176 tables. The remaining 16 tables were from Africa and Asia: 3 from Israel; 6 from Japan; 3 from Taiwan Province; and 4 from the white populations of South Africa. The 192 life tables were chosen for inclusion from an original set of 326 tables. Life tables in which age patterns exhibited large deviations from the norm were excluded. All of the 192 life tables selected were derived from the registration data and from the complete enumeration of the populations to which they refer. Most tables covered entire countries, but a few representing the mortality experience of sub regions also were included, especially when that experience showed distinctive characteristics that persisted over time. A preliminary analysis of the tables revealed that four different mortality patterns could be distinguished among them. Those patterns were labelled 'North', 'South', 'East' and 'West' because of the predominance of European countries belonging to the various regions in each category. Hence, the adjective 'regional' was applied to the entire set. The countries whose life tables underlie each of the patterns identified and the outstanding characteristics of the patterns are discussed below:

3.15.2.1 *East Model*

The life tables underlying the East model come mainly from Austria, Germany (before 1900). The Federal Republic of Germany (after the Second World War), and northern and central Italy, although some from Czechoslovakia and Poland are also included. When the pattern of these tables is compared with the 'standard pattern' (that exhibited by the majority of tables), their deviations from the standard follow a U shape revealing their relatively high mortality rates in infancy and at older ages (over age 50). A total of 31 tables were used to estimate this model. The life expectancy in those tables ranges from a low of 36.6 years for Bavaria in 1878 to a high of 72.3 years for Czechoslovakia in 1958.

3.15.2.2 *North Model*

The observed life tables underlying the North model come from Iceland (1941–1950). Norway (1856–1880 and 1946–1955) and Sweden (1851–1890). Nine tables were used to derive this pattern of mortality, characterized by comparatively low infant mortality coupled with relatively high child mortality and by mortality rates above age 50 that fall increasingly below those of the standard. The populations displaying this mortality pattern were very probably subject to endemic tuberculosis (positive deviations from the standard pattern in the middle age range, from age 10 to 40, suggest this fact). Therefore, this model is recommended as an adequate representation of mortality in populations where the incidence of this disease is high. Life expectancy in these tables ranges from 44.4 years (Sweden, 1851–1860) to 74.7 years (Norway, 1951–1955).

3.15.2.3 *South Model*

The South model is based on life tables for Spain, Portugal, Italy, southern Italy and the region of Sicily, covering a period from 1876 to 1957. The levels of life expectancy range from 35.7 years (Spain, 1900) to 68.8 years (southern Italy, 1954–1957). A total of 22 tables were used in deriving this model. Their mortality pattern is characterized by high mortality under age 5, low mortality from about age 40 to age 60. And high mortality over age 65 in relation to the standard.

3.15.2.4 *West Model*

The West model is based on the residual tables, that is, those not used in the derivation of the other regional sets. Their mortality patterns do not deviate systematically from the standard pattern obtained when all the available life tables are put together; and, in this sense, they are closer to the standard than those on which other regional sets are based. Furthermore, because this model is derived from the largest number and broadest variety of cases, it is believed to represent the most general mortality pattern. For this reason, the West model is often recommended as a first choice to represent mortality in countries where lack of evidence prevents a more appropriate choice of model. It is of interest that the age pattern exhibited by the West model is very similar to that of the earlier United Nations life tables. Life expectancy in these tables ranges from 38.6 years (Taiwan Province, 1921) to 75.2 years (Sweden, 1959).

Model life tables are convenient to use, because within a family, a unique life table can be selected on the basis of only one life table indicator. The use of model life tables thus can flexibly accommodate various data configurations of the populations under study. However, the choice of the family of life tables appropriate for application to actual populations is not always straightforward, and the full range of age variations in actual mortality experience may not be fully represented in the currently available model life tables.

Another category of mortality models is the relational model, to which the logit model developed by William Brass. Brass (1971) observed that any two life tables can be related to each other in a linear way after performing a 'logit' transformation of q (x), the probability of dying before age x. The logit system is thus a system in which a 'standard' life table can be adjusted for varying levels and age patterns of mortality across populations after solving for the two linear parameters relating empirical life table values to the standard. The Brass logit system is often used to smooth an empirical life table or to complete a life table with missing values.

3.16 MULTIPLE-DECREMENTS

Although life tables were originally developed to study mortality, the same logic can be used to study many other processes. The only requirement is that the process must be a single-decrement process, which means that there is only one mode of exiting a defined state of interest with no possible return to that state. When studying mortality, the state of interest is being alive, and the only way to leave that state, with no return permitted, is through death. The same logic can be applied, for example, to first marriages, in which case the state of interest is being never married and the event of interest is first marriage. Other single-decrement processes include first migration from place of birth, marital survival, or entry to the labour force.

In reality, single-decrement processes are rare. For a real cohort, mortality is in fact the only true single-decrement process. Other states such as 'being never married' can be left not only by marriage, but also by death. Mortality always operates in addition to other processes, and thus multiple-decrement processes are far more common than single-decrement processes. Nonetheless, single-decrement life table logic can be applied to multiple decrements if the different sources of exits can be merged into one combined source of decrement, or if sources of decrements other than the one of interest can be ignored because they are very infrequent during the age-range under study. Also, if information is available only for individuals who did not experience other sources of decrement, the process of interest can be studied as a single-decrement process. For example, data on first marriages reported by individuals aged 85 can be used to reconstruct a life table in the single state where first marriage is the only source of decrement. Such strategy will provide an unbiased single-decrement life table if survivors had the same risks of experiencing a first marriage as those who did not survive (independence of probabilities).

In a multiple-decrement environment, it is sometimes useful to present information on the various modes of exits. Such analysis is commonly performed in a multiple-decrement life table, which is a life table where several sources of decrement affect the number of people still alive, and where each source of decrement is specified in various columns. For example, in a cause-specific life table, there are as many ${}_nd_x i$ columns as there are causes of death i. The sum of ${}_nd_x i$ in an age group is equal to, the number of deaths from all causes in the corresponding single-decrement life table.

There are also methods that permit construction of a single-decrement life table in the absence of, or net of, other sources of decrement. Such life tables are sometimes called 'associated single-decrement life tables' or 'cause-deleted life tables.' This approach involves information on a population subject to various sources of decrement, but it models the process of interest by reconstructing a hypothetical cohort where that process would be the only possible source of attrition. For example, if various causes of death are taken to be different modes of exiting the cohort, an associated single-decrement life table would permit estimation of the survival of a cohort in the absence of a particular cause (or group of causes).

Life table analysis is a powerful tool that has regained interest in the social sciences with recent developments in statistical techniques. If data on cohort survival is available at the individual level and includes covariates, it is possible to use a set of techniques termed 'survival analysis' or 'event-history analysis.' The main purpose of these techniques is to estimate the influence of individual-level characteristics on the age-specific risk of attrition, the so-called 'hazard rate.' Because of their roots in classical life-table analysis, some of these procedures have been termed 'life tables with covariates.'

As noted earlier, the underlying assumption of single-and multiple-decrement life tables is that once the event of interest is experienced, individuals can never return to their original state. In reality, there are many processes where individuals can experience reverse flows. For example, if the state of interest is being 'currently married,' there are return flows as individuals who experience divorce or widowhood remarry and become 'currently married' again.

Such processes can be analyzed through increment-decrement life tables, sometimes called multi-state life tables. In an increment-decrement life table, there are as many l_x columns as there are states (excluding 'being dead'), and these l_x columns can increase or decrease depending on the observed rates of transition from one state to the other. Among other uses, increment-decrement life tables allow estimation of the expected number of years in a particular state. For example, they can permit the estimation of the number of years that a newborn can expect to live in the 'currently married' state, which could not be done using classical, single-decrement life tables.

3.17 ABRIDGED LIFE TABLES

The nomenclature of life table shown elsewhere in this chapter is an example of a 'Complete' life table because single year age groups are used throughout. Often, though, it is preferable to construct 'Abridged' life tables where most of the age groups are five years. This might be because the data being used are not sufficiently reliable for a complete life table, or because a more concise picture of mortality is preferred. In fact, in demography, abridged life tables are far more common than that of the complete life tables.

Usually abridged life tables begin with age groups 0 to1 and 1 to 4, then five-year groups until the last and an open-ended interval. The way they are constructed is very similar to that for complete life tables, but instead of calculating q_x one calculates ${}_nq_x$, where 'n' is the length of the age interval but not at its start (i.e., 0–1 and 1–4). This notation is, to say the least, a little confusing but is used universally. ${}_5q_{20}$, (i.e., for age group 20–24) for example, refers to the interval from 20 to 25 but not from 5 to 20. The equation used is:

$$ {}_nq_x = \frac{{}_nm_x}{1/n + {}_nm_x\ [1/2 + n/12\ ({}_nm_x - \log_e C]} $$

where the constant C can be estimated from the relation is as follows:

$$ C = \left(\frac{{}_nm_{x+n}}{{}_nm_x} \right)^{\frac{1}{n}} $$

under the assumption that ${}_nm_x$ follows Gompertz law ${}_nm_x = BC^X$ where B and C are constants.

It may be noted that at very young ages the Greville's approximation of ${}_nq_x$ from ${}_nm_x$ is not applicable. However, most experiences in various equations show that at higher ages mortality rates may be closely governed by Gompertz's law. For these reasons, C may be assumed as constant for the full range of life table excepting very young ages. A convenient approximation for C may be taking as **loge C = 0.09 though the values of loge C** vary between 0.08 and 0.104.

In this situation the values of ${}_nL_x$ column may be obtained by two different ways.

First approach: Under the assumption of equality between life table age-specific death rates (${}_nm_x$) and observed age-specific death rates (${}_nm_x$)

in the population under study, ${}_5L_x$ may be approximated by the following relation is of the form:

$${}_nL_x = {}_nd_x / {}_nm_x$$

Second approach: Under the assumption of a third degree polynomial of l_x curve through the four points l_{x-n} ,l_x, l_{x+n} and l_{x+2n}, Greville (1945) showed that ${}_5L_x$ may be approximated fairly well by the relation of the form:

$${}_5L_x = n/2\ (l_x +, l_{x+n}) + n/24\ ({}_nd_x - {}_nd_{x-n})$$

The other columns can be obtained as useful, as mentioned while describing various columns of a life table.

Application of Life Tables in Population Studies

The primary purpose of a life table is to present a clear picture of the mortality situation prevailing in various groups of a given population or a community. However, the life table techniques as special tools for measuring mortality that can be applied in various fields of population research.

It may be used in the measurement of population growth – in the computation of net reproduction rate (N.R.R) in particular, – and in population projection i.e., in estimating what the size and age composition of the population will be at some future date.

Different columns of the life tables of two or more communities may also be compared to determine relative mortality. Then ${}_nq_x$ –Columns, the l_x, columns, the ${}_nL_x$ columns or the e^0_x – columns may thus be compared. (incase of l_x or ${}_nL_x$ columns are used, the size of l_0 must be the same for the tables to have comparability). The most familiar of such comparison is in regard to e^0_x, the average longevity per member of a population.

Life table techniques are extensively used to prepare multiple decrement life tables for various socio economic characteristics. Examples of such life tables are school going children life tables, working population life tables, nuptiality tables, cause of death life tables, etc., which are generally prepared with two factors of attrition in which one is death and another the variable concerns.

A life table is useful from the points of view of business and government as well. Life insurance companies in determining rest of premium for policies of persons of different ages, while the government or a firm may use it for determination of rates of retirement benefits for its employees employ it. Life tables and life table techniques have been widely used in the evaluation of family planning programme as well.

3.18 LIFE TABLE FUNCTIONS (ABRIDGED LIFE TABLES)

The table given below shows the abridged life table constructed by Greville's method for West Bengal Female. Each column has been calculated from the first $_nq_x$ column, which itself was calculated using ASDRs ($_nm_x$s). Apart from a few assumptions, no other data are used.

The following paragraphs describe how each column was calculated, and how it was interpreted and used.

$_n\mathbf{q}_x$ – is the probability of dying between exact ages x and x + n. As stated earlier, $_1q_0$ is the 'true' Infant Mortality Rate (IMR) and the IMR, as conventionally calculated, is a very good estimate of this. Recall also that the figure for the last, open-ended age group q_x will always be 1.0 as every one alive at the start of the interval, dies during it.

Female life table construction (SRS, 1987–89) for West Bengal based on South Asian Pattern. $_nm_x^{obs}$ is corrected by K = 1/C (where C = 0.836) and then taking the ratio of $_nm_x^{obs}$ over $_nm_x^{model}$. The age-pattern of mortality has been constructed (1/C= 1/0.836 =1.20).

Table 3.3 Abridged life table for West Bengal Female based on SRS (1987–1989).

Age group x to x + n	$_nm_x$	$_nq_x$	lx	$_nd_x$	$_nL_x$	T_x	e^0_x
0–1	0.12842	0.12063	1,00000	12063	91266	5579186	55.79
1–4	0.02147	0.08251	87937	7255	331975	5487920	62.41
5–9	0.00364	0.01805	80682	1456	399770	5155945	63.90
10–14	0.00156	0.00777	79226	615	394593	4756175	60.03
15–19	0.00220	0.01094	78611	860	390905	4361582	55.48
20–24	0.00267	0.01327	77751	1032	386175	3970677	51.07
25–29	0.00295	0.01465	76719	1124	380785	3584502	46.72
30–34	0.00354	0.01755	75595	1327	374658	3203717	42.38
35–39	0.00424	0.02099	74268	1559	367443	2829059	38.09
40–44	0.00537	0.02652	72709	1928	358725	2461616	33.86
45–49	0.00725	0.03565	70781	2523	347598	2102891	29.71
50–54	0.01132	0.05515	68258	3764	331880	1755293	25.72
55–59	0.01789	0.08585	64494	5537	308628	1423413	22.07
60–64	0.02863	0.13408	58957	7905	275023	1114785	18.91
65–69	0.04361	0.19744	51052	10080	230060	839762	16.45
70+	0.06720	1.00000	40972	40972	609702	609702	14.88

Some Specific Methods of Constructing Abridged Life Tables

While describing various columns of an abridged life table, it is mentioned that the values of ${}_nq_x$ column which is the most fundamental column of a life table, can be obtained by making use of certain reasonable relationship between ${}_nq_x$ and ${}_nm_x$, the life table death rate in the age group (x, x + n).

Under the assumption, the observed age-specific death rates (${}_nM_x$) of the population under study during a short period of time were equated to the life table age-specific death rates (${}_nm_x$). These ${}_nm_x$ values are converted into ${}_nq_x$ under various assumptions given below.

Linear Approximation

Under the assumption that the death rates are evenly distributed within each age-interval (x, x + n), excepting the first few years of life, it can be easily shown that the age-specific mortality rates (${}_nq_x$) can be estimated from the age-specific death rates by using the following relationship

$$\frac{2n \,.\, {}_nm_x}{2 + n \,.\, {}_nm_x}$$

In this case ${}_nL_x$ may be approximated as

$${}_nL_x = \frac{n}{2}(l_x + l_{x+n})$$

The above relationship between ${}_nq_x$ and ${}_nm_x$ and between ${}_nL_x$ and l_x assume that l_x is a linear function of x within the age-interval (x, x + n).

$L_0 = 0.276\, l_0 + 0.724\, l_1$

${}_4L_1 = 0.034\, l_0 + 1.184\, l_1 + 2.782\, l_5$

${}_4L_1 = (l_1 - l_5)/{}_4m_1$

For the last half open interval, i.e., the ages y and above (y, ∞) the value of L_{y+} is given by

$$L_{y+} = l_x/m_{y+}$$

The other columns may be obtained through the interpolations among the various life table columns.

One minor detail worth noting here is that occasionally ${}_nq_0$ is written as q(n) or Q(n), particularly when using Brass-type indirect techniques, or on computers, which can not easily cope with subscripts. Very confusingly, the n often then becomes an x.

$\mathbf{{}_np_x}$ – is the probability of surviving between exact ages x and x + n. It is just the complement of ${}_nq_x$. Thus:

${}_np_x = 1 - {}_nq_x$ or, ${}_nq_x = 1 - {}_np_x$ (here we can assume $p_x = l_x$) ${}_np_x + {}_nq_x = 1$

Often ${}_np_x$, like ${}_nq_x$, is expressed per 1,000 or 10,000 population in order to avoid lots of zeros.

l_x – is the number of persons surviving at exact age x. The beginning of the age-interval (x, x + n) out of the total births l_0, is an arbitrary number called usually the ***radix*** of the life table. Usually, it will be a round number such as 1 or 1,000 or 100,000. l_x is thus the number remaining surviving at age x out of the original l_0.

To calculate l_x, first choose a suitable radix, and then work down the table using formula:

$$l_{x+n} = l_x (1 - {}_nq_x)$$

$$l_{x+n} = l_x \cdot {}_nP_x, \quad \text{where } {}_nP_x = 1 - {}_nq_x$$

In words, the number of persons surviving to age x is just the number surviving to age x – n multiplied by the probability of surviving from age x – n to age x. For example, using the figures from the above relation:

$$ {}_np_x = \frac{l_{x+n}}{l_x} $$

In words, the probability of surviving from age x to x + n is just the number of persons alive at age x + n divided by the number alive at age x.

${}_nd_x$ – the number of persons dying between the exact age x and x + n. It is just the difference between two l_xs. Algebraically:

$$ {}_nd_x = l_x - l_{x+n} $$

Thus,

$$ {}_5d_{10} = l_{10} - l_{15} $$

Note that for the last, open-ended age group the number of persons dying is the same as the number alive at its start. That is:

$$ d_{x+} = l_x $$

But ${}_nd_x$ can be calculated using:

$$ {}_nd_x = l_x \cdot {}_nq_x $$

In words, the number of persons dying during the interval is equal to the number alive at its start multiplied by the probability of dying during the interval.

For example:

$$ {}_5d_{10} = l_{10} \cdot {}_5q_{10}. $$

${}_nL_x$ – is the number of persons-years lived that would be lived by the assumed birth cohort l_0 in the age-interval (x, x + n). Thus according to the Table given here, 1,00,000 new born male babies would live 357,293 person-years between exact age 30 and 35. Of the 72,166 males who reach exact age 30, 70,697 males survive to age 35 and would live 5-years each. In other words, 72,166 males at age 30 would live 70,697 × 5 = 353,485 person-years in the age-interval (30, 35). There are various formulas through the values of ${}_nL_x$ can be approximated from the value of l_x under various assumption of the l_x–curve. Hence,

$${}_nL_x = \frac{n(l_x + l_{x+n})}{2}$$

and this is a much easier formula to use when calculating ${}_nL_x$ than the one above. In words, one simply takes the average of two l_xs and multiplies by n(n = age interval i.e. 5 years in case of abridged life table).

$${}_5L_5 = \frac{5(l_5 + l_{10})}{2}$$

There is a problem with the last, open-ended age group in that it is necessary to make an additional assumption about how many more years, on average, those alive at its start live for. There are several ways of doing this, and the method is not crucial because relatively few person-years are lived in the interval. Of course, if the old ages are of particular interest, then more care has to be taken. The usual method involves M_{x+}, the Age-Specific Death rate in the open-ended interval. First, it is approximately true that:

$${}_nM_x = \frac{{}_nd_x}{{}_nL_x}$$

In words, the ASDR is the number of life-table deaths divided by the number of person-years lived. Rearranging the equation gives:

$${}_nL_x = \frac{{}_nd_x}{{}_nM_x}$$

So $$L_{85+} = \frac{d_{85+}}{M_{85+}}$$

But, $d_{85+} = l_{85}$ since everyone eventually dies so:

$$L_{85+} = \frac{l_{85}}{M_{85+}}$$

If M_{x+} is not available, then it is probably the best to estimate L_{x+} using model life tables, or a life table for a country with a similar level of mortality.

T_x – is the total number of person-years lived after exact age x. It is thus simply the ${}_nL_x$ column cumulated from the bottom. That is:

$$T_x = T_{x+n} + {}_nL_x$$

Thus,

$$T_{85} = L_{85+}$$

From Table:

$$T_{80} = T_{85} + {}_5L_{80}$$

The main purpose of this function is in the calculation of the next – the expectation of life. e_x – is the expectation of life at age x, or the average number of years a person aged x has to live. Strictly, it should be written as e_x^0 since in actuarial science the circle is used to distinguish the conventional expectation of life from a different expectation in which deaths occurring during the year are excluded from the calculations. Since this latter statistic is not used at all in demography, the circle has become optional.

Since the total number of years left to be lived by l_x people is T_x, the expectation of life is just one divided by the other. Thus:

$$e^0_x = \frac{T_x}{l_x}$$

Thus the expectation of life at birth is:

$$e^0_0 = \frac{T_0}{l_0} \text{ (when age x = 0, i.e., at birth)}$$

P– Finally, one function of the life table which has not been mentioned so far, but which is often useful, particularly in population projections, is the survivorship Ratio. There are really two ratios, one between exact ages and one between intervals. The first, the probability of surviving between exact ages, is just the ${}_nP_x$ described above, but it is the second, the survivorship between age groups, which is more commonly required. Unfortunately, the notation for this is not quite standardized, though normally S or P is used. Shryock and Siegel, (1976: p.262)-use S. There are also notational problems about identifying the age groups involved since one needs at least three subscripts or superscripts.

The ratio is calculated simply as the ratio of any two ${}_nL_x$s. For example, the probability of surviving from age group 5–9 to age group 15–19 is

$$P = \frac{{}_5L_{15}}{{}_5L_9}$$

Some more life table functions that are used mostly

$l_0 \times P_0 = l_1; \qquad {}_4l_1 = 2(l_1 + l_5)$

$l_1 \times {}_4P_1 = l_5;$

or $\qquad {}_4l_1 = \dfrac{(l_1 - l_5)}{{}_4m_1}$

$l_5 \times {}_5P_5 = l^{10}; \quad {}_5L_{65} = \dfrac{5(l_{65} + l_{70})}{2}; \qquad L_{70} = \dfrac{l_{70}}{m_{70+}}$

$l_{x+n} = l_x \mathbf{x}\ {}_nP_x;$

$$\text{and, } m_{70+} = \frac{d_{70+}}{L_{70+}}$$

3.19 INTERPRETATION OF THE LIFE TABLE

The way the life-table functions have been described so far has assumed that 1,1,000, 100,000 or however many babies, are all born at one instant, and are then gradually killed off until eventually none are left. l_x is just the number of persons alive at exact age x, because everyone has their birthday simultaneously. ${}_nL_x$ is the number of person-years lived.

There is, however, an alternative interpretation, which may be labeled as the 'dynamic', as opposed to the 'static' one outlined above. In this 'dynamic' interpretation, 1,1,000 or 100,000 babies are assumed to be born at a constant rate during the year, and this carries on for many years, l_0 being born each year. With this interpretation the l_x and ${}_nL_x$ columns take on slightly different meanings. l_x becomes the number of persons having their birth day during the year, and ${}_nL_x$ is just the population aged between x and x + n. Now, the population described by ${}_nL_x$ column is known as a

'Stationary' population. It has a constant age structure and a constant size with l_0 being born each year and exactly the same number dying.

3.20 LIMITATIONS OF DATA AND THEIR ADJUSTMENTS

The information on children everborn (CEB), the major input for the estimation of mortality at early ages, is known to suffer from two types of errors. One arises from the underreporting of children and other from the misclassification of women in age or duration groups. The children living elsewhere and those who have died are often not reported so that proportion of such omission increases with age or duration groups of mother. On the other hand, the proportion of wrong inclusion of stillbirths or foetal deaths among children everborn causes problems. Another kind of errors that may arise is the misclassification of childless women into category 'parity not stated'. This may affect average parity downward. Data presented below for 1981 and for 1991 and NFHS (92) will prove the point.

Average parities by age groups of mother, West Bengal							
Source	15–19	20–24	25–29	30–34	35–39	40–44	45–49
1981Census	0.22	1.20	2.42	3.47	4.34	4.84	5.14
1991 Census	0.19	1.18	2.23	2.95	3.59	4.08	4.53
1992–93 (NFHS)	0.27	1.43	2.48	3.31	3.99	4.56	4.93

3.21 AN ADJUSTMENT PROCEDURE BY EL-BADRY (JASA, 1961) FOR DATA ON CHILDREN EVERBORN

In 1961, El-Badry proposed a procedure to estimate the proportion of women belonging to the category 'parity not stated' who should have been classified as childless. This procedure is based on the observed high correlation existing between the proportions childless and the proportions in the category 'parity not stated', especially when only the first four or five five-year age groups are considered.

El-Badry's method is based on a very simple model. Let Z*(i) be the true proportion childless in age group 'i' and NS (i) be the reported proportion of women classified in the category of parity not stated for the same age group. Then, it is plausible to assume that the following relation holds:

$$NS\ (i) = \alpha\ Z^*(i) + \beta \qquad A(1)$$

Where α is the proportion of women who are truly childless and who were erroneously classified as of 'parity not stated' and β is the constant, true level not stated. Since the proportion α Z*(i) of childless women has been misclassified, the reported proportion in age group 'i', Z (i) must be equal to

$$Z(i) = (1.0 - \alpha)\, Z^*(i) \qquad A(2)$$

Or $$Z^*(i) = Z(i)/ (1.0 - \alpha) \qquad A(3)$$

Substituting equation A(3) in eqn. A(1), one finds that,

$$NS(i) = \alpha\, (Z(i)/ (1.0 - \alpha)) + \beta$$

$$= [\alpha /(1.0 - \alpha)]\, Z(i) + \beta \qquad A(4)$$

Or $$NS(i) = \gamma\, Z(i) + \beta \qquad A(5)$$

where $$\gamma = \alpha/ (1.0 - \alpha)$$

Eqn. A(5) suggests a method of estimating the true value of Z*(i); fit a line to the reported points [Z (i), NS (i)] and estimate γ and β. Then the true proportion childless is

$$Z^*(i) = Z(i) + (NS(i) - \beta) \qquad A(6)$$

and an estimate of the 'zero'- parity error, α, can be obtained by

$$\alpha = \gamma/ (1.0 + \gamma) \qquad A(7)$$

Note that even though algebraically eqn. A (6) is equivalent to

$$Z^*(i) = (1.0 + \gamma)\, Z(i) \qquad A(8)$$

Eqn. A(6) and A(8) may produce slightly different results in practice, since the fit obtained is very rarely exact. For the purpose of adjustment of the zero category, eqn. A(6) is recommended.

$$\beta = \overline{NS} - \gamma\, \overline{Z}$$

In most cases, when the required final product is the best estimate of average parities by age group of women, an adjustment of the zero parity category is not of immediate use, but the true level of nonresponse is. Once β, an estimate of this level, has been calculated, the female population to be used as denominator in computing average parities by age group can be obtained by multiplying the reported female population in each age group by the factor (1.0 – β). Thus, the required output from the El-Badry correction procedure will very often be only β, obtained by fitting equation (A.5).

To conclude, it must be noted that slightly different computational procedures have to be followed according to whether the data on children ever born refer to all women or only to ever-married women. Therefore, one detailed description of the computational procedure is presented in the following section. It is also useful to note now that in the following discussions, index i, is used to denote the age group from 5i + 10 to 5i + 14.

Steps to calculate:

1. Calculation of proportion with parity not stated: If one divides by FP (i) the total number of women in age group 'i' and by FNS (i) the number of women whose parity was not stated and who belong to age group 'i', then the proportion whose parity was not stated is
$$NS(i) = FNS(i)/FP(i) \qquad (1)$$
2. Calculation of proportion childless: Let FZ (i) be the reported number of childless women in age group 'i' and FP (i) be as defined above, then the proportion childless is
$$Z(i) = FZ(i)/FP(i) \qquad (2)$$
3. Estimation of linear parameters γ and β: Once the proportion of women whose parity was not stated and those of childless women have been calculated the points [Z (i), NS (i)] should be plotted. If they follow a straight line, the use of this method of adjustment is warranted. Otherwise, no adjustment is possible and the user is advised to include all those women classified as 'parity not stated' in the denominator when computing average parities. Of course, if the proportion of women with unknown parity in each age group is small, their inclusion or exclusion from the denominator is not likely to introduce in the average parities value.
4. Calculation of true proportion childless:
As Equation
$$Z^*(i) = Z(i) + (NS(i) - \beta)$$
Indicates, the true proportion childless, Z*(i) is equal to the sum of the reported proportion childless, and the deviation of the reported proportion whose parity was not stated from the estimated constant level, i.e. (NS (i) –β). Therefore, once β has been computed, the calculation of Z*(i) is straightforward. Once the estimated Z*(i) values are available, the true number of childless women, FZ*(i) can be obtained as the product of each Z*(i) and the reported female population of age group 'i', FP (i). The values of FZ*(i) obtained in this way should be used when fertility is to be estimated by using data on first births.

5. Calculation of denominators for estimation of average parities. Let FP*(i) denotes the number of women whose parity is assumed to be known after the true proportion childless has been obtained. Then,

$$FP^*(i) = (1.0 - \beta)\ FP\ (i) \qquad (3)$$

Since according to the model presented so far, the true level of non-response is the estimated value of β.

Computation of β, the true level of nonresponse, from the data given as follows:

Female population according to different responses concerning children everborn, Rural West Bengal, India, 1991.

Age group	Index, i	Total female population, FP (i)	Female population childless, FZ (i)	Parities not stated, FNS (i)	Reported proportion childless, Z (i)	Reported proportion with parity not stated NS (i)
(1)	(2)	(3)	(4)	(5)	(6)	(7)
15–19	1	838992	485119	6850	0.5782	0.0082
20–24	2	1944015	42326	7790	0.0218	0.0040
25–29	3	2111918	208885	5550	0.0989	0.0026
30–34	4	1596944	118648	3540	0.0743	0.0022
35–39	5	1337148	84191	3040	0.0630	0.0023
40–44	6	1012552	63580	2670	0.0628	0.0026
45–49	7	916784	54273	2720	0.0592	0.0030

Age group		Reported proportion childless, Z (i)		Reported proportion with parity not stated NS (i)
15–19		0.5782		0.0082
20–24		0.0218		0.0040
25–29		0.0989		0.0026
	$\bar{Z}_1$ =	0.2330	$\overline{NS}_1$ =	0.0049
25–29		0.0989		0.0026
30–34		0.0743		0.0022
35–39		0.0630		0.0023
	$\bar{Z}_2$ =	0.0787	$\overline{NS}_2$ =	0.0024

Two methods of fitting a straight line have been presented here. If we want to fit straight lines, can fit easily. But here we have considered only a method based on group means according to which the points [(Z (i) and NS (i))] are divided into two groups, each containing three points but the middle most value is taken in common to fit a straight line (figure not shown here).

Substituting equation A(3) in equation A(1)

$$NS(i) = \alpha (Z(i) / (1.0 - \alpha)) + \beta$$
$$= [\alpha/(1.0 - \alpha)] Z(i) + \beta$$
$$NS(i) = \gamma Z(i) + \beta \text{ where } \gamma = \alpha/(1.0 - \alpha)$$
$$Z^*(i) = Z(i) + (NS(i) - \beta)$$

So,

$$\alpha = \gamma / (1.0 - \gamma), \text{ and, } Z^*(i) = (1.0 + \gamma) Z(i)$$
$$\gamma_1 = (\overline{NS}_2 - \overline{NS}_1) / (\overline{Z}_2 - \overline{Z}_1)$$
$$= (0.0024 - 0.0049)/ (0.0787 - 0.2330)$$
$$\gamma_1 = 0.0162$$
$$\beta_1 = ((\overline{NS}_2) - (\gamma_1)(\overline{Z}_2))$$
$$\beta_1 = ((0.0024) - (0.0162)(0.0787))$$
$$= (0.0024 - 0.0013)$$
$$\beta_1 = 0.0011$$

Here, the true level of non-response β is 0.0011 i.e. the result for Rural West Bengal indicates well with merely an error of $\beta = 0.0011$ which is very meagre in the sense.

Similarly we can estimate β_2 or β independently and the values would nearly be the same as that of β_1.

3.22 BRASS METHOD OF EVALUATION OF BIRTHS AND DEATH REGISTRATION USING AGE DISTRIBUTION AND CHILD SURVIVORSHIP DATA

The Brass method provides a measure of the extent of under-registration of births and cohort deaths of young children in (0–9) age group. The method makes use of data on child mortality derived from CEB/CS per woman by quinquennial age groups for women in the reproductive age groups. The proportion of children dead D_i in the childbearing age groups is then obtained. The standard proportion of children dead D^s_i have been tabulated (Brass, 1979) for different fertility patterns indicated by P_2/P_3 where P_2 and P_3 are average number of CEB per women in the age groups 20–24 and 25–29 respectively. Both the values of D_i and D^s_i refer to the probability of dyeing from birth to some age x (i.e. ${}_xq_0$) depending on i, the age group.

Transforming the values to a logit system given by logit $(1 - D_i) = \alpha + \beta$ logit $(1 - D^s_i)$, where i = 1, 2...7, where logit D_i =1/2 ln [i/1 – D_i]. The values of α and β are obtained by grouping the six sets of values corresponding to i = 2, 3, ----------, 7 into two groups. This is equivalent to averaging the logit values in the age groups 20–24 and 35–39 yielding two equations to determine.

The life table L_x values are then derived from the relation

Logit $(1 - L_x) = \alpha + \beta$ logit $(1 - L^s_x)$, where α and β are estimated values as described earlier. The values of L_x have been tabulated for single year age x (Brass, 1979). The L_x values are then obtained as

$L_x = 1 -$ antilogit $[\alpha + \beta$ logit $(1 - L^s_x)]$, where antilogit $y = [1 + e^{-2y}]^{-1}$ for any y.

An estimate of L_0 is obtained from the relation

$L_0 = p + (1 - p).l_1$, where p is the separation factor taken as 0.35 and is obtained using the logit function.

i.e., logit $(1 - l_1) = \alpha + \beta$ logit $(1 - l^s_1)$,

Then the expected births = Census population at age x/L_x

and hence, if,

$$\frac{\text{Registered Births}}{\text{Expected Births}} < 1 \Rightarrow \text{evidence of under registration of births}$$

The registered births are divided by the average number of the registered to the expected birth ratios to obtain corrected births.

Applications of the L_x values to corrected births give survivors by age. Hence, by subtraction, it provides the number of deaths to each cohort.

i.e., Cohort Deaths = Corrected Births – Number of Survivors

= Corrected Births – L_x x Corrected Births

= Corrected Births $(1 - L_x)$

These estimated deaths by age can be compared with death registered for each cohort giving a measure of the extent of death registration of young children.

3.23 EXTENT OF UNDER-REPORTING OF DEATHS

In recent years several methods have been developed for measuring the extent of under-reporting in death registration. Some of these methods are: (1) Brass Sectional Growth Balance Equation (Brass, 1975); (2) Preston-Hill's Method using inter-censal growth rate, the recorded death rate, and the age distribution of the recorded death rates (Preston and Hill, 1980; Preston, Coale, Trussell and Weinstein, 1980); (3) A Modified Sectional Growth Balance Equation (Martin, 1980); (4) An Inter-Censal Cohort Survival Method (Brass, 1979; Preston and Hill, 1980; Trussell and Menken, 1979); (5) An Extension of the Inter-Censal Cohort Survival Method (Bennett and Horiuchi, 1981); (6) Estimation of Completeness of Death Registration in a Destabilized Population (Preston and Lahiri, 1991) and (7) Forward Projection Technique Using Data from Two Censuses.

Whereas all these methods assume age-invariance of completeness in the adult age-range, the first two methods are based on the assumption of stability and remaining methods use age-specific rather than a constant overall growth rate. The latter methods normally use two censuses and provide only estimates of completeness of death reporting relative to the completeness of census enumeration. The applications of these methods to less developed countries were not successful because of the effects of age-misreporting and differential completeness of enumeration between censuses. The inter-censal cohort survival method, though not requiring the assumptions of stability, uses cohort deaths, which are not easily derivable. Moreover, the assumptions of an even distribution of deaths within each age interval to apportion death between cohorts are not clearly realistic. Though the relaxation of the condition of stability seems more appropriate for West Bengal, the non-stable methods impose the constraint of more detailed data requirements than is the case with the stable methods.

We, therefore, consider a procedure for estimating the extent of completeness of death reporting in the Sample Registration Scheme (SRS), which is more straightforward in application, but based upon the assumptions of stability. The method proposed by Preston and Hill (1980) uses the age structure of deaths and assumes that the completeness of reporting does not vary substantially with age.

If the annual average growth rate, 'r', the crude death rate, 'd', and the age distribution, (a), of recorded deaths are known, completeness, c, of death reporting is obtained from the following relationship (derivation shown in Preston and Hill, 1980) in a stable population in discrete form,

$$C = \frac{D\,(a+)/P(a+)}{r}\left[\sum_{a}^{w} \delta(a)\exp\,(ra) - 1\right]$$

D (a+) and P (a+) being the recorded deaths and the population aged 'a' and above respectively and 'w', the maximum age; average age, a, at which deaths occur in the 5-year age-interval is measured by the distance of mid-point from the lowest age considered for the analyses. For example, if we limit our analysis to mortality beyond childhood, that is, to mortality from age 10 (origin) and the mid-point of the age-interval, say, 10–14 is 12.5, the value of a equals to 12.5–10.0 = 2.5. For all age groups except the first and the last, which will, of course, be open-ended, 'a' may be taken as the mid-point of the age at death interval. The above equation may be applied to population above any age and not simply to the population above age zero, so it also provides a method of estimating the completeness of adult death registration. Indeed, since the ultimate weighting of the child deaths is rather low, and the completeness of registration of infants and child deaths is often very different from that of adult deaths, it is preferable to interpret the results as estimates of the completeness of adult death registration.

Table 3.4 Calculating the component δ (a) exp (ra) in the estimation of completeness of death reporting by sex, 1981: West Bengal

Age Interval	Proportion of recorded deaths			Mid-point of the age interval, (a)	δ (a) exp (ra), (r = 0.021)		
	Male	Female	Person		Male	Female	Person
0–4	0.34413	0.34833	0.34748	2.5	0.36268	0.36711	0.36621
5–9	0.02204	0.04346	0.03173	7.5	0.02580	0.36711	0.03714
10–14	0.01165	0.01624	0.01452	12.5	0.01515	0.05087	0.01888
15–19	0.01444	0.04072	0.02318	17.5	0.02085	0.02111	0.03347
20–24	0.01240	0.03075	0.02108	22.5	0.01989	0.05880	0.03381
25–29	0.01333	0.02733	0.01931	27,5	0.02375	0.04932	0.03440
30–34	0.01817	0.01589	0.01710	32.5	0.03595	0.04869	0.03384
35–39	0.02088	0.01936	0.02049	37.5	0.04589	0.03144	0.04503
40–44	0.03251	0.02844	0.03085	42.5	0.07936	0.04255	0.07531
45–49	0.05588	0.02884	0.04305	47.5	0.15152	0.06943	0.11673
50–54	0.05898	0.04515	0.05270	52.5	0.17763	0.07820	0.15872
55–59	0.04356	0.02110	0.03317	57.5	0.14571	0.13598	0.11096
60–64	0.07518	0.07991	0.07781	62.5	0.27933	0.07058	0.28910
65–69	0.07087	0.05011	0.06208	67.5	0.29247	0.29690	0.25619
70+	0.20599	0.20435	0.20545	*	1.07910	1.06894	1.07537
					2.75508	2.59671	2.68516

Source for e^0_0: Family Welfare Programme, Year Book, 1986–87, India.

Note: e^0_0 for
Male is 55.45
Female is 54.65, and
Person is 55.05

*Open-ended age-interval for
Male is 78.86
Female is 78.79,
Person is 78.82

Preston and Hill's (1980) method is based on the assumptions of stability as Brass's. A stable population is one that has been subject to a constant fertility and mortality for a long time. But infact, no population in the world is stable even in developed nations (Colin, Newell, 1988). According to Preston and Coale (United Nations, 1983), the violation of the assumption of stability, particularly to recent changes in fertility and to gradual changes in mortality, may not affect the estimate of the completeness of death reporting to any extent.

The population of West Bengal is not stable, but experienced gradual decline in fertility and in mortality in recent years as evidenced from SRS (1981–1993). So, it is assumed that the application of Preston-Hill's (1980) method to the data for West Bengal in 1981 may not result in biased estimation of completeness of death reporting. So, we used this method to estimate the completeness of death reporting from the SRS data of 1981. Using the common procedure of estimating annual average growth rate,

$$r = \frac{1}{t} \ln [P_2/P_1], \text{ where } t = \text{interval between } t_1 \text{ and } t_2$$

We get a value of r = 0.021 in 1981. [It may be mentioned that for 1971–1981, t = 9.92 years because 1971 Census was conducted on 1 April rather than on the usual reference date of 1 March. It may be noted that the estimates of completeness depend on the accuracy of 'r' because a too low or too high value of 'r' may under or overestimate completeness of death reporting.

To start with we illustrate the procedure with initial age 0+ and consider the average age, a, at which deaths in age-interval occur will approximately be the mid-point of the interval (e.g., 2.5 for 0–4, 7.5 for 5–9, etc.,), the exact figure being used does not seem to invalidate the working of the procedure (Preston-Hill, 1980). The last open-ended age group is more difficult to deal with, since the lower limit of the interval may vary for different data. Therefore, with the observed rate of population growth rate, r, and approximate value for the expectation of life at birth, e^0_0, the average age at death at open-ended interval has been obtained by interpolating the values from the Table 3 presented by Preston and Hill (1980). In 1981, e^0_0 for male is 55.45 and for female is 54.65; e^0_0 is given for the period of 1986–91(F W P Year Book, 1989–1990) as 59.95, 61.95 and 59.53, 61.94 for males and females respectively and the values are averaged. So, e^0_0 for males is 60.95 and for females is 60.74 and for person is 60.84 and the growth rate for both sexes combined is the same for male as well as for females in 1981. The estimate of the average age at death in the age group with no upper bound will be more sensitive to error in e^0_0 than in 'r'. With these considerations, the present estimate for the average age at death for age 70+ is 78.82 when the analysis starts at age 0+, 68.82 at 10+ and so on, for males. For females, 78.79 at 0+, 68.79 at 10+, 78.82 at 0+ and 68.82 at 10+ for Persons in 1981. The other elements are crude death rate, d, and the proportionate age distribution of deaths, δ (a) around 1981 taken from the SRS.

On the consideration of possible differential under-registration with age, especially in view of the more deficient registration in the infant and childhood ages, we again, calculate the completeness for age 10+, which is given by,

$$C = \frac{D\,(10+)/P\,(10+)}{r}\left[\sum \delta\,(x)\,\exp\,(r\,(x-10))-1\right]$$

Where x is the mid-point of the age-interval, the other symbols are similar to that described earlier. These results in unimproved estimates of completeness compared to those staring with infant age. The level of completeness of registration of infant and child deaths does not appear as expected, but is found to be different from that of young and adult deaths.

Therefore, the results obtained in Table 3.5 and 3.6 show a little variation in the estimates of completeness of death reporting, but indeed, they are fairly close. The slight variation may be due to under-registration of adult death, otherwise, the technique appears to work well.

Table 3.5 Estimating completeness of death reporting by sex, 1981: West Bengal (For age 0+).

	Annual average growth rate, r*	Crude death rate, 'd'	$\Sigma\delta(a)e^{ra}-1$	Estimated completeness 'C'
Males	0.021	0.0114	1.75508	0.953
Females	0.021	0.0110	1.59671	0.836
Persons	0.021	0.0112	1.68516	0.899

* Actually, values of $r = \ln\left[\frac{P_{1981}}{P_{1971}}\right]/9.92$ are 0.0199, 0.0222 and 0.0210 for males, females and persons respectively.

Considering some differential undercounts between census, all these figures were taken approximately as 0.021.

The use of actual values of 'r' however did not result in any appreciable different estimates.

Table 3.6 Estimating completeness of death reporting by sex, 1981: West Bengal (For age 10+).

	Annual average growth rate, r	Crude death rate, 'd'	Σδ(a)exp r (x-10)-1	Estimated completeness 'C'
Males	0.021	0.0096	2.02651	0.926
Females	0.021	0.0091	1.90376	0.825
Persons	0.021	0.0093	1.97939	0.877

*D (10+)/P (10+)

3.24 BRASS GROWTH BALANCE METHOD OF COMPLETENESS OF DEATH REGISTRATION

More than half a dozen of indirect methods are currently available for estimating the completeness of death registration. Each of the methods makes use of the age distribution of reported deaths within a certain age range. Each of these also assumes the population is to be closed to migration. Brass sectional growth balance method is one of these methods.

In 1975, Brass proposed a method to estimate the completeness of death registration of adult deaths. In a closed population, the equation applies in the 'Brass Growth Balance Method' as follows:

$$r^T_{x+} = b^T_{x+} - d^T_{x+} \tag{1}$$

where

r^T_{x+} = true growth of the population aged x and over,

b^T_{x+} = true growth 'birth day rate' of the population aged x and over, i.e., the number people reaching their x^{th} birth day in a particular year divided by the number of person years lived above x during that year.

d^T_{x+} = true death rate of the population over age x, i.e., the number of deaths in a certain year at age x last birth day and above, divided by the number of person years lived above x during that year.

Equation (1) can be written as

$$b^T_{x+} = r^T_{x+} + d^T_{x+} \tag{2}$$

Brass uses the assumption of population *stability*, so that the growth rate is constant with age and the x+ or r can be dropped. By assumption that the completeness of death registration is invariant to age within the range specified,

$$d_{x+} = C.d^T_{x+}$$

therefore, $\frac{1}{C} * d_{x+} = d^T_{x+}$

Where C is the completeness of death registration. Making these two assumptions, one has

$$b^T_{x+} = r^T + \frac{1}{C} * d_{x+} \qquad (3)$$

Equation (3) is a linear equation, the parameters of which are r^T, the intercept, and 1/C, the slope, d_{x+} is simply the recorded death rate above age x and b^T_{x+} is conventionally estimated by

$$b^T_{x+} = \frac{{}_5N_x + {}_5N_{x-5}}{10N_{x+}}$$

where ${}_5N_x$ is the number of persons recorded in the age interval from x to x + 5.

In theory, r and C could be identified by choosing any pair of ages x, since one would have two equations and two unknowns. In practice, it is more sensible to recognize that both the b_{x+} series and d_{x+} series contain errors, particularly those resulting from age mis-reporting. So one may take advantage of the linearity of equation (3) and estimate its parameters by linear regression on many data points or by other suitable fitting procedures.

There are two basic problems with the Brass procedure:

(a) At what age we start and what age we end? Errors in the data can create a scatter of points such that very different estimates of C can be produced by arbitrarily excluding various combinations of available data points from the fitting procedures. Changes in values of b_{x+} and d_{x+} at younger ages tend to be quite small so that different points add very little new information.

(b) Results are very sensitive to violations of the assumptions of stability; currently declining fertility is usually not a serious problem.

Even though Brass asserts that deviations from stability probably do not introduce much bias into the estimates of C, especially if only mortality is changing, investigation carried out by Martin of simulated population destabilized casts doubt on the robustness of the original Brass procedure. In fact, he found that the use of this method in situation in which mortality has been declining leads to underestimation of C. The degree of under registration varies with original mortality level as well as with the duration and speed of mortality change.

3.25 CHILDHOOD MORTALITY ESTIMATION

As evidenced from the earlier discussion, the available information on mortality, including infant and child mortality by age and sex, does not suggest a standard quality of reporting. United Nations' (1988) publication on 'mortality on children under age 5' stressed on the analysis of infant and child mortality, specially, on child mortality over age 1 and under age 5 in addition to infant mortality. The past 35 years have seen extensive elaboration, refinement, and application of the original Brass method for estimating infant and child mortality from child survivorship data. This experience has confirmed the overall usefulness of the methods beyond question, but it has also shown that their application is anything but routine.

It is never sufficient merely to obtain estimates from a single set of data. Estimates must be analyzed in relation to other relevant information before useful conclusions about the levels and trends in mortality can be drawn. This data analysis, unlike the derivation of estimates, cannot be reduced to mechanical routine. It requires an ability that comes only with experience and sharp acumen.

So, as a result of this, a few recently developed indirect estimation techniques based on Brass-type method (Brass, 1975) seem to be attractive. As the method proposed by Sullivan (1972) and Trussell (1975) over the original method developed by Brass (1975), we have named the methods in this chapter as Brass-Sullivan and Brass-Trussell methods respectively.

3.25.1 Brass-Sullivan Method

The proportions of children dead among those everborn to mothers in standard 5-year age groups yield life table q (x) values when multiplied by factors derived by Brass (1975) from a fertility polynomial of age and scale factor. Sullivan (1972) showed that multiplying factors based on simple linear regression model, fitted to empirical fertility schedules, yield a much more improved results than the factors developed by Brass. Thus, the probability of dying from birth to age x, q (x), is given by the equation,

$$q(x)/D(i) = a(i) + b(i)[P_2/P_3]$$

where D (i) denotes the proportion of children dead in the ith age group of mother (where i = 1, 2, 3 and 4 for 15–19, 20–24, 25–29 and 30–34), P_2/P_3, the ratio of the average parity of mothers aged 20–24 to the mothers aged 25–29 and, a (i) and b(i) are the coefficients.

The main assumption underlying the method is static, conditions for age-specific fertility and child mortality in the recent past. Unlike Brass, who used a simple mortality pattern, this method used all the four families of Coale and Demeny (1966) model life tables. Since it is very often not known whether the underlying mortality pattern conforms to West, North, East or South, Sullivan computed the effect of using wrong regression equations. The use of West regression model in the absence of definite knowledge of mortality pattern is recommended. We illustrate the Sullivan estimation with respect to West and South families of life table as these formulations are found to be suitable for India (Srinivasan et al., 1988). The information on surviving children collected from younger mothers are found to be most reliable and the regression analysis is successful with the ratios of $q_{(2)}/D_{(2)}$, $q_{(3)}/D_{(3)}$ and $q_{(5)}/D_{(4)}$. The models for estimating q (x) are as follows:

West Family	South Family
$q_{(2)} = D_{(2)}\ (1.30–0.54P_{(2)}/P_{(3)})$	$q_{(2)} = D_{(2)}\ (1.33–0.61\ P_{(2)}/P_{(3)})$
$q_{(3)} = D_{(3)}\ (1.17–0.40P_{(2)}/P_{(3)})$	$q_{(3)} = D_{(3)}\ (1.20–0.44\ P_{(2)}/P_{(3)})$
$q_{(5)} = D_{(4)}\ (1.30–0.33P_{(2)}/P_{(3)})$	$q_{(5)} = D_{(4)}\ (1.14–0.32P_{(2)}/P_{(3)})$

This method is applicable to only age-based data.

3.25.2 Brass-Trussell Method

Trussell's (1975) procedure converts the proportion of children dead among the children everborn reported by women in successive 5-year age groups into probabilities of dying before attaining certain exact childhood ages. Thus, if D (i), denotes the proportion of children dead among the children everborn to women in ith age group and q (x) = 1 – l (x), the probability of dying between birth and exact age x, the basic relation is of the form:

$$q(x) = K(i).D(i)$$

for, $x = 1, 2, 3,$ and 5

and, $i = 1, 2, 3$ and 4 for age-based

and K (i) is a multiplier according to Trussell variant of the original Brass-method. The reference time period, t (i) = a (i) +b (i) $P_{(1)}/P_{(2)}$ +c (i) $P_{(2)}/P_{(3)}$ has been used to which the mortality estimates refer. The co-efficients a (i), b (i) and c (i) are different from those of the coefficients related to K (i) (See Chapter III, UN Manual X).

The multiplier, K (i), is obtained by the equation of the form:

$$K (i) = a (i)+b (i) P_{(1)}/P_{(2)} +c (i) P_{(2)}/P_{(3)}$$

where a (i), b (i) and c (i) are the constants estimated by the regression analysis of a large number of model cases for different life tables (See Chapter III, UN Manual X).The multiplier being selected according to values of $P_{(1)}/P_{(2)}$ and $P_{(2)}/P_{(3)}$, where $P_{(1)}$, $P_{(2)}$ and $P_{(3)}$ are the average number of children everborn per woman in the age groups 15–19, 20–24 and 25–29 respectively. So, the relation of the average parity is of the form:

$$P (i) = CEB (i) / FP (i), \text{ and}$$

$$D (i) = CD (i) / CEB (i), \text{ or}$$

$$D (i) = 1- CS (i) / CEB (i)$$

Where CEB (i), CD (i) and CS (i) denote the children everborn, children dead and children surviving in the ith age group and FP (i), the female population classified by 5-year age groups. P (i) is the average parity among the women in the ith age group. The reference time period to which the q (x) values refer, is obtained by the same equation as that of K (i) with another set of regression derived co-efficients. The correspondence relating to q (x) values suggested by Brass is that the proportion dead D (i), among children everborn to women aged 15–19 is approximately equal to the probability of dying between birth and age, i; the proportion dead for women aged 20–24, to the probability of dying before age 2; that for women aged 25–29, to the probability of dying by age 3; and that for women aged 30–34 to the probability of dying by age 5. We have shown here only age-based estimates of child mortality. The main assumption underlying the method is the static condition for age-specific infant and child mortality in the recent past.

3.26 APPLICATION OF THE METHODS

The methods for estimating infant and childhood mortality have been applied to data on children everborn and surviving by five-year age groups of mother.

Though West Bengal does not have relevant data prior to 1981, child mortality is believed to have declined during the recent years. But the problems of paucity of data are taken care of by referring the estimates to different time points before the census. The sex ratios of the children everborn by age groups of mother 15–19, 20–24, 25–29 and 30–34 show an average value of around 1.07. This sex ratio implies that birth registration either is fairly complete or even if incomplete, there is no sex differential of birth recordings. On the other hand, the average parities are increasing monotonically as the age of mother increases and the proportions of children dead are also increasing. Finding the mortality levels in the Coale-Demeny West Model and South model by linear interpolation can conveniently assess the consistency in the final mortality estimates. As an illustration for l (2) in Table 3.7 (where estimated value of l (2) = 0.9257, say, l(2)obs), the interpolation factor Ø is,

$$Ø = \frac{l_{(2)}^{\text{obs}} - l_{(2)}^{\text{Model value at level 16}}}{l_{(2)}^{\text{Model value at level 17}} - l_{(2)}^{\text{Model value at level 16}}}, \text{ that is,}$$

we will get the value of Ø i.e. ($l_{(2)}^{\text{obs}}$) will lie between two $l_{(2)}$ Model level values (say, level 16 and 17) which, should be consistent with the observed value [i.e. your observed value of $l_{(2)}$ should be consistent with a family of mortality pattern as well as with its mortality level, say, west model or south model etc., and to which level, observed value of $l_{(2)}$ corresponds. If one value (at level 16) is lower than the observed $l_{(2)}$ value, the other value should be higher than the observed $l_{(2)}$ value (at level 17), and then we can interpolate in the way shown above to get the value of interpolation factor, Ø, and hence, add the value of Ø to the level 16 to get the level of $l_{(2)}^{\text{obs}}$ value that is consistent with the family of mortality pattern of our choice (see Tables 236 and 237, UN Manual X, 1983).

The dates prior to census, referred by the mortality estimates, have been calculated. Indian census of 1991 was carried out on 1 March 1991, which is equivalent to 1991.16. The decimal equivalent has been obtained (United Nations, 1983) as

Number of days from 1st January to 1st March/365

$$= 60/365$$

$$= 0.16$$

$$1991 + 0.16 = 1991.16 \text{ (i.e., our Reference date)}$$

The reference dates to which the mortality estimates i.e. q (x) values refer have been estimated by subtracting the estimated dates from the reference date of the census. Using the above-mentioned procedure, the estimates of reference dates have been found to be very close.

Table 3.7 Brass-Sullivan estimates of childhood mortality by sex, and age group of mother, 1991: West Bengal.

[Males, $P_{(2)} P_{(3)} = 0.5302$]

Age group of mother	i	x	P(i)	D(i)	d(x)	1(x)	Mortality level
(A) West family of mortality pattern							
20–24	2	2	0.6065	0.0721	0.0743	0.9257	19.0
25–29	3	3	1.1439	0.0762	0.0742	0.9258	19.2
30–34	4	5	1.5148	0.0842	0.0827	0.9173	19.0
(B) South family of mortality pattern (C)							
20–24	2	2	0.6065	0.0721	0.0726	0.9274	21.1
25–29	3	3	1.1439	0.0762	0.0737	0.9263	21.4
30–34	4	5	1.5148	0.0842	0.0817	0.9183	21.0
[Females, $P_{(2)} P_{(3)} = 0.5255$] (A) West family of mortality pattern							
20–24	2	2	0.5726	0.0780	0.0793	0.9207	17.5
25–29	3	3	1.0896	0.0845	0.0811	0.9189	17.8
30–34	4	5	1.4305	0.0926	0.0886	0.9114	17.8
(B) South family of mortality pattern							
20–24	2	2	0.5726	0.0780	0.0787	0.9213	20.0
25–29	3	3	1.0896	0.0845	0.0819	0.9181	20.2
30–34	4	5	1.4305	0.0926	0.0900	0.9100	21.0

Table 3.8 Brass-Trussell estimates of childhood mortality by sex, and age group of mother, 1991: West Bengal.

[Males, $P_{(1)}/P_{(2)} = 0.1591$; $P_{(2)}/P_{(3)} = 0.5302$]

Age group of mother	i	x	P(i)	D(i)	K(i)	q(x)	l(x)	Reference	Mortality level
(A) West family of mortality pattern									
15–19	1	1	0.0965	0.0766	1.1171	0.0856	0.9144	Mar., 1990	17.0
20–24	2	2	0.6065	0.0721	1.0308	0.0743	0.9257	Oct., 1988	19.0
25–29	3	3	1.1439	0.0762	0.9737	0.0742	0.9258	Aug., 1986	19.0
30–34	4	5	1.5148	0.0842	0.9827	0.0827	0.9173	Jan., 1984	19.0
(B) South family of mortality pattern									
15–19	1	1	0.0965	0.0766	1.0652	0.0816	0.9284	Mar., 1990	19.0
20–24	2	2	0.6065	0.0721	1.0259	0.0740	0.9262	Nov.,1988	21.0
25–29	3	3	1.1439	0.0762	0.9864	0.0752	0.9248	Sept.,1986	21.0
30–34	4	5	1.5148	0.0842	0.9943	0.0837	0.9163	Jan.,1984	21.0
[Females, $P_{(1)}/P_{(2)} = 0.1589$; $P_{(2)}/P_{(3)} = 0.5255$] (A) West family of mortality pattern									
15–19	1	1	0.0910	0.0763	1.1140	0.0850	0.9150	Mar., 1990	16.0
20–24	2	2	0.5726	0.0780	1.0322	0.0805	0.9195	Oct., 1988	17.4
25–29	3	3	1.0896	0.0845	0.9757	0.0824	0.9176	Aug., 1986	17.7
30–34	4	5	1.4305	0.0926	0.9847	0.0912	0.9088	Jan., 1984	17.6
(B) South family of mortality pattern									
15–19	1	1	0.0910	0.0763	1.0617	0.0810	0.9190	Mar., 1990	18.6
20–24	2	2	0.5726	0.0780	1.0275	0.0801	0.9199	Nov., 1988	19.9
25–29	3	3	1.0896	0.0845	0.9886	0.0835	0.9165	Sept., 1986	20.1
30–34	4	5	1.4305	0.0926	0.9963	0.0923	0.9077	Feb., 1984	19.8

Tables 3.7 and 3.8 provide the preliminary estimates of childhood mortality for West Bengal in 1991 by Brass-Sullivan and Brass-Trussell methods based on two families of mortality pattern (West model and South model) from Coale-Demeny Model Life Tables. Brass-Sullivan estimates of childhood mortality by West model show higher mortality levels compared to those of Brass-Trussell's, which are consistent with the prevailing mortality levels of West Bengal in case of both males and females but South model shows higher mortality levels than those shown by West model which are not relevant to the prevailing mortality levels of West Bengal (Saha 1997).

Note: We know that CEB and CS data by age groups (15–19, 20–24........45–49) of mother are available from Indian censuses based on which we can estimate under age five mortality, namely, ${}_1q_0$, ${}_2q_0$, ${}_3q_0$, and ${}_5q_0$. But when we wish to compare the estimates obtained from censuses with those of the estimates obtained from Sample Registration System (SRS), we are unable to compare as SRS provides only death rates by age groups and by sex i.e. for 0–4, 5–9, 10–14 and so on. We can not normally get estimates of ${}_1q_0$, ${}_2q_0$, ${}_3q_0$, and ${}_5q_0$ from age group 0-4 in SRS. So only provides ${}_5q_0$. So to split the ${}_5q_0$ we have to apply methods to derive ${}_1q_0$, ${}_2q_0$, ${}_3q_0$, and ${}_5q_0$. The method of calculation is to determine weights (α_2, α_3, and α_4) so that l_i could be estimated as $\alpha_i l_1 + (1 - \alpha_i) l_5$. Constant values of α_i are used when ${}_1q_0 \geq 0.100$ and for low levels of infant mortality (${}_1q_0 \leq 0.100$) variable weights, α'_i are used from Coale-Demeny Regional Model Life Tables, 1966.

$$\alpha'_i = \alpha_i + b_i (0.100 - {}_1q_0)$$

For example:

Comparison of ${}_1q_0$, ${}_2q_0$, ${}_3q_0$, and ${}_5q_0$ estimates, 1991: West Bengal

Sources	Males				Females			
	${}_1q_0$	${}_2q_0$	${}_3q_0$	${}_5q_0$	${}_1q_0$	${}_2q_0$	${}_3q_0$	${}_5q_0$
SRS* (1990–92)	66	81	88	97	62	77	85	95
SRS** (1990–92)	61	84	94	105	61	84	94	105
Our estimates								
Brass-Sullivan	${}_1q_0$	${}_2q_0$	${}_3q_0$	${}_5q_0$	${}_1q_0$	${}_2q_0$	${}_3q_0$	${}_5q_0$
(A) West Model	–	73	73	80	–	79	81	89
(B) South Model	–	73	74	82	–	79	82	90
Brass-Trussell								
(A) West Model	86	74	74	83	85	81	82	91
(B) South Model	82	74	75	84	81	80	84	92

* Based on Coale –Demeny West Model

** Based on South Asian Patterns of Model Life Tables

Notes: SRS deaths for the age group 0–4 have been averaged for the years 1990–92. The SRS provides only ${}_5m_0$; the values of ${}_1m_0$ and ${}_4m_1$ are derived from the Coale-Demeny West Model Life Table by taking the ratio of the closest values of ${}_5m_{10}$ (SRS) and ${}_5m_{10}$ (West Model), assuming that the age pattern of mortality under age 10 in SRS is the same as that of Coale-Demeny West Model. The values of ${}_1q_0$ and ${}_5q_0$ are calculated by the usual life table procedures. The values of ${}_2q_0$ and ${}_3q_0$ are calculated from the complements of ${}_1q_0$ and ${}_5q_0$ (i.e. l_1 and l_5) using the interpolation co-efficients of Coale-Demeny West Model given above.

Finally, in order to get the smoothed estimates of childhood mortality in West Bengal we have tried to smooth out irregularities by applying logit smoothing technique. An illustration in this context has been presented in this section.

3.27 LOGIT SMOOTHING TECHNIQUE ADOPTED FOR THE CHILDHOOD MORTALITY

In order to find out the best possible estimates of the survivorship function $l_{(x)}$ from the Brass-Sullivan and Brass-Trussell's preliminary estimates, the logit smoothing technique is adopted. Thus, the smoothed value of

$$Y(x) = 0.5 \ln (1 - l_{(x)} / l_{(x)})$$

denoted by $\hat{Y}(x)$ is derived from the estimated survivorship function l_2, l_3 and l_5 as follows:

$$\hat{Y}(x) = Y_s(x) + \frac{1}{3}\sum_x (Y(x) - Y_s(x))$$

where x = 2, 3 and 5 and $Y_s(x)$ is the logit of Brass General Standard Life Table smoothed by Hobcraft (cited in Hill and Trussell, 1977).

The smoothed l (x) values are given by

$$\hat{l}_{(x)} = 1/[1 + \exp(2\ \hat{Y}(x))]$$

Table 3.9 Logit smoothing of Brass-Sullivan and Brass-Trussell estimates of survivorship probabilities, Males: 1991, West Bengal.

Age x	Standard logit, $Y_s(x)$	Estimated $l_{(x)}$	Logit $l_{(x)}$, Y(x)	$Y(x)-Y_s(x)$	Y(x)	Smoothed $l^*_{(x)}$	Survival level
(1)	(2)	(3)	(4)	(5)	(6)	(7)	(8)
(A) Brass-Sullivan: West Model							
2	–0.7152	0.9270	–1.2707	–0.5555	–1.3112	0.9323	19.3
3	–0.6552	0.9270	–1.2707	–0.6155	–1.2512	0.9243	19.2
5	–0.6015	0.9196	–1.2185	–0.6170	–1.2185	0.9196	19.1
(B) Brass-Trussell: West Model							
2	–0.7152	0.9257	–1.2612	–0.5460	–1.3000	0.9309	19.2
3	–0.6552	0.9258	–1.2619	–0.6067	–1.2400	0.9227	19.0
5	–0.6015	0.9173	–1.2031	–0.6016	–1.1863	0.9147	19.0

(A) Brass-Sullivan: South Model							
2	–0.7152	0.9274	–1.2737	–0.5585	–1.3076	0.9318	21.5
3	–0.6552	0.9263	–1.2656	–0.6104	–1.2476	0.9238	21.2
5	–0.6015	0.9183	–1.2097	–0.6082	–1.1939	0.9159	21.0
(B) Brass-Trussell: South Model							
2	–0.7152	0.9260	–1.2634	–0.5482	–1.2961	0.9304	21.4
3	–0.6552	0.9248	–1.2547	–0.5995	–1.2547	0.9248	21.2
5	–0.6015	0.9163	–1.1966	–0.5951	–1.1824	0.9141	21.0

Table 3.10 Logit smoothing of Brass-Sullivan and Brass-Trussell estimates of survivorship probabilities, Females: 1991, West Bengal.

Age x	Standard logit, $Y_s(x)$	Estimated $l_{(x)}$	Logit $l_{(x)}$, Y(x)	$Y(x)-Y_s(x)$	Y(x)	Smoothed $l^*_{(x)}$	Survival level
(1)	(2)	(3)	(4)	(5)	(6)	(7)	(8)
(A) Brass-Sullivan: West Model							
2	–0.7152	0.9207	–1.2259	–0.5107	–1.2596	0.9255	17.8
3	–0.6552	0.9189	–1.2137	–0.5585	–1.1996	0.9168	17.6
5	–0.6015	0.9114	–1.1654	–0.5639	–1.1459	0.9082	17.6
(B) Brass-Trussell: West Model							
2	–0.7152	0.9195	–1.2178	–0.5026	–1.2487	0.9240	17.7
3	–0.6552	0.9176	–1.2051	–0.5499	–1.1887	0.9151	17.5
5	–0.6015	0.9088	–1.1495	–0.5480	–1.1350	0.9064	17.5
(A) Brass-Sullivan: South Model							
2	–0.7152	0.9213	–1.2301	–0.5149	–1.2563	0.9250	20.4
3	–0.6552	0.9181	–1.2084	–0.5532	–1.1963	0.9163	20.1
5	–0.6015	0.9100	–1.1568	–0.5553	–1.1426	0.9076	20.0
(B) Brass-Trussell: South Model							
2	–0.7152	0.9199	–1.2205	–0.5053	–1.2450	0.9234	20.2
3	–0.6552	0.9165	–1.1979	–0.5427	–1.1850	0.9145	20.0
5	–0.6015	0.9077	–1.1429	–0.5417	–1.1313	0.9057	20.0

Finally, the preliminary estimates of survival function, l (x), when smoothed by logit smoothing technique, smoothed l (x) values as indicated by the survival levels, have shown to be constant over the past years. As an illustration, logit smoothing technique has been applied to the preliminary estimates of 1991. The Brass- Sullivan estimates of smoothed $l^*_{(x)}$ values have shown higher survival levels that those shown by Brass-Trussell's, based on West model for both males and females (see Tables 3.9 and 3.10) which are consistent with the mortality pattern of West Bengal. But the estimates shown by South Model do not conform to that of the prevailing mortality pattern at childhood ages in West Bengal.

3.28 ADULTHOOD MORTALITY ESTIMATION

The United Nations and World Health Organization Working Group (Bangkok, 22–23 Oct., 1981) on mortality studies noted the lack of reliable mortality data for adults in developing countries. In view of very serious economic and social consequences of adult deaths, it is recommended that serious efforts should be made for analysis of data on the adult mortality, using a wide range of approaches and procedures. Several techniques by Brass (1975), Hill (1977), and Hill – Trussell (loc. cit) are available for estimating adult mortality based on spouse survival, parent survival and sibling survival. But, the only input available for India and its constituent states, that too not very accurately, are the widowhood data collected in the censuses.

As we know the information of the survival of the parents or spouses is an indicator only of adult mortality, since the exposure to risk of the target person begins in adulthood. Strictly speaking, such data should be used only to estimate survivorship probabilities from one adult age to another, for which both the indirect and direct estimates may be applied, but the indirect method suggested by Hill (1977) known as conditional method, has some limitations. This method does not depend much on assumed models, but more difficult to incorporate into a full life table than are the direct estimates, which, in turn, are determined, to a considerable extent, by the estimates of child mortality used in their calculation. So, however, if an estimate of the level of child mortality is available, in the form of an estimate of $l_{(2)}$, and some assumptions can be made about the form of relationship between child and adult mortality in the population under study, the information on child mortality can be combined with an indicator of adult mortality to estimate an unconditional survivorship probability, that is, the probability of surviving from birth to some adult age; this method is known as direct method which is being applied to data for West Bengal. As the method provides an indicator of the relationship between the child and the adult mortality, RSW is the ratio of l (20) and l(2) in the standard (the female level 16, model life table from the Coale – Demeny family that best approximates the pattern of the mortality experienced by the population under study) was fitted by the least square regression to data from 900 simulated cases. These cases were generated using model nuptiality, fertility and mortality schedules. The mortality schedules were obtained from the logit system using female level 16, model life tables from the Coale – Demeny's four families as standards, while the nuptiality and fertility schedules were derived from the models proposed by Coale and Mc Neil (JASA, 1972) and Coale – Trussell (loc. cit) respectively. The simulation carried out also makes some allowance for the age distribution at first marriage of spouses.

Theoretically, the information collected should refer to the survival of first spouse, but in Indian censuses questions are asked of, to the evermarried respondents on their marital status only, but the information on the order of marriage is not collected. As a result, bias in the survivorship estimates may arise and the extent of bias may not be quantified. West Bengal, is a mosaic of different culture and religion. In some society specifically in Muslims, the effect of incidence of re-marriage still exists but in case of Hindus, a wide range of results has come up in West Bengal (Malakar, 1981). So, as a first approximation, while estimating adult survivorship probabilities, it has been assumed that the marriages recorded in Indian censuses are of first order for each sex. The main assumption underlying the method is the static condition for mortality and nuptiality in the recent past. But in a changing mortality condition, Brass and Bamgboye (1981) have relaxed the assumption of constant mortality to estimate the time period to which the mortality estimates refer prior to census or survey. As West Bengal has been experiencing gradual change in mortality (F.W.P., Year Book, 1989–90; Govt. of India), the procedure proposed by brass and Bamgboye has been applied to the data for the state to estimate the time location for mortality occurred by the state, types of residence and by some selected districts in 1981.

Finally, another attempt has been made to relate the two distinct sets of mortality estimates viz.

(i) Childhood mortality estimates from children ever born and surviving data by sex and by age group of mother and (ii) Adulthood mortality estimates from widowhood data by age and sex of the evermarried respondents to complete the age pattern of mortality generated by Brass Two-Parameter Logit Life Tables System, for the state as a whole and for some selected districts of West Bengal in 1991 only.

3.29 ESTIMATION OF ADULTHOOD MORTALITY FROM THE WIDOWHOOD STATUS OF MALE AND FEMALE RESPONDENTS

Two indirect methods of estimating adult mortality as recently revised by Hill (1977) and Hill-Trussell (loc. cit) are given here as these methods are based on widowhood data, though there are other methods. The methods are as follows:

3.29.1 Conditional Survivorship Method by Hill (1977)

(A) Conditional Survivorship Method

For Male,

$$l_m(n)/l_m(20) = a(n) + b(n)\,SMAM_f + c(n)\,SMAM_m + d(n)\,NW_f(n-5) \quad (1)$$

and,
For Female,

$$l_f(n)/l_f(20) = a(n) + b(n)\,SMAM_f + c(n)\,SMAM_m + d(n)\,NW_m(n) \qquad (2)$$

where the regression co-efficients a (n), b (n), c (n) and d (n) are different for males and females in respect of each value of 'n'. SMAM's (Hajnal, 1953) are the singulate mean age at marriage for males and females. NW_m (n) and NW_f (n) are the proportions not widowered males and widowed females respectively from age 'n' to 'n + 4' whose spouse was alive at the time of survey. $NW_f(n-5)$ has been in equation (1) because the model has assumed that the wives are five years younger to husbands.

3.29.2 Unconditional Survivorship Method by Hill-Trussell (loc. cit.)

- **Male adult mortality from widowhood status of the female respondents**

The equation used to estimate the male survivorship probabilities from birth to adult ages is of the form:

$$l_m(n) = a(n) + b(n)SMAM_f + c(n)\,SMAM_m + d(n)\,NW_f(n-5) + e(n)l_m(2) + f(n)RSW,$$

where a (n), b (n), c (n), d (n), e (n) and f (n) are the regression co-efficients that depend only on male by age; $SMAM_f$ and $SMAM_m$ are the singulate mean ages at marriage for females and males respectively; $NW_f(n-5)$, the proportion of evermarried females aged n to n + 4 not widowed (assuming the wives are five years junior to their husbands) at the time of census or survey and $l_m(2)$, the probability (extrapolated) of surviving male from birth to age 2 for the spouses, and RSW, the ratio of $l_{(20)}$ and $l_{(2)}$ derived (female level 16, West model has been selected) from the Coale-Demeny Model Life Tables that best approximates the mortality pattern of West Bengal (see Annex VIII, Tables 236 and 237, U.N. Manual X, 1983).

- **Female adult mortality from widowhood status of the male respondents**

The equation used to estimate the female survivorship probabilities from birth to adult ages is of the form:

$$l_f(n) = a(n) + b(n)\,SMAM_f + c(n)\,SMAM_m + d(n)\,NW_m(n) + e(n)\,l_f(2) + f(n)\,RSW$$

where a (n), b (n), c (n), d (n), e (n) and f (n) are the regression co-efficients (will be obtained in Table 97 and 98 of Manual X) that relate to female by age; $NW_m(n)$, the proportion of evermarried males aged from n to n + 4 not widowered at the time of census or survey and $l_f(2)$, the probability (extrapolated) of surviving female from birth to age 2 for the spouses.

3.30 ESTIMATION OF REFERENCE TIME PERIODS FOR ADULT SURVIVORSHIP PROBABILITIES

In case of changing mortality, Brass and Bamgboye (1981) proposed a method of estimating reference time periods to which the mortality estimates refer. The methods of estimating reference time periods for males and females are as follows:

For Males,

$$t_m(n) = (n - 2.5 - SMAM_f)(1.0 - U_m(n))/2.0$$

where

$$U_m(n) = 0.33331\,{}_nNW_f(n-5) + Z\,(SMAM_m + n - 2.5 - SMAM_f) + 0.0037\,(27.0 - SMAM_m),$$

$$x_m = SMAM_m + n - 2.5 - SMAM_f$$

$Z(x_m) = Z$ (See U.N. Manual X, 1983, Standard Table of Z function given here in the text)

For Females,

$$t_f(n) = (n + 2.5 - SMAM_m)(1,0 - U_f(n))/2.0$$

where

$$U_f(n) = 0.33331\,{}_nNW_m(n) + Z\,(SMAM_f + n + 2.5 - SMAM_m) + 0.0037\,(27.0 - SMAM_f),$$

$$X_f = SMAM_f + n + 2.5 - SMAM_m$$

$$Z(x_f) = Z$$

The quality (n + 2.5 – SMAM) is used as an indicator of the mean duration of first marriage of the male (with subscript 'm') and female (with subscript 'f') respondents from 'n' to n + 4 and the values of the standard function 'Z' are taken from the Table 88, (pp 104), U.N. Manual X, 1983.

3.31 LOGIT SMOOTHING TECHNIQUE ADOPTED FOR THE ADULTHOOD MORTALITY

Finally to get better estimates of the two independent sets of $l_{(x)}$ values, one from childhood mortality and the other from adulthood mortality, Brass (1975, 91-6) Two Parameter Logit Life Tables System is adopted. Logit transformation of the estimated survivorship probabilities $l_{(x)}$ is given by,

$$Y(x) = \text{logit}\,(1.0 - l_{(x)})$$
$$= 0.5 \ln((1.0 - l_{(x)})/l_{(x)})$$

Selecting suitably, the two most reliable sets of points representing survivorship probabilities for childhood and adulthood ages, a line is fitted to them by a set of childhood points (l_2, l_3, l_5) and adulthood points (l_{40}, l_{45}, l_{50}, l_{55} and l_{60} respectively) for males only. For estimating the two parameters α and β by group mean method, the notations ($\bar{Y}c$ and $\bar{Y}a$) and ($\bar{X}c$ and $\bar{X}a$) representing the group means of the logit transformation of the childhood and adulthood points of estimated and standard survivorship probabilities have been used respectively only for males. Hence the value of β is given by

$$\beta = \frac{\bar{Y}a - \bar{Y}c}{\bar{X}a - \bar{X}c} \text{ and } \alpha = \bar{Y}c - \beta.\ \bar{X}c$$

Having estimated the values of α and β, the fitted logits $Y_{fit}(x)$ are then obtained and this $Y_{fit}(x)$ has been treated as logit $l_{(x)}$ for constructing life tables, logit $l_s(x)$ being the standard. So,

$$Y_{fit}(x) = \alpha + \beta\, Y_s(x)$$

Or $$\text{logit } l(x) = \alpha + \beta \text{ logit } l_s(x)$$

and the fitted $l^*(x)$ is obtained by the inverse of the logit transformation as,

$$\text{Fitted } l^*(x) = \frac{1}{1+e^{2Y_{Fit}(x)}}$$

Note: It is to be noted that if the values of α and β are not found within the range, the iteration procedure should be continued until the values converge. That is, up to fourth or fifth iteration may be continued.

3.32 APPLICATION OF THE METHODS

(A) Conditional Survivorship Method

Table 3.11 Data on proportion not widowed by age and sex for West Bengal, 1981.

Age group	Proportions not widowed	
	Male	Female
(1)	(2)	(3)
20–24	0.99562	0.98754
25–29	0.99517	0.97720
30–34	0.99348	0.95782
35–39	0.99024	0.92563
40–44	0.98173	0.85180
45–49	0.97183	0.76878
50–54	0.95271	0.61827
55–59	0.93797	0.51894

(B) Unconditional Survivorship Method

Table 3.12 Data on proportions not widowed by age and sex for West Bengal, 1991.

Age group	Proportions not widowed	
	Male	Female
(1)	(2)	(3)
20–24	0.99518	0.99030
25–29	0.99549	0.98386
30–34	0.99432	0.96870
35–39	0.99299	0.94588
40–44	0.98754	0.89819
45–49	0.98010	0.83977
50–54	0.96481	0.71013
55–59	0.94941	0.62037

Table 3.13 Estimation of survivorship probabilities by conditional method male and female in West Bengal, 1981.

Age (n)	Male survivorship			Age (m)	Female survivorship		
	$l_m(n)/l_m(20)$	Wests survival level	Reference date		$l_f(n)/l_f(20)$	West survival level	Reference date
(1)	(2)	(3)	(4)	(5)	(6)	(7)	(8)
25	0.98848	20.17	1979.73	25	0.99407	21.15	*
30	0.97950	20.74	1977.44	30	0.99274	22.56	1978.18
35	0.96309	20.11	1975.17	35	0.99100	23.19	1975.96
40	0.93475	19,06	1973.05	40	0.98153	22.66	1973.74
45	0.86731	16.46	1971.08	45	0.97029	22.54	1971.72
50	0.79636	15.21	1969.29	50	0.94740	22.09	1970.02
55	0.66306	12.36	1967.22	55	0.92854	22.47	1968.77
60	0.58318	12.59	1965.70				

* Out of line

Average level 17.09
$SMAM_m$ = 25.73 years

Average level 22.38
$SMAM_f$ =19.86 years

The results obtained by conditional method are not presented in detail in Table 3.13 but the results obtained by unconditional method are presented in detail in Tables 3.14 and 3.15 respectively. Table 3.12 presents the data on proportion not widowed by age and sex. Table shows that the proportion not widowed by sex has been decreasing as their age increases. The decrease in females up to age 35 is slow and very fast afterwards. This suggests that male mortality is increasing very fast after the females reach the age 35. On the other hand the proportion of male not widowered is seen constant up to the age 40 and afterwards they are declining but the decline is very slow. So the data exhibit that the proportions of widows are much more higher than those of the widowers. In Table 3.13 exhibits that the conditional survivorship probability estimates for each sex associated with the estimated mortality levels that are consistent with the Coale-Demeny West model and the reference dates to which the mortality estimates refer are presented.

Table 3.14 Estimation of survivorship probabilities by unconditional method for male in West Bengal, 1991.

Age group	Age (n)	Proportion not widowed, NW_f (n–5)	Reference date	West level for l_m (2)	Probability of surviving to age 2, l_m (2)	Male survivorship from birth, l_m (n)	West survival level for l_m (n)
20–24	25	0.99030	1989.9	19.36	0.93293	0.89056	19.4
25–29	30	0.98386	1987.6	19.22	0.93100	0.88472	19.6
30–34	35	0.96870	1985.3	19.08	0.92907	0.86877	19.5
35–39	40	0.94588	1983.3	18.95	0.92723	0.84727	19.4
40–44	45	0.89819	1981.4	18.83	0.92547	0.80533	18.8
45–49	50	0.83977	1979.9	18.73	0.92401	0.76095	18.5
50–54	55	0.71013	1978.1	18.63	0.92255	0.65866	17.0
55–59	60	0.62037	1977.0	18.55	0.92138	0.59707	17.1

SMAMm = 25.91 years   Average level 18.7

Note: To get the extrapolated value of l_m (2), we need child mortality estimates, q (x) values for male (i.e., $q_{(2)}$, $q_{(3)}$, $q_{(5)}$, $q_{(10)}$, $q_{(15)}$, and $q_{(20)}$) along with its complements, $l_{(x)}$ values for male (i.e. $l_{(2)}$, $l_{(3)}$, $l_{(5)}$, $l_{(10)}$, $l_{(15)}$, and $l_{(20)}$), estimated mortality levels and reference dates on one hand while on the other hand, estimated adult mortality level and reference dates for each age, 'n' (i.e., n = 25, 30, ………… 60.).

A plot of the first five mortality levels (based on Brass-Trussell estimates of childhood mortality, west level) against time would show that they define a fairly linear trend. Therefore, using the mortality levels of q (3) and q (15) to determine the trend line, its slope (change in level per annum) is calculated as

θ = (19.2, west level for q (3) – 18.63, west level for q (15) ÷ (1986.63(reference date) for q (3) – 1978.21 (reference date) for q (15).
= 0.0629.

[Here child mortality estimates from q (10) to q (20) have not been shown separately]

Therefore, for age, n (when n = 25), the extrapolated l_m (2) for age 25,

18.63 + 0.0629 (1989.89 – 1978.21) = 19.36 → adult mortality level i.e., [West level for q (15) + Slope, θ * (adult mortality reference date at age 25 – child mortality reference date at age 15] = 19.36 (adult mortality level)]. Now based on estimated adult mortality level i.e. 19.36 we should look at the two adult mortality levels (level 19 and level 20 because estimated adult mortality level (19.36) lies between level 19 and level 20 and we have to estimate our l_m (2) by linear interpolation from the Table (see Manual X) which, we will get l_m (2) = 0.93293. To calculate l_m (2) for other ages, West mortality level for q (15), Slope, θ, and Reference date for q (15) will remain the same and the reference dates of adult mortality will only vary with ages.

Table 3.15 Estimation of survivorship probabilities by unconditional method for female in West Bengal, 1991.

Age group	Age (n)	Proportion not widowed, NW_m (n)	Reference date	West level for l_m (2)	Probability of surviving to age 2, l_f (2)	Male survivorship from birth, L_f (n)	West survival level for l_m (n)
25–29	25	0.99549	–	–	–	–	*
30–34	30	0.99432	1988.2	17.80	0.92540	0.88949	18.9
35–39	35	0.99299	1986.1	17.63	0.92302	0.88609	19.3
40–44	40	0.98754	1983.8	17.46	0.92063	0.87557	19.5
45–49	45	0.98010	1981.8	17.30	0.91839	0.86241	19.6
50–54	50	0.96481	1980.1	17.17	0.91657	0.84107	19.7
55–59	55	0.94941	1978.9	17.08	0.91531	0.81996	20.0

$SMAM_f$ = 19.70 years Average level 19.5

Note: Illustration of calculating Reference Time Periods for ages n (when n = 25 and n = 40) for Males, West Bengal, 1991.

$U_m(n) = 0.3333 \ln NW_f(n-5) + Z(SMAM_m + n - 2.5 - SMAM_f) + 0.0037\,(27.0 - SMAM_m)$

$t_m(n) = (n - 2.5 - SMAM_f)\,(1.0 - U_m(n)))/2$

When n = 25

$U_m(25) = 0.3333 \ln \times 0.99030 + Z(25.91 + 25 - 2.5 - 19.70) + 0.0037(27.0 - 25.91)$

$= -0.00325 + Z(28.71) + 0.004033 = 0.09078$

$Z(28.71) = 0.29(0.90) + 0.71(0.090)$

$= 0.0261 + 0.0639 = 0.090$

$U_m(25) = 0.09078$

$t_m(25) = ((25 - 2.5 - 1970)(1.0 - 0.09078)/2$

= 1.2729 years i.e., 1991.16 – 1.2729 =1989.89 or 1989.9 (when rounded). The result indicates the time point to which the mortality estimates refer.

When n = 40

$U_m(40) = 0.3333 \ln NW_f(n-5) + Z(SMAM_m + n - 2.5 - SMAM_f) + 0.0037\,(27.0 - SMAM_m)$

$Z = (25.91 + 40 - 2.5 - 19.70)$

$Z(43.71) = 0.29\,(0.122) + 0.71(0.130) = 0.12768$

$U_m(40) = 0.11317$

$t_m(40) = (n - 2.5 - SMAM_f)(1.0 - U_m))/2$
$= ((40 - 2.5 - 19.70)(1 - 0.11317))/2$
$= 7.8928$ years, i.e., 1991.16 – 7.8928 = 1983.27(The time point to which the mortality estimates refer) but instead of 1983.27 we have put 1983.3 (when rounded).

Similarly the procedure will be applied to all other ages of males and females to estimate the reference time points but estimating equations for females are different from males.

Before we go to interpret the results analytically, we have a chance to look into the raw data provided by the Indian census for 1991. The data have appeared in Table 3.12 and it shows that the proportion not widowed by sex has been decreasing with the age of the respondents' increases. The decreasing trend of proportions not widowed upto age 35 of females is quite slow but picked up afterwards, suggesting that mortality among male spouses increases very fast after the females reach the age 35; on the other hand, the proportion not widowed is seen to be, more or less, constant upto age 40 of males and afterwards this proportion has been decreasing, but very slow and not substantially as the age of the male respondents increases. Obviously the proportions of not widowed are much higher than those widowed in this period. Besides, deficiency in the data, there are several reasons for the phenomenon. Later on, we have estimated survivorship probabilities as well as reference time periods to which the mortality estimates refer by sex for 1991.

Table 3.16 Estimation of time reference periods for male and female survivorship probabilities by unconditional method in West Bengal, 1991.

Age (n)	Length of exposure indicator, $x_m(n)$	Standard function, $Z_m(n)$	Correction function, $U_m(n)$	Reference period $t_m(n)$	Length of exposure indicator, $x_f(n)$	Standard function, $Z_f(n)$	Correction function, $U_f(n)$	Reference period $t_f(n)$
25	28.44	0.090	0.0908	1.27	21.29	*	—	—
30	33.44	0.090	0.0886	3.55	26.29	0.090	0.1151	2.92
35	38.44	0.097	0.0913	5.82	31.29	0.090	0.1147	5.13
40	43.44	0.127	0.1132	7.89	36.29	0.093	0.1155	7.34
45	48.44	0.177	0.1471	9.72	41.29	0.113	0.1336	9.35
50	53.44	0.239	0.1868	11.30	46.29	0.157	0.1719	11.01
55	58.44	0.314	0.2063	13.02	51.29	0.214	0.2239	12.26
60	63.44	0.403	0.2504	14.17	—	—	—	—

Note: An illustration of calculating the effect of incidence on re-marriage

As an example we have analyzed and calculated the effect of incidence on re-marriage in the way is given as follows:

Effect of remarriage on survival levels and life expectancy in the estimation of adult mortality by widowhood method is given as follows:

Let T and R be the true and reported proportions never widowed out of evermarried (considering survival of the first spouse) in an age group;

P = the proportion of the widowed who remarry. Thus,

$$
\begin{aligned}
R &= 1-(1-T)(1-P)\\
&= P+T-TP\\
&= P+T(1-P) \text{ so,}\\
R-P &= T(1-P), \text{ therefore, } T=(R-P)/(1-P).
\end{aligned}
$$

In the following table calculations have been shown using data on proportion not widowed for females from the 1981 Census of West Bengal with three different values of P, namely, 0.1, 0.2 and 0.3 respectively.

Proportions Not Widowed, Female, 1981: West Bengal

Age group	Reported, R	T P = 0.1	T P = 0.2	T P = 0.3
30–34	0.9578	0.9531	0.9472	0.9397
35–39	0 9256	0.9173	0.9070	0.8937
40–44	0.8518	0.8353	0.8148	0.7883

Mortality Levels
(West Model)

Age, n	Reported, R	T P = 0.1	T P = 0.2	T P = 0.3
35	20.2	19.6	18.8	17.8
40	19.1	18.4	17.5	16.4
45	16.5	15.5	14.2	12.7
Average	18.6	17.8	16.8	15.6
E^0_0	60.2	58.4	56.0	53.2

Notes:

1. The mortality levels are based on $l_m(n)/l_m(20)$ values.
2. If we allow for 10 or 20 per cent of remarriage among widowed females and the variations with different models, the range of life expectancy may be taken as from 52 to 58 years for the decade of 1971–1981. This analysis is very illuminating and the results seem to be at par with those obtained from other sources.

3.33 CONSTRUCTION OF ABRIDGED LIFE TABLES GENERATED BY BRASS TWO PARAMETER LOGIT LIFE TABLES SYSTEM

The two distinct sets of $l_{(x)}$ values, one from childhood ages estimated from children everborn and surviving data, and the other from adulthood ages estimated from widowhood data have been blended suitably at the junction to smooth the age pattern of mortality by Logit Smoothing Technique. After smoothing, abridged life table for males and females in West Bengal, 1991 have been constructed by generating Brass Two Parameter Logit Life Tables System, which is more flexible to capture the flaws that contained in the data than the other. The values of the two parameters α, the intercept and β, the slope or gradient of the straight line, are α = –0.52 and β = 1.08 for males, α = –0.47 and β = 1.10 for females. A low (i.e. –ve) value of α, the level parameter, indicates low mortality relative to the standard and a high positive value of β implies low infant and child mortality and high adult mortality relative to the standard; the estimate of data gives a general impression of the way in which the population differs. But this does not provide a detailed picture of how the standard and the population differs, but does provide the evidence of the overall pattern of adult mortality. The life table constructed for West Bengal separately for males and females show the life expectancy at birth for male as 59.70 and for female as 58.20; the estimate of life expectancy provided by Registrar General (R.G.) India (F.W.P. Year Book, 1989–90) for male as 59.95 and for female as 59.65 during 1986–91. Our estimate of female e^0_0 is slightly lower compared to the estimate provided by R.G.

Table 3.17 Brass two parameter abridged life table for males, West Bengal, 1991generated by logit $[l_{(x)}] = \alpha + \beta$ logit $[l_s(x)]$.
($\alpha = -0.52$ and $\beta = 1.08$)

Age (x)	Logit standard, $l_s(x)$	Logit estimated, $l_{(x)}$	l_x	L_x	T_x	e_x^0
0	—	—	100000	96136	59771524	59.7
1	–0.8670	–1.4564	94848	408229	5874388	61.9
5	–0.6015	–1.1696	91207	453693	5467159	59.9
10	–0.5498	–1.1138	90270	449453	5013466	55.5
15	–0.5131	–1.0741	89550	449550	4564013	51.0

Continued...

20	–0.4551	–1.0115	88319	444672	4114463	46.6
25	–0.3829	–0.9335	86611	428572	3660791	42.4
30	–0.3150	–0.8602	84818	419318	3241219	38.2
35	–0.2496	–0.7896	82909	409082	2821901	34.0
40	–0.1816	–0.7161	80724	397073	2412819	29.9
45	–0.1073	–0.6359	78105	382150	2015746	25.8
50	–0.0212	–0.5429	74755	362702	1633596	21.8
55	0.0821	–0.4313	70320	336450	1270894	18.1
60	0.2100	–0.2932	64254	300330	934444	14.5
65	0.3721	–0.1181	55878	251210	634114	11.3
70	0.5818	0.1083	44606	188168	382904	8,6
75	0.8593	0.4080	30661	117507	194736	6.4
80	1.2375	0.8165	16342	55350	77169	4.7
85+	1.7722	1.3940	5798	21819	21819	3.8

$L_0 = 0.25l_0 + 0.75l_1$
$L_1 = 1.9\, l_1 + 2.5l_5$
$L_{85+} = l_{85} \times \log_{10}.l_{85}$

Table 3.18 Brass two parameter abridged life table for female, West Bengal, 1991, generated by logit $[l_{(x)}] = \alpha + \beta$ logit $[l_s(x)]$ ($\theta = –0.47$ and $\beta = 1.10$)

Age (x)	Logit standard, $l_s(x)$	Logit estimated, $l_{(x)}$	l_x	L_x	T_x	e_x^0
0	—	—	100000	95888	5819644	58.2
1	–0.8670	–1.4237	94518	406029	5723756	60.6
5	–0.6015	–1.1316	90578	450353	5317727	58.7
10	–0.5498	–1.0748	89563	445865	4867374	54.3
15	–0.5131	–1.0344	88783	440578	4421509	49.8
20	–0.4551	–0.9706	87448	432618	3980931	45.5
25	–0.3829	–0.8912	85599	423143	3548313	41.4
30	–0.3150	–0.8165	83758	413135	31125170	37.4
35	–0.2496	–0.7446	81596	402095	2712035	33.2
40	–0.1816	–0.6698	79242	389163	2309940	29.2
45	–0.1073	–0.5880	76423	374205	1920777	25.1
50	–0.0212	–0.4933	72841	352518	1546572	21.2
55	0.0821	–0.3807	68166	324732	1194054	17.5
60	0.2100	–0.2390	61727	286895	869322	14.1
65	0.3721	–0.0607	53013	236530	582427	11.0

Continued...

70	0.5818	0.1700	41581	173650	345897	8.3
75	0.8593	0.4752	27880	105700	172244	6.2
80	1.2375	0.8912	14400	48330	66544	4.6
85+	1.7722	1.4794	4932	18214	18214	3.7

$L_0 = 0.25l_0 + 0.75l_1$
$L_1 = 1.9\, l_1 + 2.5l_5$
$L_{85+} = l_{85} \times \log_{10}.l_{85}$

[**Note:** If we do not have any death statistics by age and sex, but we have children everborn (CEB) and surviving (CS) data by age group of mother as well as if we have data on widowhood status of the respondents by age and sex for any area, we can construct life tables by sex generated by Brass Two Parameter Logit Life Tables System in the way we have shown above].

4
Reproductivity

4.1 MEASURES OF REPRODUCTION

4.1.1 Gross Reproduction Rate (GRR) and Net Reproduction Rate (NRR)

Another summary measure of period fertility rate is the GRR. It is computed only for female births but the rate is essentially a TFR, with a modification that uses life table survivorship ratios. GRR is the average number of daughters that would be born to a woman during her total reproductive period if, she passes through the childbearing ages experiencing the average age specific fertility pattern of a given period and the NRR is the same as that of the GRR but it is adjusted for mortality. The female ASFRs are calculated and summed and multiplied by five because each age group covers five years.

Table 4.1 Gross reproduction rate and net reproduction rate of West Bengal: 1981.

Age group	Female population	Total live births	ASFRs per woman	Female live $birth_x$	Age-specific maternity rates, f_x^w	*Age-specific survival rate, ${}_5L_x/l_0$	Expected female births per woman
	(1)	(2)	(3)	(4)	(5) = (4)/(1)	(6) = (5) x(6)	(7)
15–19	2721262	178940	0.0657	87288	0.0321	0.92473	0.02968
20–24	2454738	424710	0.1730	207176	0.0844	0.91154	0.07693
25–29	2122414	333400	0.1571	162634	0.0766	0.90077	0.06900
30–34	1630634	179809	0.1103	87712	0.0538	0.89005	0.04788
35–39	1464183	104274	0.0712	50865	0.0347	0.88166	0.03059
40–44	1219551	41770	0.0342	20375	0.0167	0.87440	0.01460
45–49	1049037	15475	0.0147	7549	0.0072	0.85396	0.00615
Total		1278378	0.6262 × 5	623599	0.3055 × 5		0.27488 × 5
			TFR = 3.1310		GRR = 1.5275		NRR = 1.3744

* Age-specific survival rates have been taken from Coale-Demeny Model Life Tables, Princeton, 1966 based on $e^0_0 = 58.2$ of West Bengal (through linear interpolation) and probability of surviving has been considered from birth to the mid-point of the age-group.

$$\text{NRR} = \frac{1}{l_0}\sum_{x=15}^{49} l_x f_x^w = (0.27488) \times 5 = 1.3744$$

$$\text{GRR} = \text{TFR}^* \frac{1}{1 + \text{Sex Ratio at Birth}} = \text{TFR}\ ^*0.4878$$

$$= 3.1310 \times 0.4878$$

$$= 1.5273$$

There is another way of calculating the GRR, which involves the sex ratio at birth. One can estimate the GRR just by multiplying the TFR by the proportion of births that are female. Thus for West Bengal, 1981, where the TFR was 3.1310 and there were 623599 female and 654779 male births (Sex Ratio at Birth is assumed to be of 1.05 as U.N. Standard) and the GRR was

$$\text{GRR} = 3.1310 \times \frac{1}{1+1.05}$$

$$= 3.1310 \times 0.4878$$

$$= 1.5273$$

If the true Sex Ratio at birth is not known, UN Standard of 105 is usually quite acceptable as an estimate. The GRR can be interpreted as the average number of daughters a woman would have if she survives to age 50. A GRR of 1.0 suggests that the women are approximately replacing themselves, while a figure of 2.0 may be taken to imply that the population is doubling itself in a generation; that is, each woman is producing, on average, two daughters.

4.1.2 Net Reproduction Rate (NRR)

Essentially, the Net Reproduction Rate (NRR), sometimes denoted by R_0, is a GRR adjusted for mortality. Multiplying each female ASFR by the probability of surviving from birth to that age, before summing and multiplying by five as usual perform the adjustment. The NRR will thus always be slightly less than the GRR, the extent of the difference being dependent on the level of mortality.

The probability of surviving to age x is just l_x so to calculate the NRR requires both female ASFRs and a life table. Note that a precise life table for females for the year in question is not essential. Any reasonable estimate is adequate. The calculations for West Bengal, 1981, are shown in Table 4.1.

It should be noted that the female ASFRs are here expressed per one woman rather than per 1,000. Similarly, the Radix of the life table is 1.0. This is recommended as it avoids problems of remembering to divide or multiply by 1,000 in various places. Note that the only 'Raw' data are given in Table 4.1 above. All the other columns are derived from these.

The first step is to calculate the ${}_5L_x$ — the stationary population associated with the life table. Recall that the notation ${}_5L_{15}$ refers to age group 15–19, not 5–15. ${}_5L_{15}$ is just the average of adjacent l_xs, multiplied by 5 since 5-year age groups are being used. For example:

$$ {}_nL_x = \frac{n\,(l_x + l_{x+n})}{2}, \text{ where } x = \text{age}, n = \text{interval} $$

$$ {}_5L_{15} = \frac{(l_{15} + l_{20})}{2} \times 5 $$

This procedure is repeated for each age interval and thus column 6 is calculated based on life table. Next, to calculate the GRR, and specifically, NRR one asks 'What if this Stationary population were to experience the fertility rates of the actual population?' This can be answered simply by multiplying the female ASFRs i.e. column 5 by the ${}_5L_x$ s/l_0. i.e. column 6. This gives column 7, the expected female births, sometimes known as the 'Net Maternity Distribution'. Adding these we get the NRR.The NRR for West Bengal, 1981, is thus about 1.3744. Compare this with the GRR. The difference between the two is a measure of the impact of mortality on reproductivity in West Bengal. The difference between GRR and NRR in West Bengal is very much less because mortality in West Bengal is lower compared to many states in India.

The NRR can be interpreted as the average number of daughters a woman would have during her reproductive years given the assumption of:

1. Fertility at the given rates.
2. Mortality at the given rates

And furthermore, it is generally interpreted as

NRR = 1 implies exact replacement,
NRR > 1 implies over replacement
NRR < 1 implies below replacement

Both fertility and mortality rates used are based on events occurring during a particular period, and in thinking of NRR as a number of female births per woman one is considering an imaginary that is, synthetic cohort.

This has several implications. The most important is that an NRR of less than 1.0 does not necessarily imply that the population is declining in absolute numbers. It would normally take NRRs of less than 1.0 for a considerable number of years before that happened. Nor does it imply that any real cohort will have that number of daughters. Postponement or advancement of births may be taking place, causing the fertility rates for the particular year on which the NRR is based to be unusually high or low. Alternatively, cohort fertility may be rising or falling so that the fertility rates of the 15–19 age group will not be the same as those experienced by the 45–49 age group thirty years earlier when they were 15–19. Kuczynski and others popularized NRR in the 1920s and 1930s (Shryock and Siegel 1976: 324–6).

The above method is the conventional way of calculating an NRR. However, another method exists which normally provides a very good approximation to the true value. It is not now practically useful since calculators and computers mean that the computation involved in the conventional method are no longer daunting. It is, however, included here because it serves to introduce one or two extra measures, and because it may help in understanding about the NRR. It is a slight modification of the method described by Coale (1955). The 'quick' method of calculating the NRR involves first computing $\bar{m}$ ('m bar')—the mean of the age-specific fertility distribution. This is simply a weighted average of the midpoints of the age groups; the weights being used are the ASFRs. (It is immaterial whether both sexes or just female ASFRs are used). The midpoints are multiplied by the weights, summed and then divided by the sum of the weights.

4.2 THE TIMING OF FERTILITY

Particularly, in some societies, where fertility is low and contraception is widespread, women tend to have their children at fairly young ages, whereas, in other societies, particularly those with high, 'natural' fertility regimes, women have their children, on average, a little later. The measure defined above, $\bar{m}$, the mean of the age-specific fertility distribution, is but one of a whole series of measures of the timing or location of fertility. It is easy to get confused about these, partly because of, the names and algebraic symbols used are not entirely standardized, but especially because some are often used as approximations of others.

After $\bar{m}$, the most commonly used timing measure is the 'mean age of childbearing'. This can be thought of as the mean age of mothers at the birth of their children. Keyfitz (1968: 102) labelled the measure as μ(mu) and $\bar{a}'$ (a bar prime) by Barclay (1958: 220) but Shryock and Siegel (1976: 320) do not give any name.

μ is, like $\bar{m}$, a weighted mean and is calculated in exactly the same way as $\bar{m}$ except that the weights this time are not the female ASFRs, but the births to the life table Stationary Population, which, mentioned above, is also called the Net Maternity Distribution. Thus in Table column 7 is multiplied by column 6 to give column 9 (not shown here). This is then summed and divided by the sum of the weights – the NRR – to give μ. That is:

$$\mu = \frac{\text{Sum of column 9}}{\text{Sum of column 6}}$$

This value is little less than $\bar{m}$, as it always will be because the two measures are related in exactly the same way as the GRR and the NRR. μ takes mortality into account, while $\bar{m}$ does not.

4.3 BONGAARTS PROXIMATE DETERMINANTS OF FERTILITY

Davis and Blake (1956) first identified the mechanism through which socio-economic, cultural and human behaviour interacts with the biological factors. It was demonstrated that socio-economic and cultural factors affect childbearing through biological and behavioural factors only. Eleven intermediate variables were identified and introduced within a framework that has not been widely utilized in fertility analysis. It is mainly because the framework does not lend itself to quantification and is hard to operationalize. Also the framework does not take into account the post-partum infecundability, especially the effect of lactation, which is now widely acknowledged as to have a substantial impact on fertility.

Bongaarts (1978) has refined the list of intermediate variables suggested by Davis and Blake. He has come out with a list of eight variables and termed as the proximate determinants of fertility. The eight variables are: marriage, contraception, induced abortion, lactational infecundability, and frequency of intercourse, spontaneous intrauterine mortality, sterility and duration of fertile period. It is further argued that most of the variation in fertility is mainly due to the differential impact of the first four variables. Based on the data of 41 historical, developing and developed countries it has been concluded that 96 per cent of the variation in total fertility rate of the population could be explained by the four principal proximate determinants, namely, marriage, contraception, induced abortion and lactational infecundability and the remaining four variables explain very little variation in the total fertility rate.

Thus, the framework of Bongaarts is now often quoted and widely applied in fertility studies owing to its flexibility for assessing quantitatively the effect of the proximate determinants. Despite some limitations, it gives an approximate breakdown of the contribution made by different proximate determinants to the levels and trends of fertility.

The four principal proximate variables are considered inhibitors of fertility because fertility is lower than its maximum value as a result of delayed marriage (and marital disruption), the use of contraception and induced abortion, and lactational infecundability induced by breast-feeding or abstinence. The fertility inhibiting effects of the four principal variables are measured in the model by four indices which are defined as follows:

C_m = Index of Marriage (equals 1 if all women of reproductive age are married and 0 in the absence of marriage).

C_c = Index of Contraception (equals 1 in the absence of contraception and 0, if all fecund women use 100 per cent effective contraception).

C_a = Index of induced Abortion (equals 1 in the absence of induced abortion and 0,if all pregnancies aborted).

C_i = Index of Lactational Infecundability (equals 1 in the absence of lactation and post-partum abstinence and 0, if the duration of infecundability is infinite).

Obviously, the indices take only two values, 0 and 1. When there is no fertility-inhibiting effect of a given intermediate variable, the corresponding index equals 1 and if the fertility inhibition is complete, the index equals 0.

Four different types of cumulated fertility levels are identified from which the impact of proximate variables can be derived. With the inhibiting effects of all proximate determinants present, the actual level of fertility in a population is measured by the total fertility rate (TFR). If the fertility-inhibiting effects of delayed marriage is removed, i.e., all females marry on or before 15 years of age (no delayed marriage), without other changes in fertility behaviour, fertility will increase to a level TM (total marital fertility rate). If all practice of contraception and induced abortion are also eliminated, fertility will rise further to the level TNM (the total natural marital fertility rate). If we remove the practice of lactation and post partum abstinence fertility will further rise to a level TF (total fecundity rate).

Notably, TFR, TM and TNM may vary widely among populations. However, the TFs of most population fall within the range 13–17 births per woman with an average near 15. Actually, the TF is relatively less variant because the three remaining proximate factors (natural fecundability, spontaneous intrauterine mortality and permanent sterility) which determine TF, usually causes only modest changes in fertility.

Thus, basic relations between the indices and the cumulative fertility measures are:

$$C_m = TFR/\,TM \quad (1)$$

$$C_c * C_a = TM/TNM \quad (2)$$

$$C_i = TN/TF \quad (3)$$

The above equations can be arranged as

$$TFR = C_m * TM \quad (4)$$

$$TM = C_a * C_a * TNM \quad (5)$$

$$TNM = C_i * TF \quad (6)$$

From these equations it follows that:

$$TFR = C_m * C_c * C_a * C_i * TM \quad (7)$$

$$TM = C_c * C_a * C_i * TF \quad (8)$$

$$TNM = C_i * TF \quad (9)$$

These equations summarize the basic structure of the model by relating the cumulative fertility measures to the proximate determinants.

Now let us how to estimate the indices C_m, C_c, C_a, and C_i from the measures of proximate variables.

4.4 ESTIMATION OF THE INDICES

4.4.1 Index of Marriage (C_m)

Although the index of marriage (C_m) is to be determined by the age-specific proportion currently married among females, it is not simply equal to the proportion of all women of reproductive age that are married because the fertility impact of marriage also depends on the age distribution of married women. Married women in the central childbearing age contribute more to the TFR than the youngest or eldest women as age specific marital fertility rates reach maximum in the central childbearing ages.

To take this age effect into account, the index C_m is estimated as the weighted average of the age-specific proportion of females currently married, m (a), where 'a' denotes the age with the weights taken as the age-specific marital fertility rates, g (a), i.e.,

$$C_m = \frac{\sum m(a)^* g(a)}{\sum g(a)} = \frac{TFR}{TM}$$

Where, TM denotes the total marital fertility.

4.4.2 Index of Contraception (C_c)

The index of contraception varies inversely with the prevalence and use effectiveness of contraception practices by couples in the reproductive age groups. Hence, if contraceptive practice is absent, $C_c = 1.00$, and it declines below 1 with increasing prevalence and effectiveness. C_c can be expressed by the following equation as

$$C_c = 1 - 1.08^* u ^*e$$

Where, u = proportion of married women using modern contraception; and
e = average effectiveness of contraception

The coefficient 1.08 in the above equation represents an adjustment for the fact that women (couples) do not use contraception if they know or believe that they are sterile. Therefore, the variable 'u' which measures prevalence among all women (couples), has to be inflated by the sterility correction factor to take into account the fact that the concentration of contraception is among fecund couple. Estimates of 'u' are available from the recent fertility and contraceptive prevalence surveys. The average use-effectiveness of contraceptive methods are calculated as the weighted average of the method- specific use-effectiveness (e_i), where the weights are the proportion of women using a given method (U_i), thus,

$$U = \Sigma U_i \text{ and, } e = \frac{\sum e_i U_i}{\sum U_i}$$

Then we have TFR = $C_m {}^*C_c{}^*$TNM.

This equation calculates the TFR from the natural marital fertility rate (TNM) by taking in to account the fertility reducing impact of contraception and non-marriage measured by the indices C_m and C_c respectively.

4.4.3 Index of Abortion (C_a)

It is defined as the ratio of the observed total fertility rate (TFR) to the estimated total fertility rate without induced abortion i.e. TFR +A, and hence,

$$C_a = \frac{TFR}{TFR + A}$$

Where 'A' is the reduction in fertility associated with a given level of abortion rate, and it is calculated as,

$$A = b \times TA,$$

Where, TA is the total abortion rate, describing the average number of induced abortions per woman at the end of the reproductive period, if the induced abortion rate remains at the prevailing levels for women in each age group. An exact measure would be the sum of the current age-specific abortion rate (multiplied by five if given in five-year age groups). An approximate measure suggested by Bongaarts is to calculate an annual general abortion rate by dividing the number of induced abortions in the population by the number of women aged 15–49 and then to multiply the average rate by 30, the number of years of potential exposure and 'b' is the birth averted by women which is approximately calculated by the formula, $l_o = 0.4\ (1 + u)$, where 'u' is the proportion protected by contraception among women who have had an induced abortion. Thus we have,

$$C_a = \frac{TFR}{TFR + 0.4\ (1 + u)\ TA}$$

and $TFR = C_m * C_c * C_a * TNM$.

4.4.4 Index of Infecundability (C_i)

The index C_i equals the ratio of the TNM in the presence and absence of post partum infecundability caused by breast-feeding and/or abstinence.

As post partum infecundability does not influence the duration of the reproductive years, its effect on fertility operates entirely through modification of the birth interval. Therefore, it equals the ratio of the average birth interval without and with post partum infecundability.

If the breast-feeding and post partum abstinence are in practice, the birth interval comes out, on an average, about 20 months (the sum of 1.5 months of minimum post partum anovulation, 7.5 months of waiting time to conception, 2 months of time added by spontaneous intrauterine mortality and 9 months for a full term pregnancy). Hence, in the presence of breast-feeding and post partum abstinence, the average birth interval is approximately equal to 18.5 months (7.5 + 2 + 9) plus the duration of post partum infecundability.

The index C_i is, therefore, estimated as:

$$C_i = \frac{20}{18.5 + i}$$

where, i = average duration of post partum infecundability caused by breast-feeding or post partum abstinence.

As the estimates of 'i' are not readily available, it is suggested to be estimated from the average duration of breast feeding by using the following equation:

$$i = 1.753\ e^{0.139B - 0.001872B^2}$$

where, B = mean or median duration of breast feeding, in months

Thus, we can have:

$$TNM = C_i * TF$$

and

$$TFR = C_m * C_i * C_a * TF$$

In a population, if all women married early and if breast feeding and post partum abstinence, contraception and induced abortion are not practiced, the total fecundity rate (TF) is the expected number of children a woman will have during her reproductive life span. As discussed, in the absence of breast-feeding, the post partum infecundability is, on an average, about 1.5 to 2 months. If the average natural waiting time to contraception is 7.5 months and additional 2 months are for pregnancy wastage, 9 months are for full gestation period, theoretically a woman could bear, on an average, 15 children within her 25 years (300 months) of reproductive life [300/(1.5 + 7.5 + 2.0 + 9.0)]. Although differences among population in natural fecundability, spontaneous intrauterine mortality, or permanent sterility can cause differences in the TF, but majority of populations are expected to have TF between 13 and 17 births per woman. As no direct estimates of TF are available for most of the populations we can use the standard value of it as 15.3.

For example, let us take the case of West Bengal to study the changes in the proximate determinants of fertility during 1981–1991 with the help of Bongaarts Model.

(1) The Estimation of C_m

For the state of West Bengal, we have the following information for the years 1981 and 1991 in Table 4.2.

Table 4.2 Proportion Married and ASMFR: West Bengal, 1981–1991.

Age	Proportion Married		ASMFR	
(Years)	1981	1991	1981	1991
(1)	(2)	(3)	(4)	(5)
15–19	0.37502	0.32975	0.17534	0.25807
20–24	0.78405	0.78774	0.22067	0.25630
25–29	0.90386	0.90997	0.17379	0.16649
3–34	0.92432	0.92256	0.11932	0.11133
35–39	0.90628	0.91895	0.07858	0.07062
4–45	0.83660	0.87525	0.04094	0.03987
45–49	0.75711	0.82623	0.01948	0.01900
TFR			1.19658	0.92168 × 5
	C_m		62.64	65.67

TMFR = 1.19658 × 5 = 5.9829 (1981); 0.92168 × 5 = 4.6084 (1991)

	1981	1991
Age	m (a)* g(a)	m (a)* g(a)
15–19	0.06575	0.08510
20–24	0.17302	0.20190
25–29	0.15708	0.15150
30–34	0.11029	0.10271
35–39	0.07122	0.06490
40–44	0.03425	0.03490
45–49	0.01475	0.01569
	0.62636	0.65670

Negative sign in per cent change indicates a decline

$$C_m = \frac{\sum m(a).g(a)}{\sum g(a)}$$

(2) Estimation of C_c

Officially corrected and compiled figures on couples effectively protected in West Bengal is given as follows:

Table 4.3 Percentage of couples effectively protected for West Bengal.

Number of eligible couples	Sterilization	IUD	Other methods
1981	24.1	0.7	0.9
1991	28.8	1.8	2.0

Hence $C_c = 1 - 1.08(U)(C)$

Where U is the average number users, C is the effectiveness of contraception which is taken as 1 for sterilization, 0.95 for IUD and 0.70 for other conventional methods.

Hence for 1981, $C_c = 1–1.08\ (0.2417*1.00 + 0.0090 * 0.95 + 0.009* 0.70)$
$= 0.7429$

For 1991, $C_c = 1–1.08(0.2880*1.00 + 0.018*0.95 + 0.020*0.70)$
$= 0.6798$

Therefore, the ratio of the non contraceppers in 1981 and 1991

$= 0.6798/0.7439$
$= 0.9150$

Percentage decline in the proportion non acceptors is 0.9180.

(3) Estimation of C_i

Based on the experience in the neighboring population, let us assume that the value of 'B' is about 20 months during 1981 and 18 months during 1991 under the assumptions, we have

$$i(1981) = 1.75 \exp \{0.1396(20) – 0.001872(20)2\}$$
$$i(1991) = 1.75 \exp \{0.1396(18) – 0.001872(18)\ 2\}$$

Therefore, $i(1981) = 11.23$

$i(1991) = 10.48$

$1981 = 20/(18.5+11.23) = 20/29.73 = 0.6027$

$1991 = 20/(18.5+10.48) = 20/28.98 = 0.6901$

As the value of C_i for 1981 assumes a decline in the duration of breast feeding, the birth interval which was 32.02 months in 1981 has fallen down to 30.28 months in 1991 – due to the said decline in the duration of breast feeding.

(4) Estimation of C_a

The calculation of index C_a, requires the estimation of the TFR, u and TA. If TA = 0, $C_a = 1$ and let us take the same case for the study of population.

Table 4.4 The values of indices and per cent change during 1981 and 1991 in West Bengal.

Index	1981	1991	Ratio of 1991/1981	Percentage Change |1-Ratio| 100
C_m	0.6264	0.6567	1.0478	$P_m = 4.78$
C_c	0.7429	0.6798	0.9150	$P_c = -8.5$
C_i	10.95	6.58	0.6009	$P_i = 39.91$
C_a	1	1	1	$P_a = 0$
Interaction	....	....	....	I = **
TFR	4.16	3.76	0.9038	$P_f = -9.62$

Note: –ve sign in column 5 indicates decline in the index whereas +ve sign indicates increase in the index. ** N.A

Structure of change in TFR according to the proximate determinants

$$TFR = C_m * C_c * C_i * C_a * TF$$

The above equation ascertains the trend in TFR by estimating the corresponding simultaneous trends for four indices at two points of time, say, 1981 and 1991 as follows:

$$TFR(1991)/TFR(1981) = C_m(1991)/C_m(1981) * C_c(1991)/C_c(1981) * C_i(1991)/C_i(1981) * TF(1991)/TF(1981)$$

Note that the total fecundity rate (TF) of a population is largely a function of biological proximate determinants: frequency of intercourse, natural sterility and spontaneous intercourse mortality. Let us assume; in the study of population, no significant changes have occurred in any of these factors between 1991 and 1981. Hence, TF(1981) = TF(1991) and we have,

$$TFR(1991)/TFR(1981) = C_m(1991)/C_m(1981) * C_c(1991)/C_c(1981) * C_i(1991)/C_i(1981) * C_a(1991)/C_a(1981)$$

If we take the percentage change in the above we have,

$$P_f = P_m + P_c + P_i + P_a + I$$

[where I represents an interaction factor which is to be estimated]

Where m (a) is the proportion married and g (a) is the ASMFRs given in Table 4.2.The value of C_m for 1981 is 0.6264, i.e. the proportion married in 1981 was 62.64 per cent. Similarly, the value of C_m for 1991 is 0.6567, which means in 1991, 65.67 per cent women in age group 15–49 were married as against 62.64 per cent in 1981. The ratio of the proportion married in 1981 to that 1991 being 0.953 gives a decline of 5 per cent. The net effect of decline in the proportion of married is obviously due to the rise in the age at marriage.

Let us arrange the values of these indices for both the years 1981 and 1991 as given in Table 4.5 below:

Table 4.5 Values of the Indices and per cent change during 1981 and 1991: West Bengal.

Index	1981	1991	Ratio 1991/1981	Per cent Change [1-Ration] × 100 Average
C_m	0.8153	0.7521	0.9225	$P_m = -7.75$
C_c	0.8810	0.7870	0.8933	$P_c = -10.67$
C_i	0.6250	0.6610	1.0576	$P_i = 5.76$
C_a	1.0000	1.0000	1.0000	$P_a = 0.00$
Inter-action	—	—	—	I = **
TFR	5.3	4.6	0.8679	$P_f = -13.21$

Note: Negative sign indicates decline in the index whereas, the + values are to show increase in the index. ** N.A.

Structure of Change in TFR according as the Proximate Determinants:

$$TFR = C_m * C_c * C_i * C_a * TF$$

The above equation ascertains the trend in TFR by estimating the corresponding simultaneous trends for four indices at two points of time, say, 1981 and 1991 as follows:

$$\frac{TFR\ (1991)}{TFR\ (1981)} = \frac{C_m\ (1991)}{C_m(1981)} * \frac{C_c\ (1991)}{C_c(1981)} * \frac{C_i\ (1991)}{C_i(1981)} * \frac{C_a\ (1991)}{C_a\ (1981)} * \frac{TF\ (1991)}{TF\ (1981)}$$

Note that the total fertility rate (TF) is largely a function of biological proximate determinants: frequency of intercourse, natural sterility and spontaneous intrauterine mortality. Let us assume, in the study of population, no significant changes have occurred in any of these factors between 1981 and 1991. Hence, TF (1981) = TF (1991) and,

$$\frac{TFR\ (1991)}{TFR\ (1981)} = \frac{C_m\ (1991)}{C_m(1981)} * \frac{C_c\ (1991)}{C_c(1981)} * \frac{C_i\ (1991)}{C_i(1981)} * \frac{C_a\ (1991)}{C_a(1981)}$$

If we take the percentage (or per cent) change in the above, we have

$$P_f = P_m + P_c + P_i + P_a + I$$

where I represents an interaction factor which is to be estimated.

The results given in Table 4.5 indicate that TFR has been declining during 1981–1991 and the decline is 13.2 per cent. This decline can be broken down to give the relative contribution of each proximate determinant. In the present instance, we can see from the Table that in the decrement of TFR, a decline of 9.8 per cent is due to a decrease in the proportion married, 10.67 per cent is due to decrease in non-contraception, i.e., an increase in contraceptive practice with no change in the incidence of induced abortion. Lactational infecundability has shown an increase of 5.8 per cent in the fertility level due to reduction in the practice of breast-feeding in the population.

5

Fertility: Estimation and Analysis

(Important Definitions, Basic Measures and Indirect Estimation)

5.1 INTRODUCTION

There are three basic components of population change, namely, fertility, mortality and migration, which determine the age-sex composition and distribution with respect to various other characteristics of a population. Being a positive force, fertility plays a vital role in the study of population dynamics and thereby its analysis is of great potential in the field of demography. Human fertility is responsible for biological replacement and maintenance of the human. It not only affects the size of a population but also affects the age and sex structure of the population. Age distribution of a population is more sensitive to the changes in fertility behaviour than the changes in the force of mortality. However, the process of fertility is more complex than the mortality. A number of socio-cultural, psychological and economic variables besides several biological factors affect fertility.

5.2 IMPORTANT DEFINITIONS

Natality: This is a general term representing the role of births in human reproduction. In a restrictive sense, we can say that the analysis of natality refers to certain measures of fertility.

Fecundity: The capacity of a woman (or a couple) to produce a life birth is called her fecundity.

Fertility: It refers to the actual performance rather than the capacity of the woman to produce a birth, i.e., fertility is the realization of the capacity.

Fecundability: It refers to the probability of conception in a menstrual cycle, usually taken as one month.

Family size: By family size, we mean the number of children a woman or a couple has at a point of time. The completed family size indicates the total number of children borne by a woman upto the end of her reproductive life.

Birth order and parity: When the total births at a particular point of time in the population are classified according to their occurrence, the rank we call as the order of birth. When women are classified according to the number of children born to them, they refer to their parity. As for example, the first parity women are those who have given to one child; the second parity women are those who have given birth to two children and so on. Thus, while the birth order refers to birth, parity refers to women/mothers.

Fertility and Reproduction: Fertility analysis deals with only the child-bearing activity of a population where reproduction refers to the ability of a population to replace itself and to grow.

Sterility: The lack of capacity of a woman or a couple to produce a live birth is called 'infecundity' or 'sterility'. If the woman has never been able to bear a child, such woman is called a primary sterile woman. Secondary sterility, on the other hand, arises when the woman stops producing after one or more births.

Reproductive period: The reproductive period or the childbearing period starts with the onset of menarche and continues till the menopause. In practice, the reproductive period of a woman is often made to start at 15 years or at the minimum age at marriage, and to end at 45 or 50 years.

Amenorrhea: Temporary absence of menstruation (normal or pathological) is called 'amenorrhea'. The amenorrhea period following a birth is called 'post-partum amenorrhea'.

Natural and controlled fertility: Natural fertility refers to the fertility which exists in the absence of deliberate birth control while controlled fertility is the fertility which involves a deliberate use birth control.

5.3 SOURCES OF FERTILITY DATA

The basic data for fertility analysis come from the following three sources:

1. Vital Registration System or Civil Registration System;
2. The National Periodic Censuses; and,
3. Sample Fertility Surveys.

The type of data available for each of these sources may be summarized as follows:

1. Vital Registration System: The number of births is usually registered in one calendar year.
2. Census: (a) The number of children everborn and children surviving by the age of mother; (b) Census Age Distribution, (c) The number of births during the last one year.
3. Sample Fertility Survey: (a) The number of children everborn; (b) the number of births during the last 12 months.

5.4 THE FERTILITY AND ITS BASIC MEASURES

In demographic usage the term 'Fertility' relates to the number of live births a woman has actually had. 'Fertile' thus means roughly opposite of 'Childless'. It means that a woman is or was, a mother. The physiological ability to bear children, on the other hand, is known as 'Fecundity'. 'Fecund' is thus the opposite of 'Sterile'. The words 'Fertile' and 'Fecund' are therefore used by demographers the other way round from the general public. To confuse matters further, in French, Italian, Spanish and related languages the demographic meanings 'Fecund' and 'Fertile' are reversed: fertility becomes 'fe/condite/' in French, while 'Fecund' becomes 'Fertile'. However 'Natalite' is frequently used in French as a synonym of 'fe/condite/' (See Van de Walle 1982, para 623).

It is thought of that the maximum numbers of children an average woman can theoretically produce is about fifteen if she starts child bearing as soon as possible after 'menarche', which occurs around ages 12–14 (younger in developed countries than in developing ones), and continues until 'menopause' in her middle or late forties. Of course, no population ever reaches that maximum, and there is great variability between women. Some women are, for various reasons, unable to bear any children, while, according to the '***Guinness Book of World Record***' the greatest number ever officially recorded is sixty-nine by a woman living near Moscow during the eighteenth century (sixteen pairs of Twins, seven sets of Triplets and four sets of Quadruplets). The highest recorded average for any population is about ten births per woman among the 'HUTTERITES'.

Populations in which no deliberate attempt is made to limit the number of births, such as the Hutterites, are said to experience 'Natural Fertility'. This very important and widely used concept was first identified and named by Louis Henry (1961, 1972a). Such fertility is essentially a biological phenomenon, and its level varies between populations mainly according to social customs such as varying average ages at marriage and differing breast-feeding and weaning practices. In other words, there is no fertility-limiting behaviour, which is in any way dependent upon the number of children already born.

The last frequently used concept that will be mentioned here is that of 'Fecundability'. This relates to the physiological ability to conceive, and is the statistical probability of conceiving per menstrual cycle. It is particularly important in the statistical modeling of the process of family building, and in estimation of the effectiveness of Family Planning Programme.

5.5 PERIOD AND COHORT FERTILITY ANALYSIS

There are, broadly, two ways of approaching the study of fertility: period and cohort. The essential quality of period fertility analysis is that it looks at fertility cross-sectionally, that is at births occurring during a specified period of time, normally one year. Cohort analysis, on the other hand, looks at fertility longitudinally, that is at all births occurring to a specific group of women, normally all those born or married during a particular year. One is looking over time, at their reproductive history.

Period analysis is generally simpler than cohort analysis and is more frequently used. Thus it will be considered first. Here, we will discuss a series of measures of period fertility and they are ordered roughly according to their complexity and data requirements, starting with the simplest, the Child/Women Ratio.

Samuel Preston et al. [2001] define fertility as '... the increment process by which living members of a population produce live births, that is, new living members of the population'. They also define reproductivity: 'Although often associated with fertility, the term "reproduction" in demographic parlance refers to the process by which new members of a population replace outgoing members, a process that may comprise mortality as well as fertility.' Fertility is a much more complex subject to study than mortality. Firstly, unlike mortality, it involves two individuals of opposite sex. Secondly, unlike, mortality the 'risk' of producing an offspring is not universal or identical for all females. Thirdly, unlike death, giving birth is a repeatable event. Fourthly, giving birth is an avoidable event, and can be timed or delayed. For easy of analysis, it has been customary to relate births to mothers only (to the exclusion of fathers) and study fertility rates by linking numbers of babies born to the numbers of women in their reproductive ages. A related concept is that of ***fecundity*** which refers to a woman's biological potential to reproduce. The difference between fertility and fecundity is in the fact that fertility relates to actual numbers of births per individual women whereas fecundity related to their biological potential to reproduce.

Total fertility is a cumulative process that depends on a number of factors. Moreover, a woman's past fertility may affect her future reproductive performance. Preston [3] defines cohort fertility as 'the average number of children who would be born to an actual birth cohort of women if they had all survived to the end their reproductive period, and born children at each age at the rate observed for the surviving members of the cohort at each age'. Shryock and Siegel [1974] define a cohort as follows:

'A cohort consists of a group of individuals who experienced the same significant demographic event during a specified period of time, usually a year, and who may be identified as a group at successive later dates on the basis of this common demographic experience. Examples are a birth cohort, persons born during the same year or years; a marriage cohort, persons married during the same year or years; a first parity cohort, women who had a first child in a given year…and a cohort of deceased persons, persons who died in a given year'.

There are three big problems associated with cohort analysis. The first is that it requires data in the form of a fairly long, consistent time series. Such data are rare, even in highly developed societies. The second is that of a problem known technically as 'censoring'. This refers to the fact that one does not know what will happen in the future. In other words, the later experiences of young or more recent cohorts cannot be known ahead of time. The third is that it is rather difficult to think about cohorts. Our minds are so used to thinking in a cross-sectional ways that it is hard to think in any other way [Colin Newell, 1988].

5.5.1 Child/Women Ratio

This is the simplest measure generally used in the fertility analysis and is defined as:

$$CWR = \frac{{}_5P_0}{{}_{35}W_{15}} \times 1000$$

Where ${}_5P_0$ = number of children under 5 years of age in a particular time

${}_{35}W_{15}$ = number of women in the age group 15–49 (reproductive span) in a particular time.

The subscript 15 on the right of W indicates the beginning of the age interval and the subscript 35 on the left of W indicates the duration of the interval beginning at age 15.

5.5.2 Crude Birth Rate (CBR)

The term **period** in period fertility refers to the compilation of data and reporting of results pertaining only to a very specific point in time. It shows a snapshot of the demographic event under consideration as observed at the time of the survey. 'A period rate for a population is constructed by limiting the count of occurrences and exposure times to those pertaining to members of the population during a specified period of time' [S. Preston et al., 2001].

This is the most widely used measure of fertility. It is defined as:

$$\text{CBR} = \frac{\text{Births in a year (B)}}{\text{Population at mid-year (P)}} \times 1000\ (\text{K})$$

CBR is a crude rate as it is affected by the age and sex distribution of the population. The main drawback of the CBR as a measure of fertility is that the denominator is the entire population much of which is 'non-relevant' to the reproduction process. For example, males don't give birth, and neither do children, but they are included. Thus, 'the CBR only loosely approximates an occurrence/exposure fertility rate because only women in their reproductive ages can actually give birth.... The refinement of exposure gives rise to the General Fertility Rate (GFR)' [S. Preston et al., 2001].

5.5.3 The General Fertility Rate (GFR)

The simplest overall age limited measure is the General Fertility Rate (GFR). It is defined as the number of births per year per thousand women of childbearing ages:

General Fertility Rate (GFR) =

$$\frac{\text{Births during a year}}{\text{Women 15–44 or 49 at mid-year}} \times \text{K} (= 1000)$$

$$\text{GFR} = \frac{\text{Births}}{\text{fp}_{15\text{-}44 \text{ or } 49}} \times 1000$$

where $\text{fp}_{15\text{-}44 \text{ or } 49}$ is the total number of females or women of the childbearing age 15–44 or, 49 (mid-year population).

Some demographers use 15–44 and some use 15–49 and still others prefer 20–44. For the greatest precision and the worldwide comparability, the age interval 15–44 should be adopted as standard with births under 15 and over 44 allocated to age groups 15–19 and 40–44 respectively.

This is a fertility rate rather than a birth rate because it expresses the births relative to the number of women of reproductive age. Sometimes the denominator includes women aged 45–49 and sometimes it does not. This is important because comparing a 15–44 GFR with a 15–49 GFR will be misleading.

Thus the range of possible values is roughly from 50 to 300. Note that more data are required to calculate the GFR than the CBR – one has to know the composition of the female population between ages 15 and 50, not just the overall population size.

The main advantage of GFR over CBR is that it substantially controls for age and sex structure by relating the births to roughly the women at risk of having them. But it does not control entirely for age structure since there may be substantial variations between populations within the reproductive age range. For example, in one there may be a relatively large number of girls aged 15–19, while in another there may be only a few, and because births are not spread evenly over the reproductive age range, comparisons using the GFR can be misleading. To overcome this it is necessary to move to a substantially more sophisticated level and consider fertility rates for each age group.

5.5.4 Age-Specific Fertility Rates

The frequency of childbearing varies markedly from one age group to the other within the population. As a matter of fact, there is a characteristic age pattern of fertility, which is very similar all over the world. This age pattern is the best revealed by computing age-specific fertility rates. Age is the single most important determinant of fertility, and there are great variations in the fertility of women in their late teens, late twenties or late thirties. A single measure like GFR, which encompasses the entire reproductive period, is, therefore, inadequate to reveal real fertility differences by age. Neither it is effective in showing real fertility differences spatially between women of identical age, nor those in smaller age groups, say five-year age groups. A further refinement of the GFR produces the Age Specific Birth Rates (ASBR).

Age specific fertility rates are often expressed per 1000. Normally, seven rates are calculated, one for each age group 15–19, 20–24...45–49, but calculations of single-year rates are also common. It is necessary to have birth classifications by age of the mother, but data on age is often lacking. The problem of age misreporting also complicates matters. For example, a birth to a woman whose true age is twenty-nine will fall in the 25–29 age category if she reported her true age. However, such births are often entered in the next age category if the woman reported herself to be 30. This is called rounding (by respondents) and is a common practice. It is important to note that births to women less than 15 years of age are customarily added to the births to women in the age group 15–19. Likewise, births to women reporting themselves as older than 50 are entered in the 45–49 group, with the assumption that they are overstating their age.

So, the usual definition of these is:

$$\text{Age-specific fertility rate (ASFR)} = \frac{\text{Births in a year to women aged x}}{\text{Women aged x at mid-year}} \times K$$

$$\text{Age-specific fertility rate } (\text{ASFR}_i) = \frac{b_i}{FP_i} \times 1000$$

Suppose births (b) to the women of age group 15–19(i = 1) divided by the total women or female population at mid-year in the same age group (15–19) and K is a constant, which is equal to 1000.

$$\text{Age-specific fertility rate } (\text{ASFR}_i) = \frac{b_i}{FP_1} \times 1000 = 0.2004 \times 1000 = 200.4$$

(At age 15–19, when i = 1)

Similarly for age groups 20–24, 25–29, ...45–49. (When i = 2, 3, ..., 7)

Often, though, ASFRs are expressed per 1,000. Normally, seven are calculated, one for each five-year age group 15–19, 20–24, ..., 45–49 but single year rates also common. Note there is a big jump in data requirements over the measures considered so far. It is necessary to have births classified by age of mother.

The main disadvantage of the age specific fertility rates is simply that there are a lot of numbers to look at. This makes comparisons complex and tedious' [Colin Newel, 1988]. For instance, there are sets of seven numbers corresponding to the seven age groups. Fortunately, demographers have devised a technique to allow for the computation of a single number to represent the level of completed fertility. The measure is known as the total fertility rate (TFR). The ease of interpretation as well as the possibility of comparing several populations on the basis of a simple period fertility rate, has made the TFR the most widely used measure of fertility.

5.5.5 Total Fertility Rate (TFR)

It is probably the measure of fertility that is most widely used by the demographers. It is calculated very simply just by adding up the ASFRs. However, two problems complicate matters a little. Firstly, each ASFR usually relates to five years. Thus, it is necessary to multiply the five-year rate by five (5). Secondly, the TFR is almost always expressed per woman, whereas ASFRs are often expressed per 1,000. If that is the case, then

The formula is thus:

Total Fertility Rate (TFR) = Sum of $ASFR_i \times 5 = 0.4854 \times 5 = 2.4270$

Where n = 5 (n is age-interval)

TFR is defined as average number of children that would be born to a woman if she experiences the current fertility pattern throughout her reproductive span (15–49).

An example from West Bengal data, 1991 is given below.

Table 5.1 Age-specific fertility rates, West Bengal, 1991.

Age-group (x, x + n)	Index (i)	Total women (FP_i)	Births (b_i)	$ASFR_i$
15–19	1	865323	54515	0.0630
20–24	2	865043	133130	0.1539
25–29	3	863017	100973	0.1170
30–34	4	711766	51034	0.0717
35–39	5	639310	28002	0.0438
40–44	6	464338	11376	0.0245
45–49	7	387409	4445	0.0115
$\sum_{i=1}^{7} ASFR_i$				0.4854

Where i = 1, 2, 3…7

5.5.6 Specific Fertility Rates

Ordinary Age-Specific Fertility Rates (ASFRs) are calculated by dividing the births occurring to women aged x by the total number of women aged x. However, it is also possible to define fertility rates that are specific to many other things, almost always in conjunction with age. The most common is by marital status.

Recall that GFR is a better measure of fertility than CBR because it relates the births more closely to the people at risk of having those births. Now, because in most societies births occur predominantly to married women, clearly it would be useful to have a measure similar to GFR but which uses married women rather than all women in the denominator. There are, in fact, two in common use. One is the General Marital Fertility Rate (GMFR), defined as:

General and age-specific marital fertility rates:

Restricting the base population to married women since most births occur within marriage may further refine observed fertility rates. Use of marital fertility rates of various kinds permits separating the effect of changes in the tendency to marry from the effect of changes in the level of (marital) fertility upon overall fertility.

General Marital Fertility Rate (GMFR) is defined as the total number of live births in a year, regardless of age and marital status of the mother per 1,000 married women 15–44 or 49 years of age at the middle of the year:

$$\text{GMFR} = \frac{\text{All births}}{\text{Married women 15–44 or 49}} \times 1{,}000$$

The other is the General Legitimate Fertility Rate (GLFR) is defined as the number of legitimate live births in a year per 1,000 married women 15-44, or 49 years old at the middle of the year

$$\text{GLFR} = \frac{\text{Legitimate births}}{\text{Married women 15–44 or 49}} \times 1{,}000$$

The difference between the General Marital Fertility Rate and the General Illegitimate Fertility Rate is a function of the proportion of births that are legitimate. In those countries, particularly in Latin America, where many persons live in consensual (free or common law) unions, there may be extremely large differences between the GFR and the GMFR and between GMFR and the GIFR, resulting from the fact that consensually 'married' are not included among the married and their births are not counted as legitimate. Similarly,

General Illegitimate Fertility Rate (GIFR): =

$$\frac{\text{Illegitimate births}}{\text{Single, widowed, divorced women 15–44 or 49}} \times 1{,}000$$

The curve of legitimate age -specific birth rates, like that of the general order-specific fertility rates, tends to resemble a rectangular hyperbola or the hypotenuse of a right triangle. The illegitimacy ratio is conventionally defined as the number of illegitimate live births per 1,000 total live births: i.e.

$$\frac{Bu}{B_t} \times 1{,}000$$

where Bu represents illegitimate births and B_t represents the total births.

The extent of illegitimacy in relation to the 'population at risk' is expressed by the general illegitimacy rate, defined as the total number of illegitimate live births, regardless of age of mother, per 1,000 unmarried (i.e. single, widowed or divorced) women 15–44 years of age.

It is to note that in societies where illegitimacy is negligible, such as in India and Bangladesh, the GMFR and GLFR are identical.

5.6 SEX-AGE ADJUSTED BIRTH RATE (SAABR)

The crude birth rate, as has been pointed out earlier, is not a useful measure for analytical purposes for it is affected by the age and sex distribution of the population. A rate, therefore, which would eliminate the effects of demographic composition, is required when the fertility of two populations is to be compared. The Total Fertility Rate (TFR) and the Gross Reproduction Rate (GRR) are useful for such purposes. The effects of the age-sex structure of the population on the Crude Birth Rate (CBR) can be reduced to the minimum by computing the sex-age adjusted birth rate. The United Nations has defined the sex-age adjusted birth rate' as the number of births per 1,000 of a weighted aggregate of numbers of women in various five-year age groups from 15 to 44. The United Nations has recommended a standard set of weights in computing this aggregate. These are 1, 7, 7, 6, 4, 1, which correspond to the average pattern of age-specific fertility rates for the five-year age groups, 15–19, 20–24, 25–29, 30–34, 35–39, and 40–44 respectively. The weights are roughly proportional to the typical relative fertility rates of various age groups, and have been derived from a study of the data from 52 countries, of which 15 had comparatively high fertility and 37 had low fertility.

The sex-age adjusted birth rate may be computed as follows:

Where

$$\text{SAABR} = \frac{\text{Number of live births in the year}}{1 \times W_1 + 7 \times W_2 + 7 \times W_3 + 6 \times W_4 + 4 \times W_5 + 1 \times W_6}$$

where W_1, W_2, W_3, W_4, W_5, and W_6 are the number of women in the age groups 15–19, 20–24, 25–29, 30–34, 35–39, and 40–44 respectively. The Table 5.2 shows how the sex-age adjusted birth rate is computed, in which the numerator is obtained from the vital registration system. It may be seen that the sex-age adjusted birth rate for India in 1961 was 43.1 per thousand populations.

Table 5.2 Computation of sex-age adjusted birth rate for India, 1961.

Age group (1)	Females in 1961 (in 000's) (2)	U.N. weights (3)	Actual weights (4)
15–19	17,284	1	3.6
20–24	19,134	7	6.7
25–29	18,050	7	6.1
30–34	14,855	6	4.7
35–39	11,860	4	3.2
40–44	10,774	1	1.7

The estimated number of births in India according to the Crude Birth Rate of 41.7 per thousand populations was 18,304,000:

SAABR making use of U.N. weights

$$\text{SAABR} = \frac{18{,}304{,}00}{1 \times 17284 + 7 \times 19134 + 7 \times 18050 \times + 6 \times 14855 + 4 \times 11860 + 1 \times 10774}$$

$$= 43.1$$

SAABR making use of actual weights = 42.9

The logic behind the use of the standard system of weights is that, even for countries with varying levels of fertility, the relative levels of age-specific rates for women in the age groups 15–19 to 40–44 are rather similar. It should be noted that absolute age specific fertility rates can either high or low, according to the fertility levels of the country; but the percentages of births at a given age do not suffer much.

5.7 COALE'S INDICES OF FERTILITY

In the late 1960s, Coale developed four indices of fertility. Three of these indices attempt to measure the overall marital and non-marital (illegitimate) fertility in a population and the fourth one measures the prevalence of marriage. The indices are symbolically represented as follows:

I_f = Index of overall fertility
I_g = Index of marital fertility
I_h = Index of non-marital fertility
I_m = Index of proportion married

These indices were developed essentially to study the fertility transition in Europe. The four indices are theoretically based on the technique of indirect standardization.

For computing these indices, Coale selected the fertility schedule of Hutterites as the standard. Thus, the indices computed for any given population express the level of its fertility as a proportion of the fertility the population would have had if it had experienced the highest fertility pattern on record, which is that of the Hutterites. Coale's indices show how close the fertility being measured comes to the theoretical maximum of the Hutterites. The index of overall fertility (I_f) is derived by expressing the observed number of births as a proportion of the number of expected births, if the population experiences the Hutterites ASMFRs. The expected number of births is obtained by applying the standard Hutterite marital fertility rates by age to the observed age distribution of women in the given population.

$$I_f = \frac{B}{\sum F_i \times W_i}$$

The same procedure is repeated to get index of marital fertility (I_g) by using married women and legitimate births.

$$I_g = \frac{B_L}{\sum F_i \times M_i}$$

Similarly the index of non-marital fertility is also derived as:

$$I_h = \frac{B_I}{\sum F_i \times U_i}$$

However, the index of marriage I_m provides a measure of proportions married in each age, weighted by the Hutterite fertility rate and is expressed as follows:

$$I_m = \frac{\sum F_i \times M_i}{\sum F_i \times W_i}$$

B = number of births in the population
B_L = number of legitimate births in
B_I = number of illegitimate births
W_i = number of women in the ith age interval
M_i = number of married women in the ith age interval
U_i = number of unmarried women in the ith age interval
F_i = age-specific marital fertility rate in the ith age interval in the standard Population

As a result of these definitions, the following relationship can be observed among the four indices:

$$I_f = I_m \times I_g + (1 - I_m) \times I_h$$

If in the population there are no illegitimate births, $I_h = 0$, so the relationship becomes:

$$I_f = I_m \times I_g$$

If I_g takes a value of one, it indicates that the marital fertility of the study population is the same as the Hutterite population, and if $I_g = 0.5$, it indicates that the marital fertility of the study population is half of the Hutterites.

The calculation of Coale's indices is illustrated by using the data from the Indian State of West Bengal. The expected number of births from the Hutterite Schedule for the total women as well as the married women is computed first and is provided in Tables 5.3 and 5.4 given below:

Table 5.3 Coale's index of overall fertility (I_f) for West Bengal, 1981.

Age group (i)	Female population (W)	ASFR (per 1,000 women) (f)	Hutterite fertility (F)	Number of observed births (2 × 3)/1000	Expected number of births (4 × 2)/1000
(1)	(2)	(3)	(4)	(5)	(6)
15–19	2721262	0.066	0.300	179603	816379
20–24	2454738	0.173	0.550	424670	1350106
25–29	2122414	0.157	0.502	333219	1065452
30–34	1630634	0.110	0.447	179370	728893
35–39	1464183	0.071	0.406	103957	594458
40–44	1219551	0.034	0.222	41465	270740
45–49	1049037	0.015	0.061	15736	63991
Total	12661819			1278020	4890019

Thus, I_f = Births/ Exp. Births =1278020/4890019
= 0.261

Table 5.4 Coale's index of marital fertility (I_g) for West Bengal, 1981.

Age group (i)	Married female population (W)	ASFR (per 1,000 women) (f)	Hutterite fertility (F)	Number of observed births (2 × 3)/1000	Expected number of births (4 × 2)/1000
(1)	(2)	(3)	(4)	(5)	(6)
15–19	1020526	0.175	0.300	178940	306158
20–24	1924635	0.221	0.550	424710	1058549
25–29	1918362	0.174	0.502	333400	963018
30–34	1506951	0.119	0.447	179809	673607
35–39	1326954	0.079	0.406	104274	538743
40–44	1020277	0.041	0.222	41770	226501
45–49	794237	0.019	0.061	15475	48448
Total				1278378	3815024
I_g =					

For I_g, the index of marital fertility, the same procedure is repeated, but using married women only.

$\mathbf{I_g}$ = No. of births/ Exp. Births

$\mathbf{I_g}$ = 1278378/3815024 = 0.335

A useful shortcut is that I_m can be calculated as the ratio of the expected births that would occur to married women and to all women if they experienced the standard Hutterite Fertility rates.

We have:

Expected births to married women = 3815024

Expected births to all women = 4890019

Coale's I_m

Age group	Total no. of females	Married females	Proportion married (a)	Hutterite standard (b)	(a) × (b)
15–19	2721262	1020526	0.3750	0.300	0.1125
20–24	2454738	1924635	0.7840	0.550	0.4312
25–29	2122414	1918362	0.9039	0.502	0.4538
30–34	1630634	1506951	0.9241	0.447	0.4131
35–39	1464183	1326954	0.9063	0.406	0.3680
40–44	1219551	1020277	0.8366	0.222	0.1857
45–49	1049037	794237	0.7571	0.061	0.0462
				2.488	2.0105

Hence,

$I_m = (2.0105/2.488) = 0.808$

$$I_m = \frac{3815024}{4890019} = 0.780$$

Coale's I_h = Index of illegitimate fertility, can be calculated by subtraction of legitimate from the total observed and expected births as follows:

$$\begin{aligned}\text{Obs. Illegitimate} &= \text{Obs. total} - \text{Obs. legitimate}\\ &= 1278020 - 1278378\\ &= -358\end{aligned}$$

$$\begin{aligned}\text{Expected illegitimate} &= \text{Exp. Total} - \text{exp. legitimate}\\ &= 4890019 - 3815024\\ &= 1074995\end{aligned}$$

So, $$\begin{aligned}I_h &= \text{Obs./ exp}\\ &= -358/1074995\\ &= -0.0003\end{aligned}$$

But the result of, I_h shows that the absence of illegitimate births in India or in its constituent states because in India this sort of births are not taking place.

It is important to realize that the calculations are just straightforward. The standard rates are the Hutterite ASMFRs, and the index population is, in the example above, of West Bengal, 1981. Indeed, in many cases it would be preferable to use a different standard than the Hutterite one. For example, if one was comparing the fertility levels of the regions of a country, the appropriate standard would be national rates.

5.8 BIRTH ORDER AND PARITY

A great deal of interest is given to birth order in fertility analysis because of its indirect implications to population growth. In bearing a first and second child, parents are merely replacing themselves. Bearing a third, fourth or higher order child is a contribution to population growth. The greater the proportion of births, which are of a higher order, the higher the birth rate.

A married woman having no live born child is said to be parity zero. Live birth order, on the other hand, refers to the live born child or the event of birth. If it is the first time born child of woman, then the corresponding birth order is one, and so on. Thus, parity begins with zero, while the birth order begins with one.

Parity:	0	1	2	3
Birth Order:	1	2	3	4

Note that all women of parity 'i' at time 't' do not necessarily give (i + 1) st order births at time 't + 1', as some would remain in the ith parity.

Average birth order and proportion of births of any specific order: The birth occurring in one year in a given area can be classified by the age of mother and the order of birth.

Age of mother			Order of birth			
	1	2	3	4	5	—
15–19	B11	B12	B13	B14	B15	—
20–24	B21	B22	B23	B24	B25	—
25–29	B31	B32	B33	B34	B35	—
30–34	B41	B42	B43	B44	B45	—
35–39	B51	B52	B53	B54	B55	—
40–44	B61	B62	B63	B64	B65	—
45–49	B71	B72	B73	B74	B75	—
All Ages	B1	B2	B3	B4	B5	—

The average birth order and proportion of higher order can be calculated by the age of the mother or for total woman. They can be used for comparative purposes, even when registration is incomplete. They are, however, subject to many limitations and should be used with caution.

1. Proportion of birth order 'i' = B_i/B where B_i represents birth order 'i' and 'B' the total number of births during the same interval of time i.e. sum of all B_i 's equal B.
2. Order Specific Fertility Rate (OSFR): It is defined as the number of births of the order 'i' per 1000 women of childbearing ages,

   i.e., $$OSFR = \frac{B_i}{W_{15-49}} * 1000,$$

   where, $W_{15\text{-}49}$ is the total number of women in the age group 15–49. Note that the sum of OSFRs over all orders equals the GFR, i.e.,

   $$GFR = \sum_{i=1}^{n}\left(\frac{B_i}{W_{15-49}}\right) * 1000$$

   with, 'n' is the maximum order of birth.
3. Order Age-Specific Fertility Rate (OASFR): This is the number of births of order 'i' to women of age 'x' per 1000 women of age x, i.e.

   i.e., $$OASFR_{i(x)} = \frac{B_{i(x)}}{W_x} * 1000,$$

   Where $B_{i(x)}$ be the number of births of the order 'i' to women of age x, W_x be the number of women of age x.
   Note that,

   $$\sum_{i} OASFR_{i(x)} = \sum_{i(x)}\left[\frac{B_{i(x)}}{W_x}\right] *1000 = ASFR_x$$

4. Parity-Specific Fertility Rate (PSFR): This is the number of births of the order 'i' per 1000 women of childbearing age of parity (i–1), i.e.,

   $$PSFR_i = \frac{B_i}{W_{i-1\,(15-49)}} * 1000,$$

   Where, B_i be the number of births of the order 'i' and $W_{i\text{-}1\,(15\text{-}49)}$ are the total number of women of parity i–1 in the age group 15–49.
5. Age-Parity-Specific Fertility Rate (APSFR): It is the number of births of order 'i' to per 1000 women of age 'x' and parity 'i–1', i.e.,

$$APSFR_i = \frac{B_{i(x)}}{W_{i-1\,(x)}} * 1000$$

The above rates may be compared either on a period or a real cohort basis. They may be computed with respect to all women or with respect to married women.

Relation between Birth Order and Parity: Birth order and parity are related to each other through the age-parity-specific fertility rate (APSFR). The APSFR for the ith parity and age 'x' is defined as:

$$APSFR_i = \frac{B_{i(x)}}{W_{i-1(x)}}$$

$ASFR_x$ may be expressed as a weighted sum of $APSFR_x$ and the proportion of women at each parity.

$$ASFR_x = \frac{B_x}{W_x} = \frac{B_{1(x)} + B_{2(x)} + \ldots + B_{i(x)}}{W_x}$$

$$= \frac{B_{1(x)}}{W_{0(x)}} * \frac{W_{0(x)}}{W_{(x)}} + \frac{B_{2(x)}}{W_{1(x)}} * \frac{W_{1(x)}}{W_{(x)}} + \ldots + \frac{B_{i(x)}}{W_{i-1(x)}} * \frac{W_{i-1(x)}}{W_{(x)}}$$

Remark 1: The first factor of each term on the RHS is the APSFR and the second factor of each term is the proportion of women in a parity.

Remark 2: If the APSFR and parity distribution are constant, then the ASFR also becomes constant, though the converse is not always true because the decomposition can have more than one solution.

Average Parity: Information on the number of children everborn (CEB) is collected from evermarried or currently married women through census or surveys. By cross-classifying the age of currently married women and the number of CEB to them, it is possible to compute average number of CEB per currently married women. When the average number of CEB per woman is computed for those who are beyond the reproductive ages, the measure is known as completed fertility or completed family size. It should be noted that average number of CEB per woman up to a certain age or by the end of reproductive period is a cohort measure. It is a useful measure for comparing the trend of fertility. The differentials in fertility can also be studied by average parity.

5.9 PARITY PROGRESSION RATIO (PPR)

The PPR can simply be defined as the probability of a woman having another child given that she has already had a certain number. As a matter of fact, this ratio is calculated for marriage or birth cohorts of women having completed their childbearing. The ratio can answer the question-among the women who had their third child what is the proportion who have a fourth child? The PPR being a sensitive indicator of family-building patterns reflect the sequential nature of fertility decisions. The ratio is very useful for the study of the reproductive strategies that follow in a population. The rate is generally represented by a series of a_n values; where a_0 means the proportion of women in the cohort who become mothers and a_n is the proportion of women who proceed from parity n to n + 1. It can be shown that the completed fertility rate of a cohort (CFR), which is equivalent of TFR in the period measure, can be expressed as an arithmetic series of products of PPRs. That is,

$$\text{CFR} = a_0 + a_0a_1 + a_0a_1a_2 + a_0a_1a_2a_3 + \ldots$$

The product $a_0 * a_1$, represents the proportion of women who have had at least two children.

5.10 INDIRECT ESTIMATION OF FERTILITY

5.11 BRASS METHOD OF FERTILITY ESTIMATION

The well-known Brass (1964) method of estimation of fertility, using data on births that occurred during one year preceding the census and children everborn to women of childbearing age, is also applied.

As per its requirements, the average number of children everborn (CEB) or average parity (P) is obtained by dividing the number of reported children by the number of women of reproductive age (15–49). It is, therefore, a measure of fertility experience of the cohort of women, that is, a measure of the level of fertility only containing no information about its timing. It is assumed that fertility experience of those women, who die, is the same up to the age at death as that of those who are surviving. A similar procedure can be obtained by cumulating the age-specific fertility rates (f's) taking into account the width of the age interval for which the rates are specific; the result obtained can be interpreted as the average number of children denoted by 'Φ' that would have been born to the women experiencing those fertility rates from the beginning of child bearing to the upper boundary of the highest age group included in the Cumulation.

The method suggests that these two measures should match provided the data are free from errors. They would also match if the measures are subject to errors of the same magnitude. If these measures do not match, it will indicate a change in a fertility level, either declining or increasing. This comparison provides a method of adjustment for cases where data are distorted by typical errors like omission of long dead children of those who left parental home; such distortion is most marked for older women; the reporting made by the younger women below age 30 years is usually found to be fairly accurate. Information on births occurred during one year preceding the census, may be distorted by the misperception of the length of the reference period, indicating the ill-defined period for those births. So, if errors in the reporting of current births can be assumed to be constant over age groups, the age pattern of observed current fertility may be accepted as true or nearly so, though its level may not be.

In the application of this method, the values of Φ cannot be directly comparable with the values of P because of varying age location. So Φ does not correspond to P. Usually the tabulations are done for five-year age groups that is, 15–20, 20–25 years etcetera, the cumulated 'f's' gives the mean number of children ever born at exact ages 20, 25 years etcetera. It may be noted that the current fertility experience corresponds to ages, which are about six months less than the tabulated ones. This means that the mothers were half a year younger, on the average, when giving birth than at the time of census or survey. So, the 'Φ' values corresponds to unorthodox age intervals whose limits are (14.5, 19.5), (19.5, 24.5),........., (44.5, 49.5). On the other hand average parity (P) is not a measure at exact age, rather the average, over the age group. With constant fertility, the mean number of children everborn (P's) must increase with the age of mother. The exact ages forming the lower and upper boundaries of the age interval correspond to the mid-points (17.5, 22.5), (22.5, 27.5),.........., (42.5, 47.5). Hence simple adjustments for a half-year displacement in the age groups for the current rates are to be made by assuming that specific fertility rates are equal to the mean values in the adjacent age group. If 'δf_i' is the quantity which has to be added to 'f_i' to correct for the half year displacement, the adjustments often made are

$$\delta f_1 = (f_1 + f_2)/20 \qquad \delta f_4 = (f_5 - f_3)/20$$
$$\delta f_2 = (f_3 - f_1)/20 \qquad \delta f_5 = (f_6 - f_4)/20$$
$$\delta f_3 = (f_4 - f_2)/20 \qquad \delta f_6 = (f_7 - f_5)/20$$
$$\delta f_7 = (-f_6 - f_7)/20$$

Thus for the ith interval, where Φ_i is the cumulated total of $5f_1 + 5f_2$, etc., up to $5f_{i-1}$, the estimate of the mean cumulative fertility $\Phi_i + 3.0\ f_1$ (where the mean value of the multiplying factor K = 3.0 nearly). The simple formula gives the estimated average value of cumulative fertility, which can be satisfactorily compared with observed parities to obtain an approximate idea of errors.

A sophisticated procedure, being a model distribution of age-specific fertilities in which the shape is fixed but the location may vary, has been developed for estimating multiplying factors, K's. For evenly spaced location of the model, the values calculated are:

(i) The ratio of f_1/f_2 (fertility rate in the first age interval to that in the second).

(ii) $\bar{m}$, the mean age of fertility distribution, and

(iii) for each age group, the factor K_i by which f_i value is to be multiplied in order that $\Phi_i + K_i .f_i$ should give exactly F_i, when there is a half year displacement in the current rates. The mathematical form of the model is

$$f(x) = \begin{cases} c\,(x - s)\,(s + 33 - x)^2 & s \leq x \leq s + 33 \\ 0\ , & \text{otherwise} \end{cases}$$

when the length of the childbearing period is taken as 33 years, and S is the starting age of childbearing age and c is a cohort linked to the level of fertility and is related respectively to the mean age of the childbearing ($\bar{m}$) and total fertility rate (F) by

$$\bar{m} = s + 13.2, \qquad \text{and } c = F \div 98826.75$$

these relations can easily be established by putting x – s = a, in the Brass Fertility Polynomial and integrating.

Now, the integral of f(x) from 's' to a particular age 't', gives the cumulative fertility to age 't':

$$F(t) = \int_s^t f(x)dx$$

$$= c.\ [\tfrac{1}{4}\ (s + 33 - x)^4 - 11\ (s + 33 - x)^4]_s^t$$

The age-specific fertility for age group 'i' to 'i + 5' is then given by

$$_5f_i = 1/5\ [F_{i+5} - F_i]$$

Similarly, the integral of F(x) within a 5-year age interval (i to i + 5, say) divided by the age interval gives the mean number of children everborn ($_5Mc_i$) per woman in the age group.

The adjustment factor, K, for each age group (x, x + 5) is then obtained as

$$_5K_i = [_5Mc_x - F(x)]/_5f_x$$

Now the adjusted cumulative fertility Φ_{i+5} up to age i + 5 obtained from the reported age-specific fertility rates $_5f_j$ is

$$\Phi_{i+5} = \sum_{j=0}^{i-1} {_5f_j}$$

Finally, the adjusted average cumulative fertility is given by

$$_5F_x = \Phi_x + {_5K_x} * {_5f_x}$$

But it has been found that in practice good results are obtained based on the f_1/f_2 ratio to determine K factors for the three youngest age groups and the mean, $\bar{m}$, of the recorded specific fertility rates to fix the remainder. The K-factors have been determined from the Brass-tabulation by linear interpolation (see Demography of Tropical Africa, 1968).

Brass's method has been applied here to the data for West Bengal in 1991 and the results with computational procedure are presented in Table 5.5. To select the adjustment factors, there are two provisions as suggested by Brass. The ratios of P_2 to F_2, or P_3 to F_3; or weighted average or simple average of these two may be considered for the adjustment of errors present in the observed age-specific fertility rates. But the ratio of P_2 to F_2 is best recommended (U.N., 1983) as an adjustment factor because a great majority of births will have taken place within a few years of census for which results have acceptable accuracy to reduce the memory lapses, so the ratio of P_2/F_2 is taken here as an adjustment factor and applied to the recent fertility experience to get the true age pattern of fertility for the state. The age pattern of P/F ratios may also indicate fertility trend as well as errors in the data.

Table 5.5 Estimation of age-specific fertility rates by Brass method, 1990–1991: West Bengal.

Age interval	Index, i	Reported ASFRs, f^*_i	Cumulative fertility, Φ_i	Factor, K_i	$\Phi_i+K_i.f_i = K_i$	P_i	P_i/F_i	Adjusted f^*_i
15–19	1	0.06	0.06	2.17	0.14	0.19	1.37	0.10
20–24	2	0.15	0.32	2.87	0.76	1.17	1.55	0.24
25–29	3	0.12	1.08	3.03	1.44	2.23	1.55	0.18
30–34	4	0.07	1.67	3.15	1.90	2.95	1.55	0.11
35–39	5	0.04	2.03	3.29	2.17	2.59	1.65	0.07
40–44	6	0.02	2.25	3.64	2.34	4.08	1.75	0.04
45–49	7	0.01	2.37	4.67	2.42	4.53	1.88	0.02

TFR 2.4270 3.7620
CBR 19.34 31.52
f^*_1/f^*_2 = 0.409 $\bar{m}$ = 27.49 years

The P/F ratios, which have been presented in Table 5.5, show that ratios have been increasing consistently with the increase in age. The ratio in age group 20–24 is 1.55 in 1991. The level of fertility implied by the retrospective reports on children everborn to this age group is 55 per cent higher than that implied by the current rates. The exposure to child bearing for this group of women aged 20–24 years can be at most 10 years. Despite the recent decline in fertility as reported by NFHS for West Bengal, such ratio cannot be fully explained for this short exposure period. Unless the current fertility is underestimated, the P/F ratio can yield unusually high value only if retrospective fertility is inflated, which is quite unlikely. Multiplication of the recorded f^*_i values and the total fertility by 1.55 leads to the adjusted measures for West Bengal in 1991. The sequence of P/F ratio that increases with age is an indication of recent decline in fertility. The TFR that is estimated by Brass method based on 1991 census data is 3.76.

A comparison has been made to check the accuracy in the estimates of F_i values obtained from the formulation developed by Barclay, Coale, Stoto and Trussell (1976) with that of the estimates obtained from the Brass's method (1968). The formulation developed by Barclay et al., consists in fitting a quadratic polynomial to the cumulative fertility rates and integrating the function over a 5-year period and dividing the result by 5 to find average cumulative fertility (F). The estimating equations are as follows:

$$F_1 = \Phi_0 + 3.392\, f_1 - 0.392\, f_2 \text{ and,}$$
$$F_i = \Phi_{i-1} + 3.392\, f_{i-1} + 2.608\, f_i$$

where the symbols have the same meanings as explained earlier and the values of 'i' for the age groups 15–19, 20–24, 25–29, ..., are 1, 2, 3,........ The estimates of F_i by the two methods are presented here for West Bengal. As can be seen from the Table below, the two approaches yield very similar results.

Method	Year	Age Group						
		15–19	20–24	25–29	30–34	35–39	40–44	45–49
Brass	1991	0.14	0.76	1.44	1.90	2.17	2.34	2.42
Barclay, Coale et al.	1991	0.12	0.73	1.40	1.86	2.14	2.31	2.40

The age-specific fertility rates obtained by applying Brass Fertility Method corresponds to age-groups 14.5–19.5, 19.5–24.5, ..., of mothers were converted (Trussell and Hill, 1980) into rates for conventional 5-year age groups 15–20, 20–24, ..., before calculating the birth rates.

5.12 SMOOTHING OF AGE – SPECIFIC FERTILITY RATES GENERATED BY GOMPERTZ RELATIONAL FERTILITY MODEL

The model, expressed as a linear transformation of a set of standard rates having two constant parameters α and β; has many similarities to that of Brass's (1968) logit relational system of model life tables. The logit model life table system l_xs, the proportion surviving to age x, while Barbados Gompertz model uses a specific fertility rates (ASFRs) expressed as the proportions of the total fertility rate (TFR) and then cumulated. Since there is no definite name of Gompertz transformed values, 'Gompit' has been used. Hence, the transformation is of the form;

$$\text{Gompit (p)} = -\log_e(-\log_e p), \text{ and}$$

Its inverse (or anti Gompit) is,

$$p = \exp(-\exp(-\text{Gompit})$$

As in the logit, it can be used for transforming proportions (p).

If the Gompits of the cumulative relative fertility at age x, is called Y(x) and a standard is demoted by $Y_s(x)$, the algebraical expression is of the form

$$Y(x) = \alpha + \beta\, Y_s(x),$$

Here, the standard fertility schedule generated by Booth (1984) has been used. As in the case of Brass logit system, the transformation that tends to linearize the distribution under consideration is used to relate any observed schedule to a standard pattern by the use of two constants. In the case of relational fertility model, α can be taken as determining the age location of the fertility schedule or more specifically, the age by which half of the total child bearing has occurred, while β may be interpreted as the determining spread or degree of concentration of the schedule.

Application of the model

As the observed ASFRs are calculated from the reports on births occurred during one year preceding the census, the women will have been, on an average, half a year younger at the time of birth than at the time of census. Thus, the ASFRs really refer to the exact age groups 14.5–19.5, 19.5–24.5, ….. The standard Gompits used to fit the model should therefore really be for ages 14.5, 19.5, …….., rather than conventional ages 15, 20, …….

It is also assumed here that the observed total fertility rate (TFR) is accurate. This assumption is, however, unlikely to hold in most parts of the world. To overcome this difficulty there is a technique, called the Ratio Method (Zaba, 1981), which uses the Gompertz model to estimate the total fertility; but due to the complexity of the procedure, the method is not adopted here.

The results of smoothed ASFRs in 1991 are presented in Table 5.6 (contd). The parametric values of α and β are 0.073 and 0.84 respectively in 1991. These values have been estimated from two different equations discussed earlier. Hence, when $\alpha = 0.0$, $\beta = 1.00$ and $\bar{m} = 27$, indicate the pattern of the standard schedule i.e. the pattern follows the standard. But our estimated value of $\beta = 0.84$ being slightly less than that of the standard and the value of $\alpha = 0.073$ shows much higher than that of the standard in 1991 i.e. locating the starting time of fertility is much earlier than the standard. The value of β in West Bengal indicates the spread of more fertile period than that of the standard, which is also evidenced by mean age of child bearing ($\bar{m} = 27.49$ years). So, it may, therefore, be assumed that the pattern of fertility in West Bengal is different from that of the standard.

Table 5.6 Smoothing of age-specific fertility rates (ASFRs) generated by Gompertz relational fertility model, 1991 (census-based): West Bengal.

Age group	Index, 'i'	Observed $ASFR_i$	Observed proportion, ASFRs	Age (x)	Cum. Proportion's ASFRs	Estimated $Y_{obs}(x)$	Standard Ys (x)
15–19	1	0.0528	0.1081	20	0.1088	–0.79671	–0.69130
20–24	2	0.1505	0.3100	25	0.4188	0.13885	0.02564
25–29	3	0.1208	0.2489	30	0.6677	0.90655	0.70000
30–34	4	0.0754	0.1553	35	0.8230	1.63579	1.47872
35–39	5	0.0463	0.0955	40	0.9185	2.46367	2.62602
40–44	6	0.0261	0.0539	45	0.9722	3.56866	4.80970
45–49	7	0.0136	0.0279	50	1.0000	$+\infty$	$+\infty$
TFR		2.427	1.0000				

Age (x)	Y_{fit} (x)	Fitted Cum. ASFRs	Age group	Fitted Proportions ASFRs	Fitted ASFRs (using obs. TFR)	Observed ASFRs
20	–0.51069	0.1889	15–19	0.1889	0.0917	0.0528
25	0.09564	0.4030	20–24	0.2141	0.1039	0.1505
30	0.65800	0.5958	25–29	0.1928	0.0936	0.1208
35	1.31212	0.7640	30–34	0.1682	0.0816	0.0754
40	2.27586	0.9024	35–39	0.1384	0.0672	0.0463
45	4.11015	0.9837	40–44	0.0813	0.0395	0.0261
50			45–49	0.0163	0.0079	0.0135
TFR				1.0000		2.427

5.13 USE OF BRASS RELATIONAL GOMPERTZ FERTILITY MODEL TO ESTIMATE TOTAL FERTILITY, MIZORAM, 2001

The method assumes that the fertility has been constant in the recent years, and errors in the data on current births are not correlated with the age distribution of mother. The cumulated current fertility up to a certain age x, is F_x, which is deduced from the data on births during last year should be equal to the life-time fertility (Mean number of CEB) to the same age x. Various f_i (Age-specific fertility) values are used to multiply the mid-values of the age groups and summed, and divided by the total f_i values.

The basic Gompertz Relational Model is,

$$F(x)/F = A^{Bx} \tag{1}$$

Where F_x is the cumulative fertility by age x and F, is the total fertility rate (TFR) by the end of the reproductive period. A and B are two constants, and lie between 0 (zero) and 1 (unity). The F-values can be taken as cumulative fertility derived from age-specific rates (ASFRs) or parity (P_i) data. This reduces the above function to a linear function of age by taking logarithms twice, thus,

$$Y(x) = -\ln [-\ln (F(x)/F)] = a + bx \tag{2}$$

where F(x) is the fertility up to age x and F is the TFR.

This function gives a broad representation of the pattern of fertility with age but the shape is not quite right; thus it requires a more efficient method to improve. This is done by transforming the age scale. If $Y_s(x)$ represents a standard value, then the Gompertz Relational Model is,

$$Y(x) = \alpha + \beta\, Y_s(x) \tag{3}$$

Where α and β are constants reflecting the fertility pattern of the population under study. The model also holds if F(x) is replaced by mean parity, P_i (Zaba, 1981) showed that the series of partial fertility ratios $F_x/F_{(x+5)}$ or P_i/P_{i+1} could also be represented linearly. The 's' in $Y_s(x)$ denotes the transformation for a standard age-specific fertility schedule.

Brass suggested two procedures for fitting the above equation. One is done by using *parity data*, whereas in the second, both lifetime and current fertility data are used. The estimating equations are defined as follows:

$$Z(i) = -\ln [-\ln (P_i/P_{i+1})] \tag{4}$$

$$Z(x) = -\ln [-\ln (F_x/F_{x+1})] \tag{5}$$

Where i = 1, 2, 3…7, refers to the 5 age groups, and
x = 20,25,30…50, refers to the age.

The model shown by equation (2) holds, if F_x is replaced by P_i, where P_i is the average parity of an age group of women.

Hence, $$Y(i) = \alpha + \beta\, Y_s(i) \tag{6}$$

and,

$$Y(i) = -\ln [-\ln P_i/F] \tag{7}$$

and, β is an inverse measure of the width or spread of the age-specific fertility distribution, and α is an index of central location (Henin et al., 1982) and F is estimated the total fertility rate (TFR).

The model is used to examine the age patterns of average parity (P_i) predicted by fertility models. It operates as follows: take the estimated Total Fertility Rate (TFR) and express the average parity at each age group as a proportion of the total fertility estimate (TF). Each proportion is transformed by taking its natural logarithm and changing the sign of the answer; taking the natural logarithm again and changing the signs once more. Equations (6) and (7) are utilized in this manner. Y(i) is the transformed relative parity for age 'i' and its values are compared with the model $Y_s(i)$ ratio.

Observed age-specific rates can also be compared with the model. Observed age-specific fertility rates are cumulated upward to estimate cumulative fertility to the upper limit of each age group. The cumulative fertility to each limit is then expressed as a proportion of total cumulative fertility over the whole range. The equation is the same but with only minor changes as follows:

$$Y(i) = -\ln\,[-\ln\,(F_{(x)}/F_{x+5})] \qquad (8)$$

The series, Z_i equal to $-\ln\,[-\ln\,(P_i/P_{i+1})]$ is calculated, and the $Z_i - e_i$ is compared with the 'g_i'. The values of 'e_i' and 'g_i' calculated from the standard distributions, are used. Column 4 of Tables 5.11 and 5.12 is obtained by the relation is of the form:

$$Z_{(i)} = -\ln\,[-\ln\,(P_i/P_{i+1})], \text{ where } i = 1, P_1/P_2$$

Columns 5 and 7 are standard values provided by Brass (see 1974, 1996 for details). The application of the method to cross-sectional fertility data is explained among others by Brass (1981), Zaba (1981) and Udjo (1991, 1995, 1996, 1998). For column 8 and column 9 the parameters a and b are estimated when we plot a graph of Z (i)–e (i) against g (i) values, and obtained the intercept, $\alpha = -0.253$ and the slope, $\beta = 1.065$ which is equal to putting a line to Z_1, Z_2, Z_3 and Z_4 which represent the first four age groups. The Ys (i) values are taken from the Brass standard. The fitted Y (i)'s are computed accordingly. The column 10 is computed by the relation $P_i/F = \text{Exp}\,(-\text{Exp}\,(-Y_{(i)}))$ while column 11 is computed by dividing the mean parities (P_i) by the estimated P/F ratios. The estimate of total fertility resulting from fitting the relational Gompertz model to mean parities of younger women of the age range is 4.02 which is obtained by averaging the first four values in column 11 of Table 5.11.

The same procedure is applied for Table 5.12, except that column 2 is obtained by multiplying by 5 the cumulated observed age-specific fertility rate obtained from the census. The values of the parameters α and β are

–0.406 and 0.951 respectively. These are used to estimate $Y_{(i)}$. The estimated total fertility is 3.60, which is little less but close to the earlier estimate.

The steps of computational procedure for estimating the total fertility rates by using Gompertz Relational Fertility Model are given in Tables 5.11 and 5.12. Prior to estimating TFR by using Gompertz Relational Fertility Model it is useful to estimate both observed and adjusted TFR for Mizoram, 2001. Hence, we have estimated both observed and adjusted TFR for Mizoram, 2001 in Tables 5.7 and 5.8 by Brass (1968) and Coale – Trussell's methods respectively to compare the results obtained by the two methods. The tables show similar TFR estimates by both the methods used. As a matter of fact demographic estimates are not unique, so it is recommended to use more than one method to get the consistency in the estimates. Various methods of consistency check are given later in this section.

Table 5.7 Estimating fertility by P/F ratio method (Brass, 1968) for Mizoram, 2001.

Age group (x, x+n)	Index, i	Average partities, P_i	ASFR,e f_i	Cumulative, fertility rate, Φ_i	Multiplier, K_i	Parity equivalent, $F_i = \Phi_i + K.f_i$	P_i/F_i Ratios	Adjusted ASFR
(1)	(2)	(3)	(4)	(5)	(6)	(7)	(8)	(9)
15–19	1	0.0539	0.0182	—	1.3832	0.0252	2.139	0.0264
20–24	2	0.6738	0.1329	0.0910	2.7116	0.4514	1.493	0.1927
25–29	3	1.7903	0.1677	0.7555	2.9660	1.2529	1.429	0.2432
30–34	4	2.7751	0.1162	1.5940	3.0810	1.9520	1.422	0.1685
35–39	5	3.4501	0.0652	2.1750	3.1975	2.3835	1.447	0.0945
40–44	6	4.0065	0.0417	2.5010	3.3930	2.6425	1.516	0.0605
45–49	7	4.4162	0.0325	2.7095	3.9715	2.8386	1.556	0.0471
			0.5744					0.8239
TFR			2.8700					4.1645

$TFR^{(obs)} = 2.87$; $TFR^{(adj)} = 4.16$; $f_1/f_2 = 0.137$; $\bar{m} = 30.4$ years

Table 5.8 Estimating fertility by P/F ratio method (Coale – Trussell) for Mizoram, 2001.

Age group (x, x + n)	Average parities, P_i	ASFR, f_i	Cumulative fertility rate, Φ_i	Parity equivalent, F_i	P_i/F_i Ratios	Adjusted ASFR, K = 1.43 [1/3(2 + 3 + 4)]
(1)	(2)	(3)	(4)	(5)	(6)	(7)
15–19	0.0539	0.0182	0.0910	0.0280	1.925	0.0260
20–24	0.6738	0.1329	0.7555	0.4522	1.490	0.1900
25–29	1.7903	0.1677	1.5940	1.2718	1.408	0.2398
30–34	2.7751	0.1162	2.1750	1.9656	1.412	0.1662
35–39	3.4501	0.0652	2.5010	2.3743	1.453	0.0932
40–44	4.0065	0.0417	2.7095	2.5811	1.552	0.0596
45–49	4.4162	0.0325	2.8720	2.8106	1.571	0.0465
Total		0.5744				0.8213
TFR		2.8700				4.11

$TFR^{(obs)} = 2.87$; $TFR^{(adj)} = 4.11$

Table 5.9 Mean parity, transformed relative parity, $Y_{(i)}$, and standard transformed relative parity generated by Gompertz model, Mizoram, 2001.

Age group (x, x + n)	Mean parity, P_i	Parity as a proportional to TFR = 4.11	Transformed relative parity, $Y_{(i)}$	Standard transformed relative parity, $Y_{s(i)}$
(1)	(2)	(3)	(4)	(5)
15–19	0.0539	0.01311	–1.46657	–1.07889
20–24	0.6738	0.16394	–0.59236	–0.31188
25–29	1.7903	0.43559	0.18506	0.35380
30–34	2.7751	0.67520	0.93459	1.05695
35–39	3.4501	0.83944	1.74285	1.95343
40–44	4.0065	0.97482	3.66898	3.41302
45–49	4.4162	1.07450		6.05569

Table 5.10 Smoothing of age-specific fertility rates generated by Gompertz model, Mizoram 2001.

Age group (x, x + n)	Age-specific fertility rates, ASFR (f_i)	Proportional ASFR	Cumulative proportional ASFR	Y(x)	Ys (x)
(1)	(2)	(3)	(4)	(5)	(6)
15–19	0.0182	0.0317	0.0317	–1.23879	–0.69130
20–24	0.1329	0.2314	0.2631	–0.28910	0.02564
25–29	0.1677	0.2919	0.5550	0.52969	0.70000
30–34	0.1162	0.2023	0.7573	1.28015	1.47872
35–39	0.0652	0.1135	0.8708	1.97802	2.62602
40–44	0.0417	0.0726	0.9434	2.84275	4.80970
45–49	0.0325	0.0566	1.0000	+∞	–
		1.0000			

Table 5.11 Fitting Brass Gompertz relational fertility model to mean parities of women, Mizoram, 2001.

Age group (x, x + n)	P_i	P_i/P_{i+1}	Z_i	e_i	Z_i-e_i	g_i	$Y_s(i)$	Fitted $Y_{(i)}$	P_i/F	F
(1)	(2)	(3)	(4)	(5)	(6)	(7)	(8)	(9)	(10)	(11)
15–19	0.0539	0.0799	–0.9266	1.2897	–2.2163	–1.7438	–1.0789	–1.4053	0.0170	3.18
20–24	0.6738	0.3764	0.0231	1.4252	–1.4022	–1.0157	–0.3119	–0.5861	0.1658	4.06
25–29	1.7903	0.6451	0.8248	1.3725	–0.5477	–0.3355	0.3538	0.1249	0.4137	4.33
30–34	2.7751	0.8044	1.5245	1.1421	0.3824	0.4391	1.0570	0.8758	0.6593	4.21
35–39	3.4501	0.8611	1.9004	0.7061	1.1943	1.5120	1.9534	1.8333	0.8522	4.05
40–44	4.0065	0.9072	2.3293	0.2763	2.0530	3.2105	3.4130	3.3921	0.9669	4.14
45–49	4.4162	–	–	–	–	–	–	–	–	–

¼ Σ20–39 = 4.02 TFR; $\alpha = -0.253$, $\beta = 1.068$

Table 5.12 Fitting Brass Gompertz relational fertility model to current fertility of women, Mizoram, 2001.

Age group	P_i Cum. ASFR,	Ratio of Fx/Fx+5	$Z_{(x)}$	$e_{(x)}$	$Z_{(x)}$-$e_{(x)}$	$g_{(x)}$	$Y_s(x)$	Fitted $Y_{(x)}$	P_i/F	F
(1)	(2)	(3)	(4)	(5)	(6)	(7)	(8)	(9)	(10)	(11)
15–19	0.0910	0.1205	–0.7498	1.3364	–2.0862	–1.4501	–0.7713	–1.1399	0.0439	3.59
20–24	0.7555	0.4740	0.2922	1.4184	–1.1262	–0.7430	–0.0410	–0.4436	0.2105	3.64
25–29	1.5940	0.7329	1.1686	1.2978	–0.1292	–0.0382	0.6290	0.1918	0.4380	3.24
30–34	2.1750	0.8697	1.9685	0.9670	1.0015	0.8356	1.3897	0.9170	0.6705	3.73
35–39	2.5010	0.9231	2.5248	0.4509	2.0739	2.1649	2.4781	1.9503	0.8674	3.12
40–44	2.7095	0.9434	2.8431	0.0462	2.7969	4.4564	4.5256	3.8992	0.9799	2.93
45–49	2.8720	–	–	–	–	–	–	–	–	–

$\alpha = -0.4064,\ \beta = 0.9510$

Fig. 5.1 Fitting Brass Gompertz relational fertility model to mean parity data of Mizoram: 2001

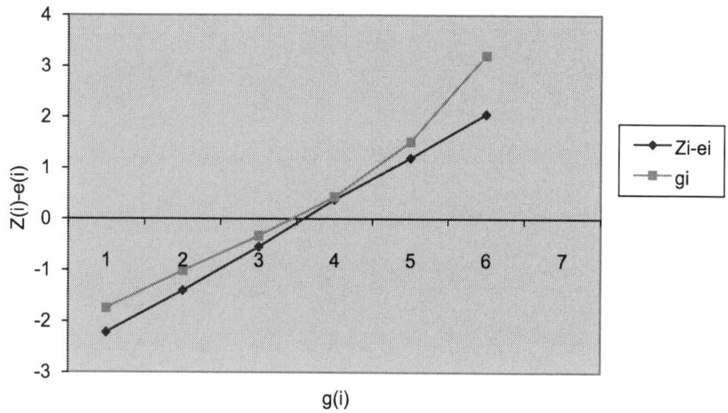

Fig. 5.2 Fitting Brass Gompertz fertility model to current fertility data of Mizoram: 2001

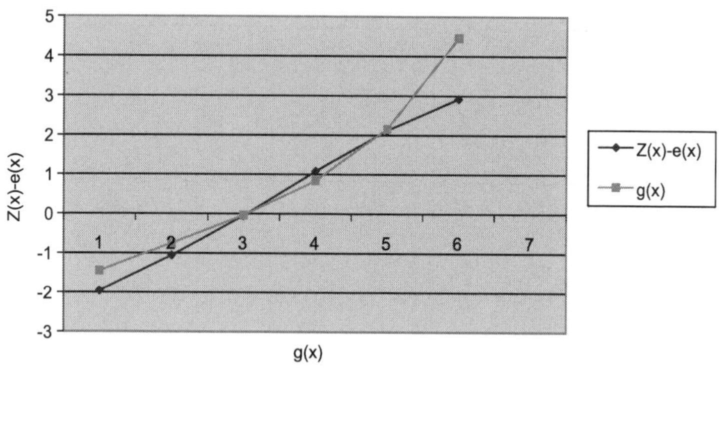

Here, it has been aimed at estimating fertility levels of Mizoram – a north eastern state of India, in 2001 using different estimating techniques with the goal of arriving at most accurate estimate of fertility levels in this area. The demographic techniques given here in this section are the most promising techniques available for deriving valid fertility measures from census and survey data. Despite, these techniques are most powerful; they do not always solve all of the problems of demographic estimation. Therefore, using Brass Consistency Check any one may check the reliability of the results that will be obtained from various methods.

Results show that the fertility rates (both the observed and adjusted TFR in Tables 5.7 and 5.8) for Mizoram derived by the two techniques are very close but the relational Gompertz model tends to give lower values, which are evinced from the Tables 5.11 and 5.12 as well as from the Figures 5.1 and 5.2 respectively. It can be seen here that the sequence of P/F ratios, which is increasing with the increase in age, clearly indicates recent decline in fertility.

Various Methods of Consistency Check

- **Brass Consistency Check**

To check the consistency of our estimates of fertility by Brass P/F Ratio Method, Brass consistency check has been used in case of Mizoram, 2001. The methodology developed by Brass for consistency check is as follows:

$$\frac{CT}{W_{15-14}} = F\left[\frac{n-m}{n} + \frac{P}{2n}(m(n-m)-40)\right]$$

Where W_{15-44} = Total number of women aged 15–44

CT = Total children everborn to women 15–44

$\bar{m}$ = Mean Age of childbearing

So, m = Mean age of period fertility distribution minus 15 years i.e.,

$m = \bar{m} - 15$ years

P = Average proportional change in the year in the number of women aged 15–44,

$2\,(W_{30-45} - W_{15-30})/15^{*}\, W_{15-44} = ?$

F = Total Fertility Rate

n = 30 year range

So by using this consistency check one can easily check the consistency with that of the estimated TFR.

5.14 PARITY RATIO METHODS OF FERTILITY

Coale and Demeny demonstrated that period total fertility rate (TFR) could be approximated as:

$$TFR = P_3^2/P_2 \qquad (1)$$

Where P_2 = Mean Number of Children Everborn (MNCEB) by women aged 20–24, and

P_3 = MNCEB/Women aged 25–29

The relationship is an empirical relationship rather than a theoretical relationship. It depends on the following assumptions:

1. P_2 and P_3 are not affected by the reference period of misplacement errors and are the least biased for omission.
2. The parities are based on women in the younger ages when reporting is assumed to be more accurate.
3. Fertility for ages 15–29 has remained constant in the recent past.

This implies that the deviations from these basic assumptions are likely to result in a biased estimate of TFR.

- In a similar way Brass (1980) developed a short-cut method of estimating fertility from mean parity by age under the following assumptions:

1. The pattern of fertility follows the Gompertz Curve.
2. The quality of the reported mean number of children everborn extends to age group 30–34. Then by using the second, third and fourth mean parities, they found that:

$$TFR = P_2\,(P_4/P_3)^4 \qquad (2)$$

where P_2 and P_3 are defined above and P_4 = MNCEB/women aged 30–34.

He stressed that this method will give a better estimation than the Coale-Demeny method if ages at births extending to age 35 are reported accurately.

As a check for the choice of the formula to be employed he suggested that the following conditions must be met:

1. If $TFR = P_3^2/P_2 < TFR = P_2\,(P_4/P_3)^4$ to the Gompertz model does not give a good fit for the reported mean parities of cohorts. In that case he recommends the use of the equation (1).
2. If $TFR = P_3^2/P_2 > TFR = P_2\,(P_4/P_3)^4$, the Brass formula is likely to give better estimates (Brass, 1980). Therefore, he recommends the use of $P_2\,(P_4/P_3)^4$.

3. Again, if the estimates are less than P_6 and P_7 there is an indication that the underlying assumptions are not met. Then the formula should not be used for our study, as the values of P_6 and P_7 are 4.0065 and 4.4162 respectively.

5.15 P/F RATIO METHOD OF ESTIMATING FERTILITY

Brass (1968) developed a useful formula of computing lifetime fertility to cumulative current fertility and the ratio of the two under the following assumptions:

1. Fertility for the population under study remained constant for sometime in the past.
2. The reported number of children everborn to women in their early ages, say 15–35 is more or less accurately reported.
3. The reported number of births for the previous year may suffer from errors resulting from inaccurate perception by the respondents of the reference period, but these errors are invariant with age.

5.16 BRASS'S P/F RATIO METHOD

In the P/F ratio analysis Brass (1968) recommended P_2/F_2. His assumption was that women in the age group 20–24 remember the number of children everborn by them sufficiently accurately because such women we have only a small number of births that could have occurred in recent years thereby reducing recall error. But some of these women could have entered into reproductive life in recent years. This can lead to false conclusion that fertility has been on decline in the years preceding the enumeration date. Also the cumulative fertility F_2 that is based on women in the age group 15–25 is assumed to have misstatement errors that will have no effect on the age structure of the current fertility schedule, but that is not the case. In order to minimize these and other shortcomings, other scholars have tried to use the average of various combinations (Somoza, 1981).

In all cases the 1/3 $(P_2/F_2+P_3/F_3+P_4/F_4)$ adjustment factor is somehow more plausible. But in lieu of the problems of assumptions and quality of data, other methods for estimating fertility should be taken into consideration.

5.17 FERTILITY ESTIMATION BY REVERSE SURVIVAL METHOD

Data required

1. The population under age 10, classified by age (5-year age groups are sufficient, though single year date are preferable) and by sex;
2. Total population at the time of enumeration, 't_0' (initial year).
3. As estimate of growth rate, r.
4. Estimates of mortality parameters that would permit the construction of a life table up to age 10. A value of l_2 obtained from information on children everborn and surviving is adequate.

Step 1 Calculation of life table estimates of person – years lived: In order to reverse-project to birth the population in age groups 0–4 and 5–9, one only needs values of ${}_5L_0$ and ${}_5L_5$, the person- years lived by the stationary population constituting the life table between birth and exact age 5, and between age 5 and exact age 10, respectively. Usually, but not necessarily, these values are obtained by assuming that mortality level associated with l_2 remained constant during the 10 years preceding enumeration. Under the assumption, the actual calculation of ${}_5L_0$ and ${}_5L_5$ is carried out by interpolating the printed values of the Coale-Demeny model life tables. Naturally, the family of models selected should be that used in estimating l_2. In some cases the mortality level selected may be the mean of those associated with l_2, l_3 and l_5 values yielded by the indirect estimation of child mortality. This mean level may represent more closely the true mortality level prevalent during the decade preceding enumeration, especially when there is evidence suggesting a recent decline in child mortality.

Step 2 Estimation of mid year population: Since the method is directed toward the estimation of an average annual birth rate, for the periods from 't_0–5' to 't_0' and from 't_0–10' to 't_0–5', 't_0' being the date of enumeration, an estimate of the total population at the mid points of these periods is required. Perhaps, the simplest way of estimating these mid year populations is by using equation

$$N_M = N_0 \exp [r(t_M - t_0)] \tag{1}$$

Where t_M is the mid-point of the period being considered; N_0, is the total count yielded by enumeration and 'r' is an estimate of growth rate between t_0 and t_1 (the time points). In such a case, the equation to estimate 'r' is of the form:

$$r = \ln [N_1/N_0] / (t_1 - t_0) \quad (2)$$

where $N_1 \rightarrow$ the total count at time t_1 and $N_0 \rightarrow$ the total count at time t_0.

Step 3 Estimation of average annual birth rates for the two five-year periods preceding the census. The average annual number of births for the first period, from t_{0-5} to t_0 is,

$$B_1 = {}_5N_0/{}_5L_0 \quad (3)$$

Where ${}_5N_0$ is the population in age group 0–4; and ${}_5L_0$ is the life table estimate obtained in step 1.

For the period from t_{0-10} to t_{0-5}, the equivalent average annual number of births is

$$B_2 = {}_5N_5/{}_5L_5 \quad (4)$$

Where ${}_5N_5$ is the population in age group 5–9. If the radix l_0, of the life table being used were not one, equations (3) and (4) would have to be modified as follows:

$$B_1 = {}_5N_0 * l_0 / {}_5L_0 \quad \text{and}$$

$$B_2 = {}_5N_5 * l_0 / {}_5L_5$$

Once B_1 and B_2 are calculated, the birth rate for each period is obtained by dividing these values by the corresponding mid-year population calculated in step 1(See U.N. Manual X, 1983).

Reverse Survival Method (An illustration)

The ways of calculating birth rates by projecting backward based on 1981 census data of West Bengal have been presented as follows:

1. Calculation of life table estimates of person-years lived: The data on children-ever born (CEB) and children surviving (CS) collected by 1981 census of India for West Bengal are used to estimate probabilities of survivorship in childhood in respect of both West model and South model by Brass-Trussell Method (Chapter 3, Mortality). The estimates provided by West model showed better approximation than that of South model of Coale-Demeny family of mortality pattern. Therefore, to obtain estimates of ${}_5L_0$ and ${}_5L_5$, $l_{(2)}$ was re-estimated by using West model. Its value 0.8930 is consistent with mortality level 16.70 (for males) in the West model. This level has been used to estimate ${}_5L_0$ and ${}_5L_5$ by interpolation. The table below shows ${}_nL_x$ values appearing in the Coale-Demeny model life tables at level 16 and 17.

Table A Values of person-years lived from exact age x to x + 5 by Stationary Population, West model by sex.

Males			Females	
Person-years lived	Level 16	Level 17	Level 16	Level 17
${}_1L_0$	0.9336	0.9389	0.9424	0.9479
${}_4L_1$	3.5040	3.5719	3.5742	3.6375
${}_5L_5$	4.2849	4.3832	4.3729	4.4680

Since the Coale-Demeny model life tables only contain ${}_1L_0$ and ${}_4L_1$, one needs to calculate ${}_5L_0$ by adding these values. Therefore, for male, 1981, West Bengal.

$$
\begin{aligned}
{}_5L_0^{16} &= {}_1L_0^{16} + {}_4L_1^{16} \\
&= 0.9336 + 3.5040 \\
&= 4.4376 \text{ (Level 16)}
\end{aligned}
$$

Similarly for,

$$
\begin{aligned}
{}_5L_0^{17} &= {}_1L_0^{17} + {}_4L_0^{17} \\
&= 0.9389 + 3.5719 \\
&= 4.5108 \text{ (Level 17)}
\end{aligned}
$$

Using these values, interpolation may be carried out as follows:

$$
\begin{aligned}
{}_5L_0^{16.7} &= 0.3(4.4376) + 0.7(4.5108) \\
&= 4.4888\text{, hence, for}
\end{aligned}
$$

$$
\begin{aligned}
{}_5L_5^{16.7} &= 0.3(4.4376) + 0.7(4.3832) \\
&= 4.3537
\end{aligned}
$$

2. Estimation of mid-year population: To estimate mid-year population, we have to find out growth rates (r) by sex (shown below)

Sex	Total Population	
	1971	1981
Male	23435987	28560907
Female	20876024	26019746

Growth rate for males $r_m = l_n [N_2 - N_1]/t_2 - t_1$

$$
\begin{aligned}
&= 17.1675 - 16.9698/1981 \text{ (March)} - 1971 \text{ (April)} \\
&= 0.1977/9.92 \\
r_m &= 0.0200
\end{aligned}
$$

For female, r_f = 17.0744 – 16.8541/9.92

= 0.220/9.92

r_f = 0.222

Child Population 1981 Census, West Bengal

Age Group	Male	Female
0–4	3186040	3157468
5–9	3790838	3673299

But during the calculation we have considered r = 0.021 as an average. The mid-year populations desired are estimated by,

N_1 = No exp [–0.021 × 2.5]

N_2 = No exp [–0.021 × 7.5]

Therefore, N_1 = (28560907) (0.94885)

= 27100017

N_2 = (28560907) (0.85427)

= 24398726

Hence, B_1 = 31,86040/4.4888

= 709775.44 (estimated no. of births)

B_2 = 37,90838/4.35370

= 870716.40 (estimated no. of births)

Where 31, 86040 (0–4) and 37,90838 (5–9) are populations for males in 1981;

Now,

b_1 = (est. B_1)/N_1

= 709775.44/27100017

= 0.026

b_2 = (est. B_2)/N_2

= 870716.40/24398726

= 0.035

Similarly, birth rates for female can be estimated.

Estimates for both sexes combined can also be obtained by adding male and female birth for the period.

5.18 RELE'S PROCEDURE FOR THE ESTIMATION OF FERTILITY

The Rele's procedure makes use of child woman ratios i.e., ratio of children of age 0–4 or 5–9 to women of age 15–49 or 20–54 respectively, and life expectancy at birth to obtain fertility rate estimates. The method is based on the linear relationship, which is shown mathematically to exist between the child woman ratio (CWR) and the gross reproduction rate (GRR) at a given level of mortality (Rele, 1976). Accordingly, linear regression equations have been fitted to a set of stable populations with a wide range of fertility and mortality levels. Thus, for the given level of mortality (measured in terms of e_0^0), it was observed that the GRR is linearly related with CWR whereas birth rate has curvilinear relationship with CWR. Also, the co-efficients to estimate GRR from CWR at fixed levels of e_0^0 are given (Rele, 1976). We have generally four types of CWRs but the CWR as defined in second and fourth row of Table 5.12 provides better estimates. Hence, two types of CWRs are used, namely, children aged 0–4 years divided by women aged 15–49 (CWR_2), and children aged 5–9 divided by women aged 20–54 (CWR_4). The e_0^0 used here corresponds to the period when the children in the CWR were born, and the fertility estimates obtained also refer to the same period. Thus, from the census, it is possible to obtain two estimates of fertility, one up to five years, and the other from five to ten years before the census.

Estimation of GRR: As mentioned above, GRR has almost linear relationship with CWR. Then for given levels of e_0^0,

$$y = GRR = a + bx$$

where x = CWR i.e.

$$CWR_1 = C\,(0\text{–}4)/W\,(15\text{–}44),$$
$$CWR_2 = C\,(0\text{–}4)/W\,(15\text{–}49),$$
$$CWR_3 = C\,(5\text{–}9)/W\,(20\text{–}49),$$
$$CWR_4 = C\,(5\text{–}9)/W\,(20\text{–}54),$$

and a and b are constants which are given in Table 5.13.

Table 5.13 Coefficients for the estimation of gross reproduction rate from child woman ratio.

Type of child-woman ratio	Regression co-efficients*	e_0^0					
		20	30	40	50	60	70
$\frac{C(0-4)}{W(15-44)}$	a	–0.0909	–0.1211	–0.1370	–0.1529	–0.1645	–0.1754
	b	4.5907	4.1829	3.9298	3.7375	3.5556	3.3878
$\frac{C(0-4)}{W(15-49)}$	a	0.0547	0.0284	0.0129	0.0059	–0.0182	–0.0309
	b	4.7680	4.3293	4.0617	3.8589	3.6628	3.4829
$\frac{C(5-9)}{W(20-49)}$	a	–0.1162	–0.1311	–0.1436	–0.1574	–0.1675	–0.1779
	b	5.2927	4.4881	4.0940	3.8301	3.5967	3.3894
$\frac{C(5-9)}{W(20-54)}$	a	0.0245	0.0106	0.0021	–0.0110	–0.0226	–0.0345
	b	5.4711	4.6398	4.2262	3.9480	3.7014	3.4821

• Coefficients of the regression equations y = a + bx for each e_0^0 derived from stable populations, where y is the gross reproduction rate and x is the child-woman ratio.

Table 5.14 can be used to obtain the corresponding coefficients to estimate TFR from CWR, obtained by multiplying by 2.05. These Coefficients are shown in Table below:

Type of CWR		e_0^0					
		20	30	40	50	60	70
C(0–4)/W(15–49)	} a	0.1121	0.0582	0.0264	–0.0121	–0.0373	–0.0633
	} b	9.7744	8.8751	8.3265	7.9107	7.5087	7.1399
C(5–9)/W(20–54)	} a	0.0502	0.0217	0.0043	–0.0226	–0.0463	–0.0707
	} b	11.2158	9.5116	8.6637	8.0934	7.5879	7.1383

Source: Derived from coefficients for the estimation of GRR from CWR (See Rele, 1976) i.e. Table 5.12

Note: The estimate of the TFR is obtained as: y = TFR = a + bx for given e_0^0.

Procedure for Estimating Birth Rate: As stated earlier, birth rate has curvilinear relation with CWR. Estimation of BR (b_c) involves two steps:

1. Estimating intrinsic birth rate (b_i); and
2. Then converting b_i into CBR (b_c).

Intrinsic birth rate (b_i) may be estimated using the following relations.

$$y = b_i = a + bx + cx^2$$

where a, b and c are given in Table 5.14 for different levels of CWR and e_0^0.

Table 5.14 Coefficients for the estimation of intrinsic birth rate (b_i) from the child woman ratio*.

Type of child woman ratio	Regression Co-efficients	e_0^0					
		20	30	40	50	60	70
$\frac{C(0-4)}{W(15-49)}$	a	–4.96	–5.37	–5.40	–5.45	–5.45	–5.25
	b	106.85	94.21	85.91	79.93	75.02	69.92
	c	–28.21	–24.92	–22.11	–19.96	–18.66	–16.94
$\frac{C(5-9)}{W(20-54)}$	a	–5.38	–5.61	–5.52	–5.52	–5.52	–5.32
	b	121.62	100.57	89.12	81.67	75.78	69.90
	c	–35.57	–28.07	–23.64	–20.75	–19.00	–16.90

* Coefficients of the regression equation $y = b_i = a + bx + cx^2$. Computed from stable populations for each e_0^0, where x is the CWR and y is the BR per 1000 population.

Once we estimate b_i, we can convert b_i to get Crude Birth Rate (b_c) by using the relationship as follows:

$$b_c = b_i \times \frac{R_A}{R_S}$$

where $$\frac{R_A}{R_S} = \frac{\text{(Weighted Sum/Total Population) for a given population}}{\text{(Weighted Sum/Total Population) for the corresponding stable population}}$$

The number R_A is calculated as'

$$R_A = \frac{1W_{15-19} + 7W_{20-24} + 7W_{25-29} + 6W_{30-34} + 4W_{35-39} + 1W_{40-44}}{\text{Total Population}}$$

The weights 1, 7, 7, 6, 4, 1 are given by United Nations based on the age pattern of fertility.

The denominator R_S of the above equation is given in Table 5.15 for different values of GRR and e_0^0.

Table 5.15 The ratio of weighted sum of women in the reproductive age groups to total population for stable populations by gross reproduction rate (GRR) and expectation of life at birth (e_0^0).

GRR	e_0^0					
	20	30	40	50	60	70
4.0	0.9667	0.9078	0.8758	0.8534	0.8299	0.8088
3.0	1.0255	0.9686	0.9396	0.9163	0.8966	0.8780
2.5	1.0470	0.9919	0.9652	0.9443	0.9270	0.9092
2.0	1.0535	1.0103	0.9782	0.9603	0.9443	0.9304
1.5	1.0338	0.9873	0.9617	0.9423	0.9354	0.9253
1.0	0.9413	0.8906	0.8697	0.8534	0.8449	0.8424

* The weighted sum is defined by $1W_{15-19} + 7W_{20-24} + 7W_{25-29} + 6W_{30-34} + 4W_{35-39} + 1W_{40-44}$ where W denotes the number of women in the age group given in the parenthesis and the weights 1, 7, 7, 6, 4, 1 correspond to average pattern of relative age-specific of fertility rates.

Remark 1: The regression coefficients for estimating GRR and Intrinsic Birth Rate (b_i), were estimated using 36 stable populations with GRR = 4.0, 3.0, 2.5, 2.0, 1.5 and 1.0 and e_0^0 = 20, 30, 40, 50, 60, and 70 years.

Remark 2: The methodology is applicable in general and can be used for national as well as sub-national population. However, it has certain strengths and weaknesses. Among the former, the estimated fertility is rather insensitive to the errors in e_0^0, so that an approximate value of e_0^0 gives fairly accurate estimates of fertility.

It is estimated that normally a variation of 1 year in e_0^0 has an effect of less than 0.8 per cent on the estimated value of TFR. Among the weakness of the methodology, derived fertility estimates depend directly on the accuracy of the CWRs. Thus, the methodology, when applied to developed countries gives excellent results. In developing countries, however, the results may be affected by errors in age reporting, especially under reporting of the number of young children in the age group 0–4 years. In such a situation, it is sometimes preferable to use a smoothed age distribution.

Remark 3: From the experience of developing countries, the estimates from CWR_1 are usually an underestimate, while that from CWR_4 may be an overestimate. Therefore, a better estimate would be a weighted mean of the two estimates. Recently, Rele (1987) has provided a refinement by using the weighted mean approach to the earlier methodology.

5.19 COALE'S MODEL OF MARITAL FERTILITY

The model of marital fertility first proposed by Coale (1971) has proved to be a powerful analytical tool. It has been shown to be a useful component of a full model of age-specific rates (Coale and Trussell, 1974) and has been employed in several procedures for estimating fertility (Coale et al., 1975) and mortality (Trussell, 1975; and Hill and Trussell, 1977) from descriptive tool in examining whether fertility is natural (Barclay et al., 1976; Trussell, 1977) in the sense of Henry (1961), in interpolating five-year rates to obtain single year rates, and in tracing the time sequence of control of fertility (Trussell, 1974; Knodel, 1977). The latter use has induced us to propose a standard technique for estimating the parameters of the model so that results quoted by different investigators would be comparable.

The model hypothesizes that in any population, the ratio of marital fertility r (a) to natural fertility n (a) at a specified age a is given by

$$r(a)/n(a) = M \exp(m \cdot v(a)) \qquad (1)$$

M is the scale factor or the level at which natural fertility is experienced at ages 20–24 where voluntary control of fertility is deemed to have no effect on the pattern; v (a) represents the universal pattern of deviation from the natural fertility and m representing the degree of which voluntary control of fertility is exercised that varies from population to population. The five-year age group (a) based on values of n (a) and v (a) shown here in tabular form were derived from empirical data (Coale and Trussell, 1974) and are assumed to be invariant over time and across populations.

Five-year values of n (a) and v (a)

	Age group						
	15–19	20–24	25–29	30–34	35–39	40–44	45–49
n (a)	0.41	0.46	0.43	0.40	0.32	0.17	0.02
v (a)	0	0	–0.28	–0.67	–1.04	–1.41	–1.67

Therefore, the model can be fitted to any population whose marital fertility rates are known just by identifying the values of the parameters M and m. The above model can be written in a simpler form so that the parameters can be estimated suitably by using the method of ordinary least square (OLS), as suggested by Coale and Trussell (1978). Thus,

$$\ln [r(a)/n(a)] = \ln M + m \cdot v(a) \qquad (2)$$

which shows that the relation between ln [r (a)/n (a)] and v (a) is of the linear form: y = c + mx. Thus, ln M and m can be estimated simply by OLS in which no single point has relatively more weight than any other. In the present study OLS considering the age groups from 15–19 to 40–44; the OLS regression equations are

$$\Sigma \ln [r(a)/n(a)] = n(\ln M) + m \bullet \Sigma v(a)$$

$$\Sigma v(a) \ln [r(a)/n(a)] = \ln M\, \Sigma v(a) + m \bullet \Sigma [v(a)]^2,$$

where n is the number of data points used.

Table 5.16 Reported and estimated age-specific marital fertility rates by types of residence, West Bengal: 1990–91.

Age group	West Bengal		Rural		Urban	
	r (a)	$\hat{r}$ (a)	r (a)	$\hat{r}$ (a)	r (a)	$\hat{r}$ (a)
15–19	0.16	0.15	0.17	0.17	0.13	0.10
20–24	0.19	0.17	0.21	0.19	0.13	0.11
25–29	0.13	0.13	0.15	0.15	0.09	0.09
30–34	0.08	0.09	0.10	0.11	0.05	0.06
35–39	0.05	0.06	0.06	0.07	0.03	0.04
40–44	0.03	0.03	0.04	0.03	0.02	0.01
P.E.		8.50		7.00		14.00
TMFR	3.23	3.17	3.58	3.56	2.23	2.03

TMFR = Total marital fertility rate
P.E. = Per cent error
$\hat{r}$ (a) = Estimated marital fertility rates by age (a)

The estimated marital fertility rates obtained by using Coale's model for West Bengal as a whole as well as by types of residence are presented in Table 5.16.

The observed and model estimates of total marital fertility rates are placed side by side in the Table 5.16 for comparison. The table shows that observed and estimated age-specific marital fertility estimates are reasonably of the same order of magnitude. The data do not permit the application of statistical test of significance for judging the fitting of Coale's model of marital fertility for West Bengal. However the fitting is being evaluated by examining the per cent errors obtained as

$$\text{Per cent error} = 100 * \Sigma |r(a) - \hat{r}(a)| / \Sigma r(a)$$

This statistic indicates the absolute error between the observed and model schedules as a percentage of the area under the observed schedule.

Here, the sum has been taken over all observed values (15–19 to 45–49), not merely over the values used in the regression to obtain M and m as suggested by Coale and Trussell (1978). From the values of observed age-specific marital fertility rates, r (a) and estimated values of $\hat{r}$ (a) given in the Table 5.16, the per cent errors have been worked out. The errors of less than 10 per cent are found in almost all cases excepting for urban areas in 1991; these are indicative of moderately good fit, which is further substantiated by the mean square error (m.s.e.) values of 0.015 in 1991 obtained by

$$\text{m.s.e.} = \Sigma[\ln r(a) - \ln \hat{r}(a)]^2 / n$$

The values, of 'm' that indicates the degree to which the fertility is controlled, have been estimated for the age groups 25–29 to 40–44 and the positive values of 'm' indicate that marital fertility in West Bengal falls increasingly short of natural fertility. This suggests that some couples have been practising the family planning methods voluntarily to limit family size.

In estimating the values of 'm' required to make the model exact for each age interval, the equation is,

$$m_a = \ln[r(a)/ M^*n(a)]/ v(a),$$

where $M = r(20\text{–}24) / m(20\text{–}24)$ as a scale factor used.

An estimate of a single value of 'm' has been obtained as the average of the m_a and the values of m_a for the individual age groups have been similar to that of average m_a. The values of 'M' and 'm' are presented in Table 5.17 for 1991.

Table 5.17 Indices of fertility level (M) and fertility control (m): 1991.

Population	Index of fertility level, M	Mean index of fertility control, m_a	m_a (by age group)			
			25–29	30–34	35–39	40–44
West Bengal	0.37	0.65	0.65	0.65	0.65	0.65
Rural	0.41	0.59	0.59	0.59	0.59	0.59
Urban	0.24	0.74	0.74	0.74	0.74	0.74

By means of the framework of the Coale's model, marital fertility of the population of West Bengal has been analyzed in relation to the natural fertility (Henry, 1961).

'If the equation used to calculate "m" were fully valid and the typical age pattern of controlled fertility appropriately estimated, the separately determined values of 'm' for each age group would all be identical (Knodel, 1977)'. The different values of 'm' (Table 5.17) across the age groups are all nearly equal in census year and the magnitudes of these values are also consistent with the patterns of family limitations practices in West Bengal. The accuracy of age pattern of marital fertility by the method could thus be attained. Since the Coale's model does not take in to account the differences in composition of population groups by marriage duration, this may however affect the above fertility estimates.

The level of fertility for each population group relative to the natural fertility schedule is indexed by M (Table 5.17). The M values are all below unity, apparently indicating substantial family limitation practices. But it seems reasonable to assume that the low level of M is not necessarily dependent solely on voluntary control of fertility in the situation of poor nutritional levels affecting fecundity (Frish, 1975).

6
Nuptiality Analysis

6.1 INTRODUCTION AND THE NEED FOR THE STUDY OF NUPTIALITY

Marriage, as a demographic phenomenon, changes population composition by exerting its influence on the population. The attention of planners and policy makers has been drawn to the role of nuptiality for the fact that delayed age at marriage can significantly contribute in reducing fertility which has direct impact on population growth. Nuptiality patterns and levels have also certain implications for non-demographic socio-economic fields such as: raising the age at marriage would permit a greater exposure to young adults for non familiar activities including education, greater mobility opportunities, and attractive labour markets for both sexes. Avoidance of very early child bearing certainly contributes to the health of the mother and children (Westoff, 1975). Lestheaghe (1971) has pointed out those classical indices characterizing nuptiality schedules such as mean age at marriage yield rather less satisfactory information since they don't allow for the specification of the age at which marriages start, nor the tempo at which nuptiality schedules proceed. Therefore, in order to have a clear and complete picture about the age patterns of marriage, it is worthwhile to know at which age marriage starts, along with the tempo of marriage, age span of first marriage and first marriage frequency. The knowledge of the nuptiality parameters helps to study the nuptiality process in depth. In exploring the importance of nuptiality studies in general, and for developing countries in particular, we may begin with D.V. Glass's (1963) comments:

'For demographers, there is ample reason to devote far more attention to marriage. It is through the intervening variable of marriage that replacement indices become sociologically meaningful. In the more developed societies, recent changes in the level and trend of fertility owe much to the changes in the amount of, and age at, marriage. The study of marital patterns and trends in less developed societies is of still greater importance.'

First, marital status is an element of population composition, which is of considerable importance. It is a significant factor in population dynamics as it affects fertility to a large extent. It has a direct bearing on the computation of reproduction rates. By examining the proportions single at various ages it is possible to judge whether first marriages are more or less frequent as well as how precocious they are. As a rule, Western countries have low intensive nuptiality, i.e., high proportion of single person aged 45–50, a proportion that is very close to the proportion of those who never marry at all. 'It is obvious', says Dorn (1936), 'that a population with two children per married woman and with 80 per cent of the women married is more fertile than a similar population with three children per married woman, but in which only 50 per cent of the women are married'. Nonetheless, the effect of nuptiality on other social economic characteristics such as school attendance, labour force participation, etc., is also not totally insignificant. In fact, proportions single are very useful indicators of socio-economic and cultural difference between regions, countries and between different segments of a population. To cite a simple example, the fact that in India about 80 per cent of males and less than 4 per cent of females in the age group 15 and above are single as against 53 and 45 per cent respectively in Ireland clearly demonstrates the socio cultural differences existing between the two societies.

Second, age at marriage is an important aspect of the study of nuptiality. A recent paper has shown (Westoff and Ryder, 1977) that the age at first marriage is the single best predictor of the level of completed fertility. This aspect of nuptiality, therefore, becomes relevant and significant in the context of a population policy, which seeks to regulate fertility.

Third, age patterns of marriage have been found to play an important role in determining growth rates of human population. A very rapid rise in population growth in Europe in the latter half of eighteenth century might have been due to the lowering of the average age at marriage and an increase in the proportions marrying. It is only quite recently that account has been taken of the effect of different marriage rates or rates of nuptiality on population growth. The combined effect of a given age structure of mortality, nuptiality and fertility of married and unmarried women on growth rate seems to be significant. In India, almost all the births occur in marriage and changes in age at marriage and marriage rates are reflected in the rates of formation of couples. It is, therefore, essential in the analysis of fertility and reproduction of certain periods and generations to consider the rate at which women at different ages marry and the rate at which married women have children. Again, duration of marriage is known to be an efficient determinant of the first few birth-intervals.

Nuptiality studies have many other uses. Marriage rates are combined into nuptiality tables and a more exhaustive mathematical analysis of population, like disaggregated projection by marital status, calculation of nuptial reproduction rates, construction of mathematical models incorporating marriage (of one or both sexes), can be made for a deeper understanding of population problems.

While discussing the importance of undertaking nuptiality studies, it has been stressed (IUSSP, 1974): 'one of the areas which has been relatively neglected in macro studies is the subject of nuptiality. The dynamics of nuptiality are still only imperfectly understood and a study of the factors, which influence the formation and dissolution of not only legal marriage, but of sexual unions, in general, would repay investigation. In particular, a study of the relation between economic variables and nuptiality in different countries and culture needs to be undertaken, and the relationship between nuptiality and fertility to be examined'.

In 1972, the Economic and Social Council of the United Nations decided to place on the agenda of the World Population Conference, 1974, and item on the World Population Plan of Action (WPPA). To achieve reduction of fertility one of the measures proposed in the Plan of Action was to establish and appropriate lower limit for age at marriage, for it was taken as an important factor influencing fertility (Conception, 1974). It had been pointed out that raising the age at marriage, at least in high fertility countries, would dampen the future population growth. In this context, analytical studies on the relationship between age at marriage and fertility would assume importance.

6.2 SOURCES OF DATA AND THEIR LIMITATIONS

The most prolific source of marriage data in India is the national population censuses. The censuses have their own limitations. They provide information only on the age distribution relating to martial status such as never married, married, divorced, separated and widowed. The census in India does not provide information on the order of marriage. It is to be noted that data relating to marital status by age and sex are available by type of residence only but not by religion nor by any other socio-economic factors since 1931 (Agarwala, 1962).

We also used data from the national population censuses of Bangladesh as well as from the Bangladesh Fertility Survey (BFS, 1976). The national population census of 1961 (erstwhile East Pakistan) has also been used. Only to draw a trend line, 1961 census has been considered. Bangladesh has conducted its first census in 1974; second one in 1981 and later on in 1991. Some other survey data of 1994 and 1996–97 have been used. Many relevant data needed to make a comparative study are not readily available from Bangladesh. So, data constraints may be the setback while we compare the results of West Bengal with that of the results of Bangladesh. It is to be mentioned that both Indian Census data for 2001 as well as Bangladesh Census data for 2001 are still yet to be published so we are handicapped due to non-availability of data to date. Therefore we have used available data sets in our study. We have a desire to study further when the data will be available later on.

6.3 DEFINITION OF NUPTIALITY

According to the latest international demographic terminology (Grebenik and Hill, 1974), the term 'nuptiality' is used to denote the whole subject of the formation and dissolution of sexual unions, including the study of marriage, consensual unions, separation, divorce, widowhood etc. It is also used, in a narrower sense, as synonym for marriage in such terms as 'nuptiality rates' and 'nuptiality probabilities'. The study of nuptiality deals with the frequency of marriage, i.e., unions between persons of opposite sexes which involve rights and obligations fixed by law and custom; with the characteristics of persons united in marriage, and with the dissolution of such unions (United Nations, 1958).

Marriage may be considered as the focus of the process of family formation. Winch (1968) has defined marriage as a culturally approved relationship of one man and one woman (monogamy), of one man and two or more women (polygyny), or of one woman and two or more men (polyandry), in which there is cultural endorsement of sexual intercourse between the marital partners of opposite sex and generally the expectation that children will be born of the relationship. The term 'nuptiality' will be used in the sense of the study of marriage only, due to the following reason:

(a) The categories divorced and separated form only very insignificant proportion of the total and the married population;

(b) The proportion widowed reflects mostly the mortality condition of the population as remarriages are assumed to be negligible;
(c) Consensual unions are practically non-existent.

6.4 TERMINOLOGY USED IN THE STUDY OF NUPTIALITY

The terminology relating to nuptiality has been described is as follows:

Marriage: Legal union of persons of opposite sex. The term has been used to denote the study of marriage.

First marriage: First legal union entered by a person. Marriages have been assumed to be first marriages. Loose synonym: Marriage.

Nuptiality: The term has been used to denote the study of marriage.

Nuptiality status or civil status: The legal status of an individual in relation to marriage. The usual range is

Single, meaning never married;
currently married or evermarried;
Widowed;
divorced or separated.

The term evermarried has been used to denote the complement of never married.

Marriage or nuptiality rate: Taken as the ratio of the number of first marriages of one sex during a period to the number of person-years lived as single by that sex in the population during the same period. Usually specified for a given age.

Marriage or nuptiality probability: The ratio of the first marriages is considered during a period to the total single population of the same sex at the beginning of the period.

Crude marriage rate: It has been computed as the ratio of the number of marriages occurring in a population during a year to the average population living during the same year.

$$\text{CMR} = \frac{\text{M}}{\text{P}} \times 1000$$

This sort of measure also suffers from the usual defects of a crude rate. The numerator of the rate uses the number of marriages. However, marriage involves two persons and if we use the number of persons getting married during the year, the rate becomes twice as large. Further, the entire population used cannot be considered as the population exposed to the risk of marriage, as the very young and the persons who are already married do not belong to the exposed category.

General Marriage Rate (GMR)

The denominator of the CMR discussed above is not wholly the population exposed to the risk of marriage. A more refined measure we can calculate is by taking the persons of marriageable ages as the denominator. The rate thus obtained is called General Marriage Rate and defined by the relation is of the form:

$$\text{GMR} = \frac{\text{M}}{\text{P}_{15+}} \times 1000$$

Here the total number of marriages in the year is again employed in the numerator and the population aged 15 above is used in the denominator. Taking account of unmarried persons in the marriageable ages and sex composition of the population can make further refinement. An alternative definition is of the form:

$$\text{GMR} = \frac{\text{M}}{\text{Unmarried persons aged P}_{15+}} \times 1000$$

This rate, anyone can calculate separately for males and females. Since rate of marriage between males and females would differ depending upon the sex ratio of the population, it calls for the calculation of marriage rates separately for males and females. As remarriage is also possible, it may be necessary to identify the numerator by the order of the marriage as first, second, etc., and the denominator should then be adjusted accordingly.

Age-specific Marriage Rate (ASMR)

As is GMR defined earlier partially controls the age distribution of the population, the internal variations in age composition within the marriageable population are not taken into these rates. It is to be noted that as generally husbands tend to be older than wives, the age-specific rate would be different for the sexes. Hence, it is more advisable to have age-specific marriage rate. The Age-specific marriage rate is of the relation as follows:

$$\text{ASMR} = \frac{{}_nM_x}{{}_nP_x} \times 1000$$

${}_nM_x$ = number of marriages in a year between ages x and x + n
${}_nP_x$ = number of persons in the age group x to x + n

We can compute ASMR separately for males and females. Instead of number of persons in the age group x, to x + n, number of unmarried persons can also be used in the denominator. As remarriages are possible, it is possible to re-enter the married state. So, it is important to have order-specific marriage rate. The generally used measure is Age-specific First Marriage Rate (ASFMR).

$$\text{Hence, ASFMR} = \frac{{}_nM_x^1}{{}_nP_x^0} \times 1000$$

${}_nM^1_x$ = number of first marriages in a year in the age group x to x + n
${}_nP^0_x$ = number of single or unmarried persons in the same age group and eligible for marriage for the first time.

Age Order-specific Marriage Rate (AOSMR)

We can define the number of marriages of a given order 'i' in a specified age category, per thousand persons of the same age group at the order i–1 during a period of time is as follows.

$$\text{AOSMR} = \frac{{}_nM_x^i}{{}_nP_x^{i-1}} \times 1000$$

${}_nM^i_x$ = number of ith order in the age group x to x + n

${}_nP^{i-1}_x$ = persons in the same age group whose (i–1)th marriage remains dissolved and they are eligible for the ith marriage.

Total Marriage Rate (TMR)

As that of TFR used in fertility analysis, it is also possible to derive a Total Marriage Rate (TMR) from the ASMR. The value of TMR indicates the total number of years in a synthetic cohort passing through life together. Thus,

$$\text{TMR} = \Sigma(\text{ASMR})$$

The rates for all ages are given equal weights in this measure,

6.5 SINGULATE MEAN AGE AT MARRIAGE (SMAM)

We can simply estimate the SMAM by using the relation given as follows:

$$\text{SMAM} = \frac{15.0 + n\sum {}_nS_x - K.S_k}{1 - S_k}$$

where the quantity 15.0 is the number of person-years lived in the single state from birth to age 15 by the hypothetical cohort (i.e. it is assumed that no one marries before age 15)

n (=5) is the age interval,

$\sum_{15}^{49} {}_nS_x$ is the sum of proportion single from age 15 to 49,

K is 50 i.e., proportion never marrying at age 50 and will remain so for the rest of the life.

S_k is the proportion remaining single between age group 45–49 and 50–54 i.e. $({}_{49}S_{45} + {}_{54}S_{50})/2)$.

Alternative Ways of Computing SMAM

Estimation of Singulate Mean Age at Marriage (Hajnal, 1953)

The steps of the computational procedure are as follows:

1. **Calculation of proportion single for a given sex (population aged 15–54):** Dividing the number of single in each age group by the total population in the same age group. The resulting proportion for the age group from 5i + 10 to 5i + 14 is denoted by U (i), with 'i' usually ranging from 1 to 8.
2. **Calculation of person-years lived in the single state:** Adding the proportion single in each age group up to and including that for the age group 45–49 (i = 7) and multiplying the sum by 5. The resulting quantity is denoted by RS_1, and $RS_2 = RS_1 + 15.0$, where 15.0 is the number of person-years lived in the single state from birth to age 15 by the hypothetical cohort of size one being considered. If the lower limit at which marriage takes place is changed to some other age x, the x should be substituted for 15 and the calculation of RS_1 should include all age groups from x to x + 4 (when x is a multiple of 5) to 45–49.
3. **Estimation of proportion who ever marries:** The proportion remaining single at age 50 is estimated as

$$RN = (U (7) + U (8))/2.0,$$

Where U (7) is the proportion single (never married) among those aged 45–49, and U(8) is the equivalent proportion among those aged 50–54. Once the proportion remaining single at age 50 is estimated, the proportion ever marrying by that age, RM, is clearly just its compliment, that is, RM =1.0–RN

4. **Calculation of number of person-years lived by those not marrying:** Since RN is estimated to be the proportion of those who have not married by age 50, the total time spent in the single state by this group is

$$RS_3 = 50.0 * RN$$

5. **Calculation of singlulate mean age at marriage (SMAM):** The value of SMAM is calculated as follows:

$$SMAM = (RS_2 - RS_3)/RM$$

That is, the value of SMAM as calculated here is, those who married before age 50 spent the average number of years in the single state. SMAM (Hajnal, 1953) can be calculated with the data presented below and the result should be equal if we apply the methods mentioned here in the text. But we have the estimates of SMAM based on the method developed by Hajnal, 1953 elsewhere in the text. The estimation of SMAM for female by Hajnal's method is given as an illustration below:

Female population in West Bengal, 1991

Age group	Total female population, TFi	Total never married female population, TNFi	Proportion single, Female ${}_nS^f_x$
15–19	2984759	1978721	0.6629
20–24	3092250	601723	0.1946
25–29	3050477	195640	0.0641
30–34	2342186	82874	0.0354
35–39	1989018	34800	0.0175
40–44	1487530	23570	0.0158
45–49	1307493	10765	0.0082
50–54	1101358	12320	0.0112

Illustration

$5x\sum_{i=1}^{7} {}_nS^f_x = 0.9985$ where ${}_nS^f_x$ indicates the proportion single for females

$$RS^f_1 = 4.9925;$$
$$RS^f_2 = 15.0 + 4.9925 = 19.99$$
$$RN^f = [0.0082 + 0.0112]/2$$
$$= 0.0097$$
$$RM^f = 1.0 - RN^f$$
$$= 1.0 - 0.0097$$
$$= 0.9903$$
$$RS^f_3 = 50.0 \times RN^f$$
$$= 50.0 \times 0.0097$$
$$= 0.485$$
$$SMAM^f = [RS^f_2 - RS^f_3]/ RM^f$$
$$= [19.99 - 0.485]/0.9903$$
$$SMAM^f = 19.70 \text{ years}$$

Note on Computational procedures of estimating Singulate Mean Age at Marriage (SMAM) by alternative way

Observed percentage never married female, West Bengal, 1991

Age group Percentage	15–19	20–24	25–29	30–34	35–39	40–44	45–49	50–54
Never married	66.29	19.46	6.41	3.54	1.75	1.58	0.82	1.12

In the standard calculation of SMAM, two key assumptions are made. Firstly, nobody will marry under the age of 15 and secondly, those still never married at age fifty will remain so for the rest of their lives. With these assumptions in mind one should preferably separate the population by sex and then extract or calculate from the census data the proportions never married in the eight quinquennial age groups 15–54 as given above. It is these that will form the basis of calculation of SMAM as given as follows:

The first stage is to calculate mean number of years of 'singleness' lived per hundred persons for the population under study (i.e., percentage).

For those aged under 15, since it is assumed that no one of this age will marry, calculation is straightforward, being 15 years of 100 per cent:

$$15 \times 100 = 1{,}500$$

To calculate the years of singleness for those aged 15–49 one simply aggregates the quinquennial means of the six age groups and multiplies the result by 5 to gain the figure in single years:

$$(66.29 + 19.46 + 6.41 + 3.54 + 1.75 + 1.58 + 0.82) \times 5$$
$$= \text{Total Years of Singleness 15–49}$$
$$99.85 \times 5 = 499.25,$$

Therefore, the total number of years of singleness experienced per hundred persons of the population until age fifty is:

$$1{,}500 + 499.25 = 1999.25$$

However, some individuals in the population will remain unmarried throughout their lives, one needs to adjust this figure to take account of this situation. On the assumption that those who are still unmarried by the age of fifty will remain so, the proportion of population who remain permanently celibate or never married can be measured from an estimation of the proportion never married at age fifty by averaging the proportions never married of two quinquennial age groups 45–49 and 49–54:

$$(0.82 + 1.12)/2 = 1.94/2 = 0.97$$

Therefore, the estimated numbers of years of singleness experienced by those never married by age fifty is:

$$0.97 \times 50 = 48.5$$

Consequently, for those in the population marrying, the total number of years of singleness experienced per hundred of the whole population is:

$$1999.25 - 48.5 = 1950.75$$

However, the actual proportion of the population who married by age fifty is:

$$100 - 0.97 = 99.03$$

This relates to 99.03 females per hundred in the 1991 population of West Bengal experiencing a total of 1950.75 years of singleness before they get married, giving a Singulate Mean Age at Marriage (SMAM) of:

$$1950.73/99.03 = 19.698 \approx 19.70 \text{ years}$$

Measure of mean age at first marriage obtained from a set of proportions single at different ages or in different age groups. Synonym: Mean Age at Marriage or Average Age at Marriage.

Gross nuptiality table

This life table may also be computed from a set of age-specific nuptiality probabilities with only one attrition, namely, marriage.

Net nuptiality table

A double decrement table is computed from a set of age-specific nuptiality probabilities together with a set of age-specific survival probabilities.

6.6 ESTIMATION OF NUPTIALITY PROBABILITIES

The basic idea for the calculation of nuptiality probabilities is the proportions single in the decade synthetic cohort (Agarwala, 1962; Census Centenary, India, 1972). The synthetic cohort is a hypothetical cohort subject to the average marriage experience of the decade in question. The basic of the method adopted here for the estimation of nuptiality probabilities for a decade is due to Mertens (1965).

Methodology

Let a cohort of single persons be traced over time from the youngest age at which marriage may occur. The incidence of mortality is assumed to be the same for the single as for the total population and the single population to be depleted by two modes of decrement, namely, marriage and death. The symbols that have been used are as follows:

P_x = Population living at age, x.

S_x = Number single at age, x.

s_x = Proportion single at age, x.

${}_5n_x$ = Five year nuptiality or marriage probability i.e., probability that a single person at age x will marry during next five year.

Following Mertens, the basic equation for the estimation of five-year nuptiality probability is as follows:

$${}_5n_x = (S_x - S_{x+5})/S_x.$$

By utilizing the proportions single in the decade synthetic cohort and using the equation given above it is possible to calculate the basic function ${}_5n_x$ in a nuptiality table. The proportions single for any decade synthetic cohort will be obtained in quinquennial age groups. As a first step, these quinquennial proportions will be converted to proportions single s_x at exact age, x, by a combination of Sprague multipliers and linear interpolation (Jaffe, 1960; Saveland and Glick, 1969).

To obtain a smooth distribution of the proportions single the multipliers may not be always suitable because they simply distribute the proportions single within the five year age groups and if any particular five year age group is in error such deficiencies are not be taken account of. In such a situation, graphic graduation (Tetley, 1946) seems to be the best and, as such, may be used to smooth further the proportions single at exact ages as obtained by Sprague multipliers and linear interpolation. The values of the graduated proportions are read off from this graph at intervals of five years of age. Having obtained these graduated values of s_x, the five-year nuptiality probabilities, $_5n_x$,are calculated. Free hand smoothing to remove any irregularities further smoothes these probabilities. It should be noted that nuptiality probabilities change very rapidly and as such the use of multipliers and graduation by graphic method is sometimes prone to produce unsatisfactory results, particularly for the younger ages of the nuptiality span.

6.7 CONSTRUCTION NUPTIALITY TABLES

(A) Gross Nuptiality Tables

Column 1: x: Age in years

Column 2: $_5n_x$: Probability that a single person at age, x will marry during next five years.

Column 3: l_x: Number single at age, x.

Column 4: $_5N_x$: Number of first marriages in the age group (x, x + 5).

Column 5: $_5L_x$: Number of years lived as single in the age group (x, x + 5).

Column 6: T_x: Number of years lived as single above age, x.

Column 7: e_x^0: Average number of years of single life remaining before marriage to a single person at age, x.

The following relations hold good:

$$l_x (1 - {_5n_x}) = l_{x+5}$$

$$l_x \cdot {_5n_x} = {_5N_x}$$

$$_5L_x = \frac{5}{2}(l_x + l_{x+5})$$

$$T_x = \sum {_5L_{5i}}; \quad e_x^0 = T_x/l_x$$

(B) Net Nuptiality Tables

Column 1: x: Age in years

Column 2: ${}_5n'_x$: Probability that a single person at age, x will marry during next five years.

Column 3: ${}_5q'_x$: Probability that a single person at age, x will die during next five years.

Column 4: l'_x: Number single and alive at age, x.

Column 5: ${}_5d'_x$: Number dying as single in the age group (x, x + 5)

Column 6: ${}_5N'_x$: Number of first marriages in the age group (x, x + 5).

Column 7: ${}_5L'_x$: Person years lived as single and alive in the age group (x, x + 5).

Column 8: T'_x : Person years lived as single and alive above age x.

Column 9: e'^0_x: Average number of years of single life remaining before marriage or death to a single person at age, x.

The following relations hold good:

$$
\begin{aligned}
{}_5n'_x &= {}_5n_x\,(1 - 1/2\,.\,{}_5q_x)\\
{}_5q'_x &= {}_5q_x(1 - 1/2\,.\,{}_5n_x)\\
l'_{x+5} &= l'_x - {}_5N'_x - {}_5d'_x\\
{}_5N'_x &= l'_x\,.\,{}_5n'_x\\
{}_5d'_x &= l'_x\,.\,{}_5q'_x
\end{aligned}
$$

$$
{}_5L'_x = \frac{5}{2}\,(l'_x + l'_{x+5})
$$

$$
T'_x = \sum_{i=x/5}^{\infty} {}_5L'_{5i}\,;\; e^{0\prime}_x = T'_x/l'_x
$$

It is to be noted that the probabilities as used in the net tables depend on two modes of decrement, marriages and death, whereas those in the gross tables are independent probabilities assuming marriage to be the only mode of decrement. The prime (′) has been used to denote functions of the two decrements, marriage and death.

Table 6.1 Gross nuptiality tables for single males for 1901–1911 to 1961–1971, India.

x	${}_5n_x$	l_x	${}_5N_x$	${}_5L_x$	T_x	e_x^0
(1)	(2)	(3)	(4)	(5)	(6)	(7)
0	—	100000	—	500000	2335679	23.35
5	—	100000	—	500000	1835679	18.35
10	0.0887	100000	8870	477825	1335679	13.35
15	0.2655	91130	24195	395162	857854	9.41
20	0.4972	66935	33280	251475	462692	6.91
25	0.6531	33655	21980	113325	211217	6.28
30	0.5120	11675	5978	43430	97892	8.38
35	0.3374	5697	1922	23680	54462	9.56
40	0.2143	3775	809	16852	30782	8.15
45	0.1212	2966	360	13930	13930	4.70

Table 6.2 Net nuptiality tables for single males for 1901–1911 to 1961–1971, India.

x	${}_5n'_x$	${}_5q'_x$	l'_x	${}_5d'_x$	${}_5N'_x$	${}_5L'_x$	T'_x	$e_x^{0'}$
0	—	0.19159	100000	19159	—	409783	1878421	18.78
5	—	0.01395	80841	1128	—	401385	1468638	18.17
10	0.0886	0.00217	79713	173	7062	380478	1067253	13.39
15	0.2634	0.01367	72478	991	19091	312185	686775	9.48
20	0.4927	0.01352	52396	708	25816	195670	374590	7.15
25	0.6457	0.01519	25872	393	16706	86612	178920	6.92
30	0.5026	0.02722	8773	239	4409	32245	92308	10.52
35	0.3265	0.05386	4125	222	1347	16703	60063	14.56
40	0.2043	0.08316	2556	213	522	10942	43360	16.96
45	0.1140	0.11121	1821	202	208	8080	32418	17.80
50	—	0.14873	1411	210	—	6530	24338	17.25
55		0.18754	1201	225		5442	17808	14.88
60		0.23181	976	226		4315	12366	12.67
65		0.28303	750	212		3220	8051	10.73
70		0.34232	538	184		2230	4831	8.98
75		0.40814	354	144		1410	2601	7.35
80		—	210	—		—	1191	5.67

Source: C.R. Malakar, 1978.

6.8 AGE PATTERNS OF MARRIAGE

Proportions single by age group of females at different times

Table 6.3 presents the proportions single by age groups of females for West Bengal (1961–1991) and Bangladesh (1961–1991) respectively. The table shows that the proportions single up to age groups 30–34 have increased over time. For example, proportions single have increased in age-group 10–14 from 0.820 in 1961 to 0.980 in 1991, in age-group 15–19 from 0.253 in 1961 to 0.663 in 1991, in age-group 20–24 from 0.075 in 1961 to 0.195 in 1991, in age-group 25–29 from 0.028 in 1961 to 0.064 in 1991 and in age-group 30–34 from 0.017 in 1961 to 0.035 in 1991 in West Bengal. Bangladesh has also observed the rising trend in proportions single up to age groups 25–29 over time. The increase in proportions single after age groups 30–34 in West Bengal and age groups 25–29 in Bangladesh are irregular which might be the result of age misreporting (as indicated by Whipple's Index ($W_{0,5}$) for females in West Bengal (in 1981is 281.36 and is 268.20 in 1991 which suggests very rough(>175), Myers' Index is 56.34 in 1981 and 56.19 in 1991 suggesting the effect of poor education though the literacy level is increased to some extent and the UN Joint Score is 59.31 in 1961 and 30.49 in 1991 indicating the inaccuracy because the value lies between 20–40, if it is < 20 it indicates accurate reporting (Saha, 1997) and misreporting of marital status but though the values of these indices for Bangladesh are not available, so, it may be assumed that the values might be similar in Bangladesh to that in West Bengal. The singulate mean age at marriage (SMAM) (Hajnal, 1953) has increased from 16.80 in1961 to 19.70 in 1991 in West Bengal. The value of SMAM provided by Sample Registration System (SRS) for 1991 is 19.3 and for 1994 are 19.5. Both the estimates provided by SRS are lower compared to the estimate of 19.70 in 1991 based on census. This might be due to under-estimation of SMAM by SRS. To cite an example, as in the case of death rate, it was underestimated in the SRS by a margin of 16 per cent for India in 1980–82. Though SRS is the best available source in India, it provides deficient estimates.

Table 6.3 Observed proportions single in different years: West Bengal and Bangladesh.

	West Bengal				Bangladesh*				
Age gr.	1961	1971	1981	1991	1961	1974	1976	1981	1991
10–14	0.820	0.974	0.976	0.980	0.674	0.905	0.912	0.930	0.968
15–19	0.253	0.466	0.611	0.663	0.083	0.255	0.298	0.310	0.487
20–24	0.075	0.123	0.188	0.195	0.013	0.032	0.046	0.051	0.105
25–29	0.028	0.052	0.058	0.064	0.005	0.009	0.010	0.013	0.024
30–34	0.017	0.019	0.021	0.035	0.004	0.006	0.002	0.010	0.011
35–39	0.009	0.013	0.010	0.018	0.002	0.004	0.004	0.004	0.006
40–44	0.007	0.007	0.007	0.016	0.002	0.005	0.001	0.007	0.006
45–49	0.006	0.006	0.005	0.008	0.001	0.003	0.005	0.003	0.004
50–54	0.005	0.006	0.005	0.011	0.001	0.003	0.005	0.014	0.005
SMAM (Hajnal, 1953)	16.80	18.24	19.36	19.70	15.52	16.43	16.73	16.71	18.07
SMAM (Trussell, 1976)	15.33	17.80	19.04	19.26	13.74	15.51	16.21	16.35	17.86
MAM (Trussell, 1976)	14.73	17.00	18.25	18.56	13.22	15.06	15.60	15.82	17.21

* Islam (1996)

Table 6.4 Percentage distribution of women ever married aged 15–19 and 45–49: West Bengal.

Age group	1961	1971	1981	1991	1992–93
15–19	74.70	53.40	38.90	33.70	41.40
45–49	99.40	99.40	99.50	99.20	98.60

Table 6.5 Singulate mean age at marriage by type of residence in different time points: West Bengal.

Residence	1961*	1961–71**	1971	1971–81	1981	1981–91	1991	1992–93
Rural	16.04	17.29	17.52	18.43	18.52	18.69	18.87	18.10
Urban	19.33	20.13	20.17	21.20	21.39	21.40	21.78	21.80

* Hajnal (1953) for one period;

** Agarwala (1962) for two periods

6.9 DERIVATION OF A COHORT SCHEDULE AND ITS ANALYSIS

The essential feature of cohort analysis is that it considers the experience of one group of women over time, usually all those born or marrying during a particular time interval. These are in contrast to period analysis in which events occurring during a particular time period are studied. It is mainly used for explaining the levels and trends, rather than forecasting. There are three big problems associated with cohort analysis. The first is that it requires data in the form of a fairly long, consistent time series, and such data are not available in West Bengal as well as in Bangladesh. It has already been mentioned elsewhere that West Bengal as a state came into its own existence in 1947 and the 1951 census is the first census taken for West Bengal. So time series data are not available for long. The second is the problem known technically as 'censoring' – that one does not know what will happen in the future so that later experience of young or more recent cohort is unknown. The third is that it seems to be rather difficult to think about cohorts. The time-series data for Bangladesh are not available. The 1974 census is the first census conducted in Bangladesh after its independence in 1971; second one in 1981 and third but the last one in 1991. Therefore to carry on with cohort analysis for Bangladesh is difficult. Hence, the cohort analysis for Bangladesh has been ignored. In such a situation an attempt has been made to study the cohort analysis for West Bengal by converting the decennial censuses into quinquennial years.

For an ideal cohort analysis, nuptiality tables should be constructed to reflect the experience of an actual generation traced forward in time. However, it is well known that adequate historical data are not always available for carrying out an ideal cohort analysis, and such is the situation for nuptiality in both West Bengal and Bangladesh. Marital status data are available for West Bengal from 1951 onwards but the problem related to use of 1951 data has been discussed elsewhere. Therefore, we have considered data from 1961 onwards for West Bengal. As the census data are available at an interval of ten years, for the reconstruction of cohort data the intercensal estimates of proportions single in quinquennial age groups have been obtained by interpolating linearly between those in the consecutive censuses (Sadique, 1965).

Symbolically, denoting the proportions single in the age group (x, x + 5) at time 't' by ${}_5s^t_x$, we have

$$ {}_{5}S_{x}^{t+5} = \frac{{}_{5}S_{x}^{t} + {}_{5}S_{x}^{t+10}}{2} $$

where t and t + 10 corresponds to census years.

Thus the census synthetic cohorts were built up as a first step at an interval of five years. Table 6.6 shows the proportions single by quinquennial age groups at five-yearly intervals of time and the diagonals give the proportions single by birth cohorts (Table 6.7).

Table 6.6 Estimated proportions single by quinquennial years, 1961–91: West Bengal.

Age group	1961	1966	1971	1976	1981	1986	1991
15–19	0.253	0.359	0.466	0.538	0.611	0.637	0.663
20–24	0.075	0.099	0.123	0.156	0.188	0.191	0.195
25–29	0.028	0.040	0.052	0.055	0.058	0.061	0.064
30–34	0.017	0.018	0.019	0.020	0.021	0.028	0.035
35–39	0.009	0.011	0.013	0.012	0.012	0.014	0.018
40–44	0.007	0.007	0.007	0.007	0.007	0.010	0.012
45–49	0.006	0.006	0.006	0.005	0.005	0.007	0.008
50–54	0.005	0.005	0.006	0.005	0.005	0.008	0.011

Table 6.7 Female proportions single by birth cohorts in West Bengal: 1941–76.

Birth cohorts	15–19	20–24	25–29	30–34	35–39	40–44	45–49	SMAM
1941–46	0.253	0.099	0.052	0.020	0.012	0.010	0.008	16.98
1946–51	0.359	0.123	0.055	0.021	0.014	0.012	–	17.56
1951–56	0.466	0.156	0.058	0.028	0.018	–	–	18.18
1956–61	0.538	0.188	0.061	0.035	–	–	–	18.77
1961–66	0.611	0.191	0.064	–	–	–	–	19.18
1966–71	0.637	0.195	–	–	–	–	–	19.64
1971–76	0.663	–	–	–	–	–	–	19.97

6.10 ANALYSIS OF MARRIAGE PATTERN BY MEANS OF A MODEL NUPTIALITY SCHEDULE

It has been suggested that the standard form of first marriage frequencies i.e., first marriage experience of a cohort can be expressed by three parameters, a_0, K and C (Coale, 1971 and Coale & McNeil, 1972).

a_0-, the earliest age at which there are a significant number of first marriages. More precisely, the model implies that about one per cent of the populations who will eventually marry have done so by age a_0, so that a_0 is close to the first percentile of the distribution (Rodriguez and Trussell, 1980).

K-, a parameter which alters the shape of the curve, essentially by making it rise more or less steeply during the years shortly after a_0. Normal values of K range from roughly 0.2, indicating a very rapid rate of marriage after a_0, up to about 1.7, indicating very slow marriage. In fact, K-expresses the rate of marriage in terms of the number of years of nuptiality in the population being modeled that is equivalent to one year in a standard population. The standard used happens to be that of Swedish women (1865–69). The value of K in the standard is of course 1.0; and a value of 0.5 indicates a rate of marriage that is double that in the standard so that marriage that instead of say, 50 per cent marrying during, say, the ten years after a_0, 50 per cent would marry within five-years. This information on the background of K is not in any way relevant for the application of the model, but it is perhaps useful for understanding its interpretation.

C-, is simply a 'level' or 'scale' parameter, which indicates that, the proportion of women who ultimately marry. It ranges from 0.7 in the population such as Nineteenth Century Ireland, up to almost 1.0 in India or Bangladesh where nearly all women eventually marry. Because it simply scales the model, whereas the main interest is normally in the shape of the model, it can genetically be ignored.

6.11 ESTIMATION OF PARAMETERS a_0, K AND C

The method of estimating parameters a_0, K and C (Coale, 1971) is based on two sets of ratios of the proportion evermarried. R_1 is the ratio of proportion evermarried in the first five-year age interval (10–14) in which marriage occurs to the proportion evermarried in the second five year age interval (15–19). R_2 is the ratio of proportion evermarried in the second five-year age interval (15–19) to the proportion evermarried in the third five-year age interval (20–24) etc. A given value of any of these ratios (R_1, R_2 and R_3) can occur with different combination of 'K' and 'a_0'. If the experiences of the cohort were perfectly consistent with the transformed standard curve, the values of a_0 and K indicated by R_1, R_2 and by R_2, R_3 would be the same. A perfect fit is rare, the recommended procedure is to combine R_2 with R_1 if $R_1 > (1 - R_3)$, and with R_3 if $(1 - R_3) > R_1$ (Coale, 1971). Recommended procedure has been applied to the data of both West Bengal and Bangladesh (only for comparison we have considered Bangladesh as it was once the part of undivided Bengal) to estimate Coale's (1971) three parameters. Combinations of R_1 and R_2 or R_2 and R_3 whichever is applicable, have been made to fit the given data. An alternative procedure (i.e. a trial for the experiment)), is to combine R_2 with R_3 if $R_1 > (1 - R_3)$ and with R_1 if $(1 - R_3) > R_1$, which is just opposite to that of the recommended procedure, has been applied to National Family and Health Survey (NFHS, 1992–93) data only in case of West Bengal as an illustration and to substantiate the values of the parameters obtained from the recommended procedure.

The values of the ratios for different years of West Bengal and Bangladesh

	West Bengal			Bangladesh		
Ratio	1961	1991	1992–93	1961	1976	1991
R_1	0.243	0.059	0.063	0.356	0.153	0. 062
R_2	0.808	0.419	0.516	0.929	0.741	0. 573
R_3	0.952	0.860	0.864	0.992	0.962	0.917

The choice of a_0 and K as the location and scale parameters of the model is certainly valid, but somewhat arbitrary (Rodriguez and Trussell, 1980). Once the parameters a_0, K and C are estimated, the frequency of the first marriage, the risk of first marriage, the proportion evermarried and the person years lived in evermarried status can readily be estimated by Coale's (1971) method. The estimated values of a_0, K and C both for West Bengal and Bangladesh are presented in Table 6.8.

Table 6.8 Coale's three parameters of nuptiality age span of first marriage (A_0) and the maximum age at first marriage (A) for females: West Bengal and Bangladesh.

	West Bengal				Bangladesh		
Parameters	1961	1991	1992–93		1961	1976	1991
			Reco.	Alt.			
a_0	10.08	13.26	11.72	11.74	10.18	10.95	12.30
K	0.462	0.528	0.630	0.628	0.313	0.463	0.489
C	0.953	0.969	0.974	0.973	0.990	0.999	1.000
A_0	18.52	21.12	25.20	25.12	12.52	18.52	19.56
A	28.60	34.38	36.92	36.86	22.70	29.47	31.86

Note:	Reco. = Recommended Ratio	Alt. = Alternative Ratio
(i) if $R_1 > (1 - R_3)$	R_1 and R_2	R_2 and R_3
(ii) if $R_3 > R_1$	R_2 and R_3	R_1 and R_2

Table 6.8 presents the values of a_0, K and C; and A_0 and A for West Bengal as well as for Bangladesh over the years. Excepting in 1961, the values of a_0 are higher in West Bengal than in Bangladesh. But both West Bengal and Bangladesh have shown an increasing trend in a_0 over the years. For example, the value of a_0 has increased from 10.08 in 1961 to 13.26 in 1991 in West Bengal followed by the increase in the same from 10.18 in 1961 to 12.30 in 1991 in Bangladesh. Similarly, the values of K have increased over time consistently both in West Bengal and in Bangladesh. Also the values of C have increased over time. This study suggests the increase in initial age at marriage and in the values of proportion ultimately marrying up to age 50 over time but the increase in the values of K implies the slower marriage rate or decrease in the speed of marriage. The value of K in the standard is of course 1.0; and a value of 0.5 indicates a rate of marriage that is double than that in the standard what is also evidenced from the results of West Bengal in 1991. But, Bangladesh with lower value of K even in 1991 indicates faster rate of marriage than West Bengal. On the other hand, the value of a_0, obtained from the NFHS (1992–93) data for West Bengal by either procedure is misleading because the value is lower than the value obtained in 1991 census, which might have resulted from the flawness in NFHS data. The value of K is rather encouraging. But the results obtained by either procedure are almost identical. Almost all women in West Bengal as well as in Bangladesh ultimately marry up to age 50, which is evinced from the value of C because the value of C is very close to unity and it is evident from the values of PEM by age 50 shown earlier. But in others the value of C is as lower as 0.75 (Lestheaghe, 1971).

Note on: Computational procedures of estimating a_0, K, and C

Determining the values of Coale's three parameters of nuptiality, namely, a_0, K and C where

a_0 = Origin or age at which most of the marriages begin to take place

K = Tempo or speed with which marriages occur

C = Proportion ultimately evermarried

The fit of the standard schedules to the nuptiality of an actual cohort is an approximation. The procedure of determining a_0, K and C is as follows:

First of all the ratios R_1, R_2 and R_3 are calculated on the basis of where a_0 lies. For example, if lies between 10 and 15 years, then

$$R_1 = \frac{\text{Cumulative proportion of evermarried women aged (10–14)}}{\text{Cumulative proportion of evermarried women aged (15–19)}}$$

$$R_2 = \frac{\text{Cumulative proportion of evermarried women aged (15–19)}}{\text{Cumulative proportion of evermarried women aged (20–24)}}$$

$$R_3 = \frac{\text{Cumulative proportion of evermarried women aged (20–24)}}{\text{Cumulative proportion of evermarried women aged (25–29)}}$$

A given value of any of these (R_1, R_2 and R_3) can occur with different combinations of K and a_0, but if two ratios (i.e., R_1 and R_2) are specified, only one combination of K and a_0 is possible. Hence, K and a_0 can be estimated by locating (through interpolation in Table of Coale (1971) the values that would yield the observed R_1 and R_2 or of the observed R_2 and R_3. If the experience of the cohort were perfectly consistent with the transformed standard curve, the values of K and a_0 indicated by R_1 and R_2, and by R_2 and R_3 would be the same. The value of C is estimated by determining the person-years lived evermarried at the beginning and end of third five-year age interval (20 and 25 if marriages begin between 10 and 15) in the transformed standard schedule with the estimated values of K and a_0. Specifically, one determines,

$$K\,Zs\left[\frac{(20-a_0)}{K}\right] \text{ and } K\,Zs\left[\frac{(25-a_0)}{K}\right]$$

where Zs = the average number of persons-years lived evermarried in standard cohort not subject to mortality. The difference between these two, divided by 5.0, is the proportion evermarried in a cohort subject to a curve characterized by the calculated values of a_0 and K, and with the ultimate proportion evermarried of 1.0. The required estimate of C is then

(Cumulative proportion evermarried 20–25)/

$$\frac{K}{5}\left[Zs\left(\frac{20-a_0}{K}\right) - Zs\left(\frac{25-a_0}{K}\right)\right]$$

Zs values are available from Table, Coale (1971).

In a population with given a_0 and K, Mean (SMAM) and median age of the population can be computed (Trussell, 1976) as:

SMAM = a_0 + 11.37 K and,

Median Age = a_0 + 10.04 K.

6.12 CONSEQUENCES OF THE PARAMETRIC VALUES OF a_0, K AND C

Both A_0 and A can be derived on the basis of two parametric values of a_0 and K. Such as

(I) A_0 = 40 k, which measures the age span of first marriage within which majority of the first marriages occur. Table 6.8 shows that value of A_0 has been consistently increasing over the years in West Bengal as well as in Bangladesh.

(II) A = a_0 + 40 k, the maximum age beyond which first marriage is unlikely to occur. Table 6.8 shows that the values of A_0 and A have been increasing as the time passes on.

The study shows that first marriage among the females completes by age 37 years in West Bengal and by age 32 years in Bangladesh and those who are not getting married within this age, remained unmarried throughout the life or a very few first marriages can take place beyond the age A. In short, all the three parameters a_0, k and c jointly influence the nuptiality schedules such as age structure of first marriage frequencies and risk of first marriages etc. (Shrestha, 1983).

6.13 ESTIMATION OF PROPORTION EVERMARRIED

Let the proportion evermarried in age group (a, a + 5). Then π (a) = [Z (a + 5) – Z (a)], where Z (a + 5) denotes the person years lived in evermarried status up to age (a + 5) by a cohort subject to the schedule of first marriage frequency of the standard form. Z (a) = C.K.Z_s (X_s), where Z_s (X_s) in the standard average number of person years lived evermarried at age (X_s) in a cohort not subject to mortality and X_s = (a – a_0)/K is not chronological age, but a standardized age relative to the standard schedule. The fitted values of proportion evermarried π (a) are estimated by the relation Z (a) = C.K.Z_s (X_s). The estimated π (a) and observed proportion evermarried p (a) in age group 'a' to '(a + 5)' and the standardized residuals are shown in Table 6.9, Where na = total number of person age (a) completed years

$$E(a) = \frac{\sqrt{n(a)}(p(a) - \pi(a))}{\sqrt{\pi(a)(1 - \pi(a))}}$$

6.14 GOODNESS OF FIT OF THE MODEL

It is required to know about the knowledge of the parameters a_0, K and C when we fit the model nuptiality schedule. To fit the model nuptiality schedules, it assumes that the variations in mortality by marital status are negligible, nuptiality remains stable in the recent past and the population is closed against migration.

Table 6.9 Fitted and observed proportion evermarried by age of females and the standardized residuals: West Bengal, 1992–93.

Parameters	Recommended	Alternative
a_0	11.72	11.74
K	0.630	0.628
C	0.974	0.973

Proportion Evermarried			
Age (a)	Observed P (a)	Fitted π (a)	Residuals E (a)
15	0.0260	0.0263	–0.0688
20	0.4141	0.4143	–0.0141
25	0.8031	0.8027	–0.0324
30	0.9291	0.9281	0.1181
35	0.9723	0.9635	1.2290
40	0.9872	0.9735	2.1307
45	0.9725	0.9725	0
50	0.9859	0.9738	1.4273
$\chi_p^2 = \Sigma$ na $[p(a) - \pi(a)]^2/\pi(a)\,(1 - \pi(a))$			

$$\chi_p^2 = 1.5305, \quad V = m - 3 \text{ d.f.}$$
$$= 5 \text{ d.f.}$$

For example, this has been tested only in case of West Bengal (NFHS, 1992–93) to see if there is any discrepancy in using the values of a_0, K and C estimated by alternative procedure (Alt.).

To test the estimated parameters a_0, K and C obtained by alternative procedure is the application of Pearson's Chi-square statistics and standardized residuals test. It is found that the parameters estimated by alternative procedure have suitable application for (NFHS, 1992–93) data.

The observed nuptiality schedule is tested by means of Pearson's chi-square $\left(\chi_p^2\right)$ statistics. In the following example,

$$\chi_p^2 = \sum \frac{na(p(a) - \pi(a))^2}{\pi(a)(1 - \pi(a))}$$

It is distributed as χ_p^2 with v = m –3 degrees of freedom, m being the number of observations under considerations and n_a = total number of persons age (a) completed years. The null hypothesis to be tested is that the nuptiality schedules can be fitted only by three parameters to an observed schedule. $\chi_p^2 = 1.5305$ is insignificant at 5% level of significance. From the table, we have $P(\chi_5^2 \geq 11.070) = 0.05$. Therefore, the critical region is $\{\omega \mid \omega \geq 11.070\}$ and we know that if the point lies inside the critical region, we reject null hypothesis and if otherwise we accept null hypothesis. Here, $\chi_5^2 = 1.5305 < 11.070 = \chi_5^2$ (0.05). That is, the point lies outside the critical region. Hence we can accept the null hypothesis and the goodness of fit is the best. Therefore, the parameter a_0, K and C estimated by the alternative procedure may represent better than that of the same estimated by the recommended procedure in the context of West Bengal.

On the basis of the standardized residuals E (a), it can be said that observed proportion evermarried does not show any significant departure from the fitted values for females excepting the only age 40 otherwise it holds true a value of E (a) > 2 indicates the significant departure as shown in Table 6.9. We could have used percentage deviation or quartile deviation etc. rather than using χ_p^2 but it has been used in case of West Bengal to see if there is any deviation as an exercise only. This may or may not be applicable to the data for other countries. Therefore, the female marriage patterns can or cannot be represented by the above-mentioned parameters estimated by the alternative procedure.

6.15 AGE STRUCTURE OF FIRST MARRIAGE FREQUENCIES

The first marriage frequency g (a) is defined as the ratio of the number of first marriages in an interval relative to the number of person years lived in that interval. In other words, it is defined as the number of first marriage in an interval of age, say a to a + 1 divided by the number persons (irrespective of marital status) in that age interval. Values of g (a) have been computed for females for different years with the help of the standard first marriage frequencies, $g_s(X_s)$, given by Coale (1971). The function of g (a) is related to $g_s(X_s)$ by the following:

$$g(a) = g_s(X_s).\ C/K \qquad 5.1$$

Where $X_s = (a - a_0)/K$ is the standardized age. The g(a) values are derived for females in single years of age and are presented in Table 6.10. Similar g(a) values can be estimated by closed form of analytical expression of probability density function of age of first marriage g. (X_s) among those who marry (Coale and McNeil, 1972). Knowing a_0, K and C a function of g. (X_s) which gives the distribution of first marriages by the following expression

$$g.(X_s) = 0.1946\, e\, [-\, 0.174\, (X_s - 6.06) - e\, (-0.2881\, (X_s - 6.06)] \qquad 5.2$$

Multiplying g (X_s) by C and dividing by K i.e. derives first marriage frequencies, denoted by g′(a),

$g'(a) = g.(X_s).\, C/K$, where X_s = Standardized age = $(a - a_0)/K$.

The values thus derived are presented in Table 6.10.

Table 6.10 First marriage frequencies among females by age for West Bengal and Bangladesh.

	West Bengal						Bangladesh					
	1961		1991		1992–93		1961		1976		1991	
Age (a)	g(a)	g′(a)	g(a)	g′(a)	g(a)	g′(a)	g(a)	g′(a)	g(a)	g′(a)	g(a)	g′(a)
11	0.0341	0.0337					.07481	0.0757	0.0017	0.0021		
12	0.1013	0.1034			0.0051	0.0051	0.2202	0.2195	0.0412	0.0412		
13	0.1584	0.1585			0.0251	0.0250	0.2426	0.2403	0.1102	0.1126	0.0213	0.0200
14	0.1683	0.1675	0.0188	0.0175	0.0607	0.0607	0.1777	0.1783	0.1609	0.1623	0.0754	0.0761
15	0.1465	0.1450	0.0622	0.0630	0.0954	0.0969	0.1132	0.1132	0.1671	0.1659	0.1349	0.1359
16	0.1121	0.1127	0.1131	0.1150	0.1166	0.1176	0.0687	0.0677	0.1422	0.1410	0.1591	0.1602
17	0.0824	0.0828	0.1408	0.1419	0.1206	0.1202	0.0407	0.0394	0.1079	0.1086	0.1514	0.1498
18	0.0590	0.0589	0.1409	0.1396	0.1115	0.1102	0.0225	0.0228	0.0791	0.0793	0.1230	0.1231
19	0.0421	0.0412	0.1215	0.1204	0.0942	0.0942	0.0147	0.0131	0.0564	0.0563	0.0937	0.0943
20	0.0296	0.0287	0.0957	0.0963	0.0767	0.0772	0.0095	0.0075	0.0403	0.0393	0.0695	0.0693
21	0.0200	0.0198	0.0731	0.0735	0.0610	0.0614	0.0052	0.0043	0.0281	0.0273	0.0502	0.0500
22	0.0136	0.0136	0.0549	0.0548	0.0482	0.0481	0.0029	0.0025	0.0189	0.0188	0.0364	0.0355
23	0.0103	0.0094	0.0408	0.0402	0.0373	0.0372	0.0009	0.0014	0.0131	0.0130	0.0259	0.0251
24	0.0080	0.0064	0.0301	0.0293	0.0292	0.0286			0.0100	0.0089	0.0177	0.0177
25	0.0056	0.0044	0.0219	0.0212	0.0225	0.0218			0.0076	0.0061	0.0125	0.0124
26	0.0037	0.0031	0.0153	0.0153	0.0171	0.0167			0.0052	0.0042	0.0097	0.0087
27	0.0025	0.0021	0.0111	0.0110	0.0126	0.0127			0.0035	0.0029	0.0076	0.0061
28	0.0016	0.0014	0.0088	0.0080	0.0097	0.0097			0.0024	0.0019	0.0054	0.0043
29	0.0007	0.0010	0.0071	0.0057	0.0078	0.0073			0.0015	0.0014	0.0037	0.0030
30			0.0052	0.0041	0.0066	0.0056					0.0025	0.0021
31			0.0037	0.0030	0.0052	0.0042					0.0017	0.0015
32			0.0025	0.0021	0.0041	0.0032					0.0009	0.0010
33			0.0018	0.0015	0.0030	0.0024						
34			0.0012	0.0011	0.0022	0.0019						
35					0.0017	0.0014						
36					0.0012	0.0011						
37					0.0008	0.0008						

It is found that the values derived by g(a) and g′(a) are quite identical to each other for the same year in all the years that can easily be depicted from the Figure 6.1.

Specifically, first marriage frequency curves for different population should differ only in origin, horizontal scale and total area (or Vertical scale). Cumulation diminishes the influence of the small differences and irregularities, so that a comparison of first marriage frequencies is a more sensitive test of the structure of nuptiality in different population than a comparison of proportions evermarried (Coale, 1971).

Table 6.10 Shows that the first marriage frequency has shifted from age 11 in 1961 to age 14 in 1991 in West Bengal and from age 11 in 1961 to age 13 in 1991 in Bangladesh suggesting an increase of 3 years at the initial age at marriage in West Bengal and of 2 years in Bangladesh within the period of 30 years. But if we pay our attention on 1976 Bangladesh Fertility Survey (BFS) results, we can easily see that there is no change in age at marriage from 1961 to 1976 in Bangladesh. The real change has taken place from 1976 to 1991 in Bangladesh. On the other hand; results from NFHS (1992–93) data, show a peculiar change caused by shifting the age at first marriage backward, which is misleading the trend in age at first marriage in West Bengal. This might have resulted from somewhat unsatisfactory collection of data samples. The first marriage frequency was the lowest at age 11 and the highest at age 14 in 1961, and the lowest at age 14 and the highest at age 18 in 1991 in West Bengal. Similarly, Bangladesh observed the lowest value of the first marriage frequency at age 11 and the highest at age 13 in 1961 followed by the lowest at age 13 and the highest at age 16 in 1991. So, West Bengal takes a hand by increasing 2 years in age at first marriage over Bangladesh within 30 years period. But this suggests that the law set up by the Act relating to the legal minimum age at first marriage in both West Bengal and Bangladesh appears to be ineffective. The maximum values of g (a) were 168 per cent in 1961, 141 per cent in 1991 in West Bengal followed by the maximum values of g (a) were 243 per cent in 1961 and 159 per cent in 1991 in Bangladesh. After the peak age of marriage, the frequency of first marriage goes on decreasing. By age 25, the corresponding values of g(a) were 6 per cent in 1961, 22 per cent in 1991 in West Bengal and all the first marriages were complete before age 25 in 1961, 8 per cent in 1976 and 13 per cent in 1991 in Bangladesh. The table shows that the first marriage frequency is very high at age 18 in West Bengal and at age 16 in Bangladesh in recent times. It can be noted that first marriages take place at very early age and it is completed by the age

34 in 1991 and by age 37 during 1992–93 in West Bengal and by age 32 in 1991 in Bangladesh.As a matter of fact, first marriages amongst females in West Bengal as well as in Bangladesh are characterized by early start, for example by age 14 in West Bengal and by age 13 in Bangladesh even in 1991. Fig. 6.1 shows that g (a) and g′(a) are identical and overlapping. So both the values i.e. g (a) and g′(a) in the Fig. 6.1 show the similar trend of first marriages, and age as well as peak age at marriage are shifting towards the higher ages in later years. The levels of frequencies of first marriages are also found changing.

Fig. 6.1 First marriage frequency among females by single years of age for West Bengal and Bangladesh

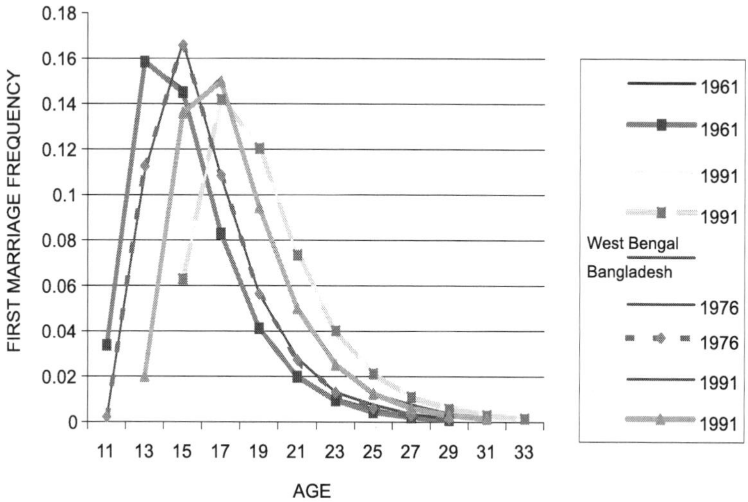

6.16 RISK OF FIRST MARRIAGE

The risk of first marriage means that chance of exposure to the marriage. It can be defined as the rate of first marriage (for those who are single). Estimation of risk of first marriage from the standard table (given by Coale, 1971) can be accomplished, knowing the values of a_0, K and C by the following relations:

The standard risk of first marriage = The standard first marriage frequency at each age / The standard proportion single.

Symbolically, $r_s(X_s) = g_s(X_s) / (1 - G_s(X_s)$ … Where, $r_s(X_s)$ is standard risk of first marriage at age (X_s), $g_s(X_s)$ is standard first marriage frequency at age (X_s), and $G_s(X_s)$ is standard proportion evermarried up to age (X_s).

Then for the observed population, the risk of first marriage R (a) is estimated as

$$R(a) = g(a) / (C-G(a)) \qquad 6.1$$

Where $G(a) = g_s(X_s)$. C/K = The first marriage frequency between ages a to a + 1 is shown in Table 6.10 and $X_s = (a - a_0)/K$.

$G(a) = C.G_s(X_s)$, proportion evermarried up to exact age a, which can be estimated from the standard schedule of proportion evermarried $G_s(X_s)$ at $X_s = (a - a_0)/K$.

According to Coale (1971) the risk of first marriage for an observed population can be estimated directly from the following double exponential analytical model.

$$r(a) = (0.174 / K)\, e\, [-4.411\, e\, (-0.309) / K)\, (a - a_0)] \qquad 6.2$$

Table 6.11 Risk of first marriage among females by age for West Bengal and Bangladesh.

	West Bengal						Bangladesh					
	1961		1991		1992–93		1961		1976		1991	
Age (a)	R(a)	r(a)	R(a)	r(a)	R(a)	r(a)	R(a)	r(a)	R(a)	r(a)	R(a)	r(a)
11	0.0346	0.0345					0.0777	0.0780	0.0017	0.0053		
12	0.1103	0.1104			0.0050	0.0059	0.2725	0.2675	0.0421	0.0421		
13	0.2002	0.2005			0.0262	0.0261	0.4236	0.4233	0.1219	0.1223	0.0214	0.0209
14	0.2716	0.2722	0.0196	0.0189	0.0654	0.0651	0.4941	0.5022	0.2104	0.2112	0.0796	0.0789
15	0.3183	0.3185	0.0673	0.0670	0.1137	0.1138	0.5244	0.5353	0.2795	0.2796	0.1603	0.1597
16	0.3386	0.3452	0.1354	0.1357	0.1593	0.1603	0.5410	0.5481	0.3222	0.3229	0.2304	0.2825
17	0.3515	0.3598	0.1959	0.2010	0.1971	0.1978	0.5552	0.5530	0.3406	0.3477	0.2839	0.2838
18	0.3595	0.3675	0.2504	0.2502	0.2252	0.2249	0.5277	0.5548	0.3532	0.3611	0.3116	0.3155
19	0.3687	0.3715	0.2820	0.2827	0.2406	0.2434	0.5956	0.5555	0.3594	0.3682	0.3264	0.3338
20	0.3752	0.3736	0.2921	0.3026	0.2503	0.2554	0.7504	0.5558	0.3699	0.3719	0.3375	0.3439
21	0.3683	0.3746	0.3065	0.3142	0.2567	0.2631	0.9403	0.5559	0.3751	0.3738	0.3419	0.3495
22	0.3579	0.3752	0.3127	0.3209	0.2628	0.2679	1.7262	0.5559	0.3649	0.3748	0.3510	0.3524
23	0.3931	0.3755	0.3201	0.3247	0.2649	0.2709			0.3615	0.3753	0.3553	0.3540
24	0.4678	0.3757	0.3264	0.3268	0.2711	0.2728			0.4021	0.3755	0.3449	0.3549
25	0.5385	0.3757	0.3289	0.3280	0.2744	0.2739			0.4732	0.3757	0.3418	0.3553
26	0.6271	0.3757	0.3175	0.3287	0.2740	0.2746			0.5385	0.3757	0.3755	0.3555
27	0.8620	0.3757	0.3165	0.3291	0.2647	0.2751			0.6397	0.3757	0.4427	0.3557
28	1.7777	0.3757	0.3458	0.3293	0.2643	0.2753			0.9164	0.3757	0.5056	0.3557
29			0.4029	0.3294	0.2786	0.2755			3.2568	0.3757	0.5841	0.3557
30			0.4530	0.3295	0.3158	0.2756					0.7545	0.3557
31			0.5211	0.3295	0.3533	0.2757					1.3077	0.3557
32			0.6146	0.3295	0.3942	0.2757						
33			0.9200	0.3295	0.4348	0.2757						
34			2.3200	0.3295	0.5000	0.2757						
35					0.6800	0.2757						
36					1.0909	0.2757						

In this model 'a' represents age. r(a) is the risk of first marriage at age 'a' during the year, a_0 is the earliest age at which there occurs a significant number of first marriages. And, lastly, K is a parameter, which alters the shape of the curve, essentially by making it rise more or less steeply during the years shortly after a_0.

Therefore, R (a) and r (a) for females are estimated separately for different years in West Bengal as well as in Bangladesh.

Table 6.11 shows that the risk of first marriage from lower ages in earlier years has shifted to the higher ages in the later years. For example, the risk of first marriage started at age 11 in 1961 and at age 14 in 1991 in West Bengal followed by the same at age 11 in 1961 as well as in 1976 and at age 13 in 1991 in Bangladesh. The result based on NFHS (1992–93) data show inconsistency with that of the result obtained based on 1991 census in West Bengal, which might be due to flawness of data.

The risk of first marriage for younger ages has decreased over the years. For example, at age 15 it was 318 per cent in 1961, 67 per cent in 1991 in West Bengal and, 524 per cent in 1961, 280 per cent in 1976 and 160 per cent in 1991 in Bangladesh. The result obtained from NFHS data shows 114 per cent at age 15 in West Bengal. Though the risk of first marriage is reduced to a reasonable extent, the decrease in West Bengal is much more appreciable than that in Bangladesh as evinced from Table 6.11. Therefore, the risk of first marriage in lower age has decreased in the later period.

Table 6.11 further shows that R(a) and r(a) values are almost identical up to age 21 in 1961, up to age 25 in 1991 and up to age 29 in 1992–93 in West Bengal followed by Bangladesh up to age 18 in 1961, up to age 23 in 1976 and up to age 24 in 1991. Afterwards there are some fluctuations in R(a) values while comparing with r(a) values in the higher ages in all the years for short age span, and finally R(a) values go on increasing near unity or more till the end of the marriageable age. While r(a) values are increasing and yielding limiting values at the end of the marriageable age, it was estimated that r (a) value was 0.3757 at age 28 in 1961, 0.3295 at age 34 in 1991 and 0.2757 at age 36 during 1992–93 in West Bengal and on the other hand, it was 0.5559 at age 22 in 1961, 0.3757 at age 29 in 1976 and 0.3557 at age 31 in 1991 in Bangladesh. Therefore, Table 6.11 reveals that r(a) value at age 28 is 0.3757 in 1961 in West Bengal which is the same as that of the r(a) value (0.3757) at age 29 in 1976 in Bangladesh. So, the similarity in r(a) value has been observed in Bangladesh with that in West

Bengal after 15 years. This might have resulted from the early marriage among females in Bangladesh.

Both the values of R(a) and r (a) show the same trend up to a certain age (as described elsewhere) over the years and later on R(a) values do not show any conformity to that of r(a) values at the higher age, which might be resulting from the fact that later risks of marriage are sensitive to errors in the cumulated values of first marriage frequencies and the first marriage frequencies at higher age in the standard schedules which are derived by somewhat arbitrary adjustments of cross-sectional data (Coale, 1971).

Furthermore, it is to be noted that both R(a) and r(a) values must be mathematically less than unity but some values of R(a) at higher ages are found to be greater than unity which might have resulted from the flawness

Fig. 6.2 Risk of first marriage among females by single years of age for West Bengal and Bangladesh (fitted by double exponential)

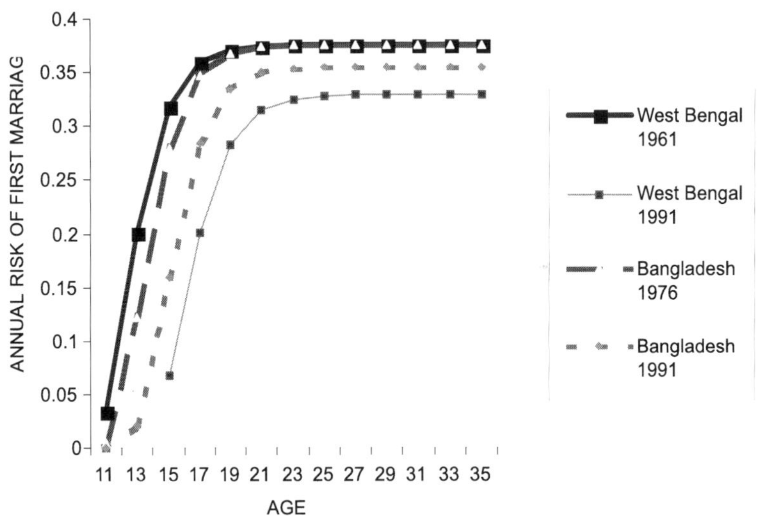

of the data. The r(a) values are shown in Fig. 6.2. The r(a) values show that the risk of first marriage rises steeply after the initial age at marriage for a very short span of ages and then it reaches the asymptote. The figure also shows that the age span of risk of first marriage is shorter, which seems to be the real phenomenon in the Bengali society either in West Bengal or in Bangladesh.

7
Migration

7.1 CAUSES OF MIGRATION

Human migration denotes any movement by human from one locality to another, sometimes over long distances or in large groups. Humans are known to have migrated extensively throughout history and prehistory.

The movement of populations in modern times has continued under the form of both voluntary migration within one's region, country, or beyond, and involuntary migration (which includes the slave trade, trafficking in human beings and ethnic cleansing). People who migrate are called migrants, or, more specifically, emigrants, immigrants or settlers, depending on historical setting, circumstances and perspective.

Causes of migrations have modified over hundreds of years. Some cases are constant, some of them do not carry the same importance as years ago (for example: 18th and 19th centuries labour migration did not have the same character like today). In general we can divide factors causing migrations into two groups of factors: Push and pull factors. Both push and pull factors are economic, political, cultural and environmentally based.

On the macro level, the causes of migration can be distilled into two main categories: security dimension of migration (natural disasters, conflicts, threats to individual safety, poor political prospects) and economic dimension of migration (poor economic situation, poor situation of national market).

Push and pull factors are those factors which either forcefully push people into migration or attract them. A push factor is forceful, and a factor which relates to the country from which a person migrates. It is generally some problem which results in people wanting to migrate. A pull factor is something concerning the country to which a person migrates. It is generally a benefit that attracts people to a certain place.

For demographic purpose, two broad types of migration are identified, international migration (across national boundaries) and internal migration (within the boundaries of a given nation).

Presently undocumented migration is gradually becoming a major issue. A comprehensive theory of undocumented migration does not yet exist. Migration theory usually assumes that documented and undocumented migration are birds of a feather. Both theories on the initiation of migration as well as on the continuation and persistence of migratory movements are perceived, and indeed do, apply to undocumented migration as well.

But the question of how documented and undocumented migratory flows relate to each other is unanswered. Does documented migration induce undocumented migration or does undocumented migration substitute documented migration, e.g. when immigration policies are restricted? Whether undocumented migration just a side effect of documented migration or they are independent and how one can estimate the undocumented part separately.

7.2 ESTIMATION AND EVALUATION OF NET MIGRATION

In view of the lack of adequate data on migration for many countries and many periods it is often necessary to estimate the volume of migration. Although there is interest on separate figures on immigration and emigration, the available methods can only be used to estimate the balance of migration.The different methods are listed below.

1. Intercensal component method for the total population.

Under this method total volume of net migration in an intercensal period can be estimated by subtracting the difference between total number of birth and death registration figures during that period from the difference of population figures obtained from census at the two end points. This residual estimate may be in substantial error due to errors in census counts and registration data.

2. Intercensal cohort component method.

This method is applicable for the estimation of net migration, by age, for the total population and for the segments of the population which are fixed with respect to gender, race and country of birth. This procedure involves the calculation of estimates by age groups on the basis of separate allowance for the components of population.

One formula this purpose is

$$I_a - E_a = P^1_a - S_a P^0_{a-t}$$

where, a = age of the cohort at the end of the period,

P^j_x = Population at age x at the census point $j.(j = 0, 1)$,

S_a = survival rate for the age group under consideration for an intercensal period of t years.

For a new born cohort this formula is, $I_a - E_a = P^1_a - S_a B$

where, B = births which occur during the intercensal period.

7.3 DIFFERENTIAL MIGRATION

Several studies have been made of differences in pattern of migration with respect to age, gender and other characteristics. Let,

M_c = number of net migrants for a particular category,

P_c = number of residents for a particular category,

M = number of net migrants for the general population,

P = number of residents for the general population.

Then an index of differential migration is given by

$100 \times ((M_c/P_c) - (M/P))/(M/P)$

7.4 MIGRATION RATES

Suppose, in a particular region and during a particular period,

I = Total number of Immigrants

E = Total number of Emigrants

P = Total Population Size.

Then the different migration rates are given by,

Crude Immigration Rate (CIR) = $(I/P) \times 1000$

Crude Emigration Rate (CER) = $(E/P) \times 1000$

Crude Net migration Rate (CNMR) = $((I - E)/P) \times 1000$

Crude Gross migration Rate (CGMR) = $((I + E)/P) \times 1000$.

7.5 INTERNAL MIGRATION AND MOBILITY

7.5.1 Concept of Mobility

The term 'Mobility' is used for different purposes in Demography and Sociology. In Demography it refers to Geographic Movements whereas in Sociology refers to a change in status. Corresponding to Geographic

Movements, by Migration we mean a change in the usual place of residence. Migration data are usually obtained from questions that compare current residence with residence at a prior date. Migratnts are those who have actually changed their residences.

7.5.2 Terms Related to Migration

1. **Migration period:** Migration period may be defined either by a prior date (which is the beginning of the period) or by specifying the length of the interval.
2. **Mover:** A person who moved from one address to another at the beginning and end of the interval.
3. **Migration status:** Migration status may be defined as **non-mover** (same residence at the beginning and end of the interval), **intra-country movers** (different residences in the same country), **intra-state movers** (different residences in the same state) etc.
4. **Local mover:** A person who moved only within an administrative area.
5. **Migrant:** A person who moved from one administrative area to another. The number of non-migrants is equal to the number of non-movers and the number of short distance movers.
6. **Area of origin:** The area from which a migrant moves (point of departure).
7. **Area of destination:** The area to which a migrant moves (point of arrival).
8. **In-migrant and out-migrant:** An in-migrant is a person who enters a migration defining area by crossing its boundary from some point outside the area but within the same country.
   An out-migrant is a person who departs from a migration defining area by crossing its boundary to a point outside it, but within the same country.
9. **Net migration:** It is the balance between in-migrants and out-migrants.
10. **Gross migration:** Gross migration is the turnover of an area defined as the sum of in-migration and out-migration.
11. **Lifetime migration:** This type of migration occurs between birth and the time of the census or survey. A lifetime migrant is one whose current area of residence is different from his area of birth, regardless of intervening migrations.

Measurement of Internal Migration

Indirect Estimates of Net Migration

The indirect estimates do not require special questions and may be computed from population counts by age and sex or even from population totals.

National Growth Rate Method

Let P^0_T and P^1_T be the national population at the beginning and end of the intercensal period respectively. Also let P^0_i and P^1_i be the population at the beginning and end of the intercensal period for the *ith* geographic subdivision. Then the estimated migration rate m_i for the area i is given by

$$m_i = \left[\left(\frac{P_i^1 - P_i^0}{P_i^0}\right) - \left(\frac{P_T^1 - P_T^0}{P_T^0}\right)\right] \times 100$$

Thus, for a geographic subdivision, a rate of growth greater than the national average is interpreted as net in-migration and a rate less than the national average is net outmigration. The name procedure can be applied to specific age-sex group. Another type of estimate is given by

$$m_i = \left[\left(\frac{P_i^1 - P_i^0}{P_i^0}\right) - \left(\frac{B_T - D_T}{P_T^0}\right)\right] \times 100$$

where $\dfrac{B_T - D_T}{P_T^0}$ = national rate of natural increase. This method assumes that the rate of natural increase is the same throughout the country. This formula gives an estimate of the total rate of net migration including international migration.

Residual Methods

1. **Vital statistics method:** This includes the use of balancing equation in various forms. The simplest form is

$$M = (P^t - P^0) - (B - D)$$

2. **Survival rate method:** The survival rate method is commonly used in statistically under developed countries because it does not require accurate vital statistics. The basic formula for estimating net migration is

$$M_{x+t} = P^t_{x+t} - SP^0_x \qquad (7.5.1)$$

where x is an age or mid point of age group
t is the interval in years between censuses
P^0_x is the population aged x at the first census
P^t_{x+t} is the population at the next census at age $x + t$
S is the survival rate
(except birth age).

Two main types of survival rates are used, those from life tables and those from censuses. Like the vital statistics method, the survival rate method does not measure net migration exactly even when there are no errors in the underlying population and vital statistics. This difference arises because the deaths are not necessarily equivalent to the number of deaths to residents of the given area during the given period. There are several ways of applying the survival rates. 7.5.1 is known as the forward survival rate method. There is another way known as reverse survival rate method given by

$$M'_{x+t} = \frac{P^t_{x+t}}{S} - P^0_x \qquad (7.5.2)$$

The survival rate may be computed from life table figures or census figures.

Some Measures Based on Place of Birth (Direct Estimates)

1. Interregional migration rate

$$m = \frac{N - \sum_i N_{ii}}{N} \times 100 = \frac{\sum_i \sum_j M_{ij}}{N} \times 100, \; M_{ij} = N_{i \neq j}$$

where $N = \Sigma_i \Sigma_j N_{ij}$
N_{ij} = Number of persons living in region i and born in region j.

2. In migration rate for rth region

$$m^I_r = \frac{\sum_j M_{rj}}{N_r} \times 100 = \frac{I_r}{N_r} \times 100$$

M_{rj} = migrants living in region r who were born in region j.
N_r = population enumerated in region r.
$\Sigma_j M_{rj} = \Sigma_j N_{rj} - N_{rr} = N_r - N_{rr}$

3. Out-migration rate for *rth* region

$$m^0_r = \frac{\sum_i M_{ir}}{\dot{N}_r} \times 100 = \frac{O_r}{\dot{N}_r} \times 100$$

where M_{ir} is the number of migrants living in region i who were born in region r.

$\dot{N}_r$ = total population born in region r.

Again $\Sigma_i M_{ir} = \Sigma_i N_{ir} - N_{rr} = \dot{N}_r - N_{rr}$

4. Net migration rate for the rth region

$$m_r^n = \frac{\sum_j M_{rj} - \sum_i M_{ir}}{N_r} \times 100$$

5. Turnover rate for region *r*

$$m_r^t = \frac{\sum_j M_{rj} + \sum_i M_{ir}}{N_r} \times 100$$

Birth – Residence Index

Net gain or loss for the *rth* area through interarea migration.

$$BR_r = \sum_j M_{rj} - \sum_i M_{ir} = I_r - O_r = N_r m_r^n$$

Intercensal Change in the Birth – Residence Index

This measure is defined as the difference in the birth – residence indices of two consecutive census periods for a given state(S) and is intended to approximate the net migration during the latter decade.

$$BR_S(2) - BR_S(1) = (I_S(2) - I_S(1)) \quad (O_S(2) - O_S(1)),$$

where 1 and 2 correspond to two successive censuses.

Gross Intercensal Interchange of Population

$$GIIP = |I_S(2) - I_S(1)| - |O_S(2) - O_S(1)|$$

Partial Migration

A partial migration rate is defined as the number of migrants to an area from a particular origin or from an area to a particular destination per 100 (or per 1000) of the population at either origin or destination. The partial out – migration rate can be expressed as (for i)

$$m_{ij}^0 = \frac{M_{ij}}{P_i} \times 100,$$

where M_{ij} is the stream from area i to area j and P_i is the population of area i.

The partial in-migration rate (for *i*) is given by

$$m^{I}_{ji} = \frac{M_{ji}}{P_i}\times 100$$

The gross rate of population interchange from *i* to *j* is

$$GRI_{i\to j} = \frac{M_{ij}+M_{ji}}{P_i+P_j}\times 100$$

The net rate of population interchange from *i* to *j* is

$$NRI_{i\to j} = \frac{M_{ij}-M_{ji}}{P_i+P_j}\times 100$$

Effectiveness of Migration

$$EM_{i\to j} = \frac{M_{ij}-M_{ji}}{M_{ij}+M_{ji}}\times 100, 0\le EM\le 100$$

Migration Preference Index

This is defined as the ratio of the actual to the expected number of migrants in a stream when the expected number is directly proportional to both the population at origin and population at destination. This indicates whether streams are greater or smaller than would be expected from considerations of population size above.

$$PI = \frac{M_{OD}\left(\sum P_i - P_0\right)}{mP_0P_D}\times 100, 0\le PI\le 100,$$

M_{0D} = actual number of migrants from 0 to *D*.
P_0 = population at origin 0.
P_D = population at destination *D*.
ΣP_i = national population.
m = population of interarea migrants in the national population.

7.6 UNDOCUMENTED MIGRATION

People migrate from one place to another due to several reasons. The primary factors responsible for migration are hunger, poverty, security threat, job opportunities etc. But only a part of the total movement is documented through immigration offices. Undocumented migration is an inherent effect of any type of restrictive immigration policy. But many countries do not have undocumented population in spite of having restrictive immigration policies. Countries like United states, India are heavily affected by undocumented migration due to having less developed neighbouring countries. The partition of Bengal at the time of independence of India has created lots of problems among the population on both sides of the border. After the initial set back the situation gradually stabilized but discrepancies with respect to living condition and other facilities became significant. At present many people from Bangladesh are regularly trying to infiltrate in different districts of West Bengal having borders with Bangladesh.

India shares 4095 kilometer border with Bangladesh the longest among all its neighbours. Of this four North East states – Tripura, Meghalaya, Mijoram and Assam account for 1879 km while West Bengal has a border running 2216 km along Bangladesh. An area of 6.5 km has not been demarcated yet, the para-military BSF deployed along the border is faced with a plethora of problems, including illegal migration from Bangladesh, transborder movement of armed sparatist rebels belonging to a number of insurgent groups from India's northeastern states, and West Bengal.

Several attempts have been made by population scientists to study undocumented migration both in India and abroad. Different approaches based on push and pull theory, network theory, transmigration theory etc have been developed to explain undocumented migration. Such migration mainly depends on information about the receiving country, travel routes, shelter at different points etc. There are different networks through which such information may be obtained. Push factors like unemployment, political unrest, attack from persons belonging to larger communities etc responsible for such moves. Pull factors like income opportunities, family reunion, political stability also responsible for undocumented migration.

Researchers like Cornelius Wayne A. (1994), Haines david W. and Rosenblum Karen E. (1999), Passel Jeffrey (1999) etc are studied such moves in United states. Holk Stobble (2000) has made an intensive study on undocumented migration in the USA and Germany.

In India studies on undocumented migration have been done by population scientists like Datta P. (2000, 2002, 2003, 2004a, 2004b, 2004c, 2005), Banerjee B.(2003), Nath D.C. (2003), Guha Ray S. (2003) and others. But most of these studies are mainly related to effects and reasons of undocumented migration. It is very difficult to measure the amount of undocumented migration directly. An indirect method may be used to estimate this amount under the assumption that people who entered a country illegally and eventually settled their residence in that country will ultimately collect some evidence of national citizenship. As a result they will be enumerated during the next census. This feature will be reflected in the rate of population growth in the migration prone regions (i.e. in districts near the Bangladesh borders). One may compare the rate of growth of these regions with a region which is far from border region (which can be treated as 'control').

7.7 INDIRECT METHOD

It is well known that some of the districts of West Bengal are very much affected by illegal migration. We have considered three police stations like Baduria, Gazole and Bashirhat as affected regions ('cases') and one police station viz Rampurhat as non affected region ('control') which is far from border area. In this connection it may be mentioned that we have not chosen regions like Kolkata, Howrah etc which are very much developed and having urban facilities. In those areas it is difficult to distinguish between internal and international migrations. We have tried to choose those areas which are not attractive to the citizens of West Bengal but which are easily accessible for the migrants of Bangladesh as the 'cases'. The area which is not only attractive to the citizens of India but also far from border has been considered as 'control'.

7.8 DATA

For our study we have used Indian census data for the years 1951, 1961, 1971, 1981, 1991 and 2001. Although there is a constant flow of migrants from Bangladesh to India but a significant number of people entered West Bengal during the time of partition of India (1946–1950) and also at the time of independence of Bangladesh (1972–74). A significant portion of this population was permanently settled in West Bengal. These features are expected to be reflected in the census figures of 1950 and 1980. We have used the 'balancing equation' to estimate the amount of 'undocumented migration'.

7.9 BALANCING EQUATION

The most basic method of demography is the decomposition of population change into its components. We may express the process in terms of the fundamental equation

$$P_t - P_0 = (B - D) + (I - O) \tag{7.9.1}$$

where P_t is the population at the end of the period t, P_0 that at the beginning of the period, B is the births, D is deaths, I is in-migration and O is out-migration. The above simple equation may have different forms and different uses. In our situation if we denote two successive census time points by t and $t + 1$ then we may write

$$P_{t+1} = P_t + R_t P_t + I_t \tag{7.9.2}$$

where P_i is the population at the census time point i ($i = t, t + 1$). R_t is the relative growth rate at the time point t and I_t is the net migration during the period ($t, t + 1$). For the regions under consideration I_t may be considered to be the total undocumented migration during the period ($t, t + 1$). Note that since the census time points are ten years apart the illegal migrants are likely to collect same evidence of citizenship during that period and are most likely to be enumerated at the census time point ($t + 1$). The relative growth rate figures are estimated from the population growth figures of the region under consideration. Then the equation (7.9.2) may be used to estimate the I_t values.

7.10 DATA ANALYSIS

The population density per sq. km. of India and the studied police stations are given in the Table 7.1 for the census years 1951, 1961, 1971, 1981, 1991 and 2001. The relative growth rate of India and the studied police stations are given in the Table 7.2. From Table 7.2 it appears that compared to the relative growth rates for India, those figures for the affected areas (cases) are higher except in a few cases whereas for Rampurhat (control) those figures are comparatively smaller except for the census year 1951. Besides this for Rampurhat the relative growth rates are decreasing over time which is around 0.2 for India but show local maxima for Baduria (1951–61, 1981–91), Bashirhat (1951–61, 1971–1981–91) and Gazole (1961–71, 1981–91). All these features indicate the effect of external population flow.

Table 7.3 shows the estimated values of migration. Here also we see that those values are relatively higher for the year 1981–91 in the affected areas viz Baduria and Bashirhat. This is likely to be the effect of birth of Bangladesh on 16th Decemder, 1971. For Gazole, the maximum is attained at the year 1961 which may be the effect of partition of Bengal. Hence the present method may be used to estimate the effects of undocumented migration. The estimated figures of undocumented migration for the above census years of different police station are given in Table 7.3 and are exhibited also in Figure 7.1.

Table 7.1 Population density per sq. km. of different police stations (P_t).

	India	Baduria	Bashirthat	Gazole	Rampurhat
1951	117	427	530	142	278
1961	142	596	757	184	369
1971	177	753	889	279	460
1981	216	911	1136	351	548
1991	267	1234	1427	454	618
2001	324	1378	1703	574	678

Table 7.2 Relative growth rate of different police stations (R_t).

	India	Baduria	Bashirthat	Gazole	Rampurhat
1951	0.1937	0.3330	0.3559	0.2554	0.2824
1961	0.2203	0.2338	0.1606	0.4163	0.2207
1971	0.1991	0.1905	0.2452	0.2296	0.1750
1981	0.2120	0.3035	0.2281	0.2573	0.1202
1991	0.1935	0.1103	0.1766	0.2340	0.0920

Table 7.3 Estimated undocumented migration per sq. km. of different police stations (I_t).

	Baduria	Bashirthat	Gazole	Rampurhat
1951	26.5505	37.9692	5.0707	12.2164
1961	17.6347	10.3083	18.4031	9.6873
1971	14.5703	29.0426	7.9487	7.4775
1981	46.5358	31.9226	12.6838	4.1232
1991	7.7891	23.6172	13.4597	2.7006

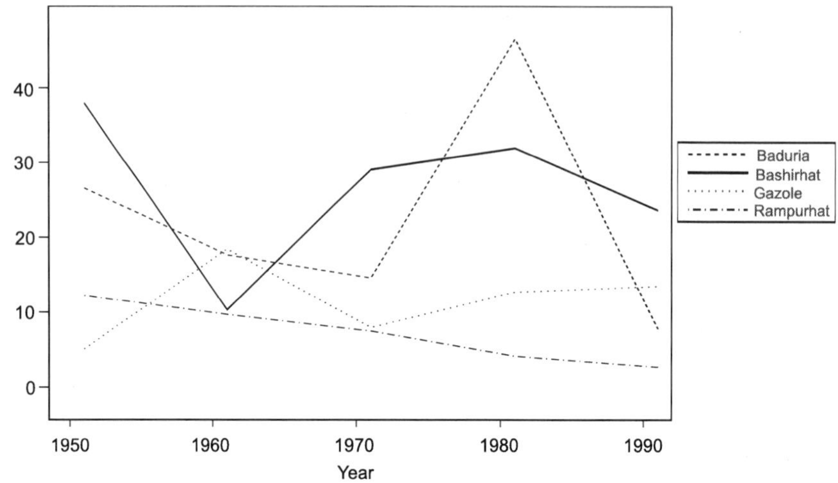

Fig. 7.1 Estimated undocumented migration per sq km of different police stations

Fig. 7.2 Relative growth rate of different police stations

8
Population Projection

8.1 POPULATION GROWTH

The mathematical expressions used to describe population growth are necessarily empirical. No exact law of population growth has yet been formulated. These methods are satisfactory only for short term predictions but are not much suitable for long term projection particularly because of the assumption that the social and economic forces that have controlled the population growth in the past will also contribute in future. There is significant uncertainty in the calculation of future population. Our knowledge regarding forces affecting underlying changes in mortality, fertility, marriage and migration is rather incomplete. The reason behind such problems is the assumption that certain policies and programmes will be sucessful at the future point of time.This is not usually true.

Projection is an illustrative calculation based upon certain given assumptions. That is why any word like estimation, forecast etc should not be used in this connection. Population projection is based only on current information about speed of growth, direction of flow etc and will be required to be amended from time to time. Population projection are usually made with regard to age and sex.

8.2 FEMALE POPULATION PROJECTION BY AGE

The following method has been developed by Leslie, P.H. (1945). By this method we compute the expected number of females, age by age, at points of time subsequent to a census or other starting points, given a set of birth and death rates. Here these rates are assumed to be fixed.

Let us define

$P(x)\, dx$ = Present population in $(x, x + dx)$

$l(x)$ = Stationary population of the life table model

= Number of persons expected to attain age x out of the cohort population l_0

$P(x)(l(x+t)/l(x))$= expected number of survivors (among those whose present age is x) at the end of t years hence.

In pratice, instead of $P(x)dx$ we observe

$$\int_0^n P(x+v)dv = {}_{-n}P_x^{(0)} = \text{ current population in the age interval } (x, x+n).$$

Among them

$$\int_0^n P(x+v)(l(x+t+v)/l(x+v))dv = {}_{-n}P_{x+t}^{(1)} \tag{8.2.1}$$

are expected to be alive at the end of t years hence.

8.2.1 Discrete Analysis

A commonly used approximation is

$$ {}_{-n}P_{x+t}^{(1)} = {}_{-n}P_x^{(0)}({}_{-n}L_{x+t}/{}_{-n}L_x) \tag{8.2.2}$$

where $\quad {}_{-n}L_x = \int_0^n l(x+t)dt$

It is customary to take $t = n = 5$. Then (8.2.2) becomes

$$ {}_{-5}P_{x+5}^{(1)} = {}_{-5}P_x^{(0)}({}_{-5}L_{x+5}/{}_{-5}L_x) \tag{8.2.3}$$

If we write ${}_{-n}P_x = P_x$ and ${}_{-n}L_x = L_x$ then (8.2.3) becomes

$$P_{x+5}^{(1)} = P_x^{(0)}(L_{x+5}/L_x) \tag{8.2.4}$$

Similarly $\quad P_{x+10}^{(2)} = P_{x+5}^{(2)}(L_{x+10}/L_{x+5}) = P_x^{(0)}(L_{x+10}/L_x)$

In a similar manner we may proceed for later points of time.

The above is the contribution for the population alive at time zero and to it the contribution for births subsequent to that date must be added.

Let F_x = annual age specific (female birth) fertility rate for females in the age group x to $x + 4$.

We know that $(P_x^{(0)} + P_x^{(1)})/2$ is the average number persons in the age group x to $x + 4$.

So the total number of live births for 5 years is given by

$$(5/2)F_x \sum_{\lambda}^{L} (P_x^{(0)} + P_x^{(1)}) \tag{8.2.5}$$

Where λ and L are the lower and upper limits of female reproductive period.

But not all of these female babies will survive to the end of the five year projection period. Hence the above should be further multiplied by $L_0/5l_0$.

So the projected population in the age group 0–4 at the end of five years age will be given by,

$$(L_0/5l_0)(5/2)\sum_{\lambda}^{L}\left(P_x^{(0)}+P_x^{(1)}\right)F_x=(L_0/2l_0)\sum_{\lambda}^{L}\left(P_x^{(0)}+P_x^{(1)}\right)F_x \quad (8.2.6)$$

As such,

$$P_0^{(1)} = (L_0/2l_0)\sum_{\lambda}^{L}\left(P_x^{(0)}+P_{x-5}^{(1)}(L_x/L_{x-5})\right)F_x \quad (8.2.7)$$

Let us take $\lambda = 15$, $L = 45$ and the highest value of x as 80 i.e. the highest age group as 80–84 l.b.d.

Then writing the equations 8.2.4–8.2.7 explicitly and considering the fact that $F_x = 0$ for $x = 0, 5, 10, 45, 50, \ldots, 80$ we have the following matrix equation

$$P^{(1)17\times 1} = L^{17\times 17}\,P^{(0)17\times 1} \quad (8.2.8)$$

where

$$L^{17\times 17}=\begin{pmatrix} 0 & 0 & L(1,3) & L(1,4) & \cdots & L(1,8) & 0 & \cdots & 0 & 0\\ L_5/L_0 & 0 & 0 & 0 & \cdots & 0 & 0 & \cdots & 0 & 0\\ 0 & L_{10}/L_5 & 0 & 0 & \cdots & 0 & 0 & \cdots & 0 & 0\\ . & . & . & . & \cdots & . & . & \cdots & . & .\\ . & . & . & . & \cdots & . & . & \cdots & . & .\\ . & . & . & . & \cdots & . & . & \cdots & . & .\\ 0 & 0 & 0 & 0 & \cdots & 0 & 0 & \cdots & L_{80}/L_{75} & 0 \end{pmatrix}$$

where

$$L(1, 3) = (L_0/2l_0)(L_{15}/L_{10})F_{15} \quad (8.2.9)$$

$$L(1, 4) = (L_0/2l_0)(F_{15} + (L_{20}/L_{15})F_{20}) \quad (8.2.10)$$

$$L(1, 8) = (L_0/2l_0)F_{40} \quad (8.2.11)$$

and

$$P^{(t)17\times 1} = \begin{pmatrix} P_0^{(t)} \\ P_1^{(t)} \\ \cdot \\ \cdot \\ \cdot \\ \cdot \\ \cdot \\ \cdot \\ P_{80}^{(t)} \end{pmatrix}$$

Thus we have the following matrix equations for future projection,

$$P^{(t)} = L^t P^{(0)} \tag{8.2.12}$$

for $t = 0, 1, 2....$

8.3 GROWTH OF FEMALE POPULATION

The following method was developed by Rhodes (1940). Let $B(t)$ denote the number of females births at time point t.

We assume that

$$B(0) = N \tag{8.3.1}$$

$$B(t) = 0 \quad \text{for } t < 0 \tag{8.3.2}$$

Let $\phi\,(x)$ denote the net female fertility function which represents the probability that a female child will survive upto age x and then give a birth to another female child.

Let λ and L denote respectively the lower and upper limits of the reproductive female age (usually $\lambda = 15$ and $L = 50$).

$$3\lambda < L < 4\lambda \qquad \text{i.e. } 45 < L < 60 \tag{8.3.3}$$

Obviously

$$\phi(x) = 0 \quad \text{if} \quad x < \lambda \tag{8.3.4}$$

$$\text{or if} \quad x > L \tag{8.3.5}$$

Here the possible cases are

1. Obviously $B(t) = 0$ for $0 < t < \lambda$

2. $B(t) = N\phi(t)$ for $\lambda \le t < 2\lambda$

3. $B(t) = N\phi(t) + \int_{\lambda}^{t-\lambda} B(u)\phi(t-u)du$ for $2\lambda \le t < 3\lambda$

   Since $t < 3\lambda$, $t - \lambda < 2\lambda$
   Then $\lambda < u < t - \lambda \Rightarrow \lambda < u < 2\lambda \quad \Rightarrow B(u) = N\phi(u)$ [by (2)]
   Hence by (3)

$$B(t) = N\phi(t) + \int_{\lambda}^{t-\lambda} \phi(u)\phi(t-u)du$$

   $= N[\phi(t) + \phi_1(t)]$ say, where $\phi_1(t) = \int_{\lambda}^{t-\lambda} \phi(u)\phi(t-u)du$

4. For $3\lambda \le t \le L$

   $B(t) = N\phi(t) + \int_{\lambda}^{t-\lambda} B(u)\phi(t-u)du$

   $t \ge 3\lambda \Rightarrow t - \lambda \ge 2\lambda$
   $t \le \mathrm{L} \Rightarrow t - \lambda \le L - \lambda < 4\lambda - \lambda = 3\lambda$ [as $L < 4\lambda$]
   Hence we have $2\lambda \le t - \lambda < 3\lambda$

   Hence $B(t) = N\phi(t) + \int_{\lambda}^{2\lambda} B(u)\phi(t-u)du + \int_{2\lambda}^{t-\lambda} B(u)\phi(t-u)du$

   By (2),

$$B(u) = N\phi(u),\ \lambda \le u < 2\lambda$$

   and by (3) $B(u) = N(\phi(u) + \phi_1(u)]$ for $2\lambda \le u < 3\lambda$
   and hence for $2\lambda \le u \le t - \lambda$ [$t - \lambda < 3\lambda$]
   Hence

$$B(t) = N\phi(t) + \int_{\lambda}^{2\lambda} N\phi(u)\phi(t-u)du + \int_{2\lambda}^{t-\lambda} N[\phi(u)+\phi_1(u)]\phi(t-u)du$$

$$= N\phi(t) + N\int_{\lambda}^{t-\lambda} \phi(u)\phi(t-u)du + N\int_{2\lambda}^{t-\lambda} \phi_1(u)+\phi(t-u)du$$

$$= N[\phi(t) + \phi_1(t) + \phi_2(t)]$$

   where $\phi_2(t) = \int_{2\lambda}^{t-\lambda} \phi_1(u)\phi(t-u)du$

5. For $L < t < 4\lambda$

$$B(t) = \int_{\lambda}^{t-\lambda} B(u)\phi(t-u)du$$

   Since the N females started with have crossed their reproductive period.

$t < 4\lambda \Rightarrow t - \lambda < 3\lambda$
$t > L \Rightarrow t - \lambda > L - \lambda > 3\lambda - \lambda = 2\lambda \; [L > 3\lambda]$
$2\lambda < \text{t} - \lambda < 3\lambda$
Hence by (5)

$$B(t) = \int_{\lambda}^{2\lambda} B(u)\phi(t-u)du + \int_{2\lambda}^{t-\lambda} B(u)\phi(t-u)du$$

$$= \int_{\lambda}^{2\lambda} N\phi(u)\phi(t-u)du + \int_{2\lambda}^{t-\lambda} N[\phi(u) + \phi_1(u)]\phi(t-u)du$$

[By (2) and (3) noting that $t - \lambda < 3\lambda$]

$$= N\int_{\lambda}^{t-\lambda} \phi(u)\phi(t-u)du + N\int_{2\lambda}^{t-\lambda} \phi_1(u)\phi(t-u)du$$

$$= N[\phi_1(t) + \phi_2(t)]$$

6. For $4\lambda \leq t < t + \lambda$ [since $L > 3\lambda$, $L + \lambda > 4\lambda$]
   Exactly as in (5) we have

$$B(t) = \int_{\lambda}^{t-\lambda} B(u)\phi(t-u)du$$

$t < L + \lambda \Rightarrow t - \lambda < L$
$t \geq 4\lambda \Rightarrow t - \lambda \geq 3\lambda$
$3\lambda \leq t - \lambda < L$

Hence $B(t) = \int_{\lambda}^{2\lambda} B(u)\phi(t-u)du + \int_{2\lambda}^{3\lambda} B(u)\phi(t-u)du +$

$$\int_{3\lambda}^{t-\lambda} B(u)\phi(t-u)du$$

$$= \int_{\lambda}^{2\lambda} N\phi(u)\phi(t-u)du + \int_{2\lambda}^{3\lambda} N[\phi(u)\phi_1(u)]\phi(t-u)du +$$

$\int_{3\lambda}^{t-\lambda} N[\phi(u) + \phi_1(u) + \phi_2(u)\phi(t-u)du$ [By (2), (3), (4) noting that $t - \lambda < L$]

$$= N\int_{\lambda}^{t-\lambda} \phi(u)\phi(t-u)du + N\int_{2\lambda}^{t-\lambda} \phi_1(u)\phi(t-u)du +$$

$$N\int_{3\lambda}^{t-\lambda} \phi_2(u)\phi(t-u)du$$

$= N[\phi_1(u) + \phi_2(u) + \phi_3(u)]$, say,

where $\phi_3(t) = \int_{3\lambda}^{t-\lambda} \phi_2(u)\phi(t-u)du$

7. $L+\lambda \le t < 5\lambda$

$$B(t) = \int_{t-L}^{t-\lambda} B(u)\phi(t-u)du$$

$\lambda \ge t-u \le L$
$t-L \le u \le t-\lambda$
Now $t < 5\lambda \Rightarrow t-\lambda < 4\lambda$
$t \ge \mathrm{L}+\lambda \Rightarrow t-L \ge \lambda$
$t \ge L+\lambda \Rightarrow t-\lambda \ge L; L \le t-\lambda < 4\lambda$
$t-L \ge \lambda$
So

$$B(t) = \int_{t-L}^{2\lambda} B(u)\phi(t-u)du + \int_{2\lambda}^{3\lambda} B(u)\phi(t-u)du + \int_{3\lambda}^{L} B(u)\phi(t-u)du + \int_{L}^{t-\lambda} B(u)\phi(t-u)du$$

$$= \int_{t-L}^{2\lambda} N\phi(u)\phi(t-u)du + \int_{2\lambda}^{3\lambda} N[\phi(u)+\phi_1(u)\phi(t-u)]du$$

$$+\int_{3\lambda}^{L} N[\phi(u)+\phi_1(u)+\phi_2(u)]\phi(t-u)du + \int_{L}^{t-\lambda} N[\phi_1(u)+\phi_2(u)\phi(t-u)du$$

[By (2), (3), (4), (5)]

$$= N\int_{t-L}^{L} \phi(u)\phi(t-u)du + N\int_{2\lambda}^{t-\lambda} \phi_2(u)\phi(t-u)du + N\int_{3\lambda}^{t-\lambda} \phi_2(u)\phi(t-u)du$$

$= N\varphi_1(t) + N\phi_2(t) + N\phi_3(t)$

where $\varphi_1(t) = \int_{t-L}^{L} \phi(u)\phi(t-u)du$

Lemma: $\phi_1(t) = \varphi_1(t)$

Proof: We have already defined $\phi_1(t) = \int_{\lambda}^{t-\lambda} \phi(u)\phi(t-u)du$

Here $L+\lambda \le t < 5\lambda$
so that $\lambda \le t-L$ and $L \le t-\lambda$

Hence $\phi_1(t) = \int_{\lambda}^{t-\lambda} \phi(u)\phi(t-u)du + \int_{t-L}^{L} \phi(u)\phi(t-u)du + \int_{L}^{t-\lambda} \phi(u)\phi(t-u)du$

$u < t-L \Rightarrow t-u > L \Rightarrow \phi(t-u) = 0$
$\Rightarrow$ the 1*st* integral on the RHS is zero.

Since $\phi(u) = 0$ for $u > L$ the 3*rd* term on RHS is zero. Hence the above relation means $\phi_1(t) = \varphi_1(t)$

Proved

Therefore for $L + \lambda \leq t < 5\lambda$ we have

$$\begin{aligned} B(t) &= N\phi_1(t) + N\phi_2(t) + N\phi_3(t) \\ &= N[\phi_1(t) + \phi_2(t) + \phi_3(t)] \end{aligned}$$

8.4 LENGTH OF A FEMALE GENERATIONS

Suppose at time point t_0 there are N female births. These N females will produce NR_0 females for the next generation where R_0 is the NRR. Thus R_0 can be interpreted as the ratio of number of female births in the $2nd$ generation to that in the $1st$ generation. By the statement 'average length of female generation T years' we mean

$$\frac{B(t_0 + T)}{t_0} = R_0$$

Later we shall see that

$$\left[\frac{B(t_0 + T)}{t_0}\right] = \frac{R_1}{R_0} (= T) \text{ where } R_1 = \sum_{x=\lambda}^{L} x\phi(x)$$

It is easy to observe that $\frac{R_1}{R_0}$ can be interpreted as the average age of mothers at the time of birth of their daughters.

8.4.1 Approximate Representation of Birth Functions

It is easy to check that for $t > L + \lambda$

$$B(t) = \int_{\lambda}^{L} B(t - x)\phi(x)dx \tag{8.4.1}$$

We try to interpret approximate $B(t)$ by the form

$$B(t) = \sum_n \theta_n e^{r_n t} \tag{8.4.2}$$

Substituting (8.4.2) in (8.4.1) we have

$$\left(\sum_n \theta_n e^{r_n t}\right) = \int_{\lambda}^{L} \left(\sum_n \theta_n e^{r_n (t-x)} \phi(x)dx\right)$$

$$\sum_n \theta_n e^{r_n t} \int_{\lambda}^{L} e^{-r_n x} \phi(x)dx$$

which holds if $\int_{\lambda}^{L} e^{-r_n x}\phi(x)dx = 1$

ie if r_n be a root of $f(r) = 1$ where $f(r) = \int_{\lambda}^{L} e^{-rx}\phi(x)dx$

Performing differentiation under the sign of integration (provided r is real) we have

$$f'(r) = \int_{\lambda}^{L} (-xe^{-rx})\phi(x)dx < 0$$

Hence for real r, $f(r)$ is strictly decreasing in r. Hence the equation $f(r) = 1$ can have exactly one real root. Let us denote this root r_0.

It is easily seen that the NRR is given by $R_0 = \int_{\lambda}^{L} \phi(x)dx$.

Suppose $r_0 = 0$ then $1 = \int_{\lambda}^{L} e^{-r_0 x}\phi(x)dx = \int_{\lambda}^{L} \phi(x)dx = R_0$

Next suppose $r_0 > 0 \Rightarrow e^{-r_0 r}\phi(x) < 1, \forall \lambda \le x \le L$

So $1 = \int_{\lambda}^{L} e^{-r_0 x}\phi(x)dx < \int_{\lambda}^{L} \phi(x)dx = R_0$.

Similarly for $r_0 < 0 \Rightarrow e^{-r_0 x} > 1 \forall \lambda \le x \le L$.

So $1 = \int_{\lambda}^{L} e^{-r_0 x}\phi(x)dx < \int_{\lambda}^{L} \phi(x)dx = R_0$.

We now consider the complex roots of the equation $f(r) = 1$. Let $u + iv$ be one such complex root. Then

$$1 = f(u + iv) = \int_{\lambda}^{L} e^{-(u+iv)x}\phi(x)dx$$

$$= \int_{\lambda}^{L} \exp^{-ux} e^{-ivx} \phi(x)dx$$

$$= \int_{\lambda}^{L} e^{-ux}(\cos(vx) - i\sin(vx))\phi(x)dx$$

$$= \int_{\lambda}^{L} e^{-ux}\cos(vx)\phi(x)dx - t\int_{\lambda}^{L} e^{-ux}\sin(vx)\phi(x)dx$$

Equating real and imaginary parts we have

$$\int_{\lambda}^{L} e^{-ux}\cos(vx)\phi(x)dx = 1$$

$$\int_{\lambda}^{L} e^{-ux}\sin(vx)\phi(x)dx = 0$$

Hence $f(u - iv) = \int_{\lambda}^{L} e^{-(u-iv)x}\,\phi(x)dx$

$$= \int_{\lambda}^{L} e^{-ux}\,e^{ivx}\,\phi(x)dx$$

$$= \int_{\lambda}^{L} e^{-ux}[\cos(vx) + i\sin(vx)]\phi(x)dx$$

$$= \int_{\lambda}^{L} e^{-ux}\cos(vx)\phi(x)dx + i\int_{\lambda}^{L} e^{(-ux)}\sin(vx)\phi(x)dx = 0$$

Here if $u + iv$ be a root of $f(r) = 1$ then $u - iv$ is also a root of $f(r) = 1$, ie the complex roots of $f(r) = 1$ occur in conjugate pairs. Further as seen earlier if $u + iv$ be a complex root if $f(r) = 1$ then

$$\int_{\lambda}^{L} e^{-ux}\cos(vx)\phi(x) = 1......(*)$$

Also by the very definition of r_0

$$\int_{\lambda}^{L} e^{-r_0 x}\,\phi(x) = 1......(**)$$

Since $\cos(vx)$ can not exceed 1 (*) and (**) imply $u < r_0$ ie the real part of any complex root is less than r_0. In particular if $r_0 \leq 0$ (ie if $R_0 \leq 1$) real parts of all complex roots are negative.

We have already seen that $f(r) = 1$ has a single real root r_0 and let the complex roots be $u_n + iv_n$, $n = 1, 2, 3, \ldots$

Hence we can express $B(t)$ as

$$B(t) = \theta_0 e^{r_0 t} + \sum_n \theta_n e^{(u_n + iv_n)t}$$

$$= \theta_0 e^{r_0 t} + \sum_n \theta_n e^{u_n t}[\cos(v_n t) + i\sin(v_n t)]$$

$$= \theta_0 e^{r_0 t} + \sum_n e^{u_n t}[C_n\cos(v_n t) + D_n\sin(v_n t)]$$

$[C_n = \theta_n, D_n = -i\theta_n]$

$$= \theta_0 e^{r_0 t}\left[1 + \sum_n \frac{1}{\theta_0} e^{(u_n - r_0)t}(C_n\cos(v_n t) + D_n\sin(v_n t))\right]$$

As already noted, for each n, $(u_n - r_0) < 0$.

Hence relative to the 1*st* term the 2*nd* term within square brackets tends to zero as $t \to \infty$. In other words as $t \to \infty$ the asymptotic from of $B(t)$ is given by

$$B(t) = \theta_0 e^{r_0 t} \tag{8.4.3}$$

This means for sufficiently old populations $B(t)$ is approximately an exponential function.

By (8.4.3) for sufficiently large t

$$\frac{dB(t)}{dt} = \theta_0 e^{r_0 t} r_0 \Rightarrow \frac{1}{B(t)}\frac{dB(t)}{dt} = r_0$$

r_0 is called the intrinsic rate or true rate of natural increase.

8.4.2 Determination of r_0

Defining $f(r)$ as before it is easy to check that

$$f'(r) = -\int_{\lambda}^{L} xe^{-rx}\phi(x)dx$$

$$= -A(r)f(r)$$

(say) where

$$A(r) = \frac{\int_{\lambda}^{L} xe^{-rx}\phi(x)dx}{\int_{\lambda}^{L} e^{-rx}\phi(x)dx}$$

$\Rightarrow \dfrac{f'(r)}{f(r)} = -A(r)$. Integrating both sides over the range 0 to r the above yields $\log(f(r)) - \log(f(0)) = -\int_0^r A(u)du$

$$\Rightarrow f(r) = f(0)e^{[-\int_0^r A(u)]} \tag{8.4.4}$$

Note that $f(0) = \int_{\lambda}^{L} e^{-0x}\phi(x)dx = \int_{\lambda}^{L} \phi(x)dx = R_0$

So that (8.4.4) gives

$$f(r) = R_0 e^{-\int_0^r A(u)du} \tag{8.4.5}$$

Define for $j = 0, 1, 2, \ldots$

$$R_j = \int_{\lambda}^{L} x^j\phi(x)dx$$

Then

$$\int_{\lambda}^{L} e^{-rx}\phi(x)dx = \sum_{j=0}^{\infty}\frac{(-r)^j}{j!}R_j = R_0 - {}_rR_1 + \frac{r^2}{2!}R_2 - \ldots \tag{8.4.6}$$

In an exactly similar manner

$$\int_{\lambda}^{L} xe^{-rx}\phi(x)dx = R_1 - {}_rR_2 + \frac{r^2}{2!}R_3 - \ldots \tag{8.4.7}$$

By (8.4.6) and (8.4.7)

$$A(r) = \frac{R_1 - {}_rR_2 + \frac{r^2}{2}R_3 - \ldots}{R_0 - {}_rR_1 + \frac{r^2}{2}R_2 - \ldots} = \alpha - \beta r + r\frac{r^2}{2} - \ldots \text{(say)} \tag{8.4.8}$$

where

$$\alpha = \frac{R_1}{R_0} \tag{8.4.9}$$

$$\beta = \frac{R_2}{R_0} - \left(\frac{R_1}{R_0}\right)^2 \tag{8.4.10}$$

and so on. Note that $\frac{R_1}{R_0}$ can be interpreted as the average age of mothers at the time of birth of their daughters. And also $\beta = \frac{R_2}{R_0} - \left(\frac{R_1}{R_0}\right)^2$ can be interpreted as the variance of the same quantity. By (8.4.8) and (8.4.5)

$$f(r) = R_0 e - \int_0^r A(u)du = R_0 e^{-[\alpha r - \beta \frac{r^2}{2} + \ldots]} \ldots \tag{8.4.11}$$

By the definition of r_0 and using (8.4.11)

$$f(r_0) = R_0 e^{-[\alpha r_0 - \beta \frac{r_0^2}{2} + \ldots]} = 1 \tag{8.4.12}$$

Therefore as a crude approximation we have $1 \cong R_0 e^{-\alpha r_0}$

or

$$\frac{1}{R_0} \cong e^{-\alpha r_0} \ldots \tag{8.4.13}$$

$$\Rightarrow \quad r_0 \cong \frac{1}{\alpha}\ln(R_0)$$

We have already noted that the statement 'The length of a female generation is T years' means

$$\frac{B(t_0+T)}{B(t_0)} = R_0 \tag{8.4.14}$$

For a sufficiently old population using (8.4.6)

$$e^{r_0T} = R_0$$

$$\Rightarrow \quad e^{-r_0T} = \frac{1}{R_0}$$

Comparing with (8.4.13) it is immediate that

$$T \cong \alpha$$

Hence by (8.4.10) $T \cong \dfrac{R_1}{R_0}$

Thus T, the length of a female generation is approximately equal to the average age of mother at the time of birth of their daughter a point noted earlier.

8.5 POPULATION ESTIMATION

There can be two kinds of population estimates.

1. Non-censal estimates
2. Censal estimates

8.5.1 Non-Censal Estimates

When census and registration data are completely lacking population estimates have been made by conjecture, by scholars, local administrators etc. The conjecture may range from a good guess of the total population to a rough estimate based on some circumstantial data related to total population. For example the number of households, tax payers, land area which is to be multiplied by a assumed ratio to convert the number to the total population. In non censal estimates acceptable counts may be available from circumstantial data related to the total population. The population estimate is obtained using a multiplier which may have to be guessed if no information is on hand.

8.5.2 Censal Estimates

8.5.2.1 *Inter Censal Estimates*

Component method: With one accurate count at two successive censuses years apart and a correct record of births, deaths and migration in the intermediate years.

We shall expect

$$P_2 = P_1 + (B - D) + (I - E)$$

where P_1 and P_2 represent population figures as enumerated during the censuses just preceding and just after the point of time under consideration, $(B - D)$ represents the natural increase and $(I - E)$ represents the net migration during the period between these two censuses. However of inaccuracy in the basic data $P_2 - P_1$ will generally differ from $(B - D) + (I - E)$. This difference $P_2 - P_1 - ((B - D) + (I - E)) = e$ (say) is called the error of closure and may be attributed to (a) error in the cesuses count P_1, P_2 (b) errors in adjustments for under registration of births and deaths and (c) errors in estimating net migration. When registration data are reliable, e is distributed over the inter censal years in proportion to the annual recorded emigration. Then to find the population estimate for some inter censal year the natural increase, net migration and allocated error of closer since the earlier census data are added to the earlier population.

Mathematical method: When the requisite data are available it is preferable to make intercensal population estimates by the component method because it takes into account the temporal features that affects population change from one year to the next. For a particular segment of population migration figures are not available, specially where internal migrations are concerned. For this, the above method is useless to estimate the population of a particular segment of the country. Mathematical methods assume same law of change in the population. However they avoid the problem of closer and they are comparatively simpler to apply.

8.5.2.2 *AP Method*

When there is reason to believe that the population changes uniformly over than inter censal period a linear interpretation between successive censuses will usually produce reasonably satisfactory results. This assuming the form

$$P_t = a + b_t$$

and denoting the points of time corresponding to two successive censuses years by 0 and n so that P_0 and P_n are known it is easy to check that the estimates of a and b are given by $a = P_0$, $b = \dfrac{P_n - P_0}{n}$

Hence $$P_t = P_0 + \frac{(P_n - P_0)t}{n}$$

will be a suitable formula for population estimation for the inter censal period.

If the population estimates for some segments of the population required we can assume on AP law and obtain the relation

$$P_t^s = P_0^s + \frac{(P_n^s - P_0^s)t}{n}$$

where P_t^s = estimated population at time t for that particular segment, and P_0^s, P_n^s denote the census figures corresponding to that particular segment.

If we consider mutually exclusive and exhaustive segments and apply the AP method it is easy to check that $\sum_s P_t^s = P_t$.

Thus for any inter censal year interpreted values for different segments will sum upto the interpolated total. This is one advantage of this method since the estimates corresponding to different segments of the populations are internally consistent.

8.5.2.3 *GP Method*

AP method assumes that the population adds a constant amount to itself each year. Since however a preferable hypothesis will be a constant rate of increase instead of a constant amount of increase. Assuming the law $P_t = k(1 + r)^t$ on the basis of P_0 and P_n estimates of k and r are given by

$k = P_0$ and $r = \left(\dfrac{P_n}{P_0}\right)^{\frac{1}{n}} - 1.$

Thus $P_t = P_0\left(\dfrac{P_n}{P_0}\right)^{\frac{t}{n}}$

Similarly for any particular segment of the population we have the law

$P_t^s = P_0^s(1 + r_s)^t$ where $r_s = \left(\dfrac{P_n^s}{P_0^s}\right)^{\frac{1}{n}} - 1$ ie $P_t^s = P_0^s\left(\dfrac{P_n^s}{P_0^s}\right)^{\frac{t}{n}}$.

Generally for any two successive censuses the values of r_s will not all be equal to r. For this reason the sum of estimates corresponding to mutually exclusive and exhaustive segments of the population for any intercensal year will not generally be equal to the total population for that year estimated independently by the GP method.

Several methods have been suggested under which only the total population is assumed to follow its own GP law while the various segments are assumed to progress in their own manner (not necessarily each following its own GP law) s.t the total of the estimates corresponding to mutually exclusive and exhaustive segments actually produce the total population as estimated on the basis of GP law.

8.5.2.4 *Modification of GP Method*

1. Here we compute the AP values for each group and then multiply each value by the constant ratio

$$\xi_t = \frac{\text{population total in GP}}{\text{population total in AP}}$$

Thus $P_t^s = \xi_t\left[P_0^s + \frac{(P_n^s - P_0^s)^t}{n}\right]$

while $P_t = P_0\left(\frac{P_n}{P_0}\right)^{\frac{t}{n}}$

It is easy to observe that

$$\xi_t = \frac{P_0\left(\frac{P_n}{P_0}\right)^{\frac{t}{n}}}{P_0 + \frac{(P_n - P_0)^t}{n}}$$

Hence the total population takes it's GP value while the segment values are brought to an approximate GP basis retaining the proportional distribution of AP.

2. Here we assume that the ratio $\frac{P_t^s}{P_t}$ changes in AP ie say $\frac{P_t^s}{P_t} = a_s + b_s t$ where a_s and b_s are constants ie

$$P_t^s = (a_s + b_s t)P_t \ldots \tag{8.5.1}$$

putting $t = 0, n$

$$P_0^s = a_s P_0, P_n^s = (a_s + b_s n)P_n$$

$$\Rightarrow a_s = \frac{P_0^s}{P_0} \ldots \tag{8.5.2}$$

$$b_s = \frac{\left(\dfrac{P_n^s}{P_n} - \dfrac{P_0^s}{P_0}\right)}{n} \ldots \tag{8.5.3}$$

Since by (8.5.2) and (8.5.3), with mutually exclusive and exhaustive segments

$$\sum_s a_s = 1, \sum_s b_s = 0$$

so that by (8.5.1) $\sum_s P_t^s = P_t$

This method, however, has a theoretical drawback. The fundamental assumption that the ratio $\dfrac{\text{group population}}{\text{total population}}$ increases in AP while the total population increases in GP can not terminate to a stationary population in any group. Since with a stationary group of size b, the total population following a GP, The ratio $\dfrac{\text{group population}}{\text{total population}}$

becomes $\dfrac{b}{P_0(1+r)^t}$ which is in GP and not in AP as assumed.

3. Here we try to express

$$P_t^s = mP_0^s + m'P_n^s \ldots \tag{8.5.4}$$

We impose the condition that if the group population is stationary in the sense $P_0^s = P_n^s$ then P_t^s must also remain stationary. Thus if

$P_0^s = P_n^s = b$ then $P_t^s = b, 0 < t < n.$

Hence by (8.5.4) $m + m' = 1$

and

$$P_t^s = mP_0^s + (1-m)P_n^s \ldots \tag{8.5.5}$$

m should be so chosen that

$$P_t = \sum_s P_t^s = mP_0 + (1-m)P_n \text{ (by (8.5.5))}$$

$$\Rightarrow m = \frac{P_n - P_t}{P_n - P_0}$$

Hence in this method $P_t^s = \left(\frac{P_n - P_t}{P_n - P_0}\right)P_0^s + \left(\frac{P_t - P_0}{P_n - P_0}\right)P_n^s$

where $P_t = P_0\left(\frac{P_n}{P_0}\right)^{\frac{t}{n}}$

8.5.2.5 *Combined Progression Method*

The assumption of GP is more applicable in the case of a population which increases mainly by an excess of births over deaths while the change in a population increasing by emigration may sometimes be represented more closely by an AP. It has therefore been suggested that a combined progression method may be used assuming that the increase in each year is a constant proportion of the previous years population plus a constant. Let at time zero population be P_0. Then population at time point 1 is

$$P_t = RP_0 + c$$

where R and c are constants.

Similarly $P_2 = RP_1 + c = R(RP_0 + c) + c = R^2P_0 + Rc + c$

$P_3 = RP_2 + c = R(R^2P_0 + Rc + c) + c = R^3P_0 + R^2c + Rc + c$

In general, for any nonnegative integral

$$P_t = R^tP_0 + R^{t-1}c + R^{t-2}c + \ldots + c$$

$$= R^tP_0 + c(1 + R + \ldots + R^{t-1})$$

$$= R^tP_0 + c\left(\frac{1-R^t}{1-R}\right)\ldots \quad (8.5.6)$$

If we have census figures for only two censuses the values of the parameters involved can be obtained only approximately. Hence we require figures for at least three censuses for determination of all the parameters involved.

Suppose census figures are available corresponding to $t = 0, n, 2n$. Thus P_0, P_n, P_{2n} are known.

By (8.5.6)

$$P_n = R^n P_0 + c\left(\frac{1-R^n}{1-R}\right) \ldots \quad (8.5.7)$$

and

$$P_{2n} = R^{2n} P_0 + c\left(\frac{1-R^{2n}}{1-R}\right) \ldots \quad (8.5.8)$$

Hence

$$P_{2n} - P_n = R^n(R^n - 1)P_0 + c\frac{R^n(R^n-1)}{R-1}$$

$$= R^n(R^n - 1)\left[P_0 + \frac{c}{R-1}\right] \ldots \quad (8.5.9)$$

Also by (8.5.7)

$$P_n - P_0 = (R^n - 1)P_0 + c\frac{R^n - 1}{R-1}$$

$$= R^n - 1\left[P_0 + \frac{c}{R-1}\right] \ldots \quad (8.5.10)$$

By (8.5.9) and (8.5.10)

$$\frac{P_{2n} - P_n}{P_n - P_0} = R^n$$

$$\Rightarrow R = \left(\frac{P_{2n} - P_n}{P_n - P_0}\right)^{\frac{1}{n}}$$

Now c may be obtained from (8.5.9) or (8.5.10).

9
Social and Occupational Mobility

9.1 SOCIAL PROCESSES

Statistics has major applications in social, biological and natural sciences. Among these, applications in social sciences are of special interest as those are mainly related to human activities. Since human nature is largely unpredictable at the individual level, it is necessary to describe the mechanism of such social processes in probabilistic terms.

Mathematical models may be deterministic or stochastic in nature. If the changes in the system can be predicted with certainty, the system is said to be deterministic. Models used in social science are usually stochastic because of the reason that either the system is not fully specified or unpredictable human behaviour as mentioned above. Hence the models include random variables and become stochastic in nature.

Some of the social processes have significant impact on the society viz social and occupational mobility, internal and international migration, diffusion of rumours etc. *In this chapter* attempts have been made to explain the above mentioned phenomenons through different probability models.

Social mobility can be defined in terms of changes in social or economic classes over generations. Such mobility affects the distribution of the total population among the constituent classes from one period of time to another. This distribution will eventually reach a steady state. In literature social and occupational mobility have been considered as intergenerational and intragenerational mobility respectively. Intergenerational mobility refers to the changes in social classes from 'father' to 'son' through succeeding generations. On the other hand, intragenerational mobility refers to changes in classes which take place during an individual's life span.

The problem of manpower planning is very much related to occupational mobility. It is often defined as the attempt to match the supply of people with the jobs available for them. There are two usual features of manpower planning problems which render them suitable for statistical treatment. The first is the concern with aggregates. Manpower planning, unlike individual career planning, is concerned with numbers. The second is the fact of uncertainty which arises both from the uncertainty inherent in the social and economic environment in which the company operates and from the unpredictability of human behaviour. A manpower planning model is a mathematical description of how changes take place in the system. A manpower planning problem can as well be solved by optimally determining the time interval between two successive recruitments or promotions of groups of persons belonging to different categories of the organisation. The famous staffing problem is a particular deterministic solution to such a problem.

Migration is another related social phenomenon that considers movement over geographical boundaries. It may be broadly classified into two categories viz internal and international migration. Migration has significant effect on population structure, social and cultural life, total manpower etc. Again depending on documentation system and other reasons, many countries suffer heavily from undocumented migration. It is very difficult to get reliable estimate of such undocumented movements.

Population dynamics is also heavily affected by migration since population change depends on the factors viz. fertility, mortality and net migration. Depending on the nature of population growth, the effect of migration on population dynamics may be studied.

All the social phenomena discussed above are based on some random movement of persons related to different categories or systems or places. Movement of information is another important area of interest and importance. Rumours, ideas, fashions, news etc. are all examples of things which spread from person to person in a population (which may be closed or open) in a random fashion. A lot of works have been done on this area. Some of the works are based on stochastic models. Although diffusion of rumour may be considered both over time and over space, most of the previous works are related to diffusion over time. Spacial diffusion theory requires a geographical context in which hearers are located at points in a two dimensional plane. However due to theoretical complexity one can consider the population distribution in one dimension on a line as many of the essential characteristics are preserved in passing from two dimensions to one.

9.2 MOBILITY AND MANPOWER PLANNING

In the field of social science the models considered are generally stochastic either because the system is not fully specified or because of the unpredictable character of human behaviour. A very simple model of social mobility can be described as below.

Let p_{ij} be the probability that the 'son' of a 'father' belonging to socio-economic category i will be in category j where p_{ij}'s are assumed to be independent of time. Suppose there are k socio-economic categories altogether. Then

$$\sum_{j=1}^{k} P_{ji} = 1$$

Let $P = ((p_{ij}))$ be the transition probability matrix. If only those family lines are considered in which each 'father' has exactly one 'son', the class history of the family will be a Markov chain.

Here by 'father' and 'son' we mean representatives of two successive generations. In case there are many representatives in a particular generation one may consider one having 'best', 'worst' or 'average' status depending on the purpose of the problem under consideration. Under this set up one may still use the same Markov models.

Let $\pi_j^{(t)}$ be the probability that the family line is in class j at time t and $\pi_j^{(0)}$ the corresponding initial probability. Then it is easy to show that

$$\pi_j^{(t+1)} = \sum_{i=1}^{k} P_{ji} \pi_i^{(t)}$$

or in matrix notation

$$\pi^{(t+1)} = P' \pi^{(t)}$$

The above model can be generalized by making the transition probability time dependent.

Occupational mobility can also be modelled through Markov processes under the assumptions that persons can change their job position only after a fixed interval of time, which is true for many organisations for promotion. Any particular person may or may not get promotion i.e. either he/she will remain in the same position or will be promoted to the next higher category.

Manpower planning problems have different aspects. Consider an organisation in which a group of n persons is recruited at same point of time. Each recruit can be in service for a period of M years at the most. However, efficiency of each recruit may be adversely affected by a long duration of service. On the other hand all the persons recruited may not continue in the service of the organisation for the entire period of M years. Such withdrawals occur due to death, resignation etc at random points of time.

To deal with the problem of random withdrawals resulting in random vacancies and the problem of reduced efficiency associated with a long service duration, the organisation may follow a recruitment policy which involves a planned recruitment of n persons after intervals of time $T(< M)$ to be determined optimally.

Study on the distribution of completed length of service is also of great importance in the context of Manpower planning problems. Distributions like exponential, lognormal, Pearsonian type XI, mixture of exponentials, mixture of weibulls etc fit observed data on completed length of service well.

9.3 MOBILITY MODELS AND MEASURES

Let us start with mobility models and some related measures. There are several models and measures based on Markov chain. Prais (1955 a, b) was probably the first author to apply Markov chain theory to social mobility. The society is characterised by the Transition Probability Matrix P and most of the measures proposed are based on this matrix. Some examples are listed in Matras (1960). In a completely immobile society, 'son' will have the same class as their father and P will be an identity matrix. Prais (1955) defined a perfectly mobile society as one in which the 'sons' class is independent of his/her 'father's'. For such a society the rows of P will be identical. A third situation can be identified as extreme movement in which every 'son' has a different class from his/her 'father'.

Bartholomew (1982) proposed an idea of social mobility based on the matrix P and the elements of π (vector giving the limiting distribution of the population among the classes).

A measure of generation dependence can be developed by considering the extent to which a son's class depends on that of his/her father's. A method of doing this is suggested by considering spectral representation of P in the form

$$P = \sum_{r=1}^{k} \theta_r A_r$$

The matrices $\{A_r\}$ constitutes the spectral set. The coefficients $\{\theta_r\}$ are the eigen values of P and since P is stochastic $1 = \theta_1 \geq |\theta_2| \geq |\theta_j|$

A measure proposed by both Shorrocks (1978) and Sommers and Conlisk (1979) is based on the second largest, in absolute values, of the θ_s. If it is denoted by θ_{max}, then the measure in $\mu_1(P) = \theta_{max}$.

Bartholomew (1982) proposed two other measures given by

$$\mu_2(P) = \frac{1}{k-1}\sum_{r=2}^{k} \theta_r$$

$$\mu_3(P) = |\theta_2 \theta_3 \ldots \theta_k|^{\frac{1}{(k-1)}}$$

By regarding the distribution of the population at times t and $(t + 1)$ as two multinomial populations, by using Bhattacharyya distance (1945–46) a measure of divergence has been suggested by Mukherjee and Basu (1979) as below

$$\cos\Delta = \sum_{i} \sqrt{\pi_i^{(t)} \pi_i^{(t+1)}}$$

where $\Delta = 0$ if $P = I$

By considering measures of association as inverse measure of mobility, Mukherjee and Chattopadhyay (1986b) proposed a number of measures based on different coefficients of association. They also proposed another measure based on minimum discrimination information statistic (MDIS) given by

$$J(1, 2) = \sum_{j=1}^{k} \left(\pi_j^{(t)} - \pi_j^{(t+1)}\right) \log\left(\frac{\pi_j^{(t)}}{\pi_j^{(t+1)}}\right)$$

Occupational mobility refers to the movement of employees between jobs or job categories. For job changes over different organisations the time interval between successive changes are likely to be random. As a result, for such situations simple Markov model does not provide a satisfactory representation. Attempts have been made to describe occupational mobility patterns in terms of semi-Markov processes (Ginsberg 1971, 1972a). Bartholomew (1982) suggested one measure based on the transition probability matrix and the stochastic process $\{m(T)\}$ where $m(T)$ is the random number of decision points in the interval $(0, T)$. Mukherjee and Chattopadhyay (1985) developed one measure based on renewal process. Starting with semi-Markov process, Mukherjee and Chattopadhyay (1989b) proposed another measure in terms of the number of occupation changes during an interval of time. The same authors have also considered the situations where the job categories may be ordered in some sense.

Occupational mobility largely affects manpower planning situations and a very well known problem in this area is known as the 'staffing problem'. Consider an organisation with r graded categories of staff, category i having k_i members. Altogether there are $k, \sum_{i=1}^{r} k_i$ staff members in the organisation. Persons are recruited at age x_1 and they retire at age x_w. Withdrawals from service at different ages occur in accordance with a stationary life table pattern (Sasieni et al. (1959)). Let λ_x = number of persons, out of a starting number , λ'_x (cohort) still in service at age x. Let persons be promoted from category i to category $(i + 1)$ at age $x_{(i)}$. Given the values of $k_1, k_2,\ldots k_r, \lambda'_x, x_1$ and x_w, the problem is to find the values of $x_{(i)}$ such that staff strength requirement of the organisation can be met.

The above problem can be easily solved if the life table function λ_x is regarded as deterministic. But under the stochastic set up the solution is difficult. Mukherjee and Chattopadhyay (1989) has developed a solution under the stochastic situation where the life table functions are assumed to be random.

9.4 MODEL FOR HALF OPEN HALF CLOSED SOCIETY

Classification of human population can be considered in several ways depending on income, occupation, social status, educational status, place of residence etc. There is a distinct difference between social mobility (movement over socio-economic categories) and occupational mobility (movement over occupational categories during one individual's lifespan). But occupational mobility can also be modelled through Markov processes under some assumptions regarding the system under consideration. These type of models will be useful to study the promotion patterns of different organizations with some common structures. Such studies always help to properly build up future plans regarding the number of new recruits and promotions which will create a good environment for proper Manpower planning.

Consider a discrete time Markov process where states of the system denote grades of the employees in an organization (Chattopadhyay and Gupta (2003)). The total size of the system is fixed. The recruitment needs are determined by the losses, together with any change in the size of the system. A specific version of the model with a fixed total size is due to Young and Almond (1961) who applied the model to the staff structure of a British University.

Suppose that the members of the organization are divided into k strata (grades) in which there are r strata where direct appointments from outside are allowed (together with the promotion of existing staff members) and in the remaining $(k - r)$ strata posts no new appointment from outside is allowed. Only internal staff members are promoted to those positions. Here we will make the following assumptions.

1. Promotion occurs after a fixed period of time.
2. The persons involved are either promoted to the next category or remains in the same category at the next time point.
3. No demotion is allowed.

Let $n_i(t)$ denote the number of people in the first type of category i at time t $(i = 1, 2, \ldots, r)$ and $z_j(t)$ denote the number of people in the second type of category j at time $t(j = r + 1, r + 2, r + 3, \ldots, k)$. The initial grade sizes are assumed to be given. Also let

$$N(t) = \sum_{i=1}^{k} n_i(t) + \sum_{j=r+1}^{k} z_j(t) \tag{9.4.1}$$

$$N(0) = \sum_{i=1}^{r} n_i(0)$$

where $N(0)$ is the total number of first type vacancies available. For $t > 0$, the grade sizes are random variables. Let us denote by $e(t)$ the number of new entrants in the system at time t and by p_{ij}, the probability of transition from grade i to grade j for an individual $\left(\sum_{j=1}^{k} p_{ij} = 1\right)$. These transition probabilities are assumed to be time homogeneous. The system from 1 to r be open system and grade $(r + 1)$ to k be closed system. The allocation of new entrants in the system is specified by p_{oj} which gives the expected proportion of new entrants to the jth grade $(j = 1, 2, \ldots, r)$. Here, we also assume that a person only moves to the next grade.

$$E(n_j(t+1)) = \sum_{i=1}^{k} p_{ij} E(n_i(t)) + e(t+1)p_{oj}, \; t = 1, 2, 3\ldots, \quad (9.4.2)$$

$$j = 1, \ldots, k$$

$$\mathrm{p}_{0j} = {}^{0\forall}\!/_{j} = t+1(1)k \quad \text{Or in matrix notation}$$

$$E(n_j(t+1)) = PE(n_j) + e(t+1)p_0$$

where,

$$P = \begin{pmatrix} p_{11} & p_{12} & 0 & \ldots 0 & 0 & 0 & 0 & \ldots 0 & 0 \\ 0 & p_{22} & p_{23} & \ldots 0 & 0 & 0 & 0 & \ldots 0 & 0 \\ \vdots \\ 0 & 0 & 0 & \ldots p_{r-1r-1} & p_{r-1r} & 0 & 0 & \ldots 0 & 0 \\ 0 & 0 & 0 & \ldots 0 & p_{rr} & p_{rr+1} & 0 & \ldots 0 & 0 \\ 0 & 0 & 0 & \ldots 0 & 0 & p_{r+1r+1} & p_{r+1r+2} & \ldots 0 & 0 \\ \vdots \\ 0 & 0 & 0 & \ldots 0 & 0 & 0 & 0 & \ldots p_{k-1k-1} & p_{k-1k} \\ 0 & 0 & 0 & \ldots 0 & 0 & 0 & 0 & \ldots 0 & p_{kk} \end{pmatrix}^{k\times k}$$

$$p_0^{k\times 1} = (p_{01}, p_{02}, \ldots\ldots, p_{0r}, 0, \ldots, 0)¢$$

where, $P = ((p_{ij}))$, $i, j = 1, 2, \ldots, k$ is the transition probability matrix and p_0 denotes the recruitment distribution.

9.5 SOME PERFECT SITUATIONS

Let us define the following two perfect situations regarding promotion.

9.5.1 Perfect Promotion Situation

Under this situation a particular individual has the equal chances of moving to next higher category or no promotion.

$$P^{k\times k} = \begin{pmatrix} 1/2 & 1/2 & 0\ldots & 0 \\ 0 & 1/2 & 1/2\ldots & 0 \\ \vdots \\ 0 & \ldots & 1/2 & 1/2 \\ 0 & \ldots & \ldots & \ldots 1 \end{pmatrix}$$

9.5.2 No Promotion Situation

Under this situation a particular individual has no chance of promotion.

$$P^{k\times k} = \begin{pmatrix} 1 & 0 & \dots & 0 \\ 0 & 1 & \dots & 0 \\ \vdots & & & \\ 0 & 0 & \dots & 1 \end{pmatrix}$$

9.6 POSSIBLE MEASURES OF CAREER PATTERN

The extent to which an individual changes his/her job from one category to another higher category can be measured by using different indices.

A measure can be defined as a continuous function $M(.)$ defined over the set of transition matrices P such that

$$0 \leq M(P) \leq 1 \quad \text{for all } P \in P$$

For this the function $M(.)$ requires no significant constraint on the set of potential measures since a change of origin and scale can always be found such that the transformed variables takes values within the chosen interval. The function $M(.)$ is monotonic in nature because the probability of movements between grades are given by the off-diagonal elements of the transition matrix. The increasing off-diagonal elements indicates the higher level of mobility among the career pattern of individuals and hence

$$M(P) > M(P') \text{ when } P > P'$$

9.6.1 Measure of Career Pattern Based on Mahalanobis Distance

We introduce a new measure of occupational mobility in terms of distance of two populations. Here, we consider occupational situation at time t as one population and at time $(t + 1)$ as another. A common distance measure is *Mahalanobis Distance.*

Let $\boldsymbol{X} = (X_1(t), X_2(t), X_3(t), \dots, X_k(t))'$

$$\boldsymbol{X} \sim \textit{Multinomial}\ (N(t), \pi_1(t), \pi_2(t), \dots, \pi_k(t)),\ \sum_{i=1}^{k} \pi_i(t) = 1;$$

$$\boldsymbol{Y} = (Y_1(t+1), Y_2(t+1), Y_3(t+1), \dots, Y_k(t+1))'$$

$$\boldsymbol{Y} \sim Multinomial\,(N(t+1), \pi_1(t+1), \pi_2(t+1), \pi_3(t+1), \ldots, \pi_k(t+1)),$$

$$\sum_{i=1}^{k} \pi_i(t+1) = 1;$$

where,

$X_i(t)$ = Number of persons belonging in category i at time t;
$\pi_i(t)$ = Probability of a person belonging in category i at time t;
$N(t)$ = Total Number of persons in entire system at time t;
$Y_i(t+1)$ = Number of persons belonging in category i at time $(t+1)$;
$\pi_i(t+1)$ = Probability of a person belonging in category i at time $(t+1)$;
$N(t+1)$ = Total Number of persons in entire system at time $(t+1)$;

$$E(\boldsymbol{X}) = N(t)\pi(t)$$

$$E(\boldsymbol{Y}) = N(t+1)\pi(t+1)$$

$$\boldsymbol{A}_1 = \begin{pmatrix} \pi_1(t)(1-\pi_1(t)) & \pi_1(t)\pi_2(t) & -\pi_1(t)\pi_3(t)\ldots & -\pi_1(t)\pi_{k-1}(t) \\ -\pi_1(t)\pi_2(t) & \pi_2(t)(1-\pi_2(t)) & -\pi_2(t)\pi_3(t)\ldots & -\pi_2(t)\pi_{k-1}(t) \\ \vdots & \vdots & \vdots & \vdots \\ -\pi_1(t)\pi_{k-1}(t) & & & \pi_{k-1}(t)(1-\pi_{k-1}(t)) \end{pmatrix}^{(k-1)\times(k-1)}$$

Let, $t' = t + 1$;

$$\boldsymbol{A}_2 = \begin{pmatrix} \pi_1(t')(1-\pi_1(t')) & -\pi_1(t')\pi_2(t') & -\pi_1(t')\pi_3(t')\ldots & -\pi_1(t')\pi_{k-1}(t') \\ -\pi_1(t')\pi_2(t') & \pi_2(t')(1-\pi_2(t')) & -\pi_2(t')\pi_3(t')\ldots & -\pi_2(t')\pi_{k-1}(t') \\ \vdots & \vdots & \vdots & \vdots \\ -\pi_1(t')\pi_{k-1}(t') & & & \pi_{k-1}(t')(1-\pi_{k-1}(t')) \end{pmatrix}^{(k-1)\times(k-1)}$$

$$M - D = (\pi(t) - \pi(t+1))'\, S^{-1}(\pi(t) - \pi(t+1)) \qquad (9.6.1)$$

where

$$S^{(k-1)\times(k-1)} = A_1 + A_2$$

Here actually we measure the shifting of the mean of population to study the mobility pattern.

9.6.2 Measure of Career Pattern Based on Entropy

Entropy as defined in a thermodynamical context arises naturally as additive quantity. Under this setup probabilities are multiplicative. It can be shown that if the entropy S is a function of the probability P of a state, then S must be proportional to lnP. When we come to consider information as a function of probability the same kind of relationship will apply.

Information is a statistical property of the set of possible messages, not of an individual message. If the probability of occurrences of symbol i in a system is p_i, Shannon (1949) observed the following requirements for a measure H of 'information' produced, which is continuous in the p_i. He then showed that only measure confirming to these requirements is

$$H_1 = -\text{ const} \sum_{i=1}^{n} p_i \ln(p_i) \tag{9.6.2}$$

where p_i is the probability of a person belonging to the ith category. Under the present setup an appropriate measure on the absolute difference between the entropies of the classifications (distributions) corresponding to t and $t + 1$ is defined as,

$$E = \left| \sum_{i=1}^{k} \pi_i(t) \ln(\pi_i(t)) - \sum_{i=1}^{k} \pi_i(t+1) \ln(\pi_i(t+1)) \right| \tag{9.6.3}$$

9.6.3 Values of the Measures from the Model

The model based values of the two measures may be obtained by using the relation $\pi(t + 1) = P'\pi(t)$ i.e.

$$\begin{pmatrix} \pi_1(t+1) \\ \pi_2(t+1) \\ \pi_3(t+1) \\ \vdots \\ \pi_{r-1}(t+1) \\ \pi_r(t+1) \\ \pi_{r+1}(t+1) \\ \vdots \\ \pi_{k-1}(t+1) \\ \pi_k(t+1) \end{pmatrix} = \begin{pmatrix} p_{11} & 0 & . & . & 0 & 0 & 0 & \cdots & 0 & 0 \\ p_{12} & p_{22} & . & . & 0 & 0 & 0 & \cdots & 0 & 0 \\ 0 & p_{23} & . & . & 0 & 0 & 0 & \cdots & 0 & 0 \\ \vdots & \vdots & \vdots & \vdots & \vdots & \vdots & \vdots & \vdots & \vdots & \vdots \\ 0 & 0 & . & . & p_{(r-1)(r-1)} & 0 & 0 & \cdots & 0 & 0 \\ 0 & 0 & . & . & p_{(r-1)r} & p_{rr} & 0 & \cdots & 0 & 0 \\ 0 & 0 & . & . & . & p_{r(r+1)} & p_{(r+1)(r+1)} & \cdots & 0 & 0 \\ \vdots & \vdots & \vdots & \vdots & \vdots & \vdots & \vdots & \vdots & \vdots & \vdots \\ 0 & 0 & . & . & 0 & 0 & 0 & \cdots & p_{(k-1)(k-1)} & 0 \\ 0 & 0 & . & . & 0 & 0 & 0 & \cdots & p_{(k-1)k} & p_{kk} \end{pmatrix} \begin{pmatrix} \pi_1(t) \\ \pi_2(t) \\ \pi_3(t) \\ \vdots \\ \pi_{r-1}(t) \\ \pi_r(t) \\ \pi_{r+1}(t) \\ \vdots \\ \pi_{k-1}(t) \\ \pi_k(t) \end{pmatrix}$$

From this relation we get,

$$\pi_1(t + 1) = p_{11}\pi_1(t) \tag{9.6.4}$$

$$\pi_i(t + 1) = p_{(i-1)i}\pi_{i-1}(t) + p_{ii}\pi_i(t) \quad \forall i \geq 2 \tag{9.6.5}$$

Under Perfect promotion situation

$$\pi_1(t+1) = \frac{\pi_1(\mathrm{t})}{2} \text{ and } \pi_i(t+1) = \frac{\pi_{i-1}(t) + \pi_i(t)}{2} \quad \forall i \geq 2 \tag{9.6.6}$$

Under No promotion situation it become

$$\pi_i(t+1) = \pi_i(t) \quad \forall i \geq 1 \tag{9.6.7}$$

Value of the Measure Based on Entropy from the Model

Using the relationship (9.6.4, 9.6.5) we get the value of measure E is

$$E = \left| \sum_{i=1}^{k} \pi_i(t)\ln(\pi_i(t)) - p_{11}\pi_i(t)\ln(p_{11}\pi_i(t)) \right.$$

$$\left. -\sum_{i=2}^{k} (p_{(i-1)i}\pi_{i-1}(t) + p_{ii}\pi_i(t))\ln(p_{(i-1)i}\pi_{i-1}(t) + p_{ii}\pi_i(t)) \right| \tag{9.6.8}$$

Under Perfect promotion situation (9.6.8) become

$$E = \left| \sum_{i=1}^{k} \pi_i(t)\ln(\pi_i(t)) - \frac{\pi_1(t)}{2}\ln\left(\frac{\pi_1(t)}{2}\right) \right.$$

$$\left. -\sum_{i=2}^{k} \left(\frac{\pi_{i-1}(t)+\pi_i(t)}{2}\right)\ln\left(\frac{\pi_{i-1}(t)+\pi_i(t)}{2}\right) \right| \tag{9.6.9}$$

Under No promotion situation (9.6.8) become

$$E = 0 \tag{9.6.10}$$

Value of the Measure M-D from the Model

Using the relationship (9.6.4, 9.6.5) the values of measure *M–D* can be obtained under different situations.

Under Perfect promotion situation using the relation (9.6.6) it is difficult to obtain any closed form of *M–D*.

Under No promotion situation we use the relations (9.6.7) and get the value of *M–D* as 0.

9.7 AN EXAMPLE

M–D and E can be estimated by replacing the $\pi(t)$ and $\pi(t+1)$ values by their corresponding MLE.

Consider the following real life example on the non-teaching stuff of Calcutta University officer class of the year 1990 and 2000. This was a six-grade hierarchical system. Here, $r = 3$ i.e. direct appointment be allowable upto 3*rd* category. The estimated transition probability matrix from the flow data for the years 1990–91 and 2000–01 is as follows:

$$P = \begin{pmatrix} 0.7 & 0.3 & 0 & 0 & 0 & 0 \\ 0 & 1 & 0 & 0 & 0 & 0 \\ 0 & 0 & 0.5 & 0.5 & 0 & 0 \\ 0 & 0 & 0 & 0.834951 & 0.165049 & 0 \\ 0 & 0 & 0 & 0 & 0.457143 & 0.542857 \\ 0 & 0 & 0 & 0 & 0 & 1 \end{pmatrix}^{(6\times6)}$$

$$\hat{\pi}(t) = (0.134, 0.109, 0.369, 0.276, 0.093, 0.276, 0.093, 0.016)'$$

$$\hat{\pi}(t+1) = (0.093, 0.1501, 0.184987, 0.41555, 0.088472, 0.067024)'$$

For the above example the values of *M–D* and *E* measures as well as the values of those measures under Perfect Promotion and No Promotion are given in the following table:

Table 9.1 The values of *M–D* and *E* under two perfect promotion situations

	Observed	Perfect Promotion	No promotion
$\widehat{M\text{–}D}$	0.05	0.085	0
E	0.024201	0.0468460	0

Since the observed value of *M–D* and *E* measures are near to the values under Perfect promotion situation, it may be inferred that the chances of promotion are very high.

9.8 MODEL BASED ON JOB MARKET SITUATION

Let the service life of an individual be comprised of k intervals of equal fixed width, t (Chattopadhyay and Khan (2004)). The individual gets at least one job offer within each such interval. The worth of an offer being determined by the associated salary (reward). The individual (assumed to be in service already) decides to leave the present job or not, at the end of each interval. One moves to a new job for the first time at the end of an interval in which the maximum of the remunerations associated with different job offers (within that interval) exceeds a fixed amount. This is the minimum wage at which the individual is willing to enter the job market for the first time. Subsequently, one changes the current job at the end of a particular interval only when the maximum of the wages associated with the offers received during that interval exceeds the wage of the current job. A change of job in this paper means that an individual may move from one occupation to another or within the same occupation. Let the individual gets N_i new job offers in the ith interval and let X_{ij} be the salary corresponding to the jth job offer in the ith interval, for $j = 1, 2, \ldots, n_i$, and $i = 1, 2, \ldots, k$. Note that to reflect the real life situation it is necessary to assume that n_i is strictly greater than zero since none can enter into the job market without a job offer. Both X_{ij} and N_i are assumed to be independently and identically distributed with pdf $g(x)$, $0 < x < \infty$, and pmf $h(y)$, $y = 1, 2, \ldots, \infty$ respectively. Define

$$Z_i = \max(X_{i1}, X_{i2}, .., X_{ini}). \tag{9.8.1}$$

Here Z_i is the maximum wage of all job offers during the ith interval. Since Z_i is the largest order statistic, for a given n_i, the pdf of the conditional distribution of Z_i is

$$f(z_i|n_i) = n_i[G(x_{ij})]^{n_i-1}g(z_i)$$

where $G(\cdot)$ is the cdf of the distribution of X_{ij}. The pdf of the joint distribution of Z_i and N_i becomes

$$f(z_i, n_i) = n_i[G(x_{ij})]^{n_i-1}g(z_i)h(n_i)$$

Hence the marginal distribution of Z_i is given by

$$f(z_i) = \sum_{n_i=1}^{\infty} n_i\left[G(z_i)\right]^{n_i-1} g(z_i)h(n_i) \tag{9.8.2}$$

where $g(\cdot)$ and $h(\cdot)$ have the same specifications as before.

Let $F_{Zi}(z)$ denote the the corresponding cdf. Let z_0 be the minimum wage for which the individual accepts the first job offer at the ith interval. Then we can define

$$F_{Z_i}(z_0) = P[Z_i < z_0] \tag{9.8.3}$$

and its complement

$$\bar{F}_{Z_i}(z_0) = 1 - F_{Zi}(z_0) = P[Z_i > z_0] \tag{9.8.4}$$

9.8.1 Distribution of the Number of Job Changes

In this section we derive the distribution of the number of job changes during the service life of an individual. Define $N(k)$ = total number of job changes within the service life of the individual and $p_r^{(k)}$ = the probability of r job changes in the entire service life of the individual. Then

$$p_r^{(k)} = P[N(k) = r] \tag{9.8.1}$$

Theorem 9.8.1 Under the above definition of $F_{Z_i}(z_0)$ and $p_r^{(k)}$, we have

$$p_r^{(k)} = F^k \quad \text{if} \quad r = 0 \tag{9.8.2}$$

$$p_r^{(k)} = F^{k-1}\bar{F}\left[\sum_{m=0}^{k-1}(r+m-1)_{C_m}(2F)^{-(r+m-1)}\right] \text{if} \quad 1 \le r \le k \tag{9.8.3}$$

where, for notational convenience, we write $F = F_{Z_i}(z_0)$ and $\bar{F} = 1 - F_{Z_i}(z_0)$

Outline of proof:

Note that $P[Z_i > Z_j] = P[Z_i < Z_j] = 0.5$ for $i, j = 1, 2, \ldots, k$, but $i \neq j$, and

$$P[Z_i > \max(Z_1, Z_2, \ldots, Z_{i-1})] = P[Z_i < \max(Z_1, Z_2, \ldots, Z_{i-1}] = 0.5 \tag{9.8.4}$$

Now define S_i as the event that there is a job change in the ith time interval which depends only on the maximum wages of the ith and $(i-1)^{th}$ time intervals, for $i = 1, 2, \ldots, k$ and T_i as the event that there is a job change in the ith interval which depends on the maximum wages of all intervals upto the ith including z_0, the initial minimum acceptable wage, for $i = 2, 3, \ldots, k$, that is

$$S_i = [z_i > z_{i-1}], \text{ for } i = 1, 2, \ldots, k \text{ and} \tag{9.8.5}$$

$$T_i = [z_i > \text{Max}(z_0, z_1, \ldots, z_{i-1})]; \text{ for } i = 2, 3, \ldots, k: \tag{9.8.6}$$

Then $p_r^{(k)}$ can be obtained by adding the probabilities of the $(k - r + 1)$ events $E_0, E_1, \ldots, E_{k-r}$ where

E_0 = there is no change in the first $(k - r)$ intervals and r changes in the last r intervals.

E_1 = there is no change in the first $(k - r - 1)$ intervals, one change at the $(k - r)^{th}$ interval and $(r - 1)$ changes among the last r intervals.

E_2 = there is no change in the first $(k - r - 2)$ intervals, one change at the $(k - r - 1)^{th}$ interval and $(r - 1)$ changes among the last $(r + 1)$ intervals....

E_{k-r} = there is a change at the first interval and $(r - 1)$ changes among the last $(k - 1)$ intervals.

Let S^c denote the complement of the event S. Then from the fundamental rule of probability we have

$$P(E_0) = P\left[S_1^c S_2^c \ldots S_{k-r}^c T_{k-r+1} \ldots S_k\right]$$
$$= F^{k-r}\bar{F}(0.5)^{r-1} \quad (9.8.7)$$

Similarly

$$P(E_1) = F^{k-r-1}\bar{F}r_{C1}(0.5)^r$$
$$P(E_2) = F^{k-r-2}\bar{F}(r+1)_{C1}(0.5)^{r+1}$$
$$\ldots$$
$$P(E_{k-r}) = \bar{F}(r+(k-r-1))_{C_{k-r}}(0.5)^{r+(k-r-1)} \quad (9.8.8)$$

Hence the proof is complete by adding the above probabilities.

Illustration: Consider the situation when $k = 3$ and $r = 2$.

$$p_2^{(3)} = P(S_1S_2S_3^c) + P(S_1S_2^cT_3) + P(S_1^cT_2S_3)$$
$$= P(Z_1 > z_0)P(Z_2 > Z_1)P(Z_3 < Z_2)$$
$$+P(Z_1 > z_0)P(Z_2 < Z_1)P(Z_3 > Z_1)$$
$$+ \mathrm{P}(Z_1 < z_0)P(Z_2 > z_0)P(Z_3 > Z_2)$$
$$= \bar{F}(0.5)(0.5) + \bar{F}(0.5)(0.5) + F\bar{F}(0.5)$$
$$= (0.5)\bar{F}(1+F) \quad (9.8.9)$$

When $r = 0$

$$p_0^{(3)} = P(S_1^cS_2^cS_3^c)$$
$$= P(Z_1 < z_0)P(Z_2 < z_0)P(Z_3 < z_0) = F^3 \quad (9.8.10)$$

Theorem 9.8.2 Under the above setup $p_r^{(k)}$ is a probability distribution, i.e.

$$\sum_{r=0}^{k} p_r^{(k)} = 1 \quad (9.8.11)$$

Proof: Write $s = r + m - 1$. Then

$$\sum_{r=0}^{k} p_r^{(k)} = F^k + F^{k-1}\bar{F}\left[\sum_{r=1}^{k}\sum_{m=0}^{k-r}(r+m=1)_{C_m}(0.5F)^{(r+m-1)}\right]$$
$$= F^k + F^{k-1}\bar{F}\left[\sum_{s=0}^{k-1}(0.5F)^s\sum_{m=0}^{s}S_{C_m}\right]$$

$$= F^k + F^{k-1}\bar{F}\left[\sum_{s=0}^{k-1}(0.5F)^s 2^s\right]$$

$$= F^k + F^{k-1}\bar{F}\left[\sum_{s=0}^{k-1}(1/F)^s\right] = F^k + 1 - F^k = 1 \qquad (9.8.12)$$

9.9 MEASURE OF OCCUPATIONAL MOBILITY

In this section we obtain a measure of occupational mobility using $p_r^{(k)}$ as defined in section 3. From the previous specifications the momemts of the number of job changes are reasonable choices as measures of occupational mobility. For practical reasons, the first raw moment has better intuitive appeal in interpreting the phenomenon of job changes than any other moments. Therefore, we suggest, the expectation of the number of job changes can be considered as a measure of occupational mobility. This should of course be normalised with respect to k. Then we have

$$E[N(k)] = \sum_{r=0}^{k} r p_r^{(k)}$$

$$= F^{k-1}\bar{F}\sum_{r=1}^{k}\sum_{m=0}^{k-r} rC_m^{(r+m-1)}(0.5F)^{r+m-1}$$

$$= F^{k-1}\bar{F}\sum_{s=0}^{k-1}(0.5F)^s\sum_{m=0}^{s}(s-m+1)C_m^s$$

$$= F^{k-1}\bar{F}\sum_{s=0}^{k-1}(0.5F)^s(s+2)2^{s-1}$$

$$= F^{k-1}\bar{F}\left[\sum_{s=0}^{k-1}(s/2)(1/F)^s + \sum_{s=0}^{k-1}(1/F)^s\right]$$

$$= (0.5)F^{k-1}\bar{F}\sum_{s=0}^{k-1}s(1/F)^s + (1-F)^k$$

$$= \left[(K+1)\bar{F} - \bar{F}F^k - F(1-F^k)\right]/2\bar{F} \qquad (9.9.1)$$

In the computation of E[N(k)] different binomial and geometric series are involved. After normalization with respect to k, the measure becomes $E[N(k) = k]$.

In a similar way it can be shown that,

$$E[\{N(K)\}^2] = (0.5)F^{k-1}\bar{F}\sum_{s=0}^{k-1}(1/F)^s(s^2+5s+4) \qquad (9.9.2)$$

Hence the variance of $N(k)$, $Var[N(k)]$ is readily available from (4.1) and (4.2). As a measure of spread of the above measure of occupational mobility one uses the estimated value of $Var[N(k)]/k^2$.

9.10 MODELLING SURVEY DATA

With a view to applying the proposed measure of occupational mobility a survey among the employees of the University of Southern Queensland (USQ), Australia has been conducted. The main objective of the survey is to gather data on the number of job offers received by the individual employees during the entire employment period, including the offer(s) of the current employer. In addition, wages associated with each of the job offers for the employees have been collected. The data on the number of job offers and the associated wages have been classified according to the staff category, academic and non-academic, as well as gender, male and female. Separate analysis of the data have been provided based on the above four categories and the values of the proposed measure of occupational mobility have been obtained for all those cases. An overall analysis of the data from all the respondents across the categories has been also provided.

The sample consisted of 221 employees of the USQ. This comprises of 83 academic and 138 non-academic staff. Among these respondents there are 93 males and 128 females. In the survey we limited the maximum number of offers for any individual to 20 and the range of wages has been equally divided into 6 intervals.

9.10.1 The Survey

The general distribution of the survey data with respect to the number of job offers and associated wages is provided in this subsection. Table 9.2 below represents the means and standard deviations of the number of job offers of the respondents by various categories.

Table 9.2 Table of summary statistics of job offers by gender and staff category.

	Academic			Non-Academic			Total		
	Count	Mean	Std.	Count	Mean	Std.	Count	Mean	Std.
Male	58	5.40	4.26	35	6.20	4.31	93	5.70	4.27
Female	25	6.20	4.07	103	5.60	4.24	128	5.72	4.20
Total	83	5.64	4.20	138	5.75	4.25	221	5.71	4.22

The average number of job offers received by the employees in the sample is 5.71. The corresponding figure for the academics is 5.64 and that of the non-academics is 5.75. Thus the average number of job offers for non-academics is slightly higher than the academics. The female respondents have higher average number of job offers than their male counterparts, although the difference is negligible. However, a clear dominance of the females with respect to the average number of job offers over the males is observed among the academics. The opposite picture is reflected in the case of non-academic staff. The value of the measure of spread remains almost the same across the categories.

The distributions of the number of job offers and the wages are given in Figure 9.1. The first graph in Figure 9.1 shows that the distribution of the number of job offers is highly skewed to the right. From the shape of the distribution it appears that the geometric distribution would be an appropriate model for the data. The second graph gives the observed distribution of the wages of all employees.

9.10.2 Fitting of Distributions

First we have fitted the geometric distribution with pmf

$$h(y) = p(1-p)^{y-1}, \quad y = 1, 2, 3, \ldots, \infty \qquad (9.10.1)$$

to the number of job offers for all respondents as well as by all the categories. Here the estimate of the parameter p is $\hat{p} = \frac{1}{\bar{y}}$ where $\bar{y}$ is the sample mean of the observed number of job offers.

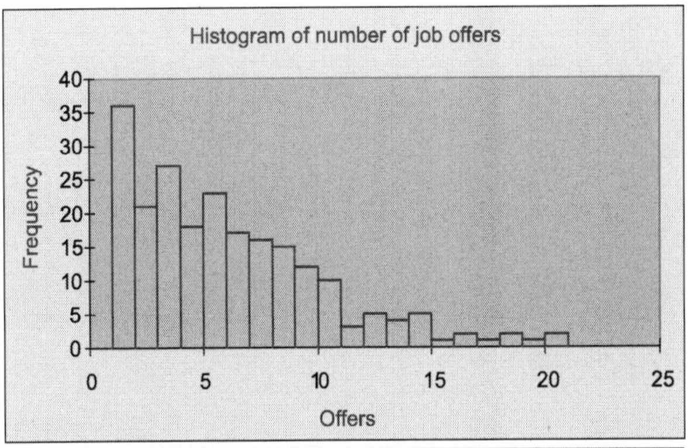

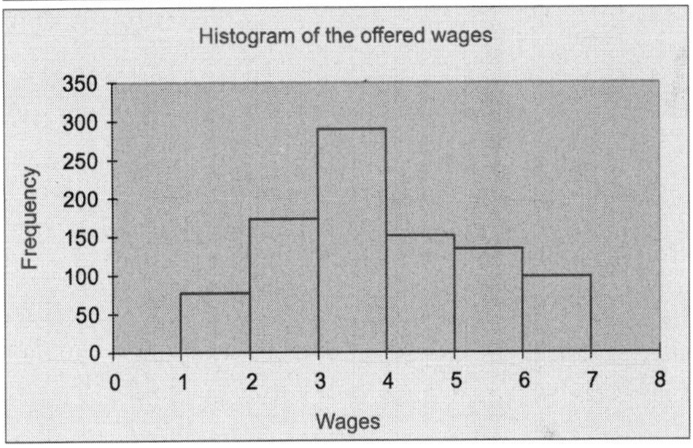

Fig. 9.1 Histogram of Distributions of Observed Job Offers and Wages for all employees

From Table 9.3 it is evident that the data fit very well with the geometric distribution for all respondents as well over all the categories.

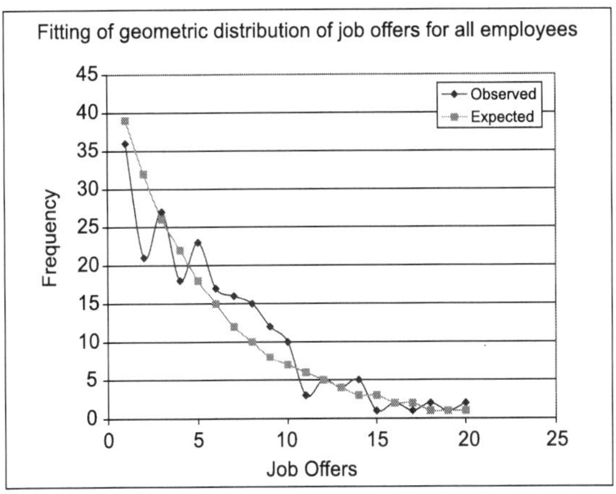

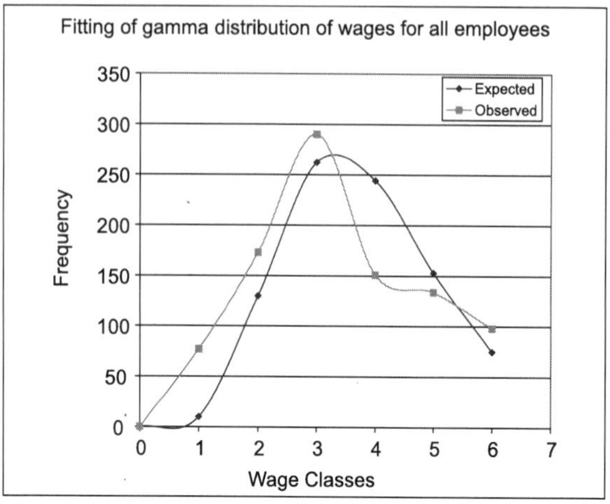

Fig. 9.2 Graphs of Observed and Fitted Distributions of Job Offers and Wages for All Employees

Table 9.3 Table of expected and observed frequency distributions of job offers by gender and staff category.

	Academics		Non-Acads.		Male		Female		Total	
Offers	Exp.	Obs.	Exp.	Obs.	Exp.	Obs.	Exp.	Obs.	Exp.	Obs.
1	15	12	25	24	16	15	22	21	36	39
2	12	9	20	12	13	8	18	13	21	32
3	10	11	17	16	11	14	15	13	27	26
4	8	6	14	12	9	7	13	11	18	22
5	7	11	11	12	8	9	10	14	23	18
6	6	5	9	12	6	8	9	9	17	15
7	5	7	8	9	5	6	7	10	16	12
8	4	6	6	9	4	6	6	9	15	10
9	3	3	5	9	3	5	5	7	12	8
10	3	4	4	6	3	3	4	7	10	7
11	2	2	3	1	2	1	3	2	3	6
12	2	1	3	4	2	3	3	2	5	5
13	1	0	2	4	2	2	2	2	4	4
14	1	2	2	3	1	2	2	3	5	3
15	1	0	2	1	1	0	2	1	1	3
16	1	2	1	0	1	2	1	0	2	2
17	1	0	1	1	1	0	1	1	1	2
18	1	1	1	1	1	1	1	1	2	1
19	0	0	1	1	1	0	1	1	1	1
20	0	1	1	1	0	1	1	1	2	1

Then we have fitted the gamma distribution with pdf

$$g(x) = \frac{1}{\beta^{\alpha}\Gamma(\alpha)} e^{-\frac{x}{\beta}} x^{\alpha-1}, \; 0 < x < \infty, \alpha > 0, \beta > 0 \qquad (9.10.2)$$

to the wages for all respondents as well as by all the categories. The estimates of the parameters α and β are $\hat{\alpha} = \left[\frac{\bar{x}}{s_x}\right]^2$ and $\hat{\beta} = \left[\frac{s_x{}^2}{x}\right]$ respectively where $\bar{x}$ is the sample mean of the observed wages and s_x is the corresponding standard deviation. For further details see Cohen and Whitten (1988).

From Table 9.4 it is observed that the data fit more or less well with the gamma distribution for all respondents as well over all the categories.

Table 9.4 Table of expected and observed frequency distributions of wages by gender and staff category.

	Academics		Non-Acads.		Male		Female		Total	
Wages	Exp.	Obs.	Exp.	Obs.	Exp.	Obs.	Exp.	Obs.	Exp.	Obs.
0	0	0	0	0	0	0	0	0	0	0
1	2	27	11	48	1	25	10	50	10	77
2	38	41	123	127	21	25	114	146	130	173
3	89	67	198	223	85	94	180	193	262	290
4	94	62	139	89	119	88	124	63	244	151
5	64	80	63	52	95	98	55	34	153	134
6	34	70	22	25	53	79	19	17	75	98

Figure 9.2 displays the observed and fitted distributions of the number of job offers and wages of all respondents. Looking at the observed and the fitted distributions of the number of job offers in the first graph it is evident that the geometric distribution fits the data very well. The same feature of the distributions of job offers for different categories of respondents is observed from Figure 9.3. In all the above mentioned graphs the geometric distribution provide a better fit than any other distribution for the number of job offers.

The distributions of the observed and the expected values of the wages are given in Figure 9.4. It is observed that the gamma distribution fits very well to the observed data for the non-academics and the female employees. Although for the other categories of respondents the fitting is not as good. Figure 1 displays that the observed data for the wages show some irregular pattern at some points. Hence the fitting of the gamma distribution is not so good for some parts in the right side of the distribution when all respondents are considered. Nonetheless empirically the gamma distribution provides a better fit than all other relevant distributions.

9.10.3 Computation of Measure

Here we derive the expression for the measure of the occupational mobility under the above specifications of distribution of the number of job offers and wages. We also compute the values of the measure as well as the variance of the number of job changes during the employment period for all respondents. The same is also obtained for different categories of respondents to compare the mobility of employees over categories.

From (9.8.2), assuming α to be an integer (cf. Evan et al. 1993, for instance), the pdf of the distribution of the maximum wage is

$$f(z_i) = \frac{1}{\beta^\alpha \Gamma(\alpha)} p e^{-\frac{z_i}{\beta}} z_i^{\alpha-1} \left[(1-p)\left(1 - e^{-\frac{z_i}{\beta}} \sum_{r=0}^{\alpha-1} \frac{1}{r!}\left\{\frac{z_i}{\beta}\right\}^r\right)\right]^{n_i-1} \quad (9.10.1)$$

and the corresponding cdf is given by

$$F(z_0) = p\sum_{k=1}^{\infty} k(1-p)^{k-1}\Gamma_k(\alpha,\beta,z_0) \quad (9.10.2)$$

where

$$\Gamma_k(\alpha, \beta, z_0) = \int_0^{z_0} \frac{1}{\beta^\alpha \Gamma(\alpha)} e^{-\frac{z_i}{\beta}} z_i^{\alpha-1} \left(1 - e^{-\frac{z_i}{\beta}} \sum_{r=0}^{\alpha-1} \frac{1}{r!}\left\{\frac{z_i}{\beta}\right\}^r\right)^{k-1} dz_i \quad (9.10.3)$$

Table 9.5 Table of empirical distribution function, expectation, variance of job changes and measure of mobility by different categories.

Variable	$\hat{\alpha}$	$\hat{\beta}$	$\hat{p}$	$F(z_0)$	E[N(k)]	Var[N(k)]	$E\left[\frac{N(k)}{k}\right]$
Academic	6.54	0.61	0.1773	0.00060	10.49969	4.73451	0.52498
Non-Acad.	6.38	0.48	0.1795	0.00200	10.49883	4.75000	0.52494
Male	8.23	0.50	0.1754	0.00020	10.49992	4.75000	0.52500
Female	6.00	0.48	0.1748	0.00400	10.49809	4.75000	0.52490
Overall	5.70	0.60	0.1751	0.00200	10.49896	4.75000	0.52495

Table 9.5 describes the expectation and variance of number of job changes for all respondents as well as categories and the values of the proposed measure. From the expected values it appears that for any particular

individual, on the average, the number of job offers with wage associated with a new job offer exceeding the maximum wage earned from a previous offer is a little over 10. The computed values of measure for the survey data enable us to infer that an employee is more mobile (than expected in the job market) in the occupational life depending on whether the observed value of the measure (computed on the basis of the employee's job changes) exceeds the above computed value of the measure. This is valid under the assumption that the job changes occur only on the basis of wage consideration. The same conclusion can be extended over all the categories considered in the study. The measure reveals the fact that the expected number of job changes is about the same for all employees regardless of the gender and the staff category.

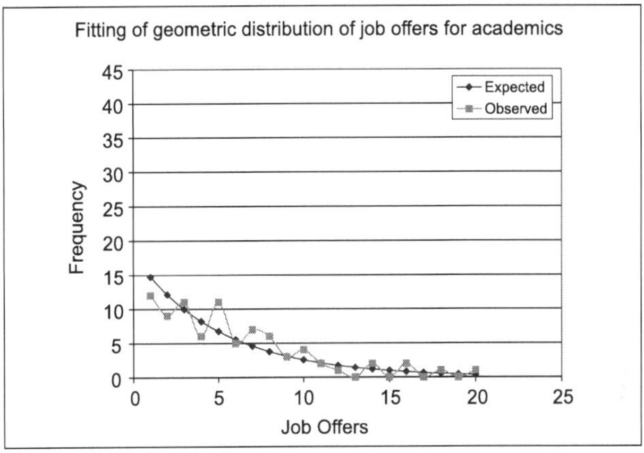

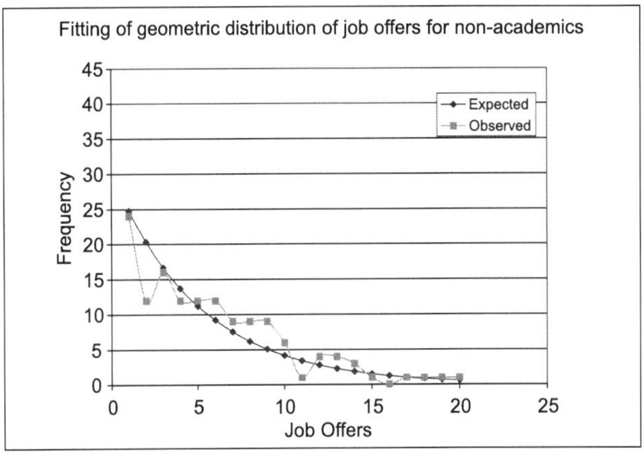

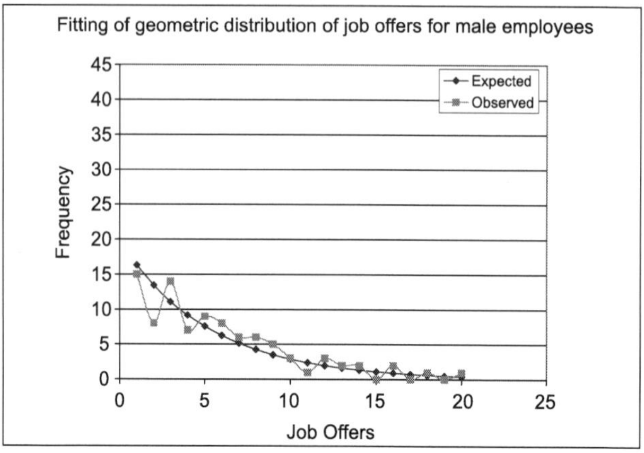

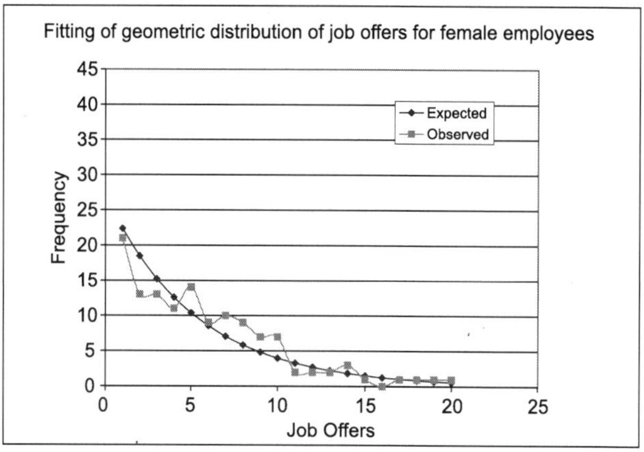

Fig. 9.3 Graphs of Observed and Fitted Distributions of Job Offers

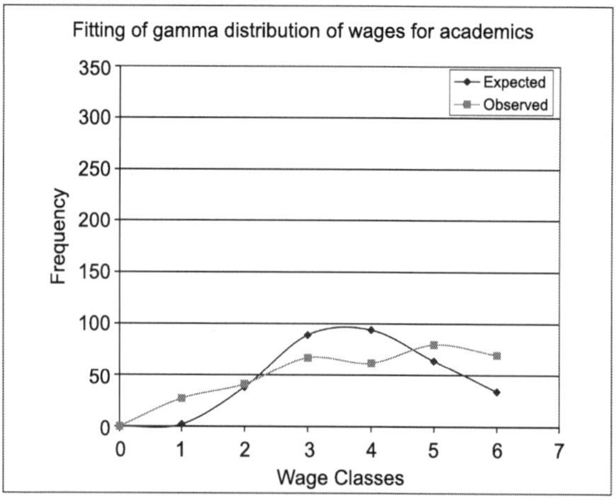

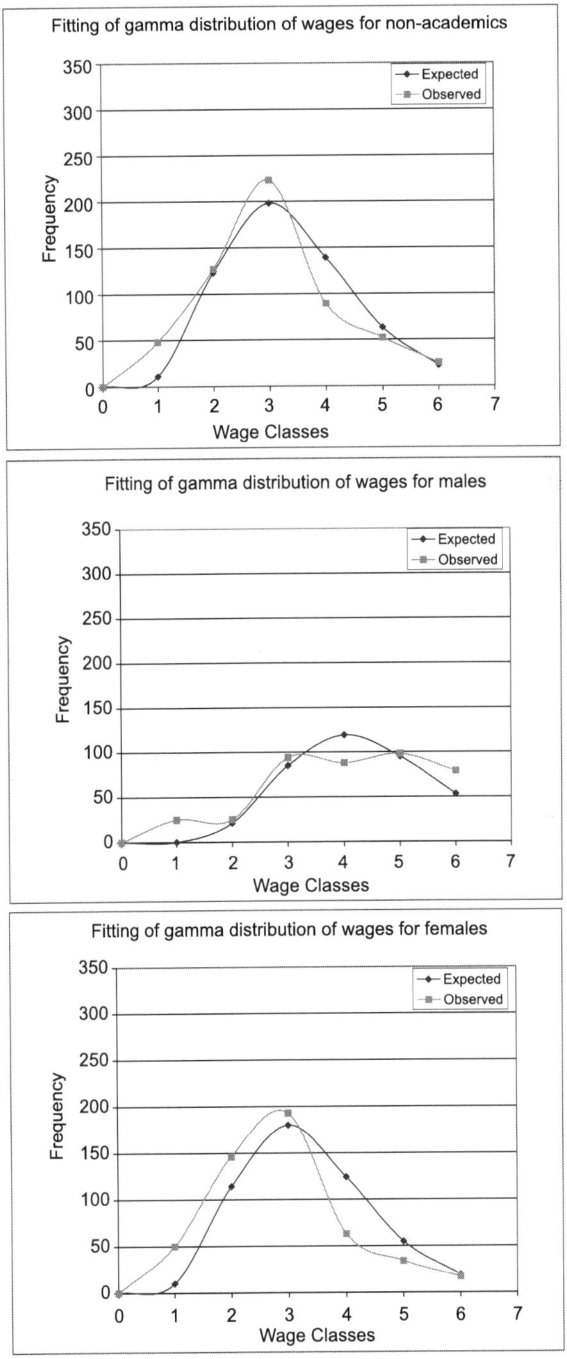

Fig. 9.4 Graphs of Observed and Fitted Distributions of Wages

References

1. Agarwala, S.N. (1962). Age at marriage in India. Kitab Mahal Pvt. Ltd., Allahabad, India.
2. Anker, R. and Knowles, J.C. (1978). 'A microanalysis of female labour participation in Africa' in *Standing*, G. and Sheehan, G. (Ed.) Labour forces participation in low-income countries. Geneva, ILO.
3. Banerjee, B. (2003, January). *Infiltration and border problem*, Paper presented in the workshop at the Indian Statistical Institute on the undocumented migration from Bangladesh to West Bengal organised by Population Studies Unit, Kolkata, India.
4. Bangladesh Bureau of Statistics (BBS), (1977). National Volume: *1974 Bangladesh Population Census Report*, Dhaka, Statistics Division, Ministry of Planning, Bangladesh.
5. Bangladesh Fertility Survey (BFS), (1978). *The 1976 Bangladesh fertility survey: Country report.* Ministry of Population Control and Family Planning, Dhaka, Bangladesh. No. 1.
6. Bangladesh Population Census, (1991). Dhaka: 1981. Dhaka, Bangladesh.
7. Bangladesh Bureau of Statistics (BBS), (1996). *Statistical Year Book of Bangladesh.*
8. Barclay, George, W. (1958). 'Techniques of population analysis,' John Wiley and Sons, Inc., New York.
9. Barclay, George, W., Coale, A.J., Stoto, Michael, A. and Trussell, T. James, (1976). 'A re-assessment of demography of traditional rural China.' *Population Index*, Princeton, NJ., 42 (4): 606–632.
10. Bartholomew, D.J. (1982). *Stochastic Models for Social Processes*, Third Edition. John Wiley, New York.
11. Beaujot, R. (1986). Dwindling families. Policy Options Politiques. 7(7): 3–7.

12. Bennett, N.G. and Horiuchi, S. (1981). 'Estimating the completeness of death registration in a closed population.' *Population Studies*; 47(2): 207–21.
13. Bhattacharyya, A. (1945–46). 'On a measure of divergence between two multinomial populations,' *Sankhya*, 7, pp. 401–406.
14. Bongaarts, John, (1978). 'A framework for analyzing the proximate determinants of fertility.' *Population and Development Review*. 4(1): 105–132.
15. Bongaarts, John and Roher, R.G. (1983). 'Fertility,' *Biology and Behaviour*. Academic Press, New York.
16. Booth, H. (1979). 'Estimation of fertility from incomplete cohort data by means of the transformed Gompertz model.' *Ph.D. Thesis*. Faculty of Medicine, University of London (London School of Hygiene and Tropical Medicine).
17. Booth, H. (1984). 'Transforming Gompertz's function for fertility analysis.' The development of a standard for the relational Gompertz function. *Population Studies*, 38. 495–506.
18. Bougue, D.J. (1969). 'Principles of Demography'. John Willey and Sons, New York, USA.
19. Brass, William and Coale, A.J. et al., (1968). 'Demography of Tropical Africa.' *Princeton*, New Jersey.
20. Brass, William, (1971). 'On the scale of mortality.' *in Biological Aspects of Demography*, (Ed.). W. Brass. London: Taylor and Francis Ltd.
21. Brass, William, (1974). 'Perspectives in population prediction: Illustrated by statistics of England and Wales.' *Journal of the Royal Statistical Society*, Series A–137, Part 4: 532–583.
22. Brass, William, (1975). 'Methods for estimating fertility and mortality from limited and defective data', Chappel Hill, N.C., 27514, USA.
23. Brass, William, (1979). 'A procedure for comparing mortality measures calculated from intercensal survival with corresponding estimates from registered deaths.' *Asian and Pacific Census Forum*, Honolulu. 6(2), 5–7.
24. Brass, William, (1980). 'Screening procedures for detecting errors in maternity history data.' *In Regional Workshop on Techniques of Analysis of World Fertility Survey Data*. pp. 30–49. The Hague. WFS, International Statistical Institute.
25. Brass, William, (1981). Use of relational Gompertz model to estimate fertility in proceedings of the international union for the scientific study of population (IUSSP) conference, manila.

26. Brass, William and Bamgboye, E.A. (1981). 'The time location of reports of survivorship estimates for maternal and paternal orphanhood and the ever widowed'. Working paper no. 81–1, London School of Hygiene and Tropical Medicine, Centre for Population Studies.
27. Brass, William, (1996). 'Demographic data analysis in less developed countries: 1946–1996.' *Population Studies*, 50 (1996), 525–536.
28. Caldwell, et al., (1989). 'Is marriage delay a multi-phasic response to pressures for fertility decline? The case of Srilanka.' *Journal of Marriage and the Family*. 51(2): 39–46.
29. Carl, E. Taylor and Marie-Françoise Hall (1967). Health, 'Population, and economic development international health programs have an important role in promoting economic development and population control division of international health,' Johns Hopkins University School of Hygiene and Public Health, Baltimore, Maryland. *Science* 11 August 1967: Vol. 157. No. 3789, pp. 651–657, DOI: 10.1126/ Science.157.3789.651
30. DC Annual Seminar, (1983). 'Age patterns and dynamics of nuptiality in Nepal in Shrestha', K.P. (Ed.). *Research Monograph Series*. Studies in African and Asian. Demography. No. 12.
31. Centenary, India, (1972). *Pocket Book of Population Statistics*, New Delhi.
32. Chattopadhyay, Asis Kumar and Gupta, Arindam, (2003). 'A model based study on the career prospects of individuals in an Indian University,' *Journal of Statistical Research*, Vol. 37 (2).
33. Chattopadhyay, Asis Kumar and Khan, Shahjahan, ((2004). 'A general occupational mobility model-a salary based measure,' *Hacetappe Journal of Mathematics and Statistics*, Turkey, Vol. 33.
34. Cherlin, A.J. (1983). 'Marriage, Divorce and Remarriage.' Cambridge, Harvard University Press.
35. Coale, A.J. (1965). 'Birth rates, death rates and rates of growth of human populations in Sheps, M.C. and Ridley, J.C. (Eds.).' *Public Health and Population Change*. Current Research Issues, University of Pittsburgh, Pittsburgh, USA.
36. Coale, A.J. (1971). 'Age patterns of marriage.' *Population Studies*. 25(2): 193–214.
37. Coale, A.J. and McNeil, D.R. (1972). 'The distribution by age of the frequency of first marriage in a female cohort.' *Journal of American Statistical Association*. 67(340): 743–749.

38. Coale, A.J. and Trussell, T. James, (1974). 'Finding the two parameters that specify a model schedule of marital fertility.' *Population Index*, April, 1978. 44(2).
39. Coale, Ansley J., and Paul Demeny, (1983). 'Regional model life tables and stable populations.' New York: Academic Press. (First edition 1965, Princeton: Princeton University Press).
40. Coale, A.J. and Demeny, P. (1983). 'Regional model life tables, and stable populations.' Princeton: Princeton University Press. Second Edition.
41. Coale, A.J. 'An overview of demographic analysis as a method for evaluating census coverage in the United States.' *Population Studies* 58(4), 597–607, Winter 1992.
42. Cohen, A.C. and Whitten, B.J. (1988). 'Parameter estimation in reliability and life span models,' New York: Mercell Dekker.
43. Conception, Mercedes B. (1974). 'A demographic view of the world population plan of action.' *International Union for the Scientific Study of the Population* (IUSSP). Lecture Series on Population, Bucharest.
44. Cornelius, Wayne A., Martin, Philip L., Hollifield, James F. (Ed.). (1994). *Controlling Immigration. A Global Perspective, Stanford.*
45. Datta, P. (2000). *Migration to India with special reference to Nepali migration, unpublished doctoral dissertation*, University of Calcutta, Kolkata,West Bengal, India.
46. Datta, P. (2002, June). *Nepali Migration to India*, Paper presented in the regional population conference, South East Asias population in a changing Asian context, organised by International Union for the Scientific Study of Population, Bangkok, Thailand.
47. Datta, P., Sadhu, S., Bhattarchya, B.N., Majumdar, P.K. (2003, January). *Undocumented migration from Bangladesh to West Bengal: A perception study*. Paper presented in the workshop at the Indian Statistical Institute on the undocumented migration from Bangladesh to West Bengal organised by Population Studies Unit, Kolkata, India.
48. Datta, P. (2004a). 'Push-Pull factors of undocumented migration from Bangladesh to West Bengal: A perception study.' *The Qualitative Report*, 9(2), 336–358, 2nd June, North Southern University, Florida, USA.
49. Datta, P., Sadhu, S., Bhattacharya, B.N., Majumdar, P.K. (2004b). *Undocumented Migration from Bangladesh to West Bengal.* Peace and Conflict, Institute of Peace and Conflict Studies, Vol. 7, No. 7 pp. 15–16.

50. Datta, P., Sadhu, S., Bhattacharya, B.N., Majumdar, P.K. (2004c). *Impact of undocumented migration from Bangladesh to West Bengal refugee watch South Asia Forum for Human Rights and Calcutta Research Group* (SAFHR and CRG), Vol. 22 pp. 14–16.
51. Datta, P. (2005). *Effects of Undocumented Migration from Bangladesh to 11 West Bengal: A Perception Study*, Paper presented in session 111, Forced migration, IUSSP XXV International Conference France. Tours,18–23 July.
52. Dorn, Harold F. (1936). 'Demographic factors affecting fertility.' Unpublished paper read before a joint meeting of American Statistical Association and the Population Association of America. Chicago, Illinois, December 30, 1936.
53. Dublin, L.I. and Lotka, A.J. (1925). On the true rate of natural increase, JASA, 20.305–339.
54. Dupâquier, Jacques, (1996). L'invention de la table de mortalité: de Graunt à Wargentin: 1662–1766. Paris: P.U.F.
55. Duza, M. Badrud and Mokhatari, A. Aziz, (1976). *Age at Marriage in Souk-Eltenine: A Case Study in Algeria Research Monograph Series*, No. 7, CDC, Cairo, pp. 419–446.
56. Economic and Social Commission for Asia and the Pacific, (1978). Population of the Philippines. ESCAP Country Monograph, Bangkok, Thailand. Series, No. 5.
57. El-Badry, M.A. (1961). 'Failure of enumerators to make entries of zero: Errors in recording childless cases in population censuses,' *Journal of the American Statistical Association* 56(296): 909–924.
58. Evans, M., Hestings, N., and Peacock, B. (1993). Statistical Distributions, New York: Wiley.
59. F.W.P., Year Book, (1981–82), 1997. Ministry of Health and Family Welfare, Department of Family Welfare, Govt. of India, New Delhi.
60. F.W.P., Year Book, (1989–90), 1997. Ministry of Health and Family Welfare, Department of Family Welfare, Govt. of India, New Delhi.
61. F.W.P., Year Book, (1991–92), 1997. Ministry of Health and Family Welfare, Department of Family Welfare, Govt. of India, New Delhi.
62. F.W.P., Year Book, (1996–97). Ministry of Health and Family Welfare, Department of Family Welfare, Govt. of India, New Delhi.
63. Fernando, D.F.S. (1975). 'Changing nuptiality patterns in Sri Lanka, 1901–1971.' *Population Studies*. 29(2): 179–190.

64. Frisch, Rose E. (1975). 'Demographic implications of biological determinants of female fecundity.' Soc/a/fl/o/og>'22:17–22. 1975.
65. Ginsberg, R.B. (1971). 'Semi-Markov processes and mobility,' *J. Math. Sociology*, 1, pp. 233–262.
66. Ginsberg, R.B. (1972a). 'Critique of probabilistic models: Application of the semi-Markov model to migration,' *J. Math. Sociology*, 2, pp. 63–82.
67. Glass, D.V. (1963). Introductory Comments. Session on marriage, divorce and widowhood. *International Population Conference*. Vol. 2, 1961, New York: 143, London, 1963.
68. Grabhil, W.R. (1945). 'Attrition life tables for single population.' 40: 364–375. *Journal of Marriage and the Family*. 40.364–375.
69. Grebenik, E. and Hill, A. (1974). 'International demographic terminology: Fertility, family planning and nuptiality.' *International Union for the Scientific Study of Population*. IUSSP Paper No. 441–53.
70. Guha Roy, S. (1986). Estimation of demographic parameters for India, *Unpublished Ph.D. Thesis*. Indian Statistical Institute, 203 B.T. Road, Kolkata 700 035, India.
71. Guha Roy, (2003, January). *Some observation on Bangladeshi Migration to India with special reference to West Bengal*, Paper presented in the workshop at the Indian Statistical Institute on undocumented migration from Bangladesh to West Bengal Organized by Population Studies Unit, Kolkata, India.
72. Haines, David, W., Rosenblum, Karen, E. (1999). Illegal immigration in America: *A Reference Handbook*, West Port.
73. Hajnal, J. (1953). 'Age at marriage and proportion marrying. Population Studies.' *Journal of the American Statistical Association*. 7(2): 111–136.
74. Henin, et al. (1982). 'Linkages between socioeconomic factors and demographic change (139–167) of the KFS birth histories'. *Population Dynamics of Kenya*.
75. Henry, Louis, (1976). 'Population' – Analysis and Models. Edward Arnold Ltd., 25 Hill Street, London., WIX8LL.
76. Hill, K. (1977). 'Estimating adult mortality levels from information on widowhood,' *Population Studies*, 31(1).
77. Hill, K. and Trussell, J. (1977). 'Further developments in indirect mortality estimation.' *Population Studies*. 31(2).

78. Hobcraft, J.N. et al., (1982). 'Advances in P/F ratio method for the analysis of birth histories.' *Population Studies*, 36, 291–316.
79. Holk Stobble, (2000). 'Undocumented migration in the USA and Germany: An analysis of the German case with cross-references to the U.S. situation,' *Working Paper 4, February, The Center for Comparative Immigration Studies University of California, San Diego*.
80. India, Office of the Registrar General. Census of India, (1931). *Bengal and Sikkim: Report*. Vol. 5. Part I.
81. India, Office of the Indian Civil Service, Superintendent of Census Operations and Joint Development Commissioner, Census of India, (1951). Vol. VI, West Bengal, Sikkim and Chandernagore, Part II Tables.
82. India, Office of the Registrar General, Census of India, (1961). West Bengal and Sikkim, Vol. XVI, Part II–C (i), Social and Cultural Tables, West Bengal.
83. India, Office of the Registrar General, Census of India, (1961). West Bengal and Sikkim, Social and Cultural Tables. Part II C(I).
84. India, Office of the Registrar General, Census of India, (1971). West Bengal Social and Cultural Tables. Part II. C(ii).
85. India, Office of the Registrar General, Census of India, (1971). Series–22, Part II–C, Social and Cultural Tables, West Bengal.
86. India, Office of the Registrar General, Census of India, (1981). Social and Cultural Tables, West Bengal. Series–23. Part V–A.
87. India, Office of the Registrar General, Census of India, (1981). Fertility and child mortality estimates, West Bengal.
88. India, Office of the Registrar General, Census of India, (1991a). Census data floppies.
89. India, Office of the Registrar General, Census of India, (1991b). Religion Series–1: India.
90. India, Office of the Registrar General, Census of India, (1991c). Primary Census Abstract, *General Population*. Part II. B(I). Vol. 1.
91. India, Office of the Registrar General, Census of India, (1981). Series–23, Part V–A, Social and Cultural Tables, West Bengal.
92. India, Office of the Registrar General, Census of India, (1991). Census Data Floppies (C and F–Series), West Bengal.

93. India, Office of the Registrar General, Census of India, (2001). Social and Cultural Tables, F–2 and F–3 Series, Mizoram.
94. International Union for the Scientific Study of Population (IUSSP), (1974). Demographic Research Needed. IUSSP Paper No. 1.
95. Islam, M.N. (1996). Living arrangements of women and their children in developing countries: A demographic profile. Dept. for Economic and Social Information and Policy Analysis Division.
96. Jacobson, P.H. (1959). American marriage and divorce. Richart & Co. New York, USA.
97. Knodel, John, (1977). 'Family limitations and fertility transition: Evidence from the age patterns of fertility in Europe and Asia'. *Population Studies*. 31(2), 219–249.
98. Keyfitz, Nathan, (1968). 'Introduction to mathematics of population'. University of California, Berkeley, Addison Wesley Publishing Co., Massachusetts.
99. Keyfitz, Nathan, (1985). *Applied Mathematical Demography*, 2nd edition. New York: Wiley.
100. Keyfitz, Nathan and Wilhelm Flieger, (1990). World population growth and aging: Demographic trends in the late twentieth century. Chicago and London: University of Chicago Press.
101. Laing, L. and Krishnan, P. (1976). 'First marriage decrement tables for males and females in Canada: 1961–1966'. *Canadian Review of Sociology and Anthropology*. 13(2): 217–228.
102. Leslie, P.H. (1945). 'On the use of matrices in certain population Mathematics', *Biometrix*, 35: 183–212.
103. Lotka, A.J. (1907). 'Relation between birth and death rates', *Science*, New Series, Vol. 26, No. 653, pp. 21–22.
104. Lotka, A.J. (1922). 'The stability of the normal age distribution'. *Proceedings of the National Academy of Sciences* 8, 339–345. Re-printed in D. Smith and N. Keyfitz, (1971). Mathematical Demography. Selected Pages. pp. 101–108. Berlin: Springer-Verlag.
105. Lestheaghe, R. (1971). 'Nuptiality and population growth', *Population Studies*, 25(3): 415–432, November.
106. Lestheaghe, R. (1980). 'On the social control of human reproduction.' *Population and Development Review*. 6(4): 527–548.
107. Linder, E. (1959). Elements of **Demography**. Introduction to Part III 15. World **Demographic** Data Forest E. **Linder** 16. Population Composition Amos H. Hawley 17.

108. Malakar, C.R. (1978). 'Study of indian nuptiality', *unpublished Ph.D. dissertation*. Indian Statistical Institute, 203 B.T. Road, Kolkata 700035.
109. Malakar, C.R. (1981). 'Evaluation of widowhood data in indian censuses: A life tables investigation.' *Genus*, 37 (3–4), 165–178.
110. Malakar, C.R. and Crook, N. (1989). 'Use of widowhood data for estimating adult mortality: A district level analysis', *Demography India*, 18(1, 2).
111. Martin, K. (1998). 'The role of animal behavior studies in wildlife science and management.' *Wildl. Soc. Bull.* 26: 911–920.
112. Matras, J. (1960). 'Comparison of intergenerational occupational mobility patterns, an application to the formal theory of social mobility', *Population Studies*, 14, 163–169.
113. Mertens, Walter, (1965). 'Methodological aspects of the construction of the nuptiality tables.' *Demography* 2 (3): 317–348.
114. Milne, J. (1815). 'A treatise on the valuation of annuities and assurances on lives and survivorship; on the constructions of tables of mortality; and on the probabilities and expectations of life.' Vol. 1, Farnborough, Germany, Gregg Int. pp. 300.
115. Mohan, R. (1985). Labour force participation in a developing metropolis: Does sex matter? World Bank Staff Working Papers. Washington, D.C., USA. No. 749.
116. Mukherjee, S.P. and Basu, R. (1979). 'Measures of social and occupational mobility,' *Demography India*, VIII, 1 and 2, pp. 236–246.
117. Mukherjee, S.P. and Chattopadhay, A.K. (1986b). 'Measures of mobility and some associated inference problems,' *Demography India*, Vol. 15(2), pp 269–280.
118. Mukherjee, S.P. and Chattopadhyay, A.K. (1989). 'A stochastic analysis of a staffing problem,' *J.Operation Research Society*, Vol. 40, No. 5, pp. 489–494.
119. Nath, D.C. (2003, January). U*ndocumented migration in India with special reference to West Bengal: A big security threat*, Paper presented in the workshop at the Indian Statistical Institute on undocumented migration from Bangladesh to West Bengal organised by Population Studies Unit, Kolkata, India.
120. National Family and Health Survey (NFHS, 1992–93). International Institute for Population Sciences (IIPS), Mumbai 400088.

121. Newell, Colin, (1988). Methods and Models in Demography. Belhaven Press. A Division of Printer Publishers, London.
122. Odimegwu, Clifford Obby, (1998). 'Application of demographic estimation models to fertility in a Nigerian ethnic group: Implications for population growth and family planning programmes.' *Development and Society*. 27 (2).
123. Office of the Census Commissioner, (1962). Population census of Pakistan, 1961: Age, sex and marital status. Ministry of Home and Kashmir Affairs, Karachi, Pakistan. *Census Bulletin* No. 3.
124. Office of the Registrar General, (1981–1993). Sample registration system (SRS), Ministry of Home Affairs, Govt. of India, New Delhi.
125. Passel, Jeffrey, (1999). Undocumented Migration in the U.S. in: Haines, David, W., Rosenblum, Karen, E. (Ed.): *Illegal Immigration in America: A Reference Handbook*. West Port.
126. Population Control and Family Planning Division, (1976). An outline of the national population policy of Bangladesh (mimeo). Dacca Ministry of Population Control and Family Planning.
127. Prais, S.J. (1955a). 'Measuring social mobility', *J.R. Statistics Society A*, 118, pp. 56–66. Prais, S.J. (1955b). 'The formal theory of social mobility', *Population Studies*, 9, pp. 72–81.
128. Pressat, Roland, (1972). *Demographic Analysis: Methods, Results, Applications.* Chicago: Aldine-Atherton.
129. Preston, Samuel H., Patrick Heuveline, and Michel Guillot, (2001). *Demography: Measuring and Modeling Population Processes*. London: Blackwell Publishers.
130. Preston, Samuel H. and Hill, K. (1980). 'Estimating the completeness of death registration'. *Population Studies*. 34 (2). LSE, Houghton Street, London WC 2A 2AE.
131. Preston, Samuel H., Coale, A.J., Trussell, J., Weinstein, M. (1980). 'Estimating the completeness of adult deaths in populations that are approximately stable.' *Population Index*; 46: 179–202.
132. Preston, Samuel H., and Lahiri, Subrata, (1991). 'A short-cut method for estimating death registration completeness in destabilized populations.' *Mathematical Population Studies*, Vol. 3, No. 1.
133. Preston, Samuel, H. et al., (2001). *Demography: Measuring and Modeling Population Processes*. Oxford, Blackwell Publishers.
134. Rogers, A. (1975). 'Introduction to multiregional mathematical demography.' New York. John Wiley.

135. Rodriguez, C. and Trussell, J. (1980). 'Maximum likelihood estimation of the parameters of Coale's model nuptiality schedule from survey data.' *WFS Technical Bulletin*, 7: 1261.
136. Rele, S.R. (1967). Fertility analysis through extension of stable population concepts. Institute of International Studies. University of California, Berkley. Republished by Greenwood Press, Westport, Connecticut, 1976.
137. Rhodes, E.C. (1940). 'Population Mathematics, I, II and III'. *J.R. Statistical Society A*, 103, 61–89, 218–245 and 362–387.
138. Sharp, F.R., and Lotka, A.J. (1911). 'A problem in age distribution.' *Philosophical Magazine*, Series 6, Vol. 21, 435–438.
139. Sekar, C.C. and Deming, W.E. (1949). 'On a method of estimating birth and death rates and the extent of registration,' *JASA* 44, 101–115.
140. Sadique, Nasim, M. (1965). 'Estimation of nuptiality and its analysis from census data of Pakistan.' *The Pakistan Development Review* 5: 229–248.
141. Schoen, Robert, (1988). Modeling multigroup populations. New York: Plenum Press. 114.
142. Shryock, H.S., et al., (1971). 'The methods and materials of demography.' U.S. Department of Commerce.
143. Shryock, S., Henry, Jacob, S. Siegel and Associates, (1973). 'Methods and materials of demography', Vol. 2, U.S. Department of Commerce, Washington: Chapters 14 and 15, pp. 389–455.
144. Shryock, S., Henry and Jacob, S., Siegel, (1976). 324–6. *Methods and materials of demography*, Vol. 2, Washington: U.S. Bureau of Census.
145. Sasieni, M., Yaspan, A. and Friedman, L. (1959): *Operations Research: Methods and Problems*, J. Wiley and Sons, Inc.
146. Saha, Anuj Kumar, (1993). 'Use of Indirect methods for estimating childhood mortality for West Bengal prior to 1981.' *Demography India*, Vol. 22 (2), 211–223.
147. Saha, Anuj Kumar, (1996). 'Use of widowhood data for estimating adult mortality for West Bengal', 1981. *Demography India*, Vol. 25 (1), 71–81.
148. Saha, Anuj Kumar, (1997). 'Study of fertility and mortality in West Bengal: Trends, levels and patterns'. *Unpublished Ph.D.Thesis*. International Institute for Population Sciences, Deonar, Mumbai 400088, India.

149. Saha, Anuj Kumar and Roy, Debasish, (2002). 'Generating life tables for the districts of West Bengal: A model approach.' *Journal of Combinatorics, Information and System Sciences* (JCISS), Vol. 27 (1–4), 23–40. Forum for Interdisciplinary Mathematics (FIM). USA.
150. Saha, Anuj Kumar, (2004). 'On the proportionate age structure of the population of West Bengal.' *Indian Journal of Regional Science*, Vol. 36, No. 1. Regional Science Association, India.
151. Saha, Anuj Kumar, (2007). 'Female nuptiality in an Indian State and Bangladesh: An episode.' Published in a book, namely, *Environment Concerns and Perspectives*, edited by Sudip Data Banik, Saikat Kumar Basu and Amit Krishna De by A P H Publishing Corporation, 5 Ansari Road, Daryaganj, New Delhi 110002.
152. Saveland, W. and Glic, P.C. (1969). 'First marriage decrement tables by color and sex for the United States in 1958–1960.' *Demography*. 6: 243–268.
153. Singh, K. (1976). National Population Policy, New Delhi, India.
154. Smith, P.C. (1978). Index of nuptiality. Asia and Pacific Census Forum. No. 5 (2).
155. Shahidullah, M. (1980). 'Differential nuptiality patterns in Bangladesh.' *ISRT*, Dacca University, Dacca, Bangladesh.
156. Spiegelman, Martiner, (1968). Introduction to Demography. Harvard University Press, Cambridge (Revised Edition), Chapters 4 and 5, pp. 80–182.
157. Sullivan, J.M. (1972). 'Models for the estimation of probability of dying between birth and exact ages of early childhood'. *Population Studies*, 26: 71–97.
158. Srinivasan, et al., (1980). 'Family planning targets by states for India.' *Methodology and Input Data*. 1 & 2, IIPS, Bombay.
159. Srinivasan, K. (1995). 'An overview of demographic transition in India since 1970 in Srinivasan,' K (Ed.) *Population Policy and Reproductive Health*. Hindustan Publishing Corporation, India.
160. Srinivasan, K. (1997). *Basic Demographic Techniques and Applications*. Sage Publications, New Delhi.
161. Somoza, Jorge L. Somoza, (1981). Indirect estimates of emigration: Applications of two procedures using information on residence of children and siblings.
162. Sommers, P.M. and Conlisk, J. (1979). 'Eigenvalue immobility measures for Markov Chains', *J. Math. Sociolog*, 6, pp. 169–234.

163. Shorrocks, A.F. (1978). 'The measurement of mobility', *Econometrics*, 46, 1013–1024.
164. Trussell, T.J. (1976). 'A refined estimator of location of the age of first marriage.' *Demography*. 13(2): 225–234.
165. Trussell, T. James, (1974). Knodel, J. (1977). 'Family limitations and the fertility transition: Evidence from the age patterns of fertility in Europe and Asia', *Population Studies*, 31(2): 219–249.
166. Trussell, T. James and Menken, Jane, (1979). 'Estimating the completeness and relative under enumeration in two successive censuses.' *Asian and Pacific Census Forum*, Honolulu. 6(2), 9–11.
167. Tetley, H. (1946). *Actuarial Statistics*, Vol. 1, *Statistics and Graduation*. Institute of Actuaries and Faculty of Actuaries.
168. Taylor, C.L. and Hall, (Ed.). *Aggregate Data Analysis: Political and Social Indicators in Cross-Sectional Research.*
169. The Population of Central America (including Mexico), 1950–1980, ST/SOA/Ser. A, *Population Studies*, No. 16.
170. The Statesman, (1978). Daily News Paper. Kolkata, India. Issue: Oct., 2, 1978.
171. The United Nations and World Health Organization Working Group (Bangkok, 22–23 Oct., 1981).
172. United Nations (UN), (1958). 'Population Studies'. *Multilingual Demographic Dictionary*, 29: 31–34. Census.
173. United Nations, (1958) 'Principle and recommendations for national population censuses', *Statistical Papers*, Series M, No. 27.
174. United Nations, (1967). 'Methods of estimating basic demographic measures from incomplete data'. Manual IV, *Population Studies* No. 42, ST/50 Series A–42, New York.
175. United Nations, (1973). 'The determinants and consequences of population trends', *Population Studies*, No. 50, Department of Economic and Social Affairs (1).
176. United Nations, (1982). Model life tables for developing countries. New York: United Nations Population Studies, No. 77.
177. United Nations, (1983). Manual X. Indirect techniques for demographic estimation, Department of International, Economic and Social Affairs, *Population Studies*, No. 81.
178. United Nations, (1984). 'World population trends, population and development inter-relations and population policies', *Monitoring Report* (1).

179. United Nations (UN), (1985). *Report of the world conference to review and appraise the achievements of the United Nations decade for women: Equality, development and peace.* Nairobi, July 15–26, 1985.
180. United Nations (UN), (1990). Patterns of first marriage: Timing and prevalence. Dept. International Economic and Social Affairs.
181. United Nations (UN), (1995). Living arrangements of women and their children in developing countries: A demographic profile. Dept. for Economics and Social Information & Policy Analysis Division.
182. Udjo, E.O. (1997). Fertility and mortality trends in South Africa, The evidence from the 1995 october household survey and implications on population projections. Central Statistical Service, Pretoria.
183. Van de Kaa, D.J. (1987). 'Europe's second demographic transition'. *Population Bulletin.* 42(1): 3–17.
184. Vallin Jacques and Lopez, Allan, (1985). a, b. Health policy, social policy and mortality prospects. Liege, UIESP, Ordina Editions, pp. 558.
185. Van de Walle, E. (1982). *Multilingual Demographic Dictionary.* Belgium: International Union for the Scientific Study of Population. Ordina Editions.
186. Westoff, C.F. (1975). The population debate: Dimensions and perspectives. United Nations, New York. 11: 313–317.
187. Westoff, C.F. and Ryder, N.B. (1977). 'The contraceptive revolution'. Princeton. Princeton University Press.
188. WHO Experts' Committee on health statistics and adopted by the third world health assembly, Geneva, 08–27 May 1950.
189. Young, A. and Almond, G. (1961). Prediction distribution of Staff, *Comp. J.*, 3, 246–250.
190. Zaba, B. (1981). Use of relational Gompertz model in analyzing fertility data collected in retrospective surveys, Centre for Population Studies, Working Paper 8, 1–2 London School of Hygiene and Tropical Medicine.

Index

D

E

I

J

K

L

M

N

O

P

R

S

T

U

V

W

Z